HOW TO SEE IT, HOW TO DRAW IT

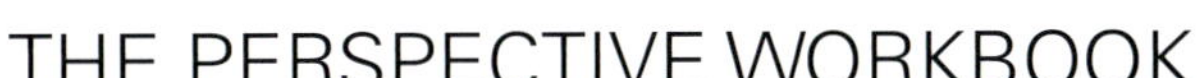

THE PERSPECTIVE WORKBOOK

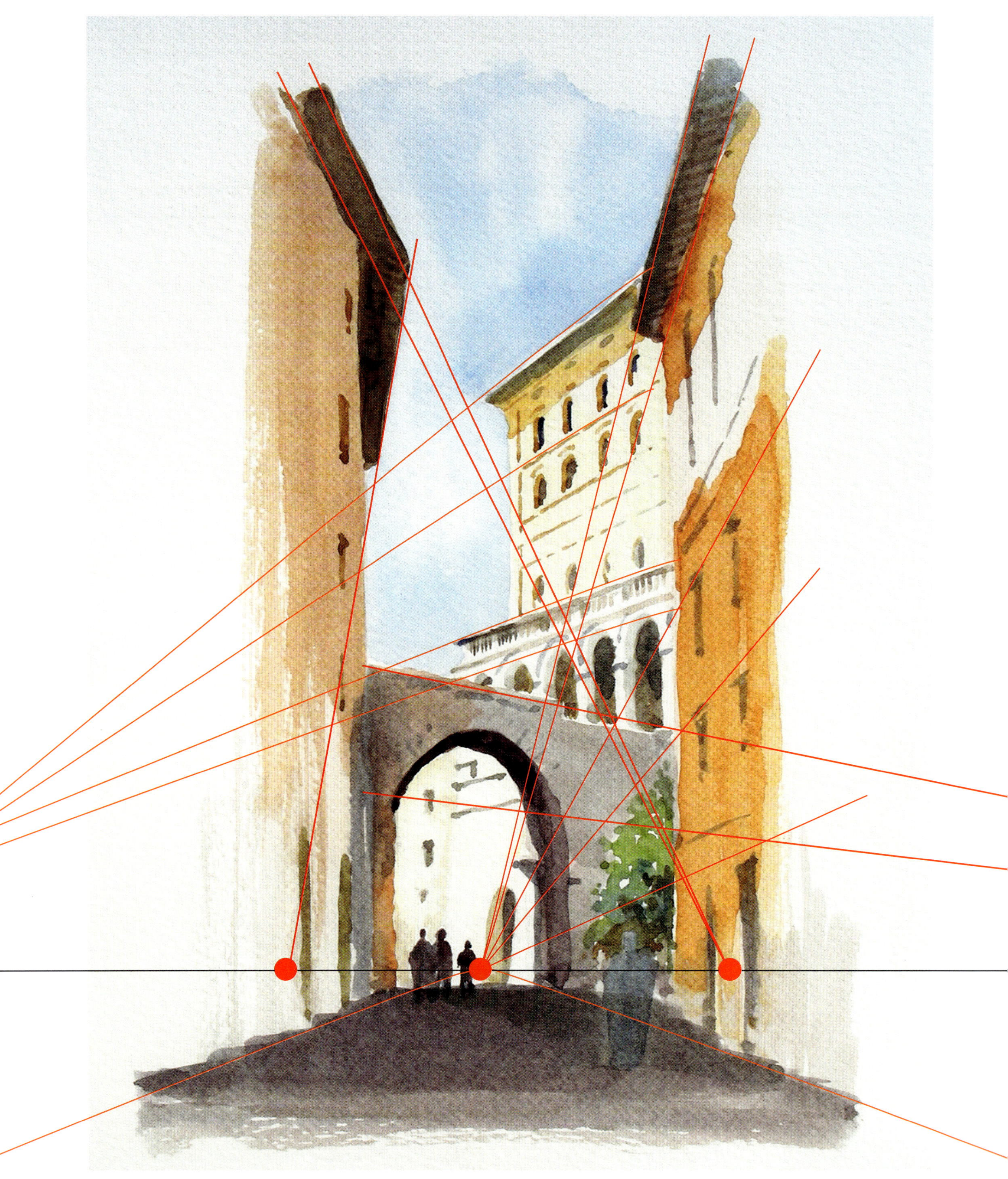

HOW TO SEE IT, HOW TO DRAW IT

THE PERSPECTIVE WORKBOOK

MATTHEW BREHM

Search Press

CONTENTS

1

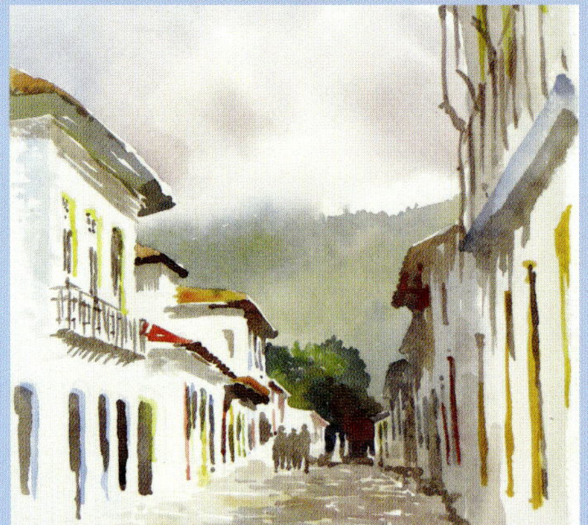

2

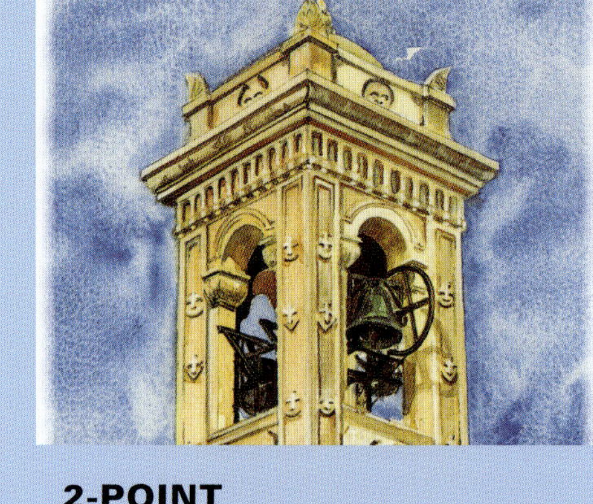

3

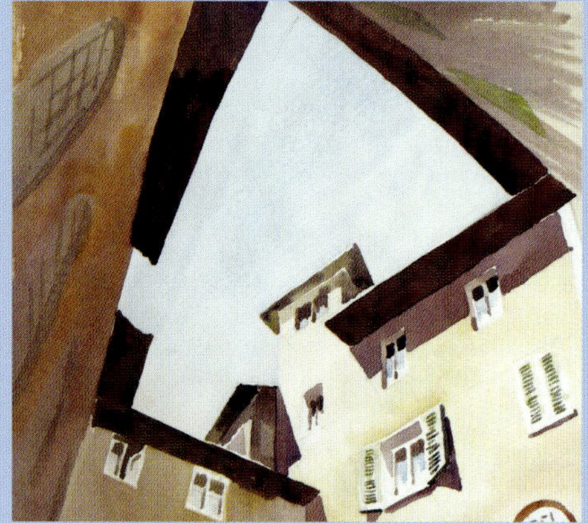

A QUARTO BOOK
DRAWING PERSPECTIVE

Published in 2016 by
Search Press Ltd
Wellwood
North Farm Rd
Tunbridge Wells
Kent TN2 3DR

Reprinted 2017, 2018, 2019, 2020, 2021, 2024

ISBN: 978-1-78221-276-8
QUAR.DRPE

MULTI
POINT

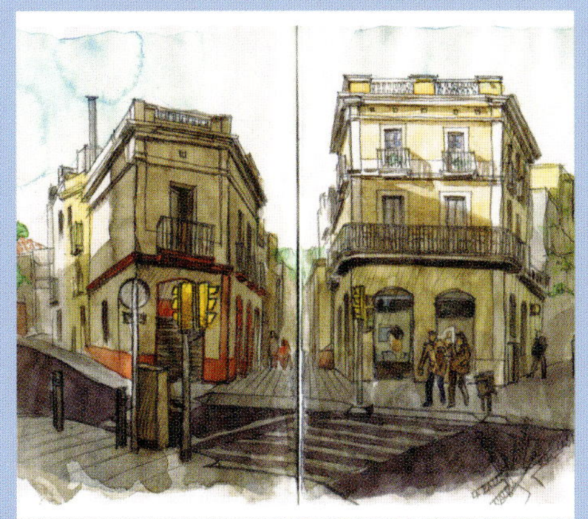
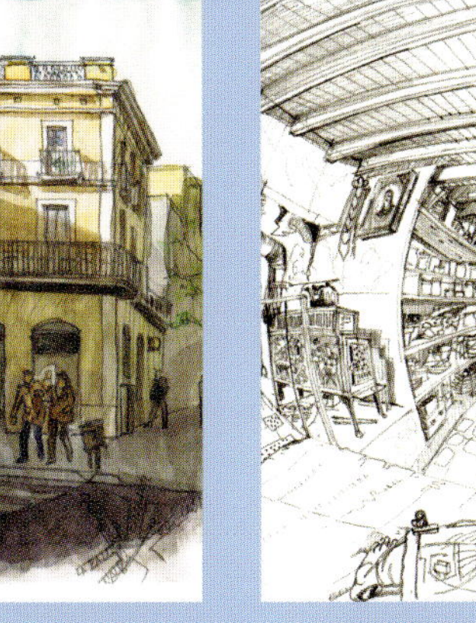

CURVI-
LINEAR

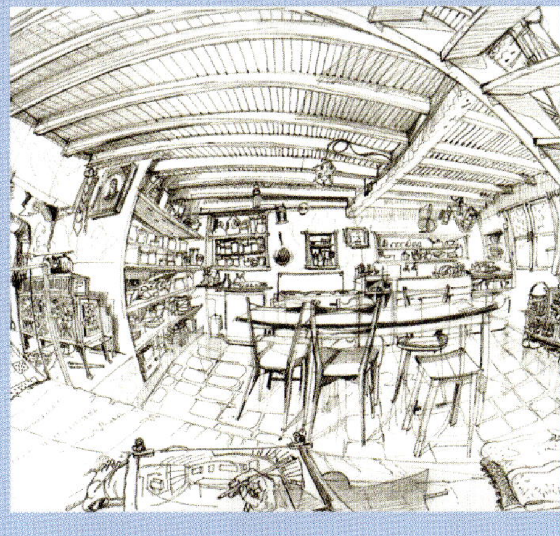

WORK-
BOOK

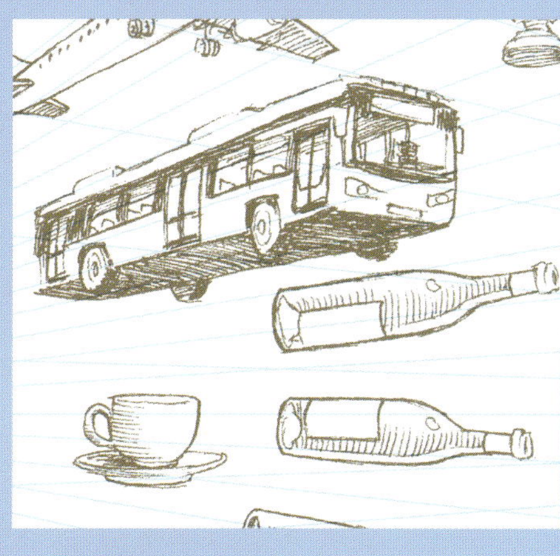

Conceived, designed and produced by
Quarto Publishing plc
The Old Brewery
6 Blundell Street
London N7 9BH

Senior editor: Chelsea Edwards
Designer: Nick Clark
Copy editor: Sarah Hoggett
Picture research: Sarah Bell
Proofreader: Emma Hill
Indexer: Helen Snaith

Creative director: Moira Clinch
Publisher: Paul Carslake

Colour separation by PICA Digital Pte Ltd,
Singapore
Printed in Malaysia

9 8 7 6 5

Introduction

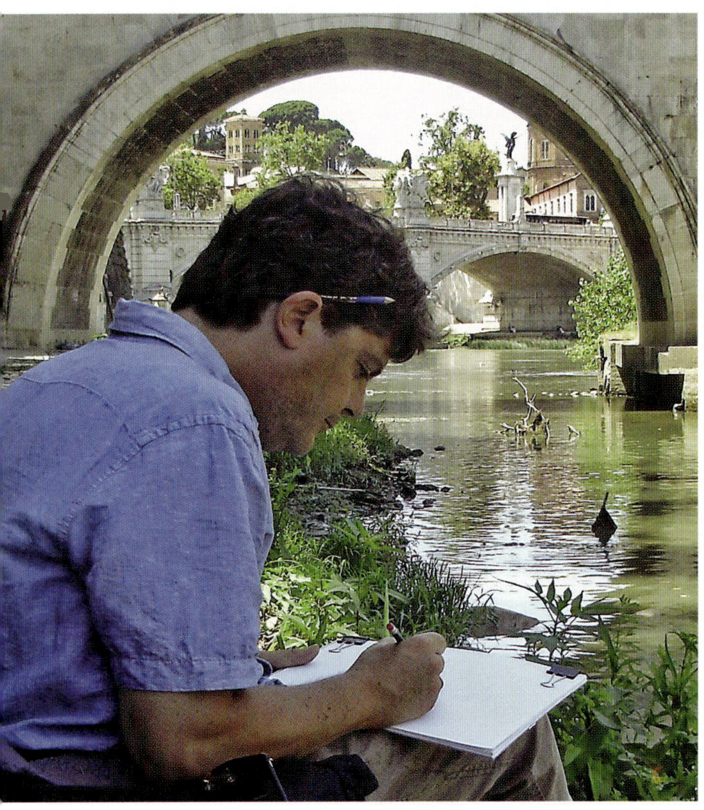

This book will help you develop a working knowledge of how perspective appears in the world around you, why it appears the way it does and how to apply these understandings in your sketching work.

Too often, it's assumed that a thorough knowledge of perspective is required before someone can incorporate perspective techniques into their drawings. In my experience, a little knowledge goes a very long way – some understanding of the basics of perspective, and the ability to see the effects of perspective in your daily life – this is all that's really needed to have a truly positive effect on your drawing ability.

We should remember that perspective drawings are only an approximation of what we see, and we should always retain some degree of freedom from the constraints of being overly 'correct' in the construction of a perspective drawing. In fact, I often draw without thinking much about perspective at all. But understanding the basics of perspective frequently gets me out of a jam – it helps me greatly to solve visual problems as I encounter them. And that's the primary goal of this book; to provide easy access to an understanding of perspective that will actually help you see the world around you and record it more accurately through drawing.

Matthew Brehm

About this book

Each type of perspective is broken down and analysed in a comprehensive way using helpful text, diagrams and artwork from a range of artists. The simple structure of 'Seeing it', 'Understanding it' and 'Applying it' will help you to identify what you're looking at, interpret it and then reproduce it. The structure of the book is outlined here:

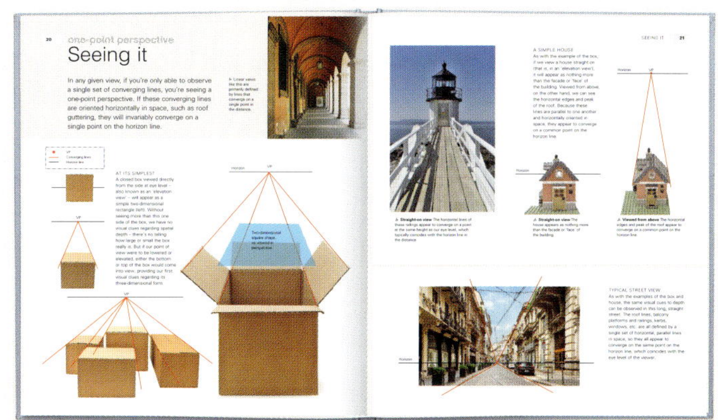

'Seeing it'
Simple, recurring objects are used to demonstrate the shift in placement of the vanishing point(s) and horizon line for each type of perspective. Photographs and drawings which typify the view being described are included.

'Understanding it'
Using diagrams and existing artworks as a starting point enables you to see how perspective principles can be broken down. Annotations help to illuminate the underlying structure of each piece.

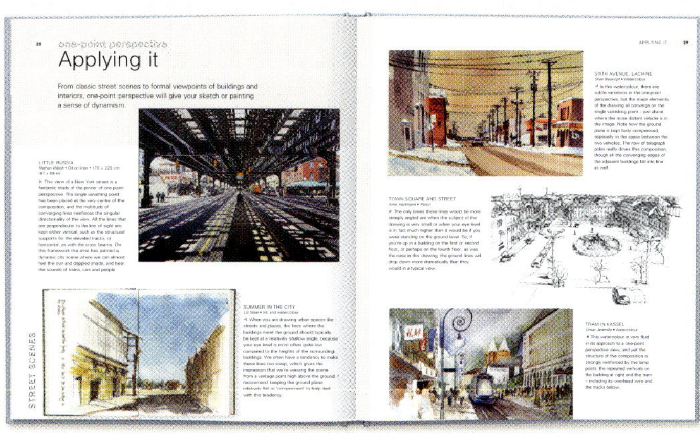

'Applying it'
Once you've understood the rules for each type of perspective, you can begin to apply them to your own work. These pages pull together a whole host of artists' works to showcase that particular viewpoint.

Workbook (pages 110–140)
This section gives you the chance to get hands-on with perspective. Blank grids are included so that you can photocopy them and then draw in your own scene. Alternatively, you can dive in and draw directly on to the page. Also featured are partially completed scenes that you can finish off using the lists of missing items provided.

Downloadable grids
Visit searchpress.com/how-to-see-it-how-to-draw-it to download the blank perspective chambers and unfinished artworks from the workbook. You can print them out and practise drawing your chosen scenes on them.

A brief history of perspective

To varying degrees, humans have had the ability to depict spatial depth on a flat surface throughout history. The full development of perspective as an aspect of drawing and painting is a complex and lengthy story, but what follows is a brief description of some notable points along the way.

The dawn of perspective

Even some cave paintings from more than 30,000 years ago, such as those in the Chauvet Cave in southern France (*right*), show the use of overlapping forms to render some objects as being further in the distance than others. Egyptian wall paintings and low-reliefs show a more precise, yet similar, approach to spatial depth, where animals and human figures often overlap one another. But in these very early cases, any depictions of architectural space are either non-existent or, at best, extremely flat.

It's generally assumed that the Ancient Greeks had some grasp of perspective, though no conclusive archaeological evidence of this survives. In ancient Rome, from about the 1st century BC onwards, perspective was a fairly well-developed practice and was used primarily as a way to decorate interior living spaces. Most often this was in the form of trompe l'œil frescoes on walls, which created an optical illusion of spatial depth as a means of extending the perceived size of a room, or to mimic exterior gardens.

A fine example can be seen in the House of Livia on Rome's Palatine Hill (*below*). Livia Drusilla was the wife and also an advisor of the Emperor Augustus, and the interior rooms of her house are decorated with trompe l'œil frescoes of gardens and pavilions. In the image shown here, the two central columns are in the foreground, while the bases and entablatures of the two outermost columns clearly converge on a single vanishing point. Other examples of ancient perspective can be found at Pompeii and Ostia

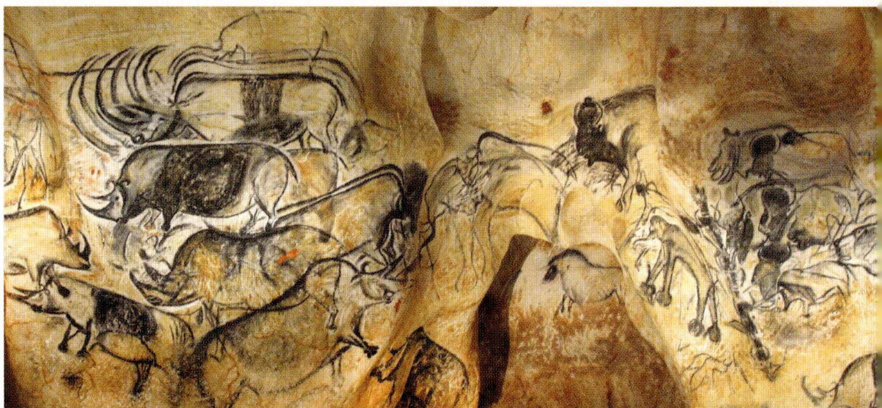

Antica, which suggests that perspective was widely understood and practised by artists for several centuries.

The rise of the Eastern Church began to take hold as the seat of the Roman Empire moved to Constantinople and there was a change in how artists depicted depth on flat surfaces. What is now called 'Byzantine perspective' began to appear in religious iconography. Also referred to as 'reverse perspective', this approach to drawing places the viewer between the subject and the vanishing point, so that objects appear to get larger rather than smaller as they recede into the distance. This image of *The Virgin and Child Enthroned* (*right, above*), from the 13th century, demonstrates Byzantine perspective, with the lines of the chair and footstool converging towards the viewer rather than away.

Losing perspective

The ability to create perspective images seems to have been lost after the Roman Empire, during the medieval era. The reasons for the diminished use of perspective, particularly in religious painting, are not well understood; it may have as much to do with the intentions of artists and their patrons as it does with any lack of drawing skill or knowledge. Regardless, it can safely be said that perspective as the ancients used it fell out of use and/or favour until at least the 12th or 13th century. Buildings are generally very flat – more elevation drawings than perspectives – yet there is some suggestion of spatial depth; one side may be lighter than the other, rooflines may be at angles. Figures, too, lack form. Nonetheless, there is some understanding that objects appear to change based on their relative proximity to the viewer – in other words, some

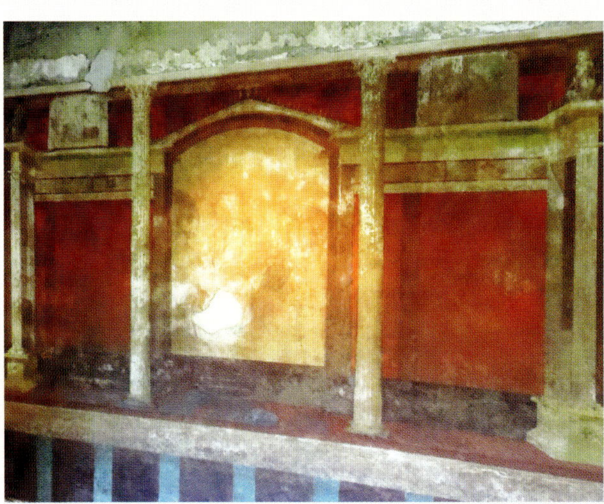

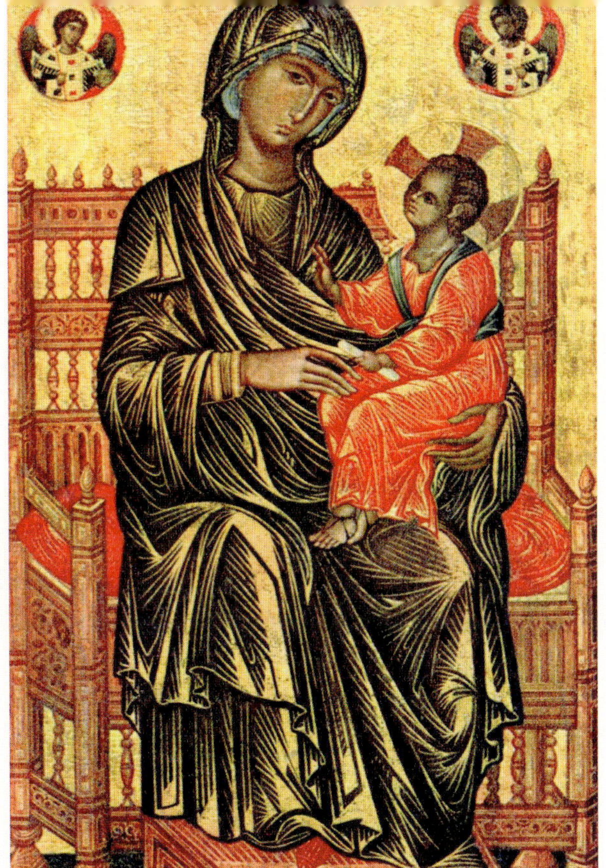

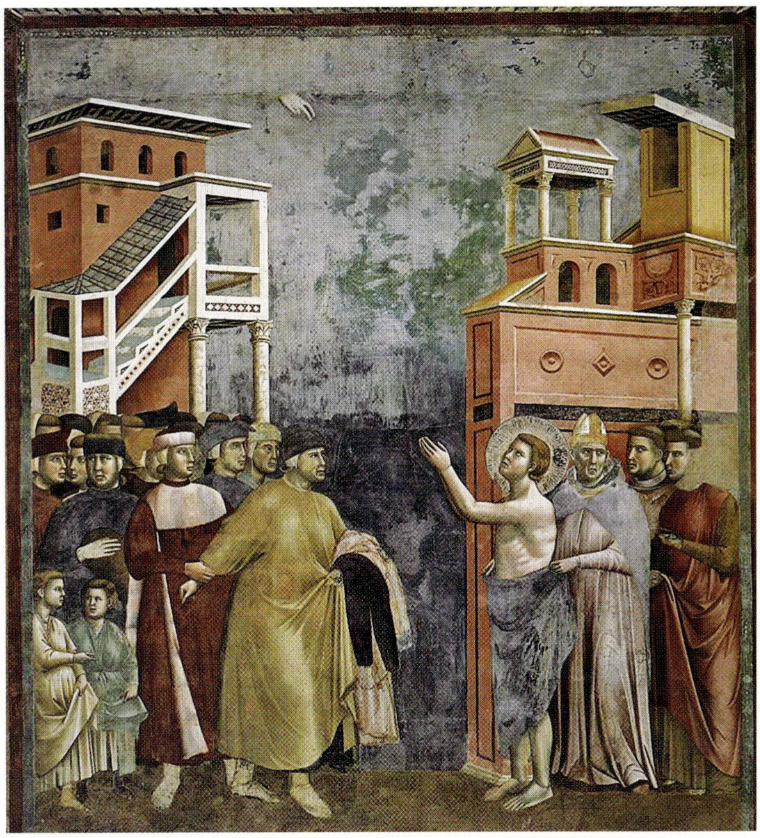

understanding of perspective, but without much geometric precision or consistency.

The principles of perspective

By the late 13th century, however, artists were on the verge of 'rediscovering' how to draw in perspective, but they weren't quite there yet in a comprehensive way. They seemed to understand that lines would appear to converge on vanishing points, but the points they established for their views were seldom in agreement with one another. In this fresco from the Basilica of Saint Francis in Assisi, Italy (*above, right*), painted around the 1290s, note the small stair landing at far left as it compares to the landing at the top of the stairs or the little temple at upper right. Both appear to converge on distant vanishing points, but it would make more sense if they converged on the same point. Note, too, how the human figures appear more three-dimensional, thanks primarily to their modelling and lighting.

As the Italian Renaissance began to develop in the 14th and 15th centuries, the rules of perspective were rediscovered, or perhaps reinvented, by a few individuals and ultimately became widespread throughout pictorial art. In 1344, Ambrogio Lorenzetti painted *Annunciation* (*right*) that clearly demonstrates the use of one-point perspective, at least in his design for the floor, in what is one of the very earliest known examples of carefully structured perspective during the Renaissance. Filippo Brunelleschi conducted perspective experiments and is widely believed to have 'invented' linear perspective around 1420.

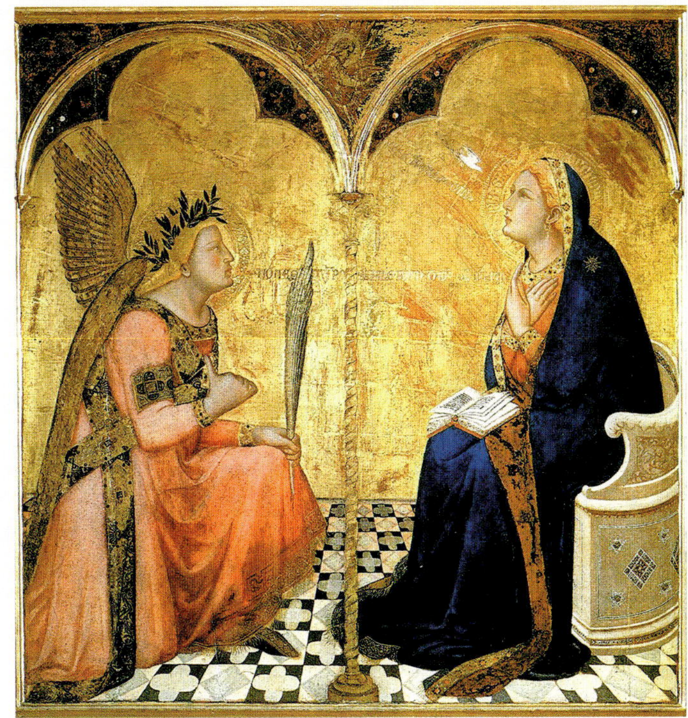

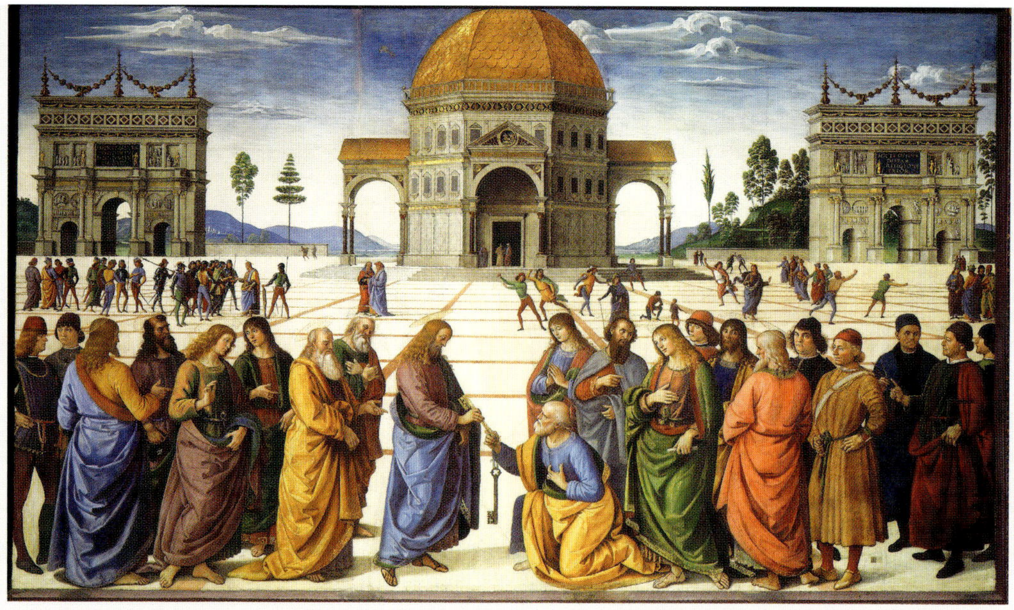

Leon Battista Alberti, in his treatise *On Painting* (1435), was the first writer of the Renaissance to codify the procedures for crafting linear perspective, and gave credit to Brunelleschi for developing the technique. From this time onwards, artists' attempting to render spaces with accurate perspective became the norm. The great majority of these images were based on one-point perspective as a way to reinforce an emphasis on ideal form that relied on bilateral symmetry. An early example is Pietro Perugino's fresco in the Sistine Chapel of *Christ Giving the Keys to St Peter* (*above*), completed in 1482. It is a rigorous study in one-point perspective that sets the scene for the story, and utilises not only linear perspective, but also overlapping figures and, in the distance, atmospheric perspective.

Perspective in three dimensions

While perspective representations on two-dimensional surfaces continued to develop, architects began to experiment with ways to manipulate three-dimensional space to alter visitors' perceptions of spatial depth. By and large, these places continued to rely on the formality provided by axial symmetry. In the mid-1500s, Michelangelo designed the Piazza del Campidoglio, in Rome, to have buildings that were set at angles to the central axis of the space (*right*). When the visitor stands at the entry to the piazza, the capitol building at the far end appears to be closer than it actually is, and the effect is reversed when viewed from the opposite direction. It's an optical illusion on a grand scale, intended to manipulate one's understanding of physical space through the use of perspective principles. This has become known as a 'forced perspective': the arrangement of the spaces 'forces' our perception of spatial depth, in one direction or the other. Another famous and roughly contemporary example was designed by Andrea Palladio in 1585. His Teatro Olimpico, in Vicenza, Italy, uses a forced perspective view as part of a permanent stage set. The backdrop to the stage is a formal facade with openings that reveal what appear to be streets going off into the distance. In reality, the floor slopes upwards and the walls angle inwards, which gives the impression that the spaces beyond the openings are much deeper than they actually are.

Pushing boundaries

As the Baroque era developed in the 17th century, the desire for ever-more daring perspective images grew. One of the most incredible examples is Andrea Pozzo's trompe l'œil ceiling fresco at Sant'Ignazio in Rome (*opposite, right*), painted in 1684–95. It's a tour de force in perspective construction, all the more impressive when we consider that it was painted on a curved, barrel-vaulted ceiling.

Giovanni Battista Piranesi, from about 1748–1774, created an extensive series of etchings of Rome, including the decrepit ruins of the ancient city (*opposite, far right*). The views were a departure from the ideal formality of Renaissance painting – they were less rigid and more about the off-centre view of a casual visitor, so Piranesi more frequently used two-point perspective. Partly because the etchings were available as prints, these images had great influence on later artists, helping lead them in the direction of the more romantic, natural (or

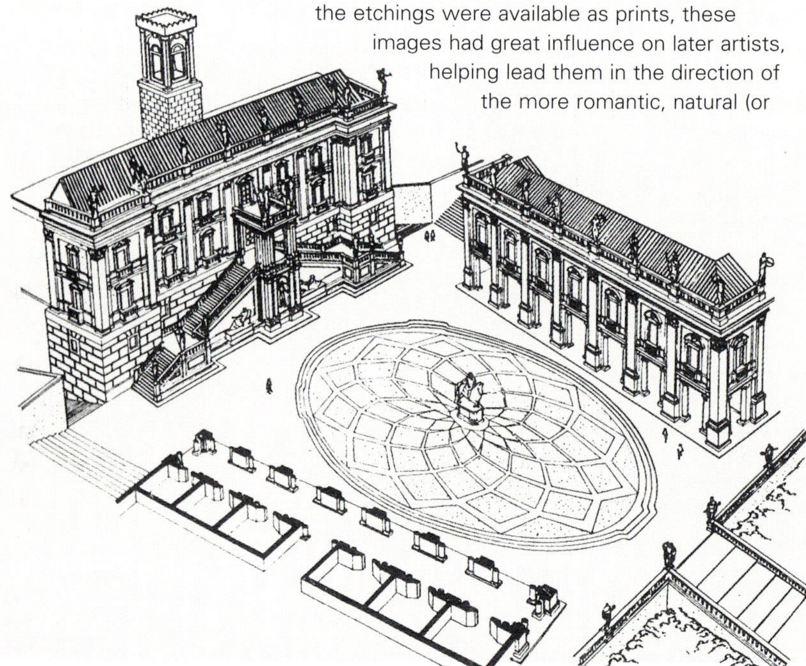

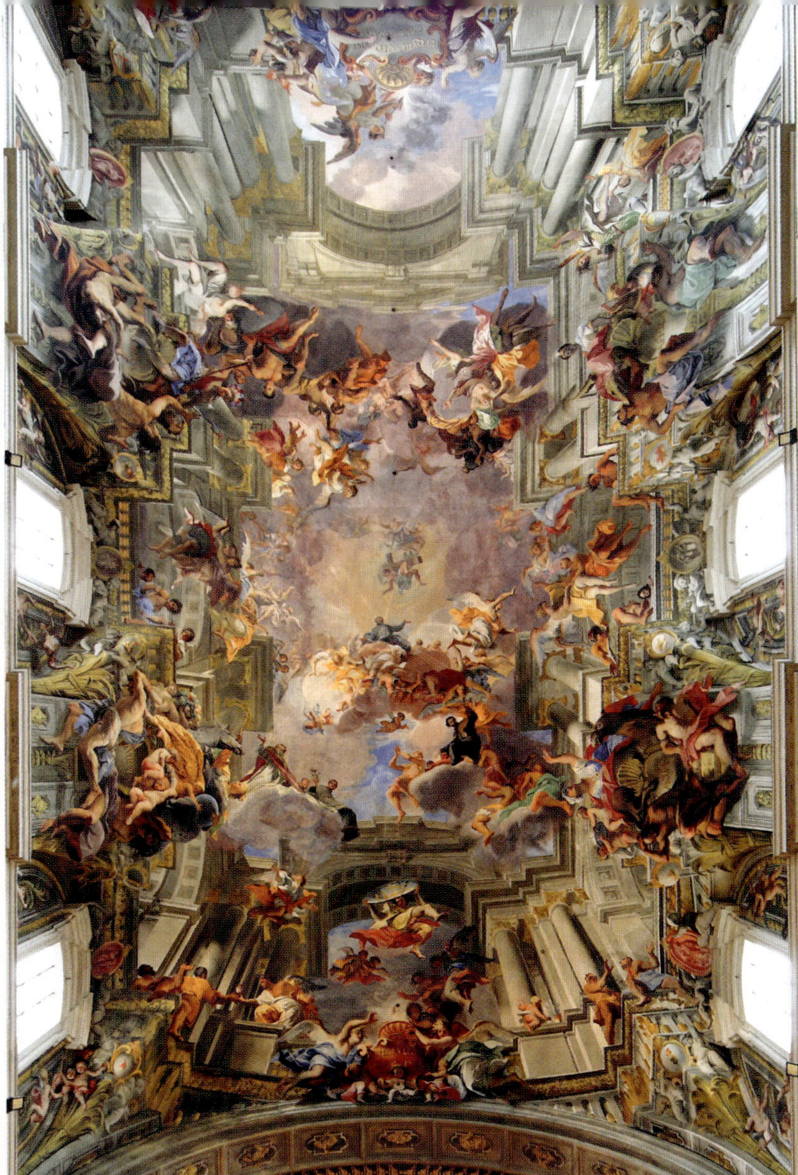

perspective to draw a complete view of the interior of the Collégiale Saint-Denis in his hometown of Liège, Belgium.

More recently, digital tools have advanced our ability to create virtual three-dimensional models, and from these we can take complex perspective views, but they haven't replaced our desire to use some simple knowledge of perspective to draw what we see from direct observation. This leads back to the basics of perspective drawing: we don't need to be experts or to use advanced technology to make good use of perspective in drawing the endlessly fascinating world around us.

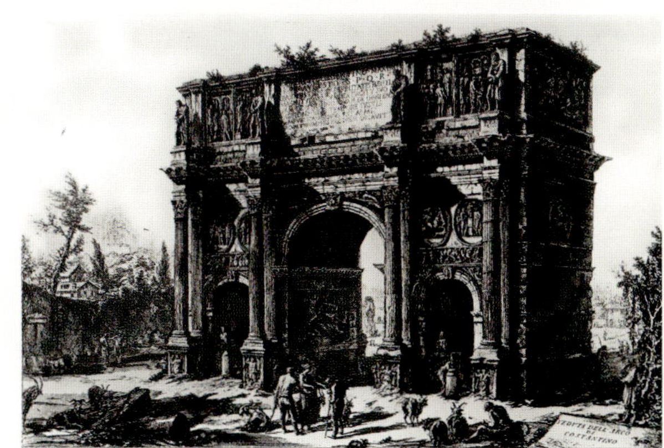

even supernatural) visions to come in the 19th century.

Building on the romantic notions of other artists and writers, painters of the American landscape in the 1800s used light, scale and atmosphere to depict the grandeur of untrammelled wilderness. These paintings were not about the urban world, so there are few, if any, lines of convergence to speak of. The way in which spatial depth was portrayed had to work for this type of subject matter. Strong shafts of light, overlapping forms and diminished detail and colour saturation in the distance – all these strategies combine in the works of artists such as Albert Bierstadt to give a strong sense of limitless depth.

Perspective in modern art

In the past century, experimentation with perspective has continued. M.C. Escher regularly explored ways to play with perspective and our perception of spatial depth. Continuing a long tradition, Gérard Michel (*right*) has conducted his own experiments with perspective on both two- and three-dimensional surfaces. In this case he used spherical

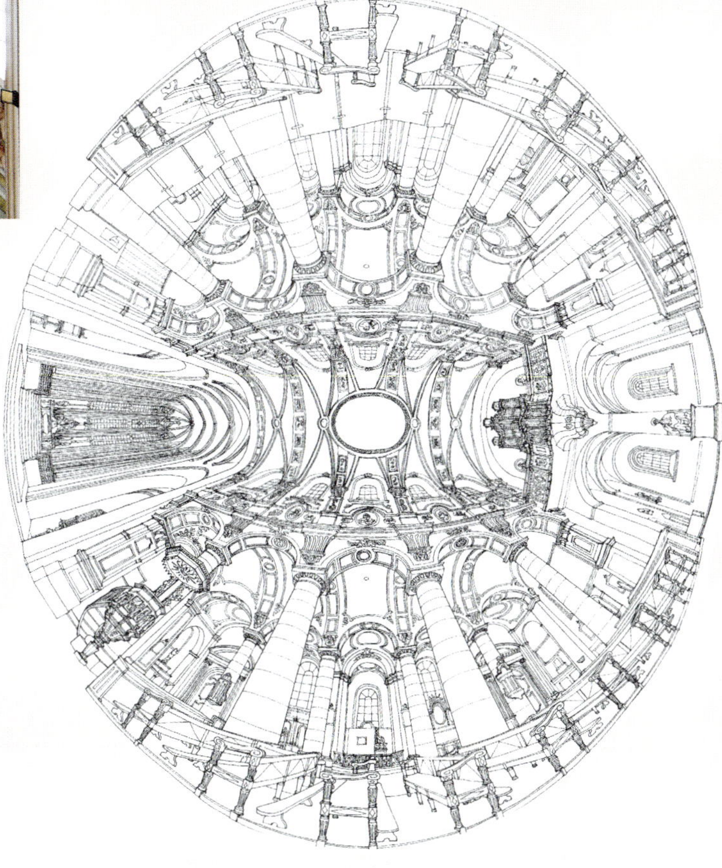

Perspective basics

Perspective is the means by which we can create the illusion of three-dimensional space on a two-dimensional surface. To be able to draw with perspective, it helps to have some understanding of basic terms and concepts that are applicable to all types of perspective drawing. When we can see and identify these basics, and we understand why things appear as they do, it becomes easier to observe the scenes we see and recreate them as sketches.

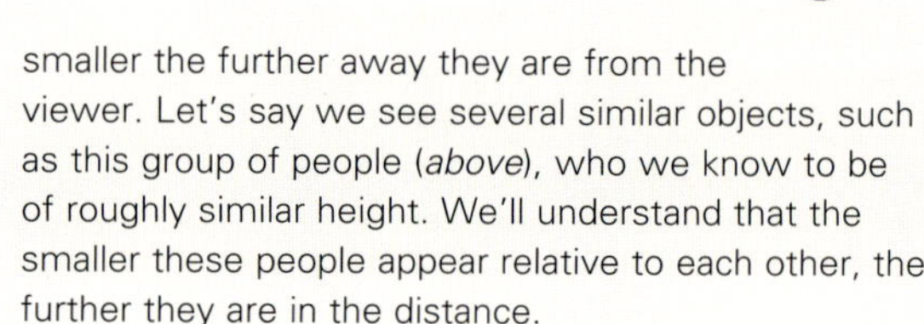

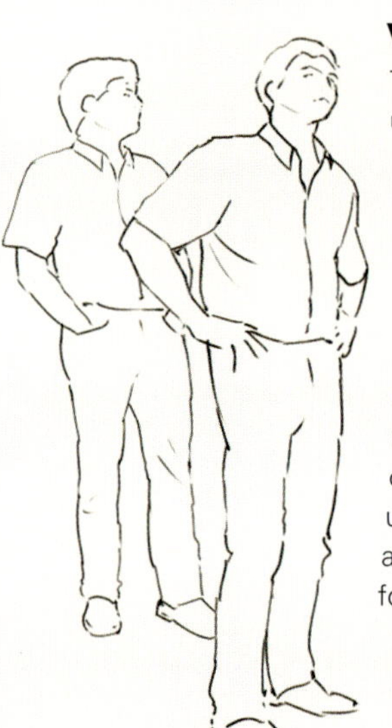

Visual depth cues

There are several visual cues that help us understand spatial depth – that is, how near or far we are from what we see.

OVERLAP

If one object overlaps another (*left*), the object that is partially hidden will be understood to be further in the distance from the object that's obscuring our view. So if we see two people, and our view of one is partially blocked by the other, we understand immediately that one is further away, as seen in this simple sketch. The same holds true for any group of objects that appear to overlap.

RELATIVE SIZE

Perhaps the most basic principle of visual depth, and the one that has the greatest effect on perspective drawing, is this: objects appear to get smaller the further away they are from the viewer. Let's say we see several similar objects, such as this group of people (*above*), who we know to be of roughly similar height. We'll understand that the smaller these people appear relative to each other, the further they are in the distance.

ATMOSPHERIC PERSPECTIVE

When we see objects at a significant distance, often when we view landscapes at long range, we're seeing them through more 'atmosphere' – that is, through more dust particles and water vapour that affect what we're able to see. The most distant objects will appear to be fainter in value (less contrast between the darks and lights), and sometimes cooler in colour (fewer warm tones and more blues and purples). Conversely, objects in the near distance appear to be sharper, showing more detail and value contrast, and exhibit a more complete range of warm and cool colours. It can be a subtle distinction, but it's one of the ways in which we perceive spatial depth and it can be used to emphasise great distance in drawing or painting.

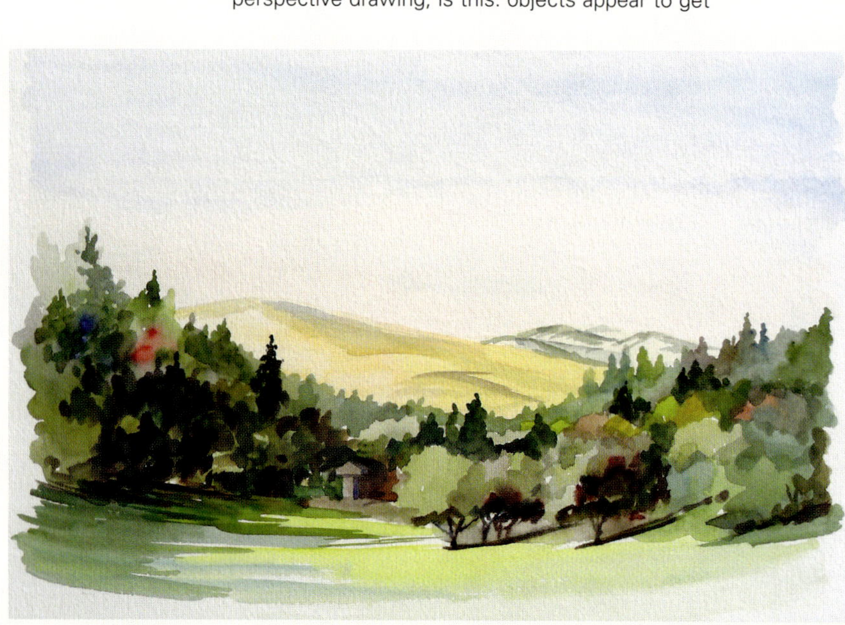

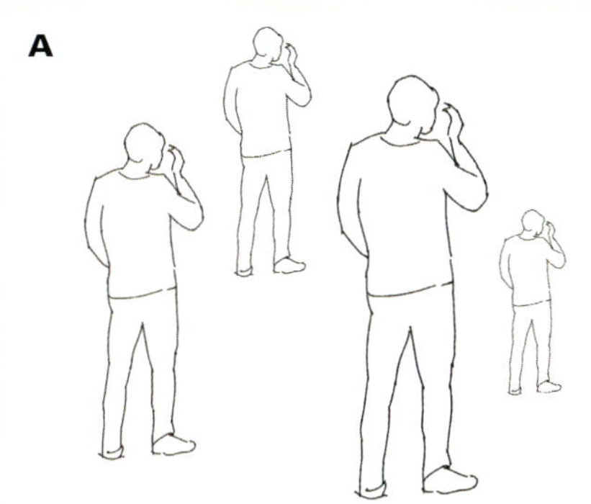

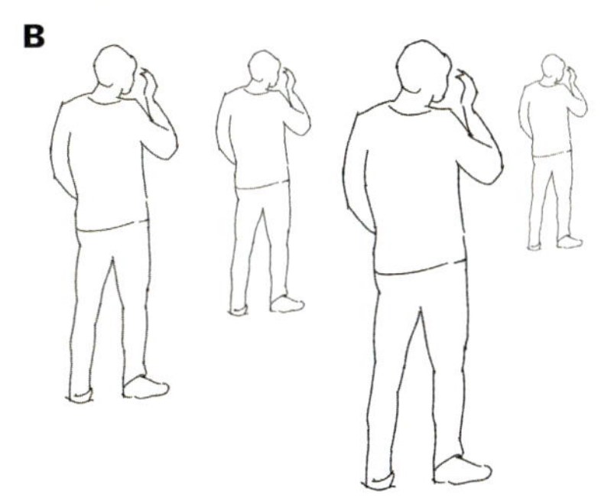

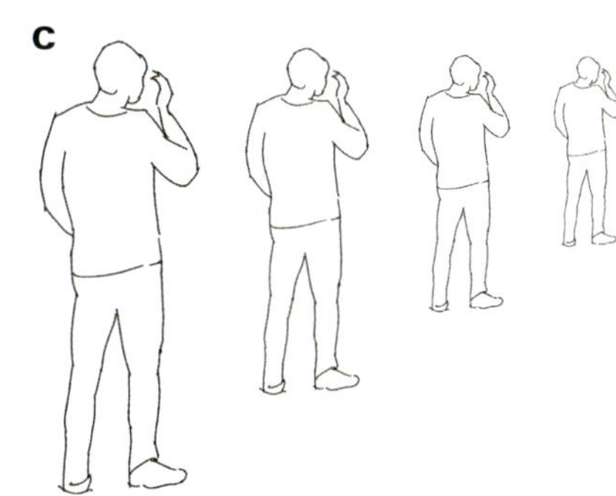

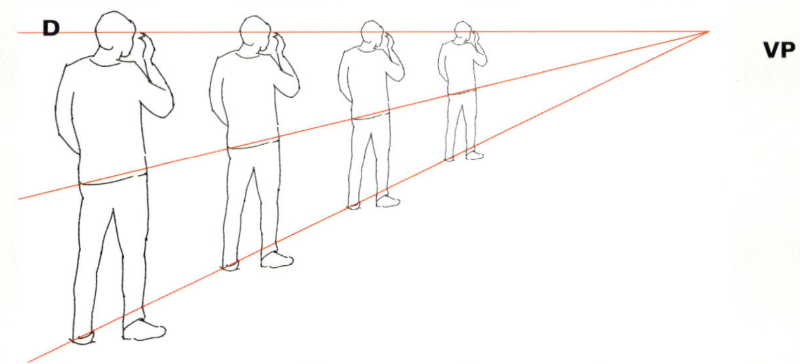

RELATIVE POSITION

Overlap, atmosphere and relative size are effective cues that help us to understand spatial depth. But the relative positions of objects – particularly of similar objects – also helps us understand the distance between our viewpoint and our subject. What if we see the same figure, at various sizes, but also positioned randomly in our view (**A**)? The result doesn't tell us very much about spatial depth. But if the same group of figures is arranged with their heads all at approximately the same level (**B**), we begin to understand that the largest figure is the nearest, and the smallest is the furthest from our point of view. If the same group of figures is arranged from the largest at left to the smallest at right (**C**), it becomes even more apparent that they are diminishing into the distance. If we draw lines connecting their eyes, their waists and their feet (**D**), we see that these lines all converge on the same point.

Lines of convergence

Once they have been established in a drawing, these lines can be used to determine the size of additional figures that are nearer or further away from our point of view. Any set of parallel lines, anywhere in space, will appear to converge on a single point as they recede into the distance, because the space between each pair of lines will appear to become progressively smaller as their distance from the viewer increases.

The same is true for any set of objects of similar height, arranged along a straight line, like the columns in this photo (*below*). Except for the two broken columns in the foreground, all of the tops and bottoms are aligned along lines of convergence that appear to 'vanish' at a single point in the distance (the *vanishing point* or **VP** as labelled in this book). By establishing these lines, we can begin to visualise what this scene would look like if the row of columns were extended in either direction.

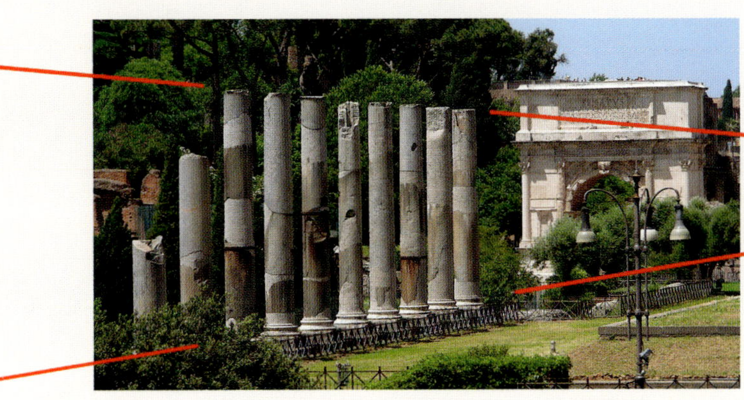

Vanishing points

As seen on the previous page, vanishing points are the precise spots at which groups of lines that are parallel in space will appear to converge. These groups of lines may be oriented vertically, horizontally or at some angle in space, but if they are parallel to one another, they will appear to meet at vanishing points as they recede into the distance, away from the viewer. In this photograph *(right)*, there are numerous lines that are oriented horizontally in space – the rail tracks, the power lines overhead, the yellow line on the platform, etc. Because all of these lines are parallel to one another, they will all appear to converge on the same vanishing point, which is located just to the right of the oncoming train.

Horizon line

Two very important concepts regarding perspective are 'horizon line' and 'eye level', which are closely related but not the same thing. The horizon line is where the earth and the sky appear to meet in the extreme distance. When we're standing on a beach and looking out to sea, the horizon line is very apparent. It's usually less easy to spot in other situations, because buildings and trees and other objects are in the way. However, when any set of parallel lines is oriented horizontally *(right)*, its vanishing point will invariably be located on the horizon line. In this case, if we follow the lines of convergence to the vanishing point just to the right of the train, and then envision a horizontal line running through that point, we will see the horizon line – and this strategy will work in most situations. As you'll see in the coming chapters, the location of the horizon line can be of great help in determining the locations of vanishing points for as many sets of parallel horizontal lines as you might encounter in a particular view.

Eye level

Each of us has our own eye level that we take with us wherever we go. It's simply the height and orientation of our eyes at any given time and place. Think of your eye level as a flat plane, stretching out in the direction of your gaze *(below)*. Depending on your positioning the resulting perspective will be different from what others are seeing. So your unique position in space – and specifically the position of your eyes – will greatly contribute to how you perceive a particular subject.

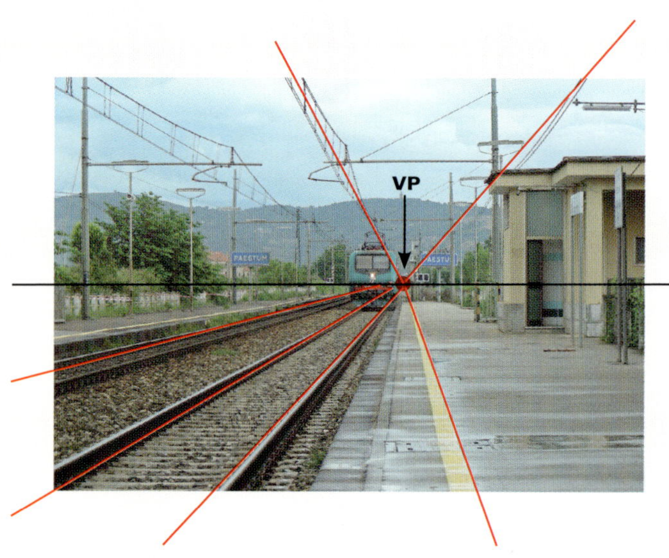

Line of sight and cone of vision

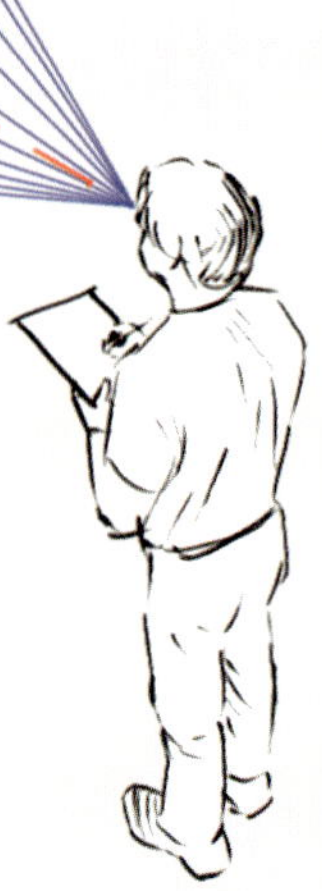

Closely related to eye level is our 'line of sight' – the specific direction in which we're looking at any given time. Think of it as a straight line emanating from a point right between your eyes and running outwards in the direction of your view *(right)*. Most often we're looking straight ahead, and when we draw, we usually face directly towards our subject. But there are times when we need to look up or down at a subject (as in a three-point perspective). So our line of sight is usually, though not always, parallel to the ground. In most views, what we see and what we're trying to draw will be limited to a central 'cone of vision'. This is the area of our vision with the greatest focus and the least distortion. For what it's worth, the cone is usually assumed to be about 60 degrees, but it is obviously somewhat variable as it relates to our peripheral vision, which is defined by a wider cone of approximately 140 degrees vertically and perhaps 180 degrees horizontally. This broader peripheral vision, and the way that objects will appear to distort outside the central cone of vision, is taken into account when we consider curvilinear perspective views.

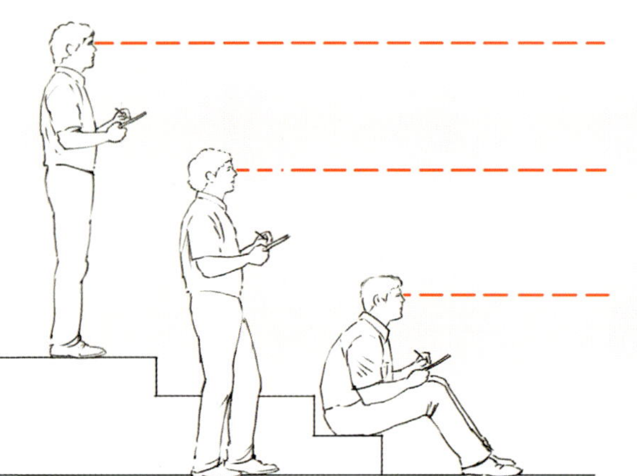

If you are seated, your eye level will be lower than if you were standing on the ground and it would be different again if you were on a platform above.

Techniques for seeing and sketching

In the brief moment between looking at a subject and looking down at your sketchbook, your brain does a lot to analyse what you've just seen – subconsciously, without you even thinking about it. This has a significant effect on the drawing; it usually means that what you draw doesn't look like what you see. Thankfully, there are a few simple strategies that will help enormously, provided you make them part of your regular workflow for sketching.

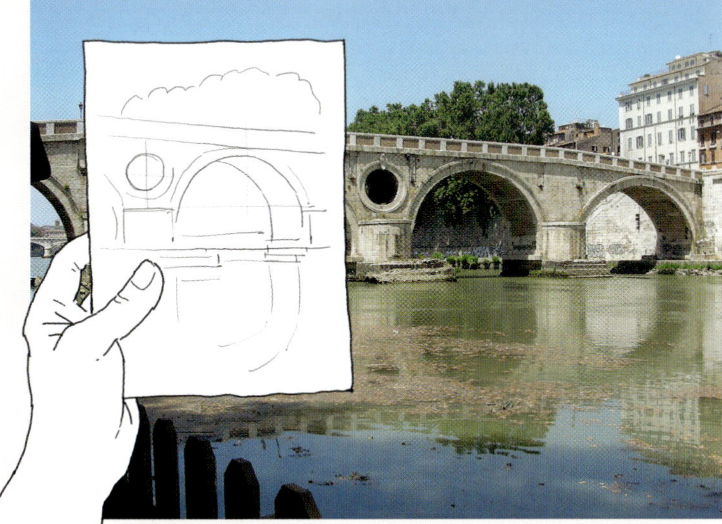

▲ Hold your sketchbook all the way up so that your initial lines and the subject are side by side, and at the same size.

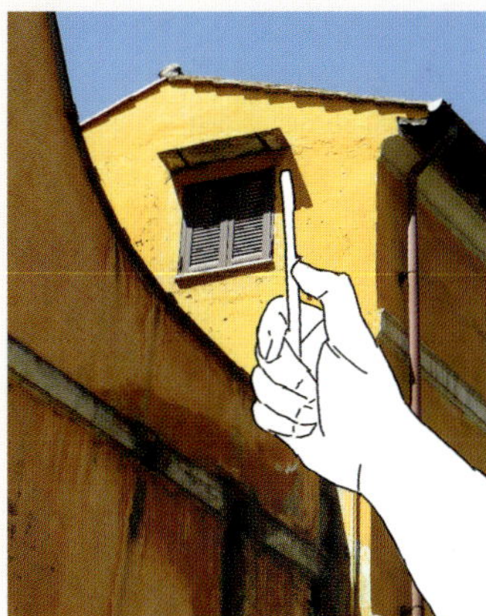

▲ Use a portion of the pencil, as marked with your thumb, to compare the size of one object to another.

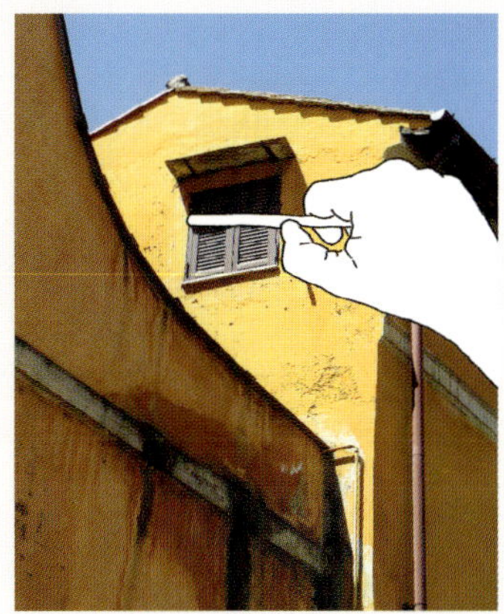

▲ Using this method you can judge that the window is roughly as tall as it is wide.

SIGHT SIZING

This is the single most effective way to check your progress as you're laying out the rough guidelines for any sketch, yet for some reason people often seem reluctant to use the technique. Simply hold your sketch up, right next to the subject beyond, and move your book nearer to or further from your eyes until the sketch and the subject are about the same size (*left*). Are the shapes and sizes correct? Are the angles of the perspective accurate? If not, make the necessary corrections to the layout lines and go through this process again until you achieve the level of accuracy you're after.

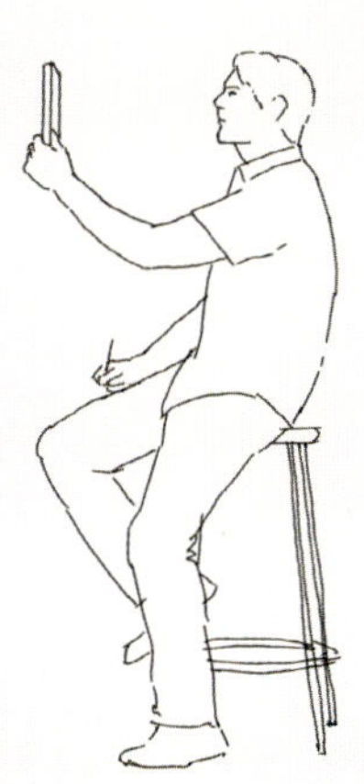

PENCIL SIGHTING

This technique uses your pencil (or pen) as a rough measuring device. While closing one eye, hold your pencil as shown in these diagrams (*below*). It's not necessary to hold your arm perfectly straight, as long as you keep the distance between the pencil and your eye consistent when making any set of measurements. Your measurements don't need to be very precise, but they can really help to create an overall level of accuracy in the drawing. Pencil sighting can also be used to help determine angles of perspective, and will also be covered in the step-by-step sequences later in the book.

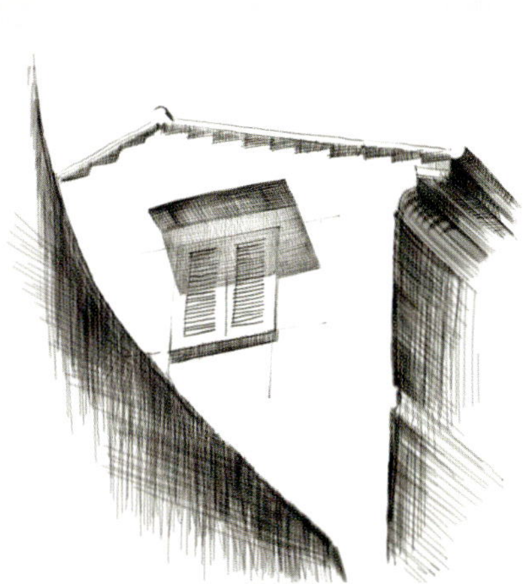

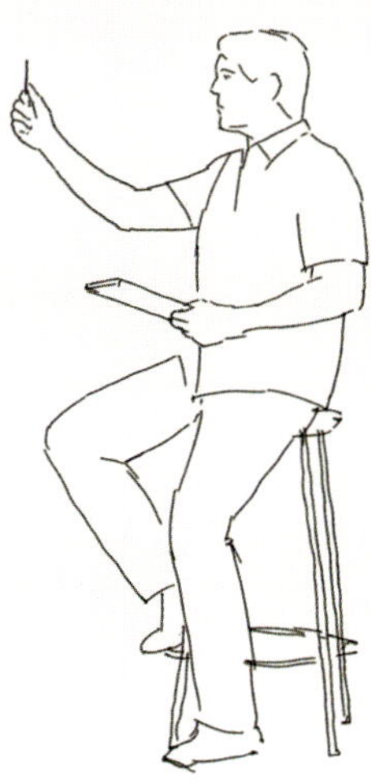

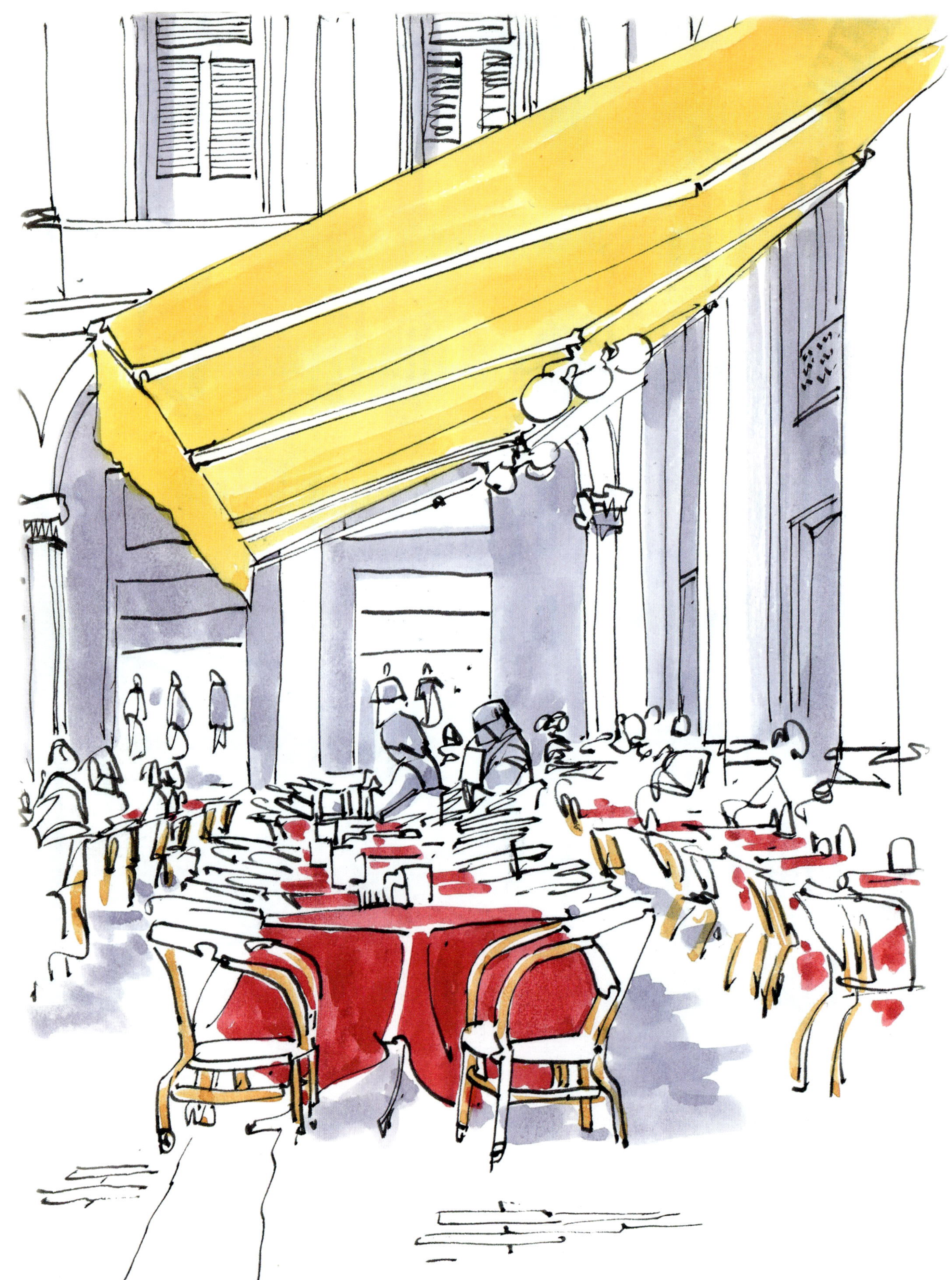

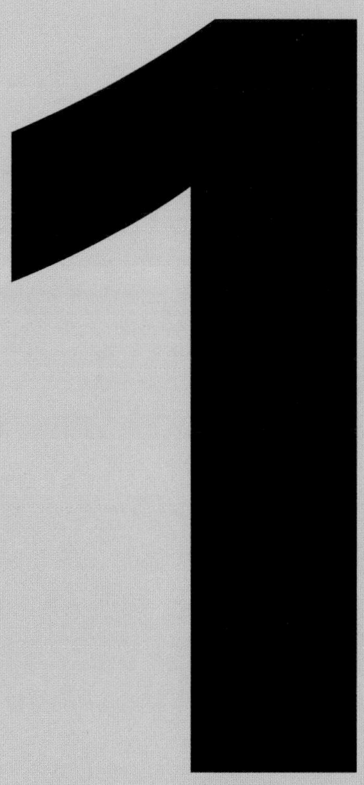

1

POINT PERSPECTIVE

The simplest type of perspective drawing is called 'one-point' because we're only dealing with a single vanishing point. One-point perspective is very commonly seen in street views or at any time when our line of sight is parallel to one set of horizontal lines and perpendicular to other sets of lines in the view.

◀ CAFE SCENE • *Miguel Herranz* • Fountain pen and watercolour

Introduction

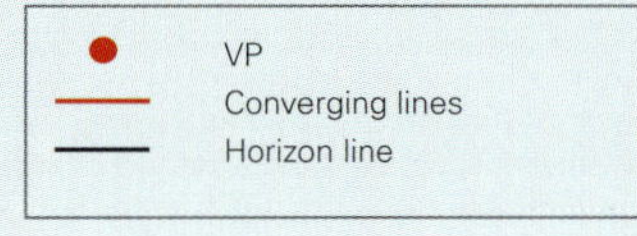

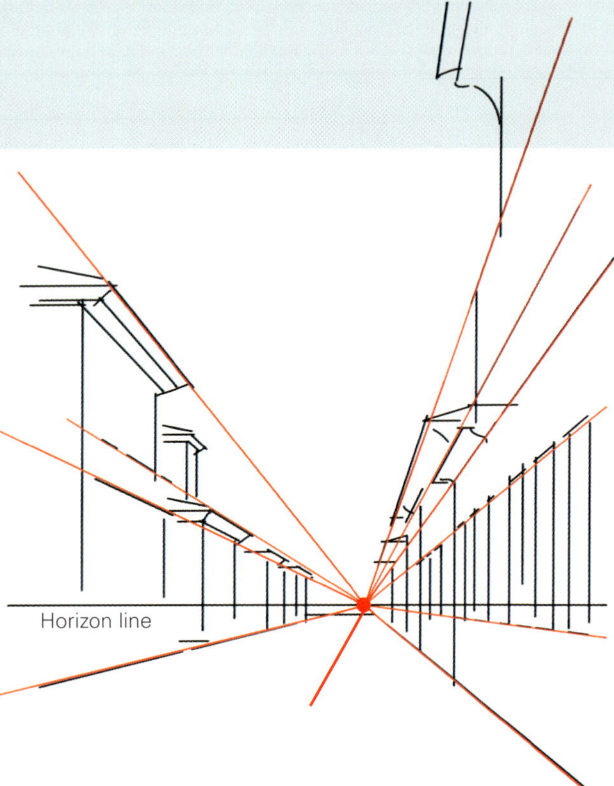

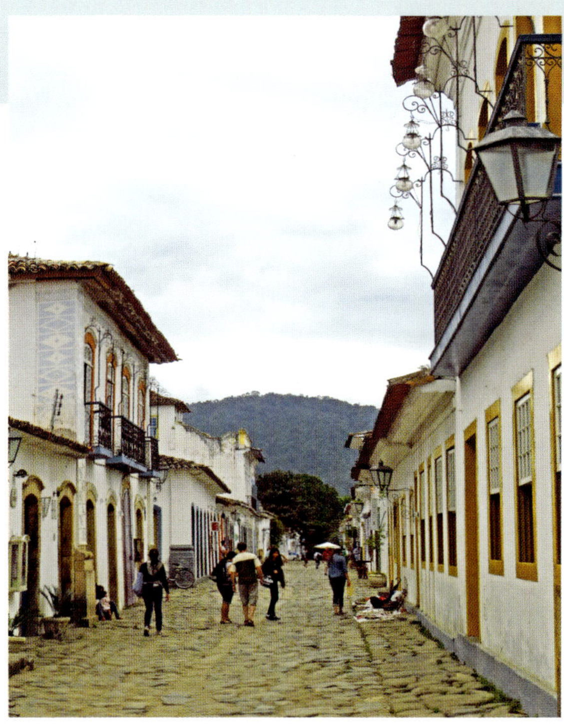

What is one-point perspective?

It happens when your line of sight is parallel to the horizontal set of lines that diminish to, or converge upon, a single point in the distance. If you're not looking up into the sky or down towards the ground, this point will be on the horizon line, and that line will coincide with your eye level.

One-point perspective can be challenging to see in the real world, because our peripheral vision will make lines appear to warp and converge on other points as well. But if we focus on the view in the middle distance and beyond, the relatively simple structure of the perspective becomes apparent. Ideally, you could look at a building in real life and see glowing lines along the edges with arrows pointing to the vanishing points, just like in this book.

In a modern city that's arranged on a rectilinear grid, there will be one set of parallel lines running in one direction, and another set of parallel lines running perpendicular to the first set. If we look straight down a street in a gridded city, we'll see a one-point perspective: the lines running parallel to our line of sight will appear to converge on a single point in the distance, while the opposing set of perpendicular lines will appear to be horizontal in the view, and the vertical lines will appear to remain vertical.

▲ ▶ This long, straight street in Paraty, Brazil is an excellent example of one-point perspective – all the major lines of the buildings that run parallel to the street (and to your line of vision) appear to converge on a single point at the far end, at the same height as your eye level.

▶ RUA DO COMÉRCIO, PARATY, BRAZIL
Matthew Brehm • Graphite and watercolour

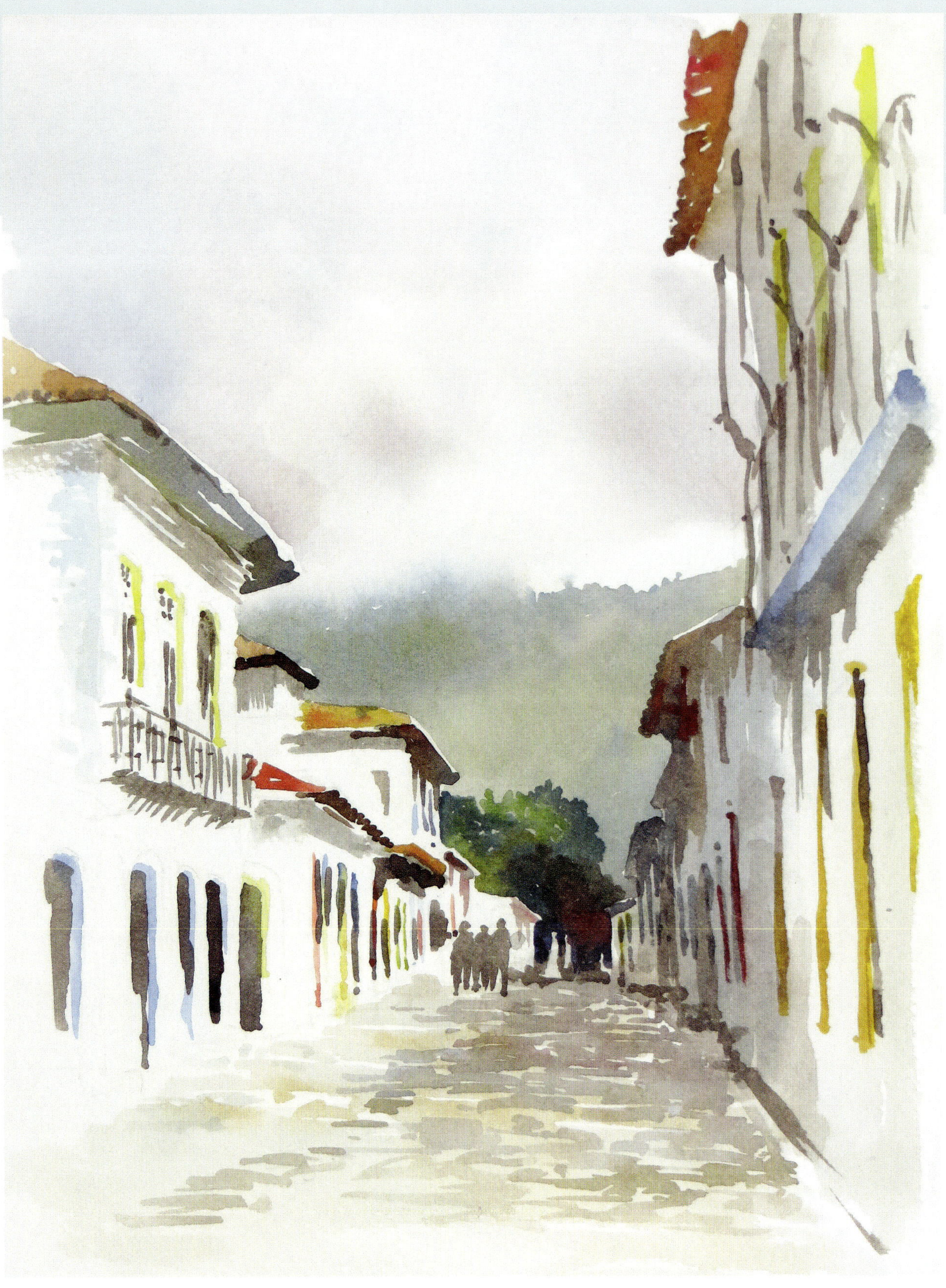

one-point perspective
Seeing it

In any given view, if you're only able to observe a single set of converging lines, you're seeing a one-point perspective. If these converging lines are oriented horizontally in space, such as roof guttering, they will invariably converge on a single point on the horizon line.

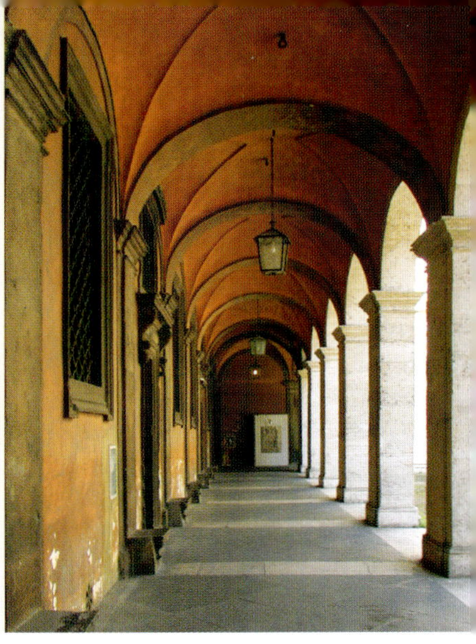

► Linear views like this are primarily defined by lines that converge on a single point in the distance.

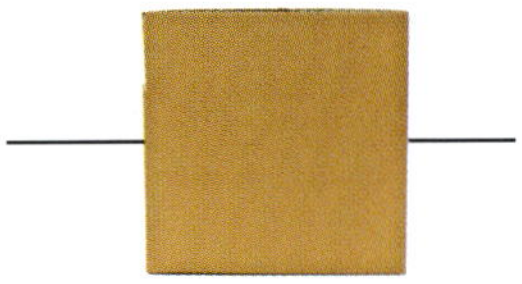

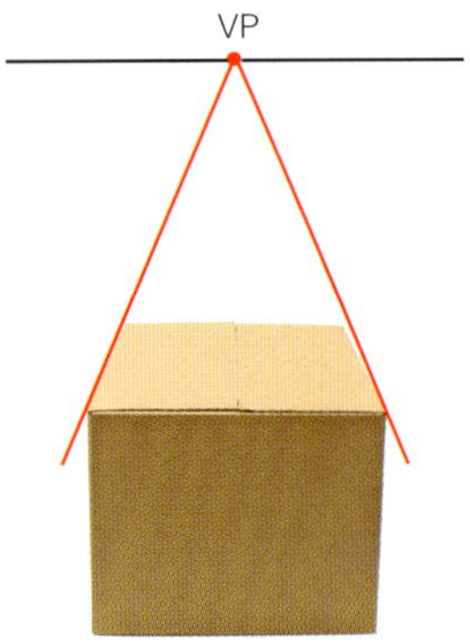

AT ITS SIMPLEST
A closed box viewed directly from the side at eye level – also known as an 'elevation view' – will appear as a simple two-dimensional rectangle (left). Without seeing more than this one side of the box, we have no visual clues regarding spatial depth – there's no telling how large or small the box really is. But if our point of view were to be lowered or elevated, either the bottom or top of the box would come into view, providing our first visual clues regarding its three-dimensional form.

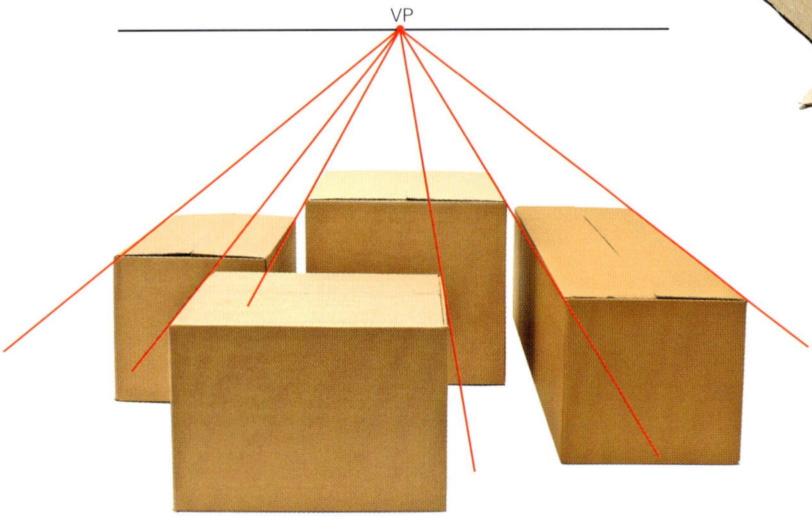

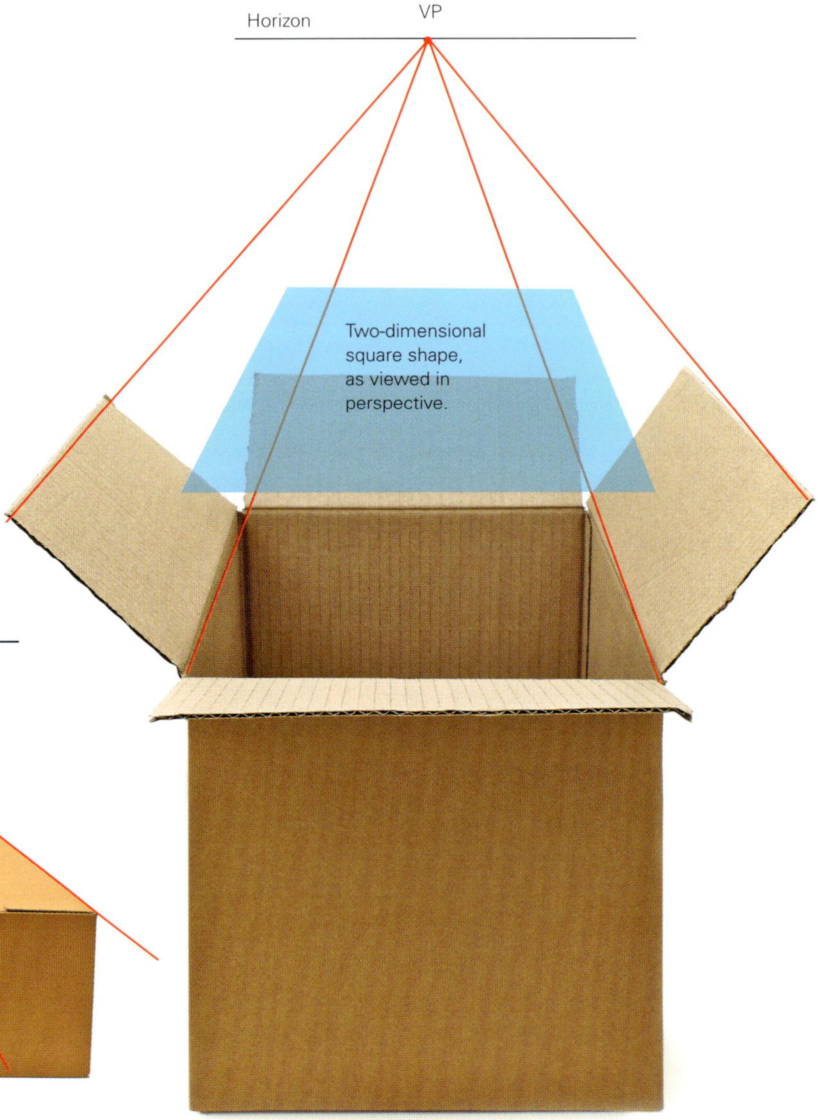

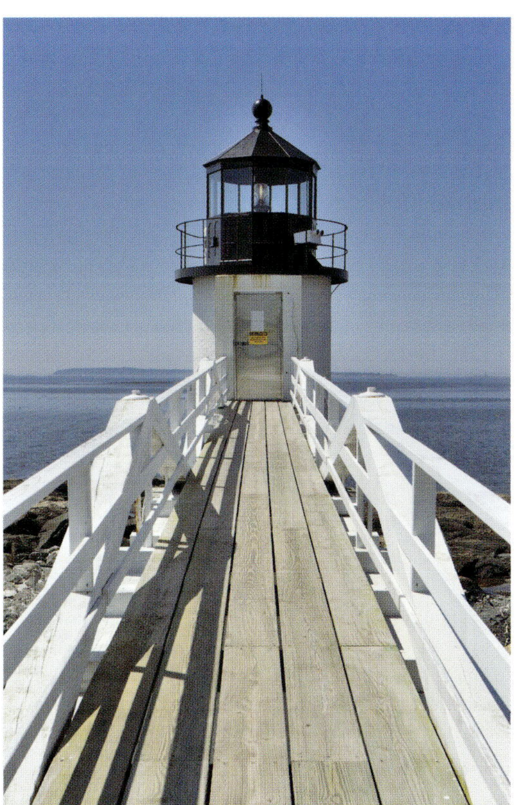

▲ **Straight-on view** The horizontal lines of these railings appear to converge on a point at the same height as our eye level, which typically coincides with the horizon line in the distance.

A SIMPLE HOUSE

As with the example of the box, if we view a house straight on (that is, in an 'elevation view'), it will appear as nothing more than the facade or 'face' of the building. Viewed from above, on the other hand, we can see the horizontal edges and peak of the roof. Because these lines are parallel to one another and horizontally oriented in space, they appear to converge on a common point on the horizon line.

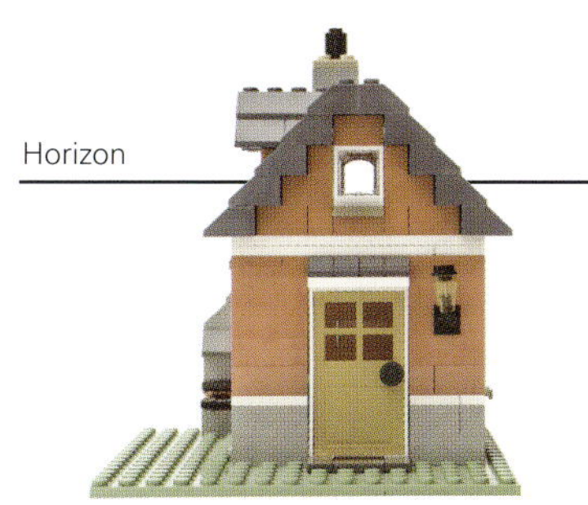

▲ **Straight-on view** The house appears as nothing more than the facade or 'face' of the building.

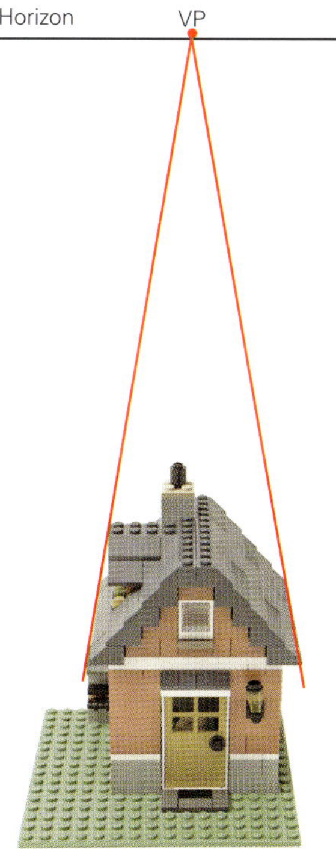

▲ **Viewed from above** The horizontal edges and peak of the roof appear to converge on a common point on the horizon line.

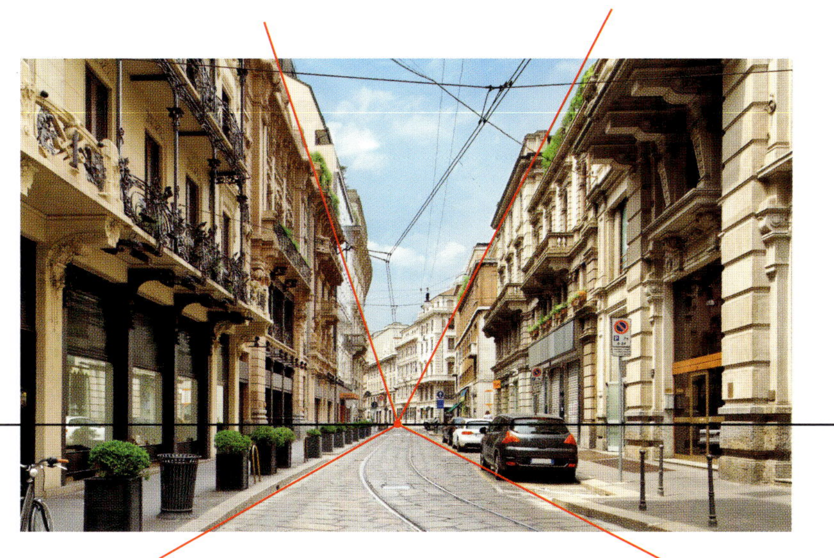

TYPICAL STREET VIEW

As with the examples of the box and house, the same visual cues to depth can be observed in this long, straight street. The roof lines, balcony platforms and railings, kerbs, windows, etc. are all defined by a single set of horizontal, parallel lines in space, so they all appear to converge on the same point on the horizon line, which coincides with the eye level of the viewer.

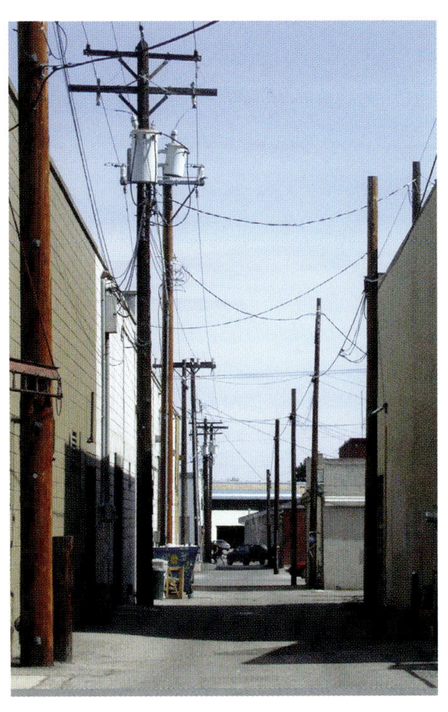

LOOK FOR A CONTINUOUS GUIDELINE

Even though the tops of the telegraph poles aren't perfectly even – some are slightly shorter or lean just a bit this way and that – they can be located with the use of a continuous guideline that links their tops and another that links the points where they meet the ground.

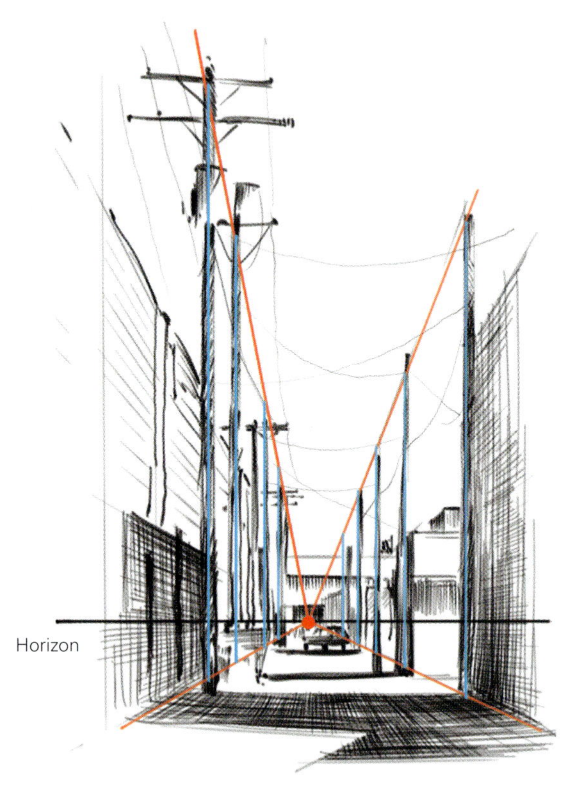

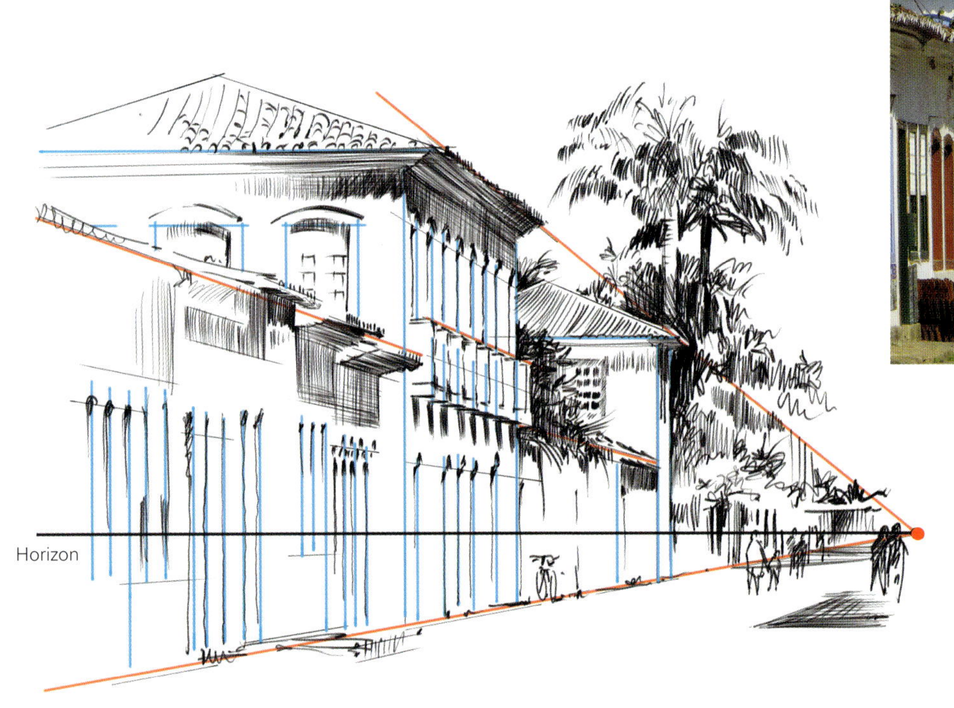

KEEP VERTICAL LINES VERTICAL

In a one-point perspective, the vertical lines of building edges, windows and doors (the blue lines in this sketch) will appear to remain vertical for the drawing. In other words, these vertical lines do not converge on vanishing points – only the lines that are parallel to your line of sight (the red lines) will converge.

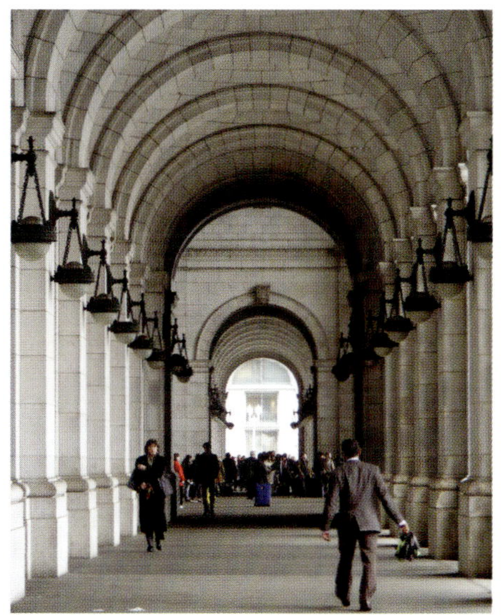

ESTABLISH THE LINES OF CONVERGENCE

The arches in this view also align along the major lines of convergence. Observe where the pilasters meet the ground and where they spring into the arches – these are the essential lines of the one-point perspective. It can also help to give yourself additional lines that will define the semicircular arches – it would be wise to sketch out one line right along the very tops of the arches as a guideline when you're first establishing the overall layout.

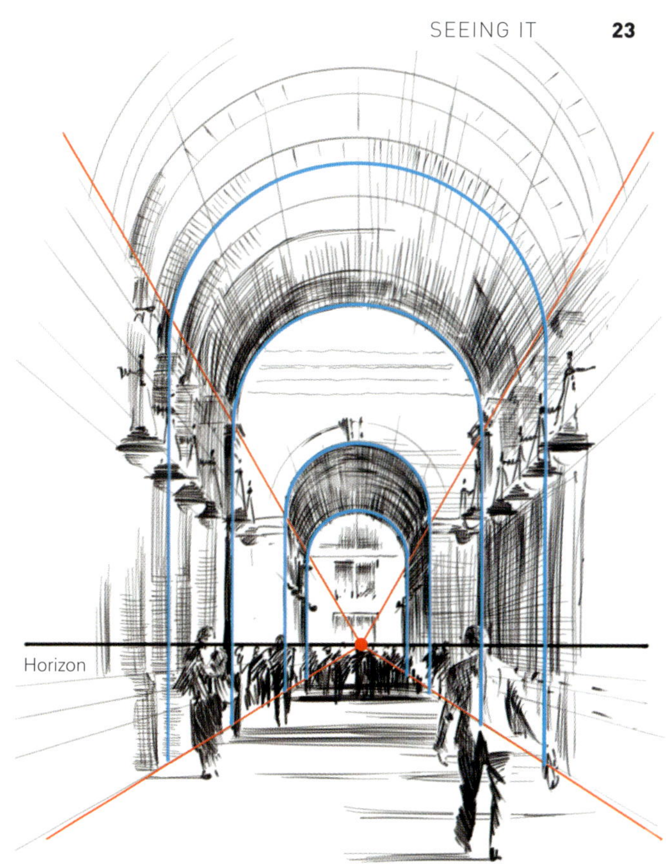

MAKE SURE THAT LINES PERPENDICULAR TO YOUR LINE OF SIGHT DO NOT CONVERGE

Like the vertical lines in the example at far left, any lines that are perpendicular to your line of sight will not appear to converge on a vanishing point. The group of horizontal lines identified in blue will remain horizontal in the drawing. The tracks in the foreground of this view are uneven and begin to deviate from the vanishing point, but they are generally parallel to your line of sight, so they converge on a single vanishing point in the distance. Incidentally, I took this photo from an adjacent platform that was a bit lower than the others, so my eye level was below that of the people in the distance.

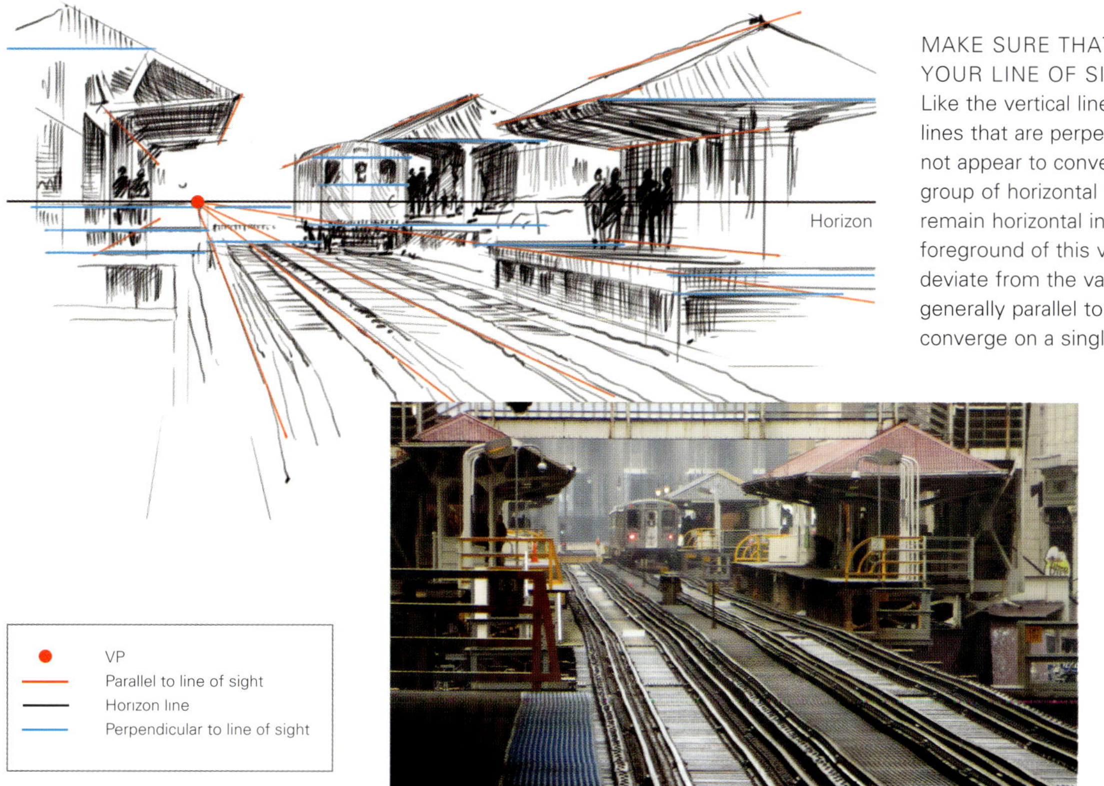

●   VP
—   Parallel to line of sight
—   Horizon line
—   Perpendicular to line of sight

Understanding it

When you're dealing with irregular or complex shapes, it's sometimes hard to see how to apply the rules of perspective. Reducing your subject to a simple shape, or even a flat plane such as a wall, makes it easier to see where the lines of convergence fall.

GO TO THE WORKBOOK

To help you understand one-point perspective, read this section then turn to pages 112–115 and try the range of exercises shown in the grid chambers.

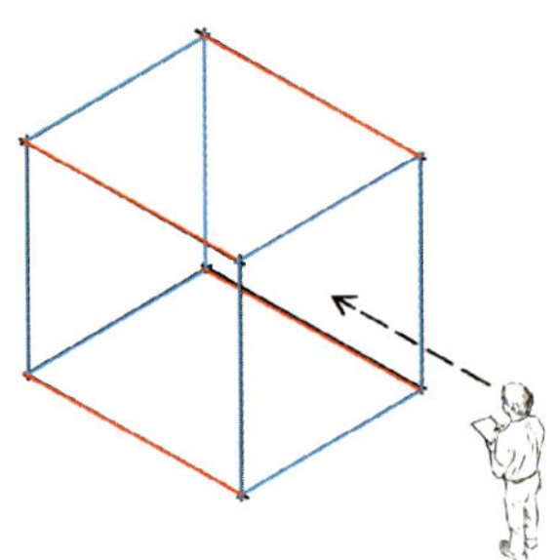

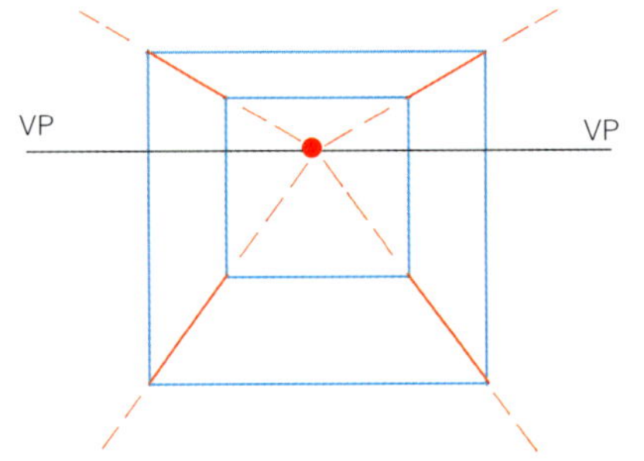

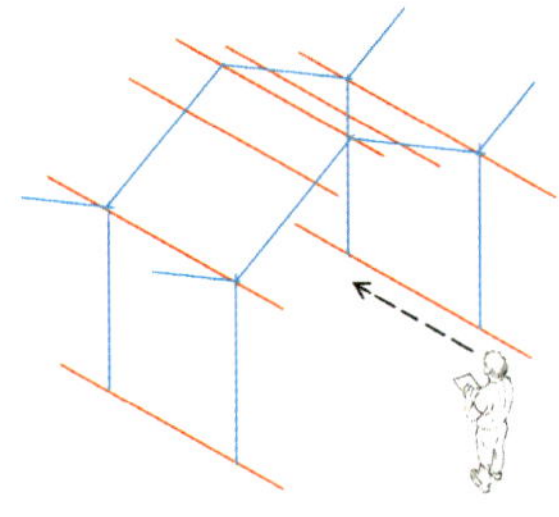

CUBE-SHAPED STRUCTURES
Imagine you are looking at this cube, and your line of sight is represented by the black dashed arrow. The red lines are parallel to your line of sight, while the blue lines are perpendicular to your line of sight.

Because the red lines are horizontal in space, they will converge on a vanishing point on the horizon line. If they were angled up or down, they would converge on a point either above or below the horizon line.

The red lines are parallel to the viewer's line of sight; the blue lines show the elements of the space that are perpendicular to the line of sight.

FOLLOWING THE RULES
This drawing by Eduardo Bajzek is of a slightly more complex view than just a simple cube – but the same rules for one-point perspective apply.

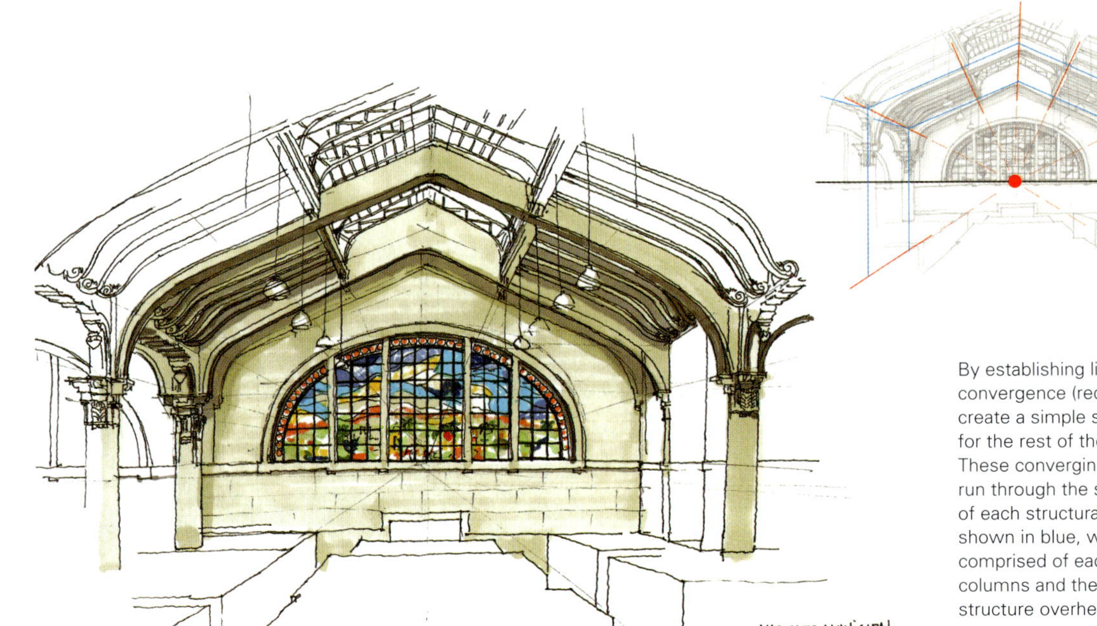

By establishing lines of convergence (red), you can create a simple structure for the rest of the image. These converging lines run through the same points of each structural frame shown in blue, which are comprised of each pair of columns and the arching structure overhead.

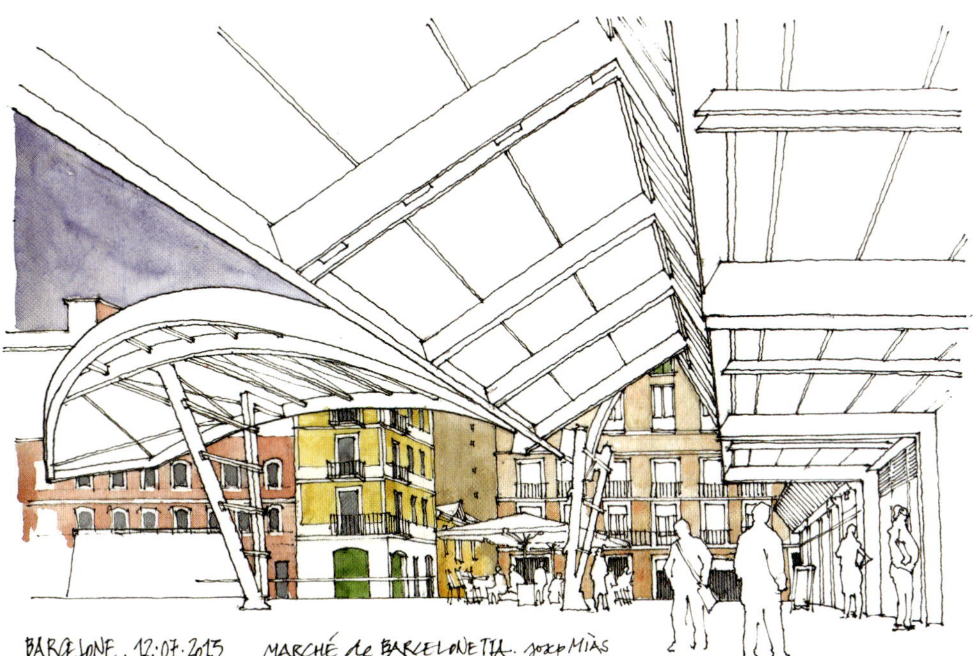

CHANGING EYE LEVEL

In this drawing by Gérard Michel, the subject is even more complex than the previous examples, yet the very same rules apply. Apparently Gérard was seated when he made this drawing, because the horizon line is evidently lower than the eye level of the people in the view. If he had been standing, the horizon line would be roughly at their eye level, and their heads would generally appear to align with each other horizontally along this line.

The lines parallel to the artist's line of sight (in red) all converge on a single vanishing point, while the lines perpendicular to his line of sight (in blue) do not converge. These blue lines might be vertical, horizontal or sloping in space – but if they are truly perpendicular to your line of sight, they do not converge towards a vanishing point.

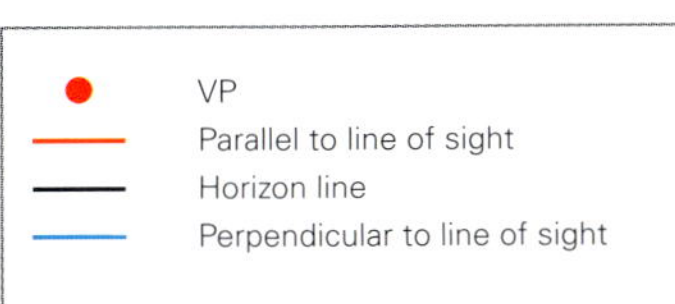

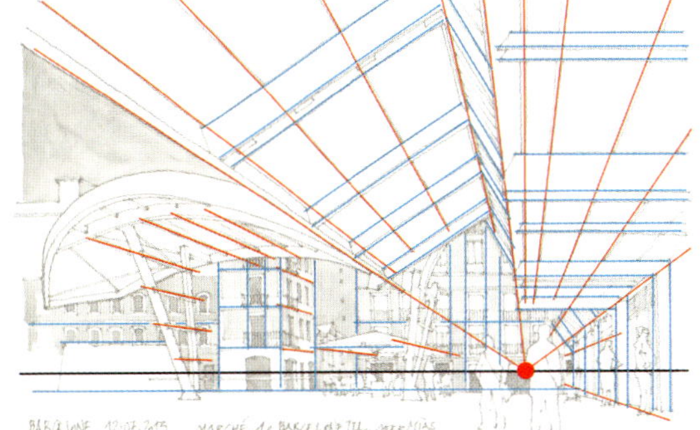

SIMPLIFY THE SHAPES

The converging lines in a one-point perspective can also be seen in many situations involving planted landscape elements. These umbrella pines in Rome, for example, are arranged along a broad, straight street that leads to the Arch of Constantine. The trees are not perfectly linear elements, but we can use the basic principles of perspective to arrange them in the drawing. Think of them in the same way as the sides of the cube (opposite) and establish how the lines converge on the horizon; don't get distracted or confused by their apparently complex shapes.

Note the tops of the trees, and the places where the trunks split into smaller limbs. These points can be visually connected to form lines that converge on the vanishing point.

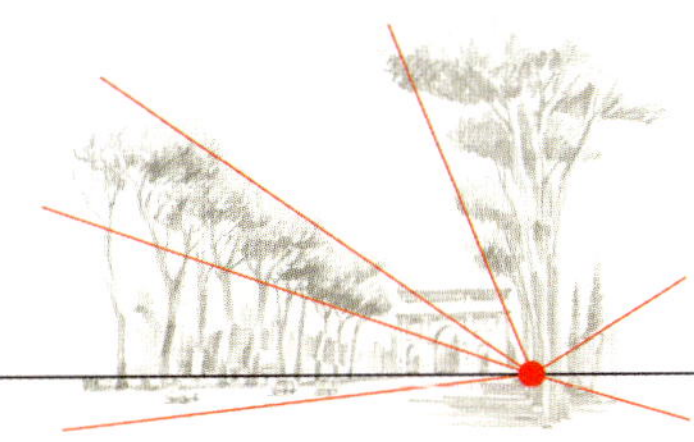

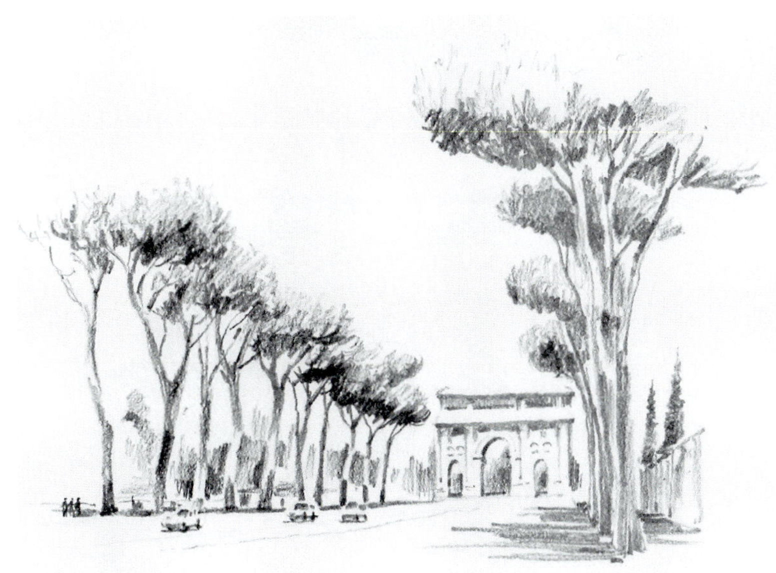

DEALING WITH EVENLY SPACED, REPEATED ELEMENTS IN A SCENE

There are many occasions when you may need to evenly distribute 'modules' in a perspective drawing. If you begin by establishing the overall rectangular forms using the ideas on the previous pages, you can use a few simple geometric strategies to distribute evenly spaced divisions of elements in the view. These strategies are also applicable in two- and three-point perspective views.

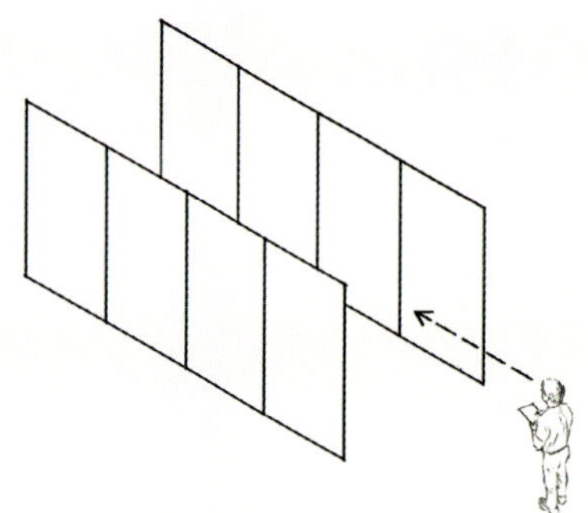

Imagine being the person in this image, looking straight between the two sets of vertical panels.

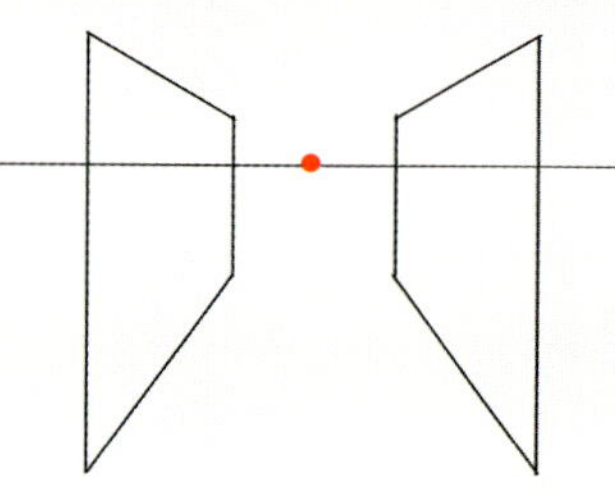

The left and right walls, taken as a whole, would appear as they do here.

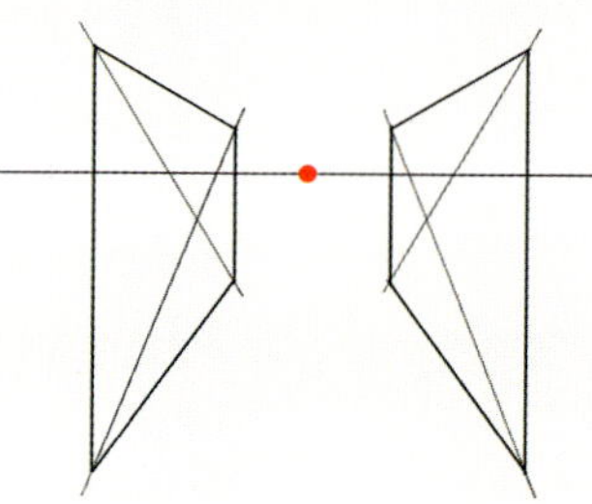

Now draw diagonals that connect the corners of each side wall to establish the centre points of the wall planes.

DIVIDING THE SPACE

Florian Afflerbach's drawing of a railway station employs a strategy similar to that explained above, and his diagonal guidelines for working out the measurements are clearly visible, especially on the far left part of the drawing.

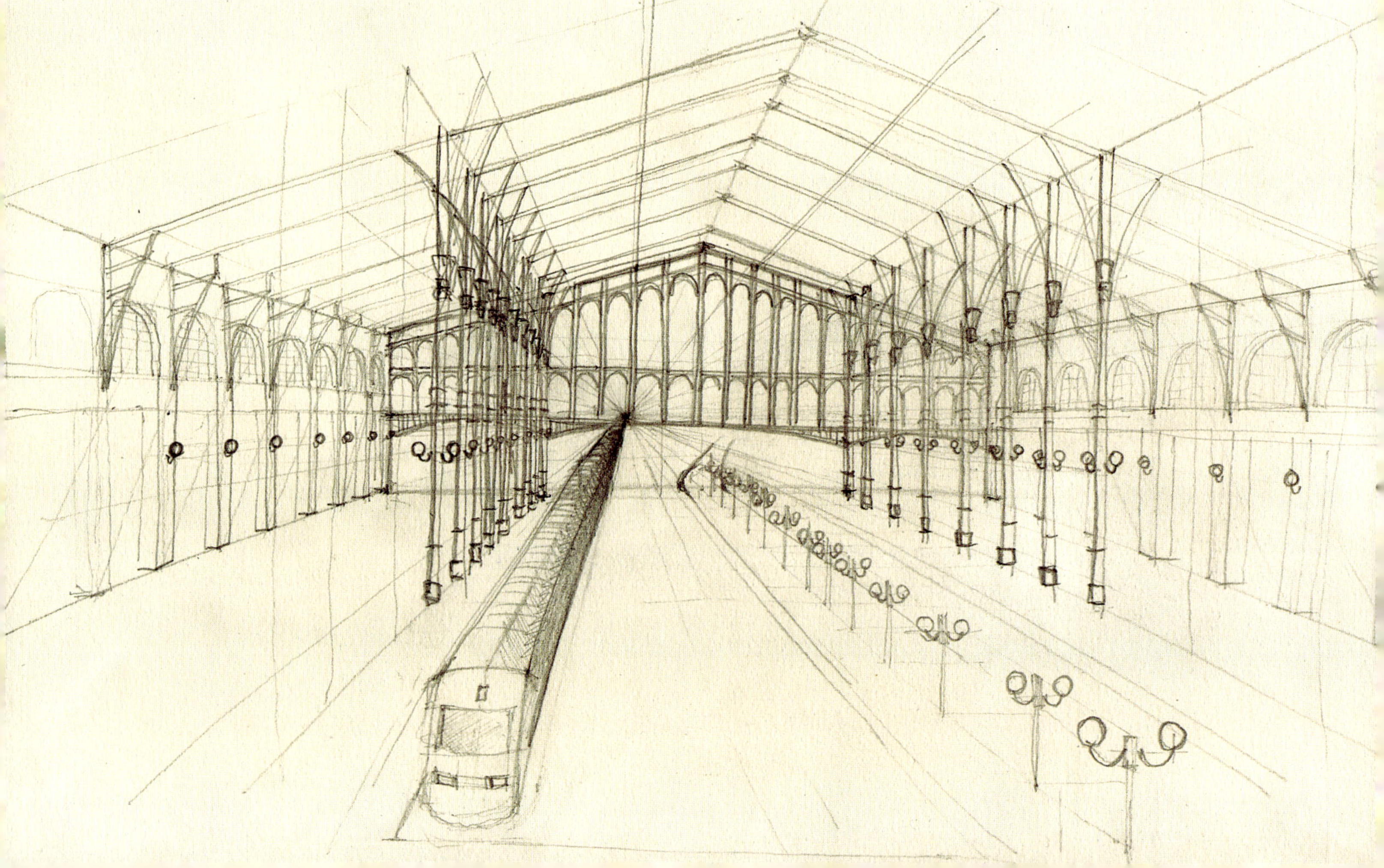

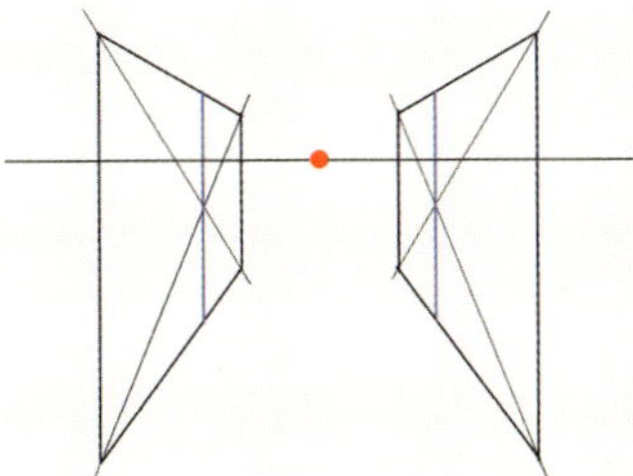

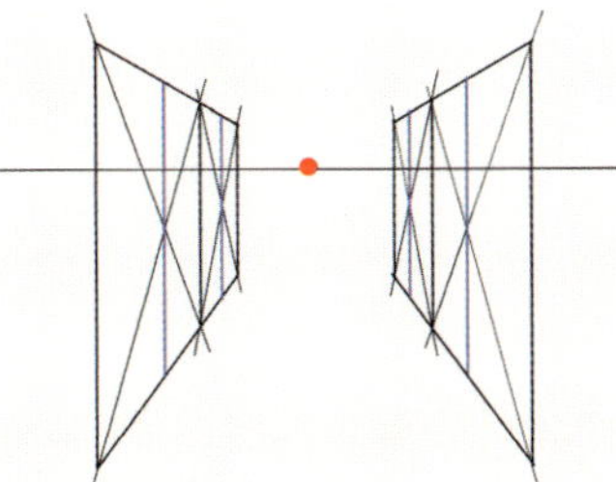

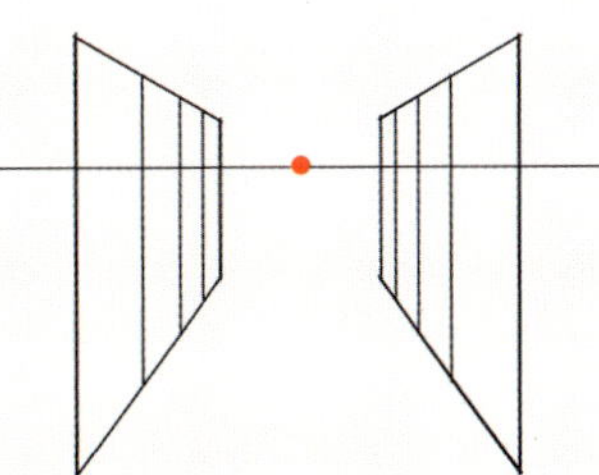

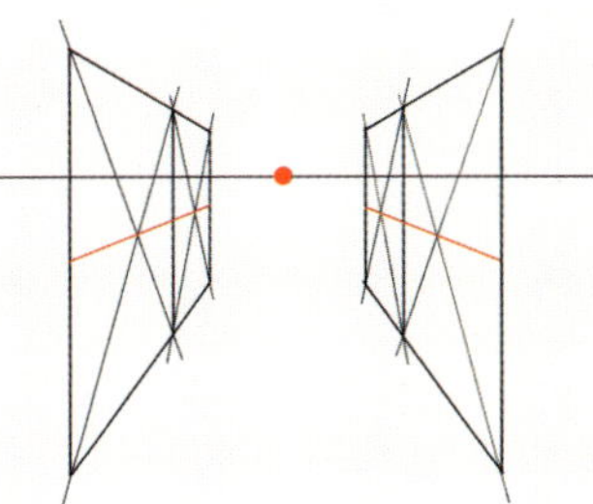

Draw lines vertically through these centre points (the blue lines).

These subdivided planes may be further subdivided. Use light guidelines to connect the corner points of a given plane and then draw a vertical line through the point where the guidelines intersect.

Going through this process, it's easy to accurately depict any evenly spaced group of modules in a view.

By drawing lines from the vanishing point through the centre points (the red lines), you can also divide the planes along horizontal lines in space.

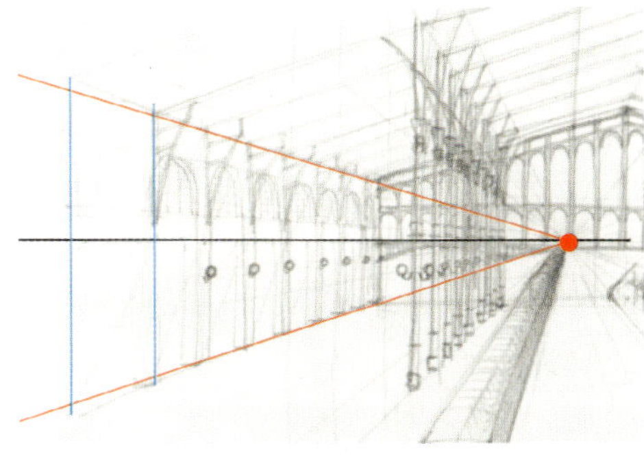

First, establish the converging lines (red, in these diagrams) and a line midway between them (the black line, which roughly coincides with the horizon line in this case). Next, draw a pair of the vertical lines, perhaps using a method such as pencil sighting (see page 15) to determine their spacing. This can be easier if you start with the nearest pair, because they will be more widely spaced than other pairs of vertical lines in the distance.

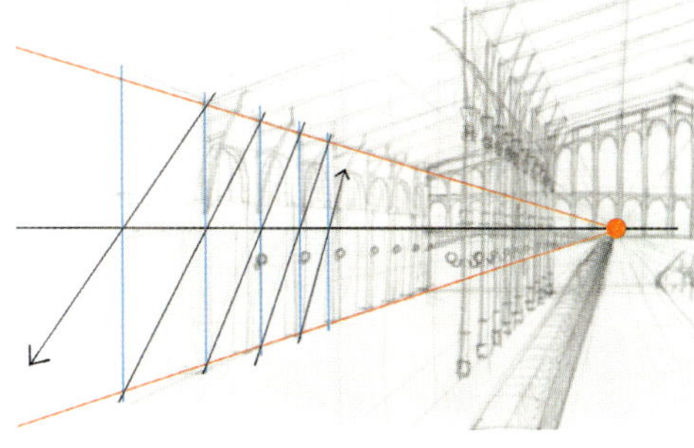

Then, by drawing a diagonal guideline through the intersections of vertical and converging lines, you can determine where the next vertical line should be placed.

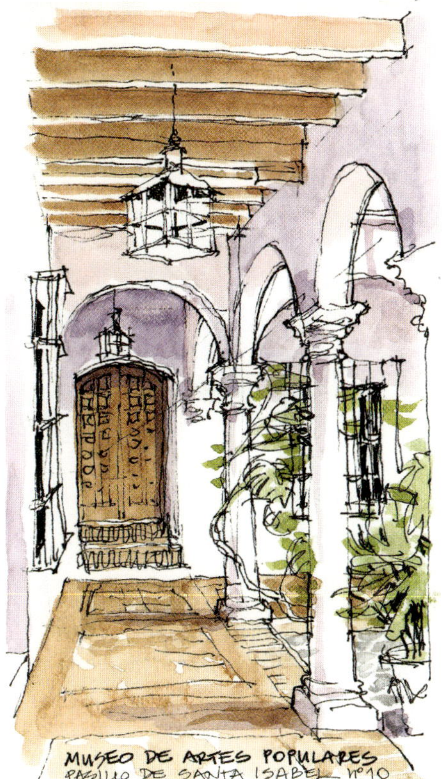

ADDING PEAKS

Finding the centre of a rectangular plane also enables you to locate the peak of a triangular pediment. Simply extend the centre line vertically from where the diagonals cross (top right). Unfortunately, this technique

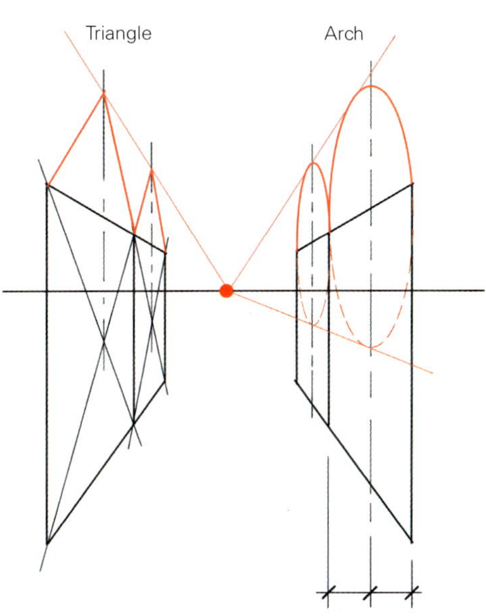

doesn't work when dealing with arches. When viewed in perspective, circular arches will appear as elliptical forms, which have one long axis and one short axis. In the case of a vertical arch, the long axis of the ellipse is roughly midway between the vertical supports of the arch (top right). This axis is not precisely between the supports, but it's close enough for the purpose of setting up a sketch, as you can see in this example by Luis Ruiz (top left).

Applying it

From classic street scenes to formal viewpoints of buildings and interiors, one-point perspective will give your sketch or painting a sense of dynamism.

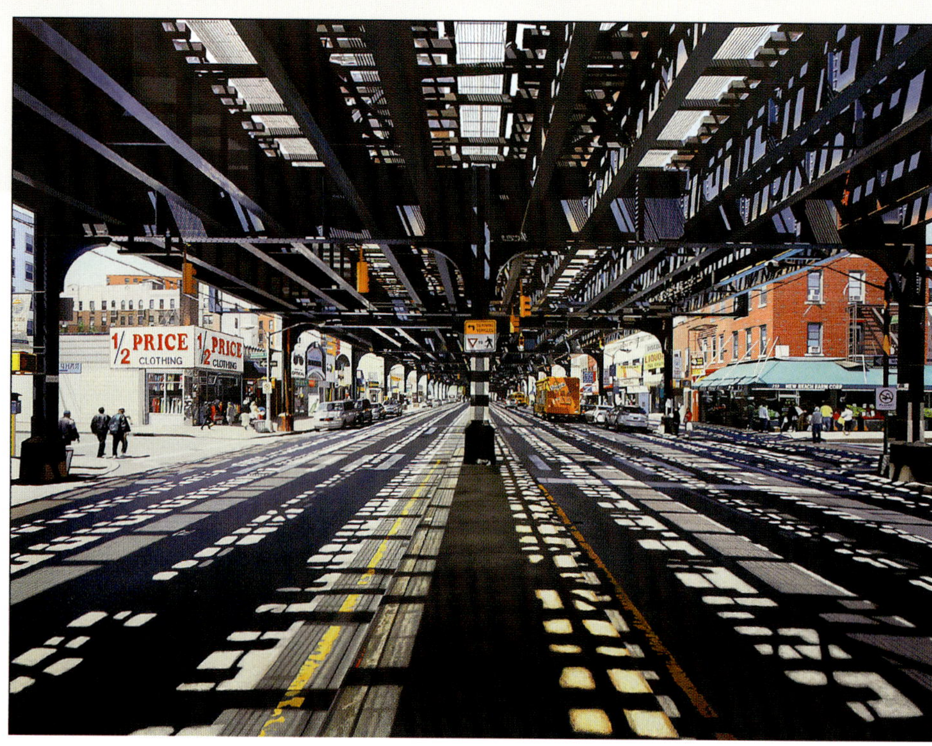

LITTLE RUSSIA
Nathan Walsh • Oil on linen • 170 × 225 cm (67 × 89 in)

▶ This view of a New York street is a fantastic study of the power of one-point perspective. The single vanishing point has been placed at the very centre of the composition, and the multitude of converging lines reinforces the singular directionality of the view. All the lines that are perpendicular to the line of sight are kept either vertical, such as the structural supports for the elevated tracks, or horizontal, as with the cross beams. On this framework the artist has painted a dynamic city scene where we can almost feel the sun and dappled shade, and hear the sounds of trains, cars and people.

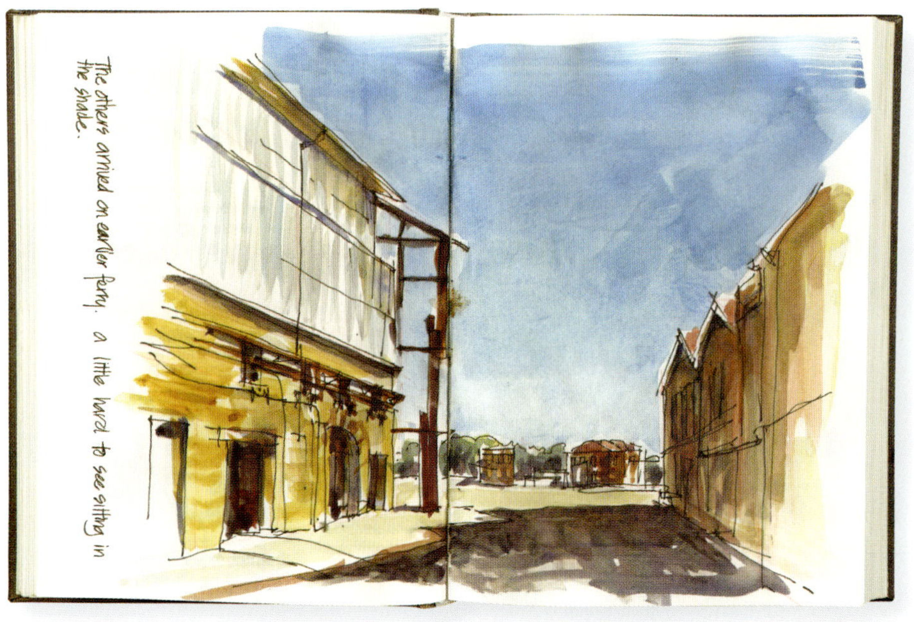

SUMMER IN THE CITY
Liz Steel • Ink and watercolour

◀ When you are drawing urban spaces like streets and plazas, the lines where the buildings meet the ground should typically be kept at a relatively shallow angle, because your eye level is most often quite low compared to the heights of the surrounding buildings. We often have a tendency to make these lines too steep, which gives the impression that we're viewing the scene from a vantage point high above the ground. I recommend keeping the ground plane relatively flat or 'compressed' to help deal with this tendency.

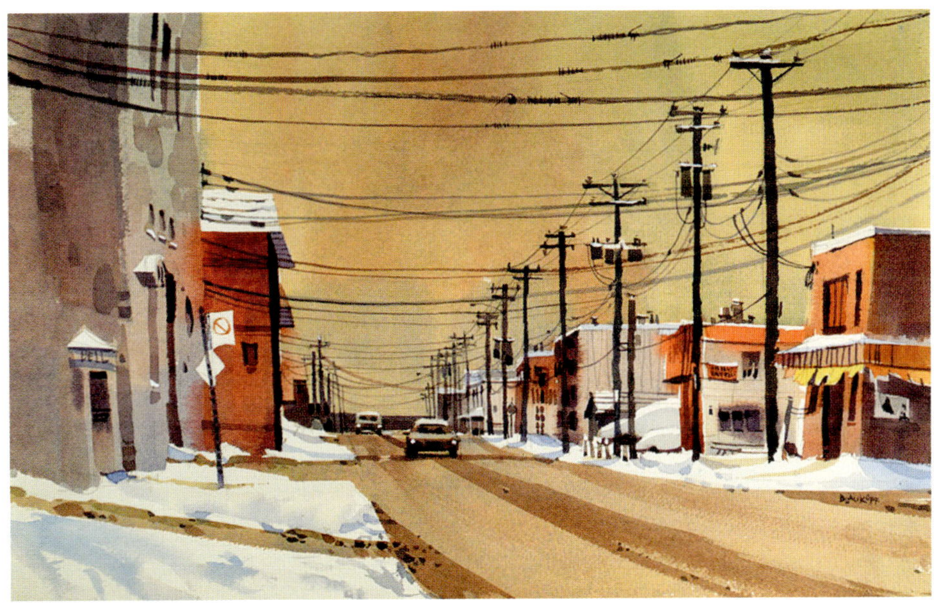

SIXTH AVENUE, LACHINE
Shari Blaukopf • Watercolour

◀ In this watercolour, there are subtle variations in the one-point perspective, but the major elements of the drawing all converge on the single vanishing point – just about where the more distant vehicle is in the image. Note how the ground plane is kept fairly compressed, especially in the space between the two vehicles. The row of telegraph poles really drives this composition, though all the converging edges of the adjacent buildings fall into line as well.

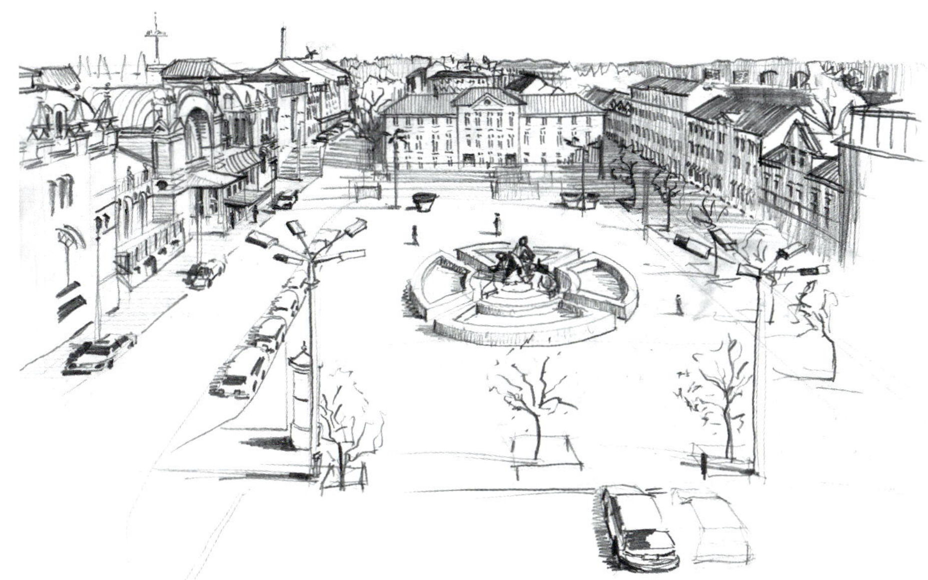

TOWN SQUARE AND STREET
Arno Hartmann • Pencil

▶ The only times these lines would be more steeply angled are when the subject of the drawing is very small or when your eye level is in fact much higher than it would be if you were standing on the ground level. So, if you're up in a building on the first or second floor, or perhaps on the fourth floor, as was the case in this drawing, the ground lines will drop down more dramatically than they would in a typical view.

TRAM IN KASSEL
Omar Jaramillo • Watercolour

◀ This watercolour is very fluid in its approach to a one-point perspective view, and yet the structure of the composition is strongly reinforced by the lamp posts, the repeated verticals on the building at right and the tram – including its overhead wire and the tracks below.

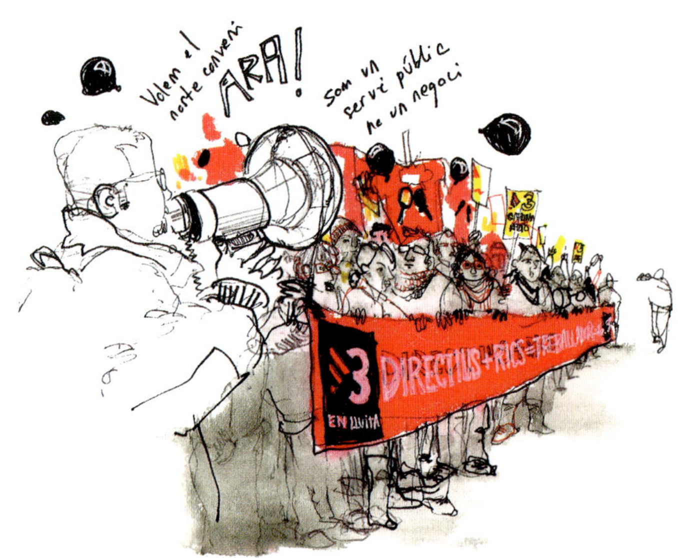

DEMONSTRATION
Cristina Curto • Fountain pen and markers

▲ The red banner adds to the dynamism of this one-point perspective work. The viewer's eye is led from the large, cropped, detailed figure in the foreground through the ever-decreasing height of the figures in the crowd to the little 'agent provacateur scamp' in the distance.

LONG HAUL TRIPPERS
Lapin • Ink, pen and watercolour

▼ One-point perspective can also be used to deal with non-linear subjects, though there may be less precision in these cases. This drawing of airline passengers is an interesting study of the way objects appear to diminish as they get further from the viewer. In this case, the 'objects' are actually people at close range; while they don't align strictly with any converging lines, it may help you to draw them in as you lay out your drawing.

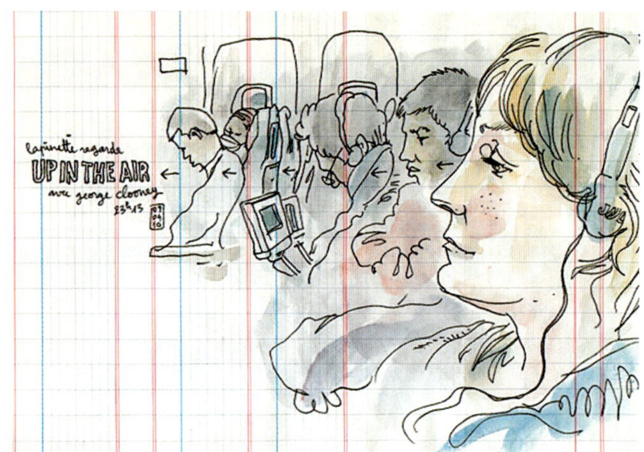

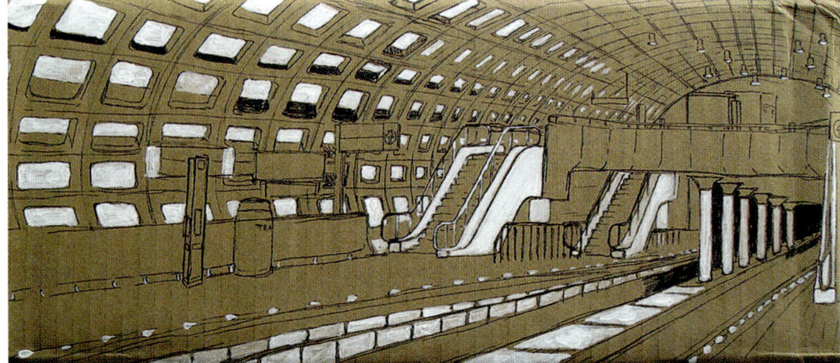

WASHINGTON METRO
Christian Tribastone • Ink

▲ Sometimes you'll want to draw a long interior space, as in this sketch of a metro stop in Washington, DC. Placing the single vanishing point in the centre of the page would emphasise the tunnel-like quality of the space and could result in a rather static image. Here, the dynamic coffered structure is highlighted because the vanishing point has been placed at the far right edge of the page.

INTERIORS

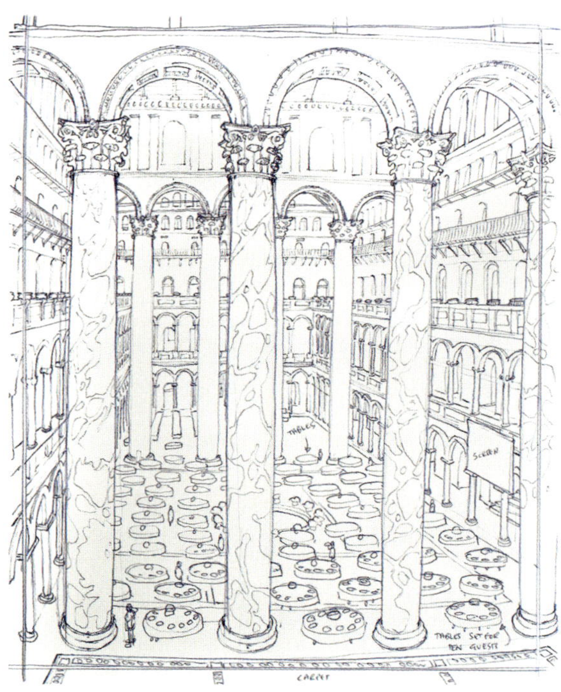

NATIONAL BUILDING MUSEUM
Richard Johnson • Line and ink

▶ One-point perspective can be an effective way of simplifying very complex subjects. This ink drawing of the National Building Museum (Washington, DC) is a fine example, with the many repeated arches all being organised by the converging lines on the left and right.

WATERSCAPES

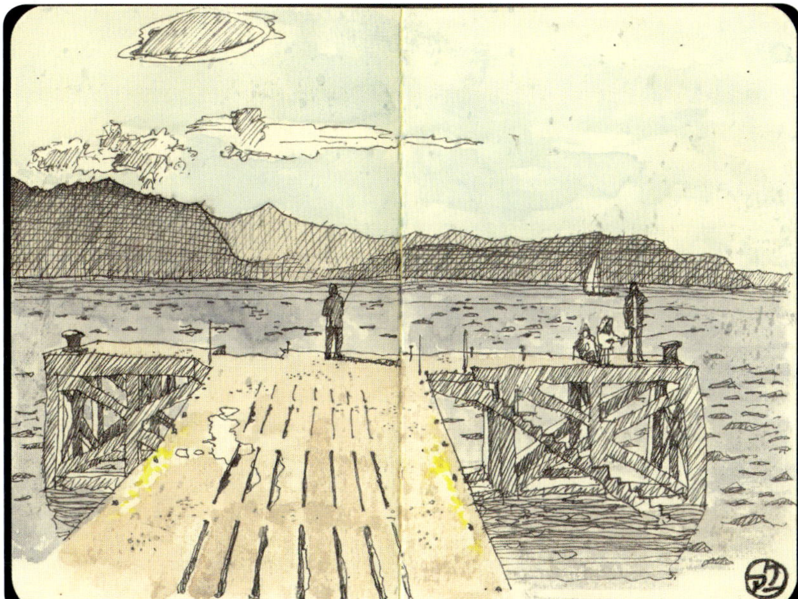

FISHING ON THE QUAYSIDE
Stuart Kerr • Ink and wash

◀ One-point perspectives are useful for a variety of subjects – from small spaces to expansive views like this dock scene by Stuart Kerr. The key to laying out these drawings is to keep in mind the relationship between your eye level and the elements of the view. In Stuart's drawing, the eye level coincides perfectly with the horizon in the distance, with the mountains and sky above the eye level and everything else below it.

BUILDING EXTERIORS

CAPTURING GRANDEUR
Liz Steel • Ink and watercolour

▶ The formality of the subject is increased by the straight-on viewpoint giving a balanced composition; only the inner walls of the towers and the wings 'show' the converging lines going towards the central vanishing point. The expansive nature of the building is exaggerated by the low level of the horizon.

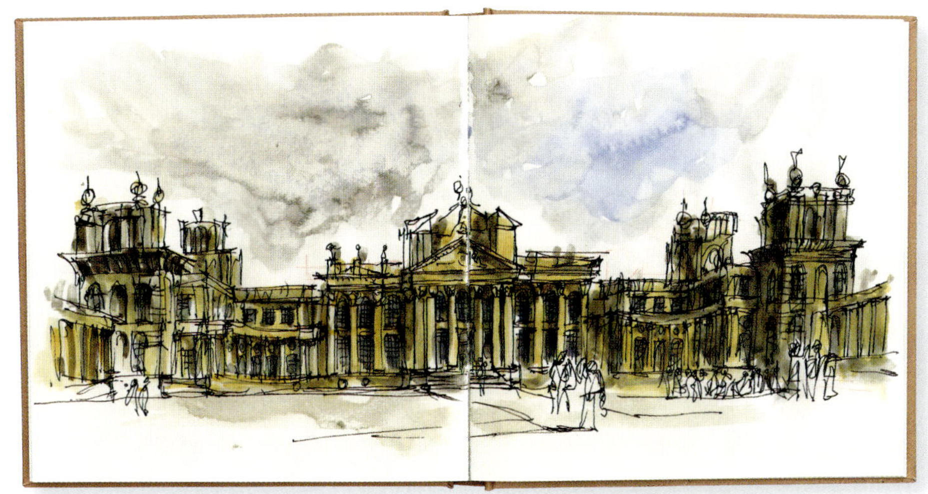

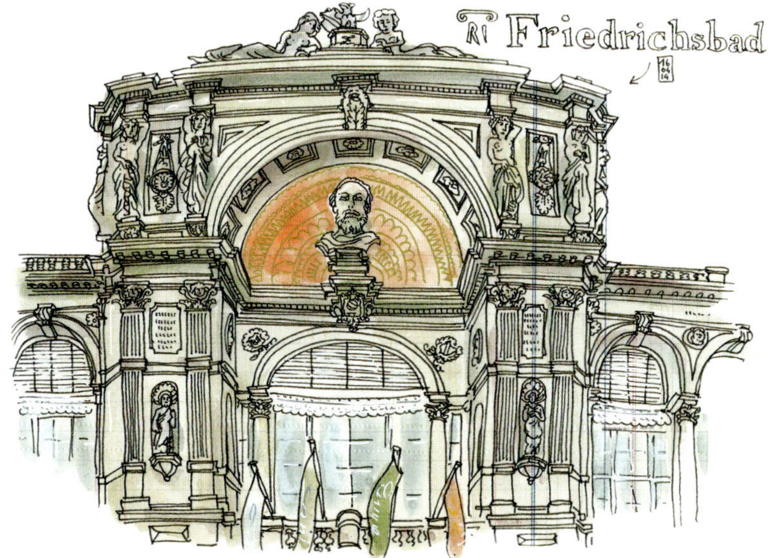

FINDING DEPTH
Lapin • Ink, pen and watercolour

◀ This close-up of a straight-on viewpoint could have made for a flat facade were it not for the depth of the arch with its receding cornicing. Notice how the outer arch is much bigger than the inner roof arch – this gives good visual depth to the building structure.

How-to sequence

Here, Florian Afflerbach demonstrates how to complete an interior scene using pencil sighting in one-point perspective.

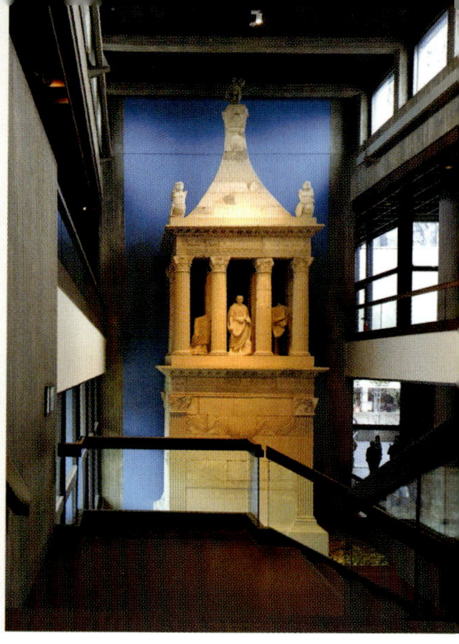

▶Head-on view
Although the main subject is the tomb directly in front of us, the different levels – the steps, the big interior space and the light that comes in – make this a particularly interesting scene to draw.

MEASURING METHOD

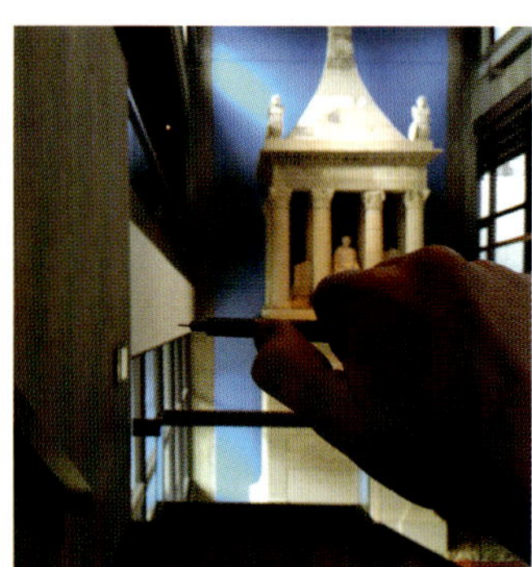

Use a pencil as a measuring instrument for both distances and angles. When measuring distances or proportions, make sure to transfer the distance not as the actual length, but as a unit. Remember to always measure with your arm outstreched.

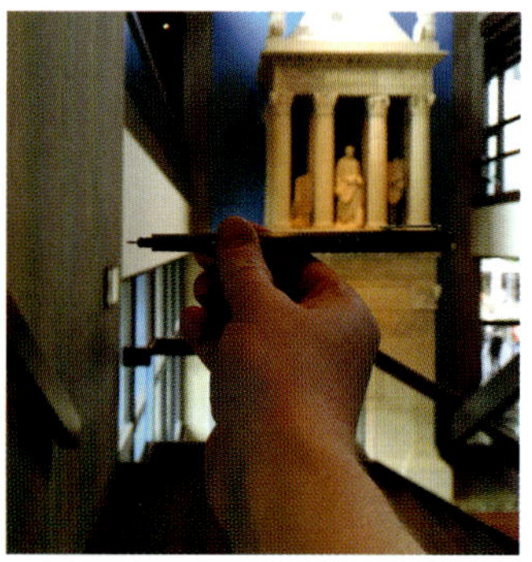

If you hold your drawing instrument horizontally in front of your eyes and imagine the line produced, you obtain the position of the horizon. This imagined line can now be transferred on to your sheet as a horizontal line.

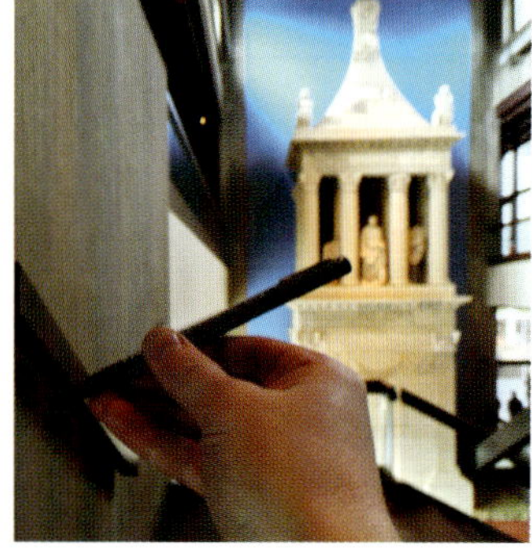

If you measure the angles of the lines running from the end points of the building element edges into the space towards the horizon, you will find the vanishing point. These angles can be transferred precisely on to the paper. Some people imagine a clock face and name times (for example: two o'clock) for a more certain transfer.

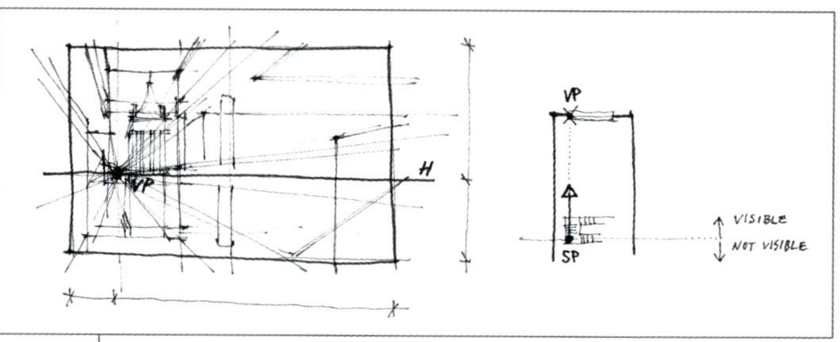

A preparatory drawing will help you to visualise the single vanishing point (VP).

Begin by making a station point drawing – a little sketch of the location and your line of sight as an abstract floor plan. The station point (SP) is where the sketcher is.

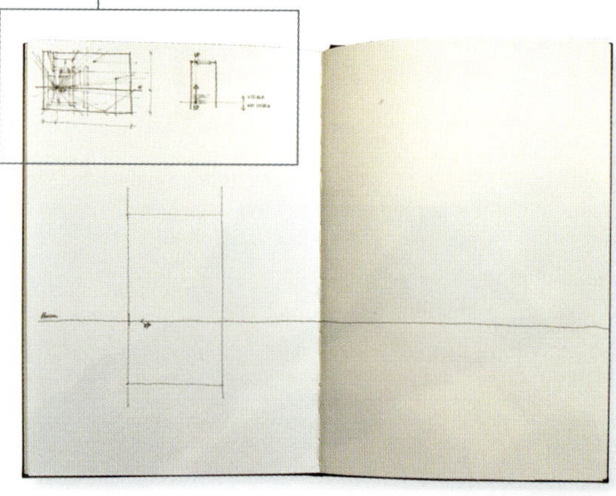

STEP 1 ▲ Start by establishing the horizon line: this is always level with the sketcher's eye level, and here it lies at the bottom of the columns on the tomb. Then establish where the vanishing point falls: looking back at the station point drawing and the preparatory drawing, you can see that the vanishing point is on the left, on the horizon line. The main subject of the drawing is the blue background wall with the tomb in front of it. Referring to your previous measurements, place the edges of the blue wall on the sheet, always in relation to the vanishing point and the horizon.

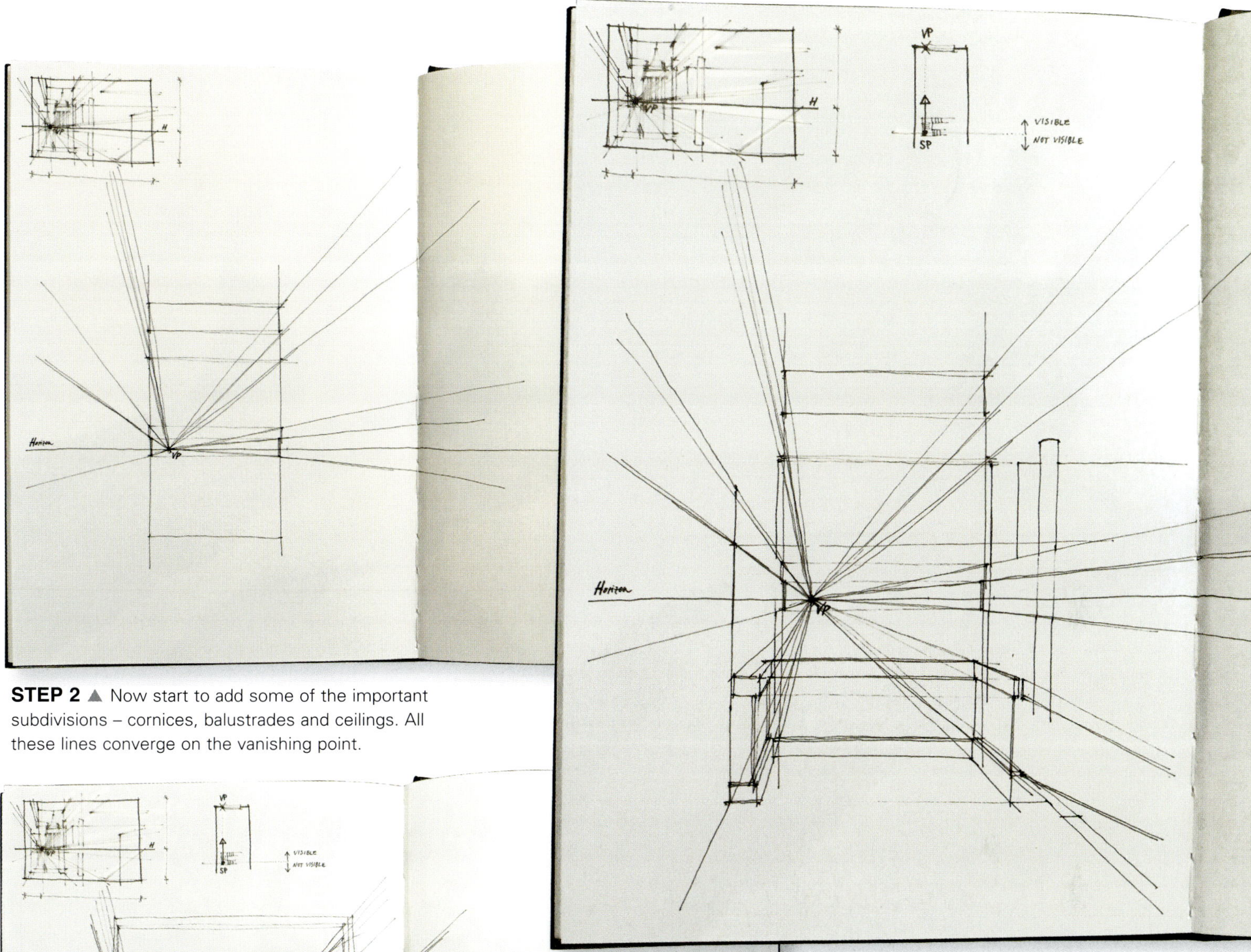

STEP 2 ▲ Now start to add some of the important subdivisions – cornices, balustrades and ceilings. All these lines converge on the vanishing point.

STEP 3 ▲ Now it should be easier to locate other important elements, like the column in the background and the platform with the handrail in the foreground. Refer back to your station point sketch to differentiate between elements that are parallel to the horizon (and thus have no vanishing point) and elements that converge towards the vanishing point.

STEP 4 ◄ Add more details of the surrounding architecture, such as the right part of the skylight. The position of the left part can be found via the horizontal carrying structure.

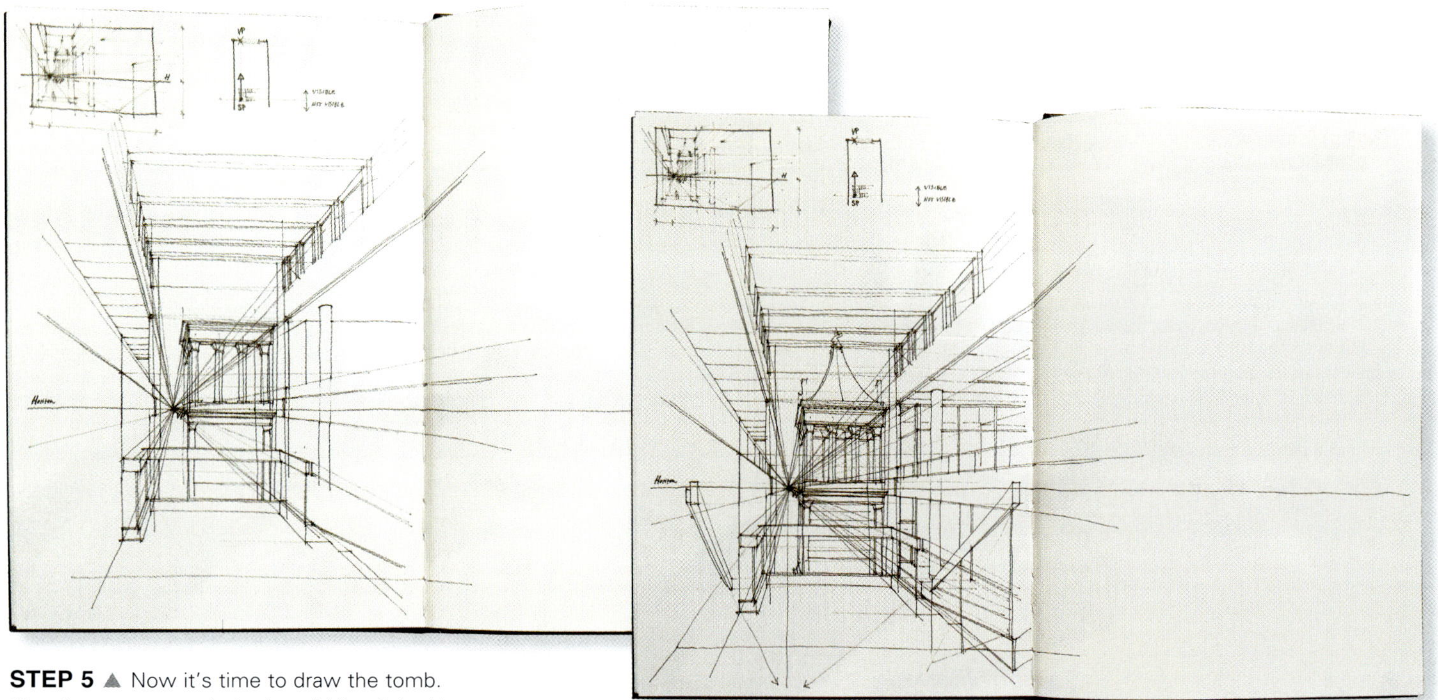

STEP 5 ▲ Now it's time to draw the tomb. Sketch out a rectangle in the middle of the blue background wall, then draw vanishing lines from the four corners of the rectangle. Add the underpart elements of the tomb, too. As it is quite far away, don't make it too detailed.

STEP 6 ▲ Gradually add more details, such as the handrails of the stairs in the foreground; these rails form an inclined plane, rectangular to the whole architecture, that has its own vanishing point on a vertical line below the original vanishing point. Refine the details in the background, too, such as the details of the tomb's facade.

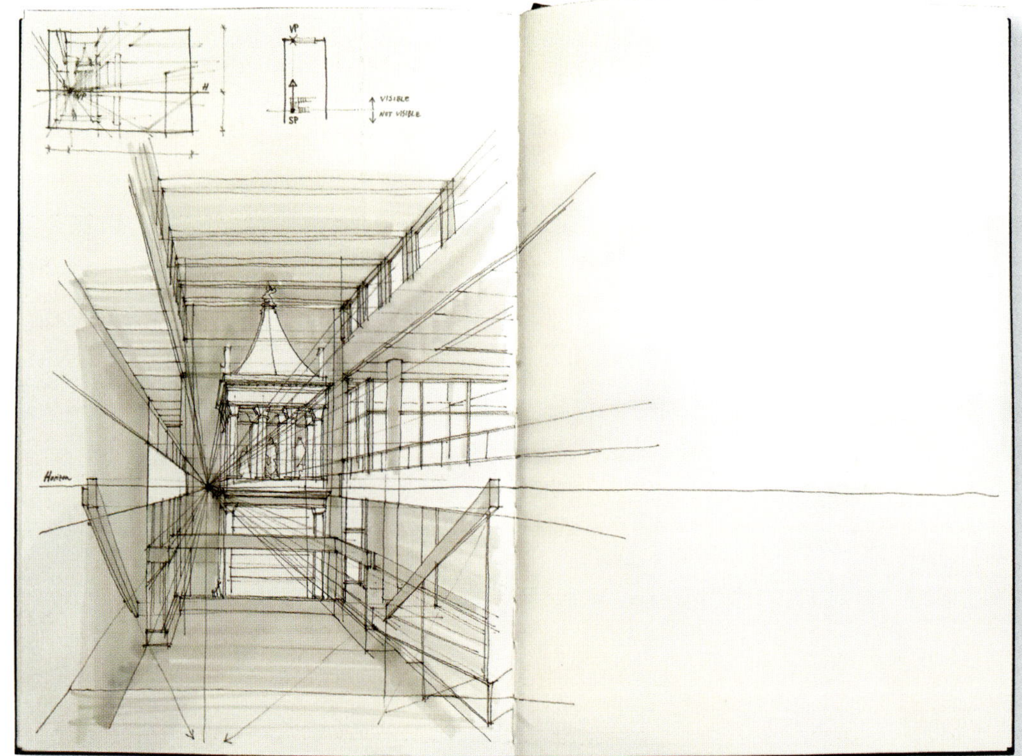

STEP 7 ▶ Now begin to add some tones of grey. Start with the lightest grey, applying it over everything except white surfaces or the spaces where daylight streams through the skylights. Use alcohol-based marker pens, as they won't blur the pigment-based lines laid down earlier.

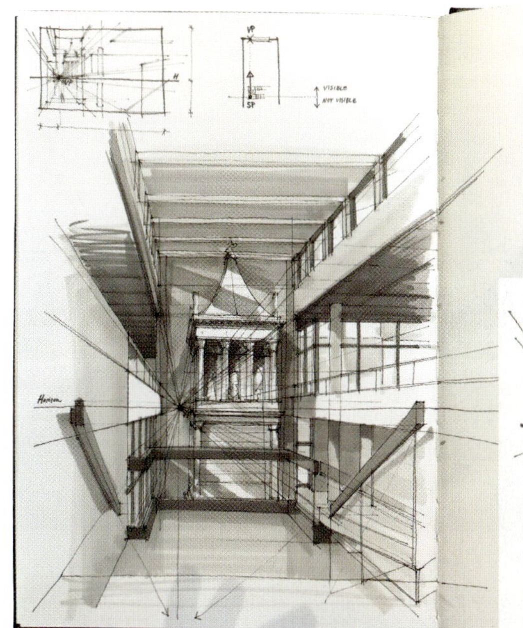

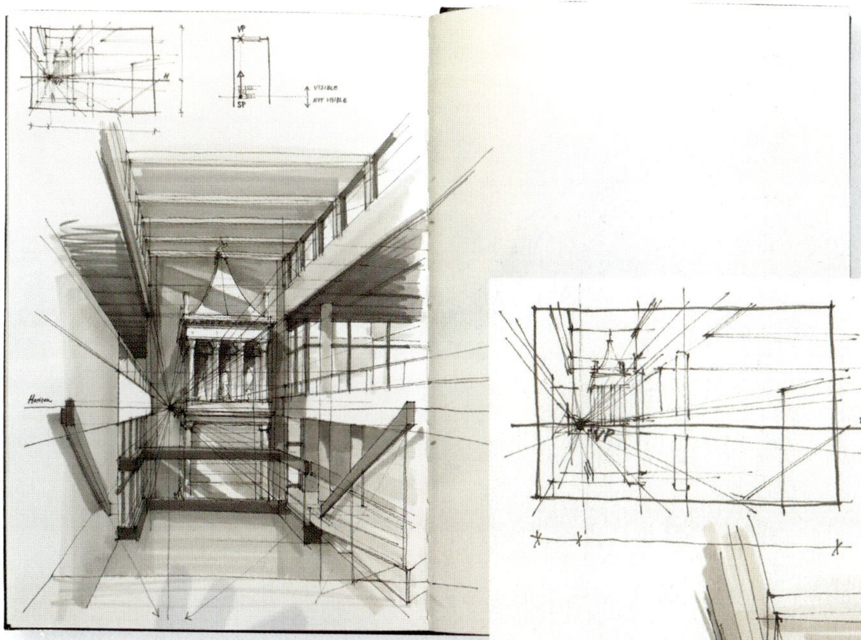

STEP 8 ▲ Define darker zones, corners or materials with darker greys in two or more stages. Add secondary shadows to the columns, handrails and other parts of the interior, using a medium grey, and use the darkest grey for the hard shadows cast by the sunlight coming in from the left of the scene. Make sure to be more accurate in the centre of the drawing and to let it fade out towards the edges.

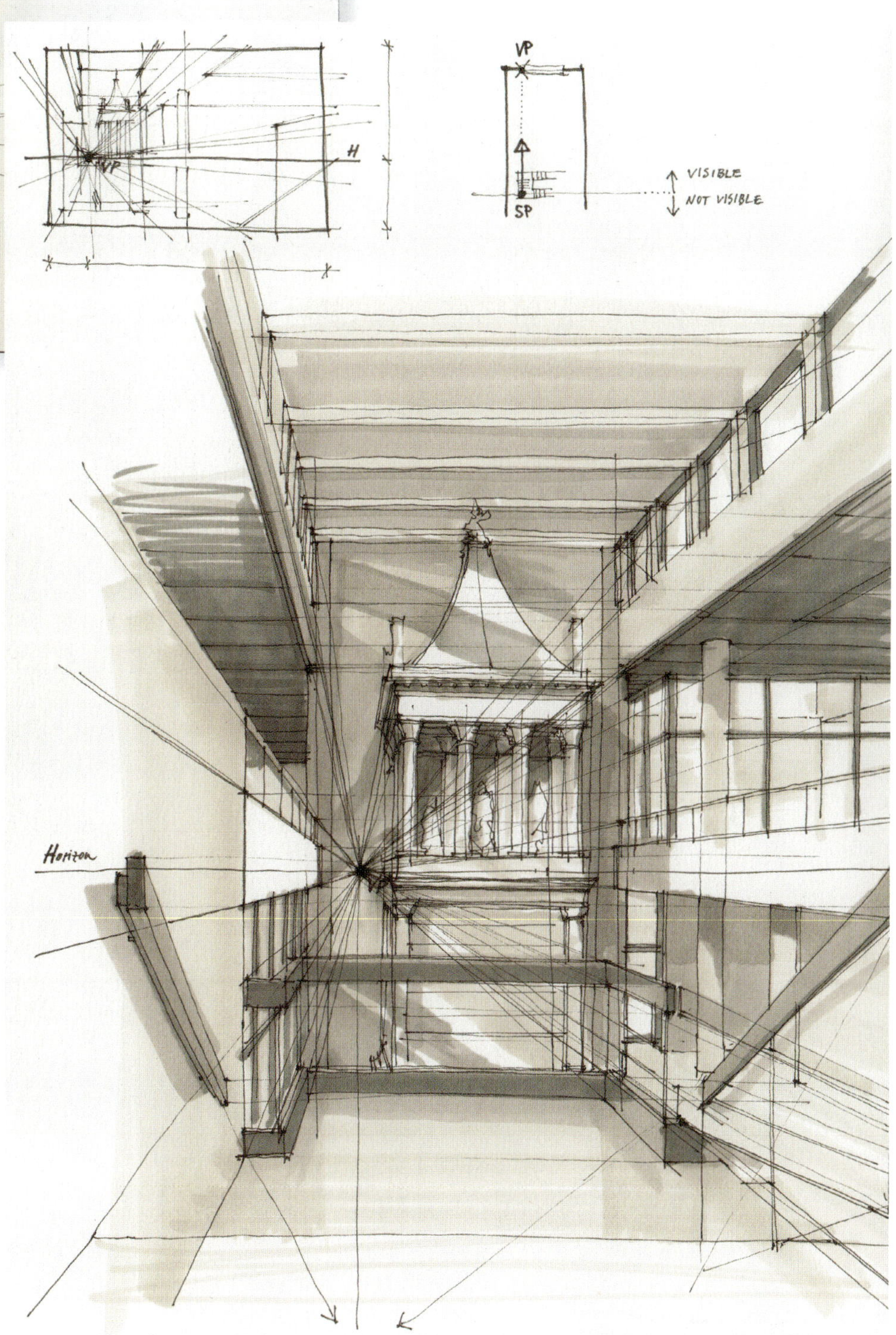

THE FINISHED DRAWING

At first glance, this scene looks rather complicated, but by establishing the lines of convergence from the very outset and carefully measuring both distances and proportions you can create a drawing that is both spatially accurate and full of visual interest.

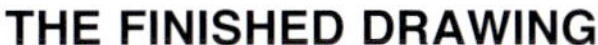

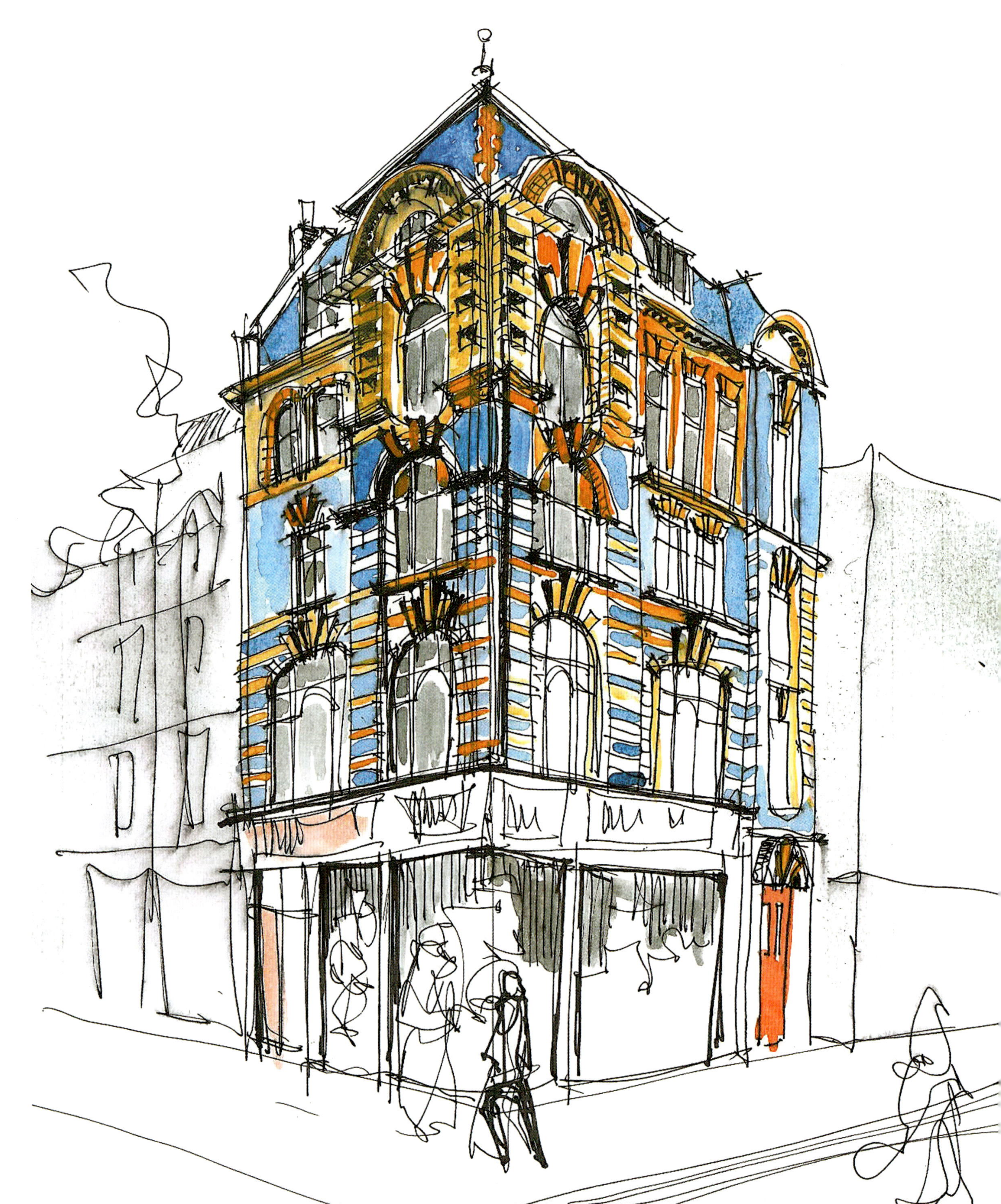

2 POINT PERSPECTIVE

Two-point perspective builds on our understanding of one-point, and is the result of our line of vision being at an angle to the horizontal lines in our view. This type of perspective is often more dynamic and engaging than one-point, because we're able to see the volumes of objects and spaces more clearly.

SHAFTESBURY AVENUE, LONDON • *Hans Muerkens* • Pen and watercolour

Introduction

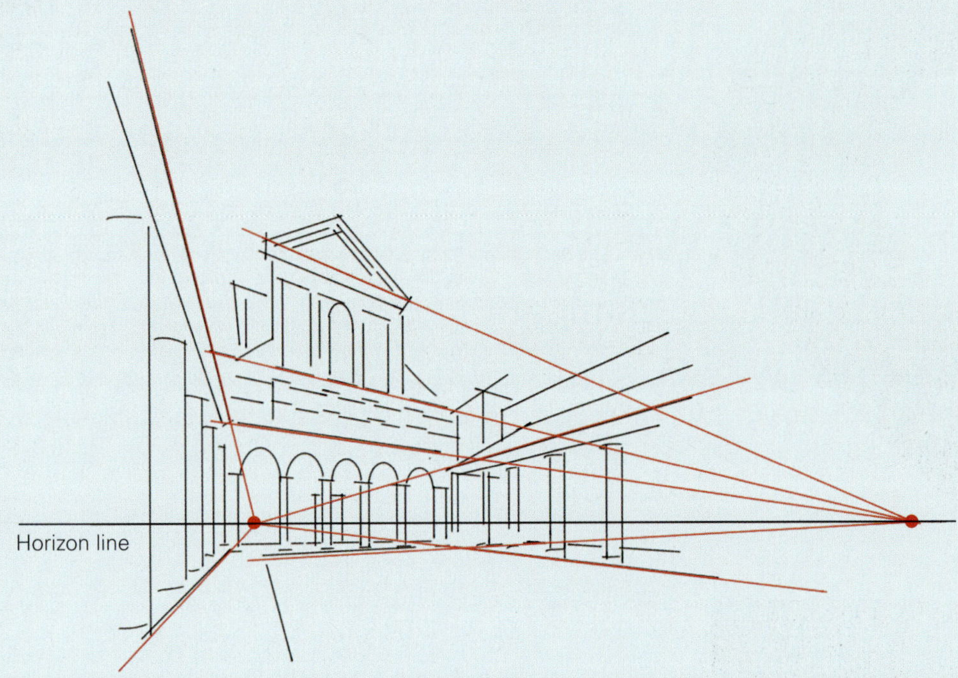

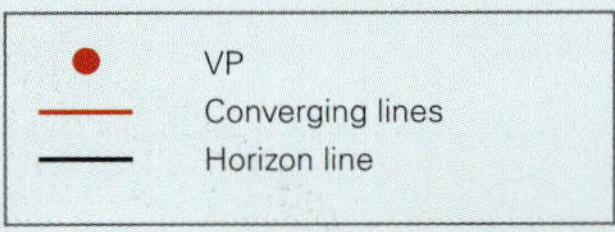

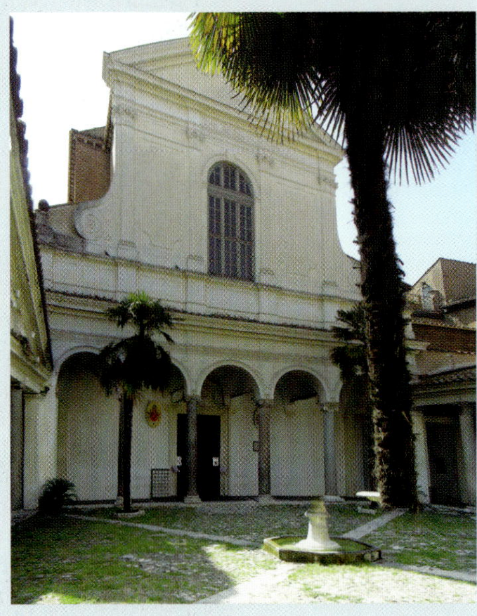

What is two-point perspective?

In a two-point perspective view or drawing, there are two clearly identifiable vanishing points, with both most often occurring on the horizon line. Two-point perspective comes into play when your line of sight is at an angle to the horizontal sets of lines that converge upon, or 'vanish' towards, points in the distance. In our gridded modern cities, two-point perspective is quite common to see, because there are only two sets of parallel horizontal lines in these environments. Interior views are also commonly drawn as two-point perspectives, as the vast majority of rooms we occupy tend to be rectangular. With their sets of lines almost visibly 'moving' at angles to one another, two-point perspective views are typically much more dynamic than one-point.

While you will certainly encounter one-point perspective views on your quest for worthwhile sketching subjects, it's actually somewhat rare to be looking into space with your line of vision perfectly parallel to the horizontal lines around you. It's more common for your desired line of sight to be at some angle to the typically grid-oriented lines of the built environment, and the resulting subjects are almost always more dynamic in character and therefore more appealing to draw. When there are two sets of converging lines in a drawing, the place that's being described is almost invariably more 'spatial' – which means that the observer can understand the three-dimensional qualities of the place much better because it's a closer approximation of how we typically perceive the world around us. Two-point perspectives can be more challenging to draw, as you'll see in the pages that follow, because there will be times when one or both of the two vanishing points will be far off the page. In these cases, you'll need to do some creative visualisation to locate the points and use them to help set up the drawing.

▲ Standing in one corner of a courtyard like this one in Rome, and looking diagonally across the space, presents a good example of a two-point perspective view. There are two sets of parallel horizontal lines – those that run across the church facade, and those that define the left and right sides of the courtyard, running perpendicular to the facade. Each set of lines has its own vanishing point, with both at your eye level.

▶ BASILICA DI SAN CLEMENTE, ROME, ITALY
Matthew Brehm • Graphite and watercolour

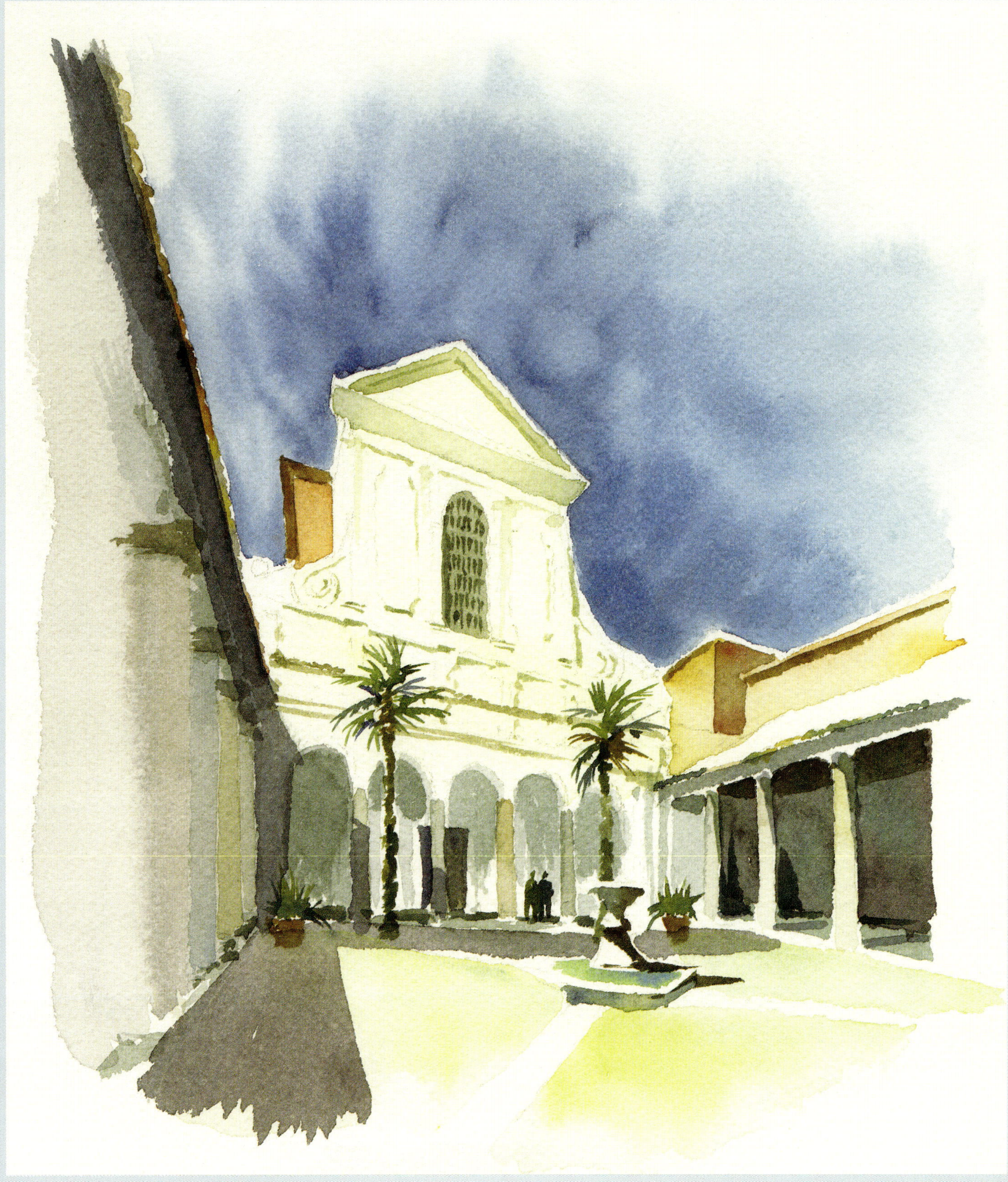

two-point perspective
Seeing it

In a two-point perspective view, two sets of converging lines are clearly visible. Both sets of converging lines will appear to recede to vanishing points on the horizon line, while vertical lines in space will appear to remain vertical in the drawing.

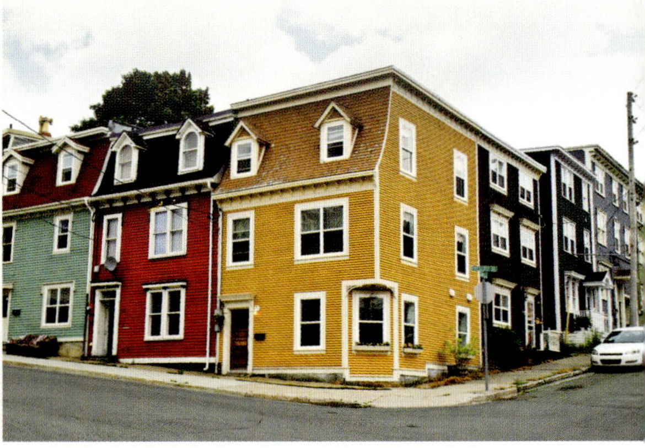

▼ Two-point perspectives are most often used to depict outside corner conditions, such as this view of two streets intersecting at a right angle to one another.

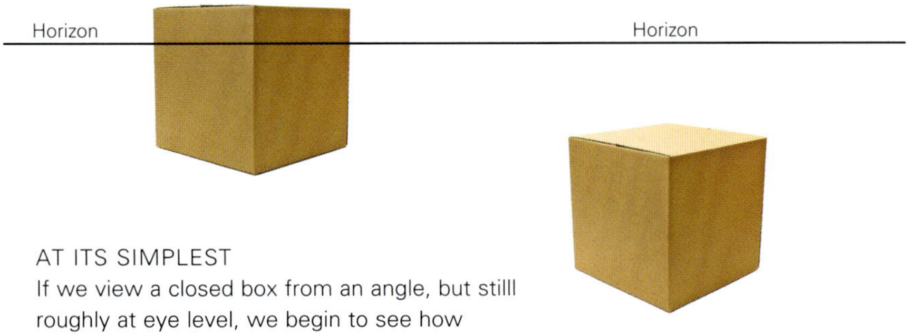

Horizon

Horizon

● VP
— Converging lines
— Horizon line

AT ITS SIMPLEST
If we view a closed box from an angle, but stilll roughly at eye level, we begin to see how perspective gives us clues to understanding visual depth. The near vertical edge appears to be the tallest, with the left and right visible corners appearing to be smaller. The faces of the box appear to diminish in size as they recede into the distance, with the top and bottom edges of the box receding towards vanishing points – one to the left and the other to the right. If our point of view were to be lowered or elevated, the lines would still recede to the same points on the horizon line.

← ● VP 1   Horizon

VP 2

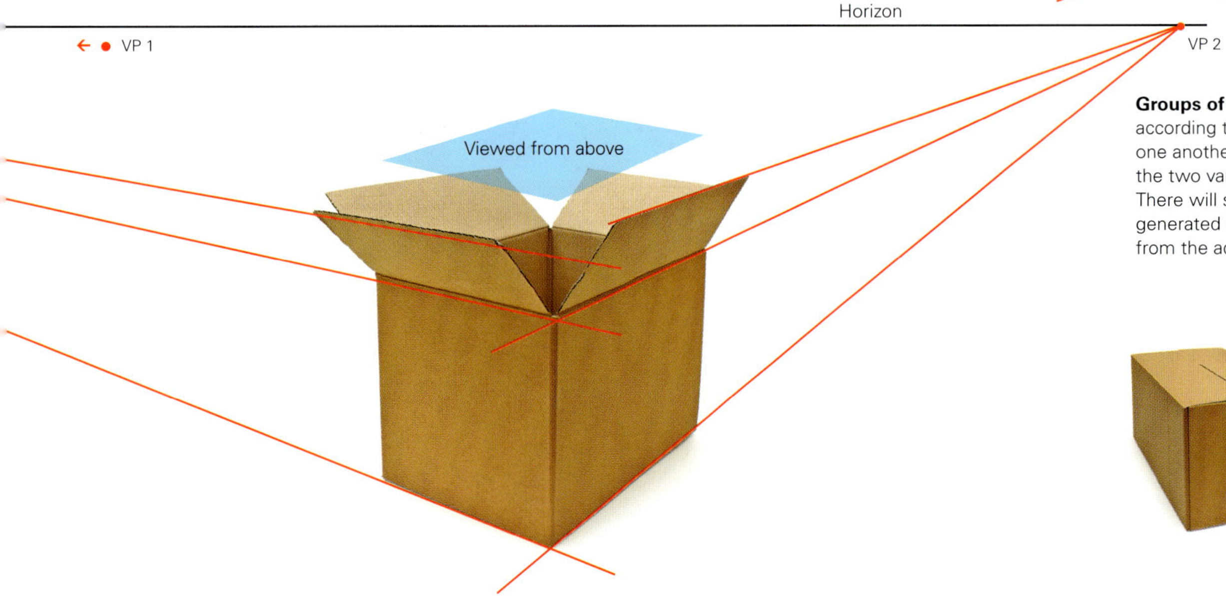

← ● VP 1   Horizon   VP 2

Viewed from above

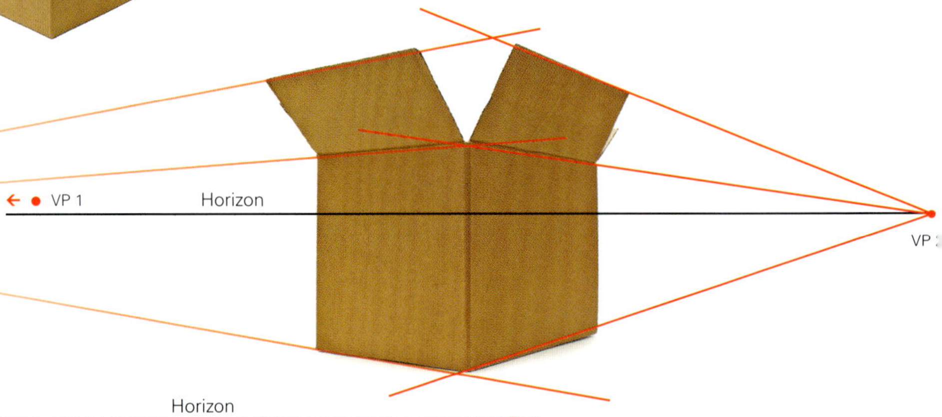

Groups of boxes, if they are arranged according to a grid such that they all align with one another, will show the same relationship to the two vanishing points and the horizon line. There will simply be more converging lines, generated by the greater number of edges from the additional boxes.

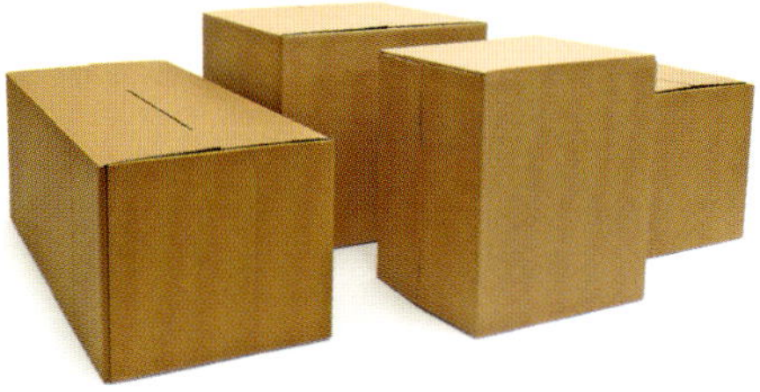

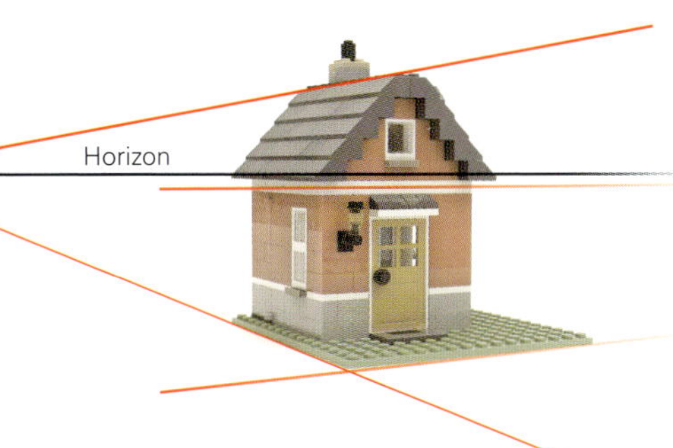

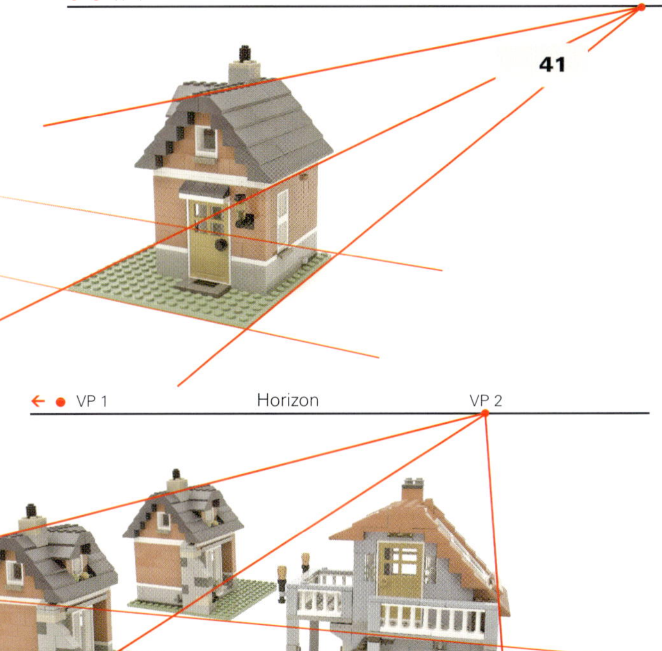

INDIVIDUAL HOUSES

These objects are more complex than a simple cardboard box, yet the same principles of two-point perspective still apply. There are two sets of converging lines, each comprised of edges that are parallel to one another in space.

A GROUP OF HOUSES

Here we also see two sets of converging lines, but there are simply more lines in each set – because there are additional roof lines, ground lines, etc. Tracing these lines back towards the horizon reveals the two vanishing points, one on on either side of the subject in view. Our line of vision is directed more towards the right, so the right vanishing point is closer to the centre of the view while the other vanishing point is far off to the left.

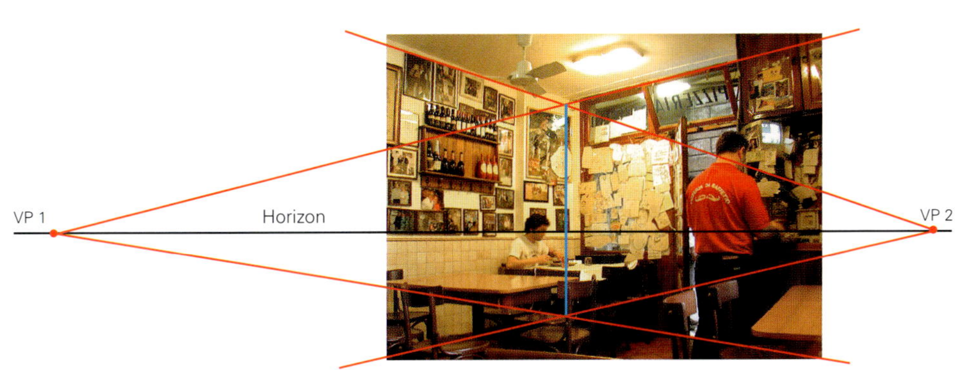

INTERIOR VIEWS

Two-point perspective is also a useful strategy when dealing with interior views. Rather than defining an outside corner, the converging lines combine to form an inside corner, indicated here by the blue line. Lines that are vertical in the space, such as this interior corner, are perpendicular to your line of vision, so they will be truly vertical in the drawing as well – just as we learned with respect to one-point perspective.

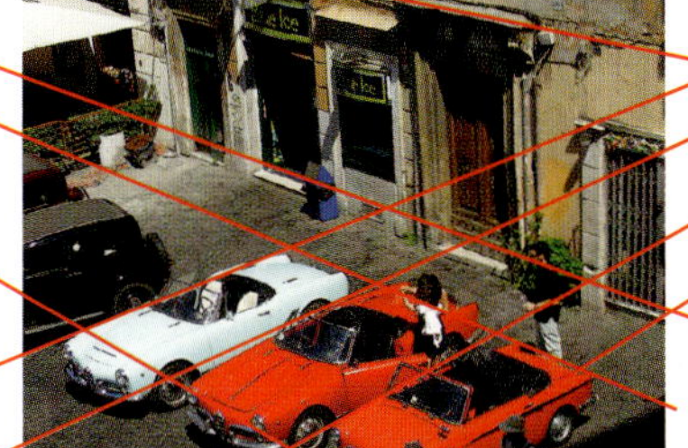

ELEVATED EYE LEVEL

When your eye level is well above the subject in view, the lines of convergence will ascend to the right and left, as seen in this diagram.

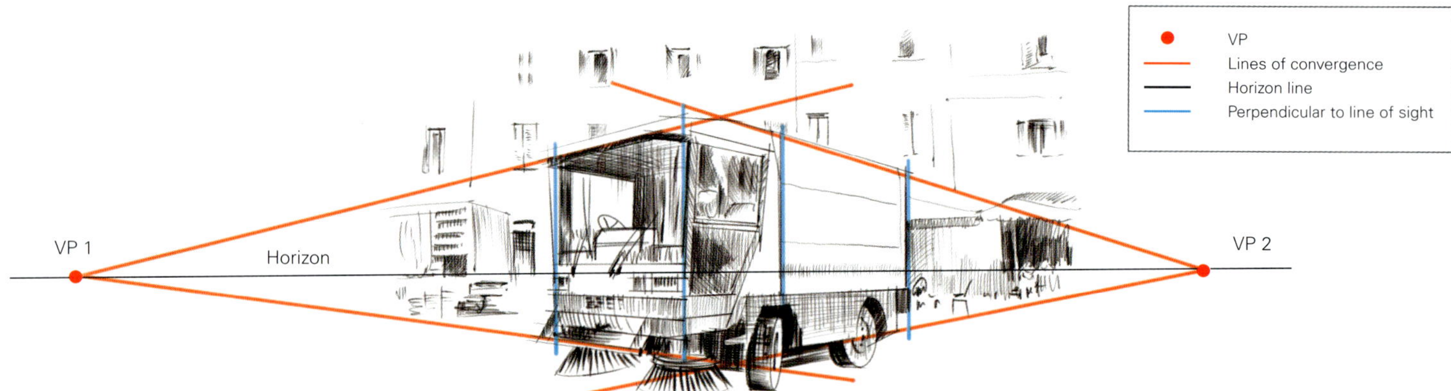

45-DEGREE VIEW

When viewing a basic rectangular object, such as this vehicle, from a 45-degree angle, the two vanishing points will be roughly equidistant from the centre of the image. When you are relatively close to the subject, the vanishing points will be fairly close to one another. In this case, the green striped marking and the bottom of the windscreen form a level, horizontal line that coincides with the eye level.

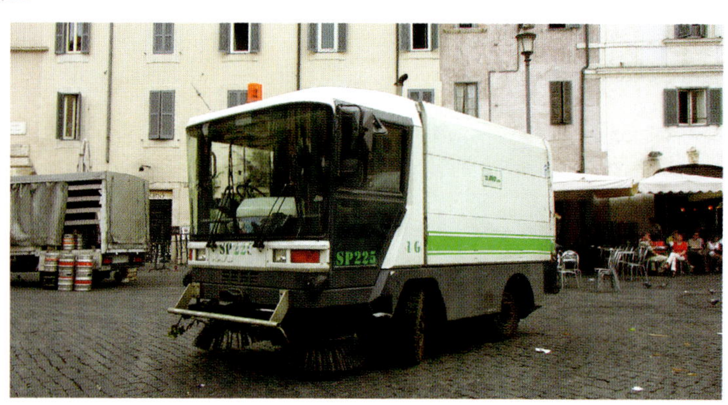

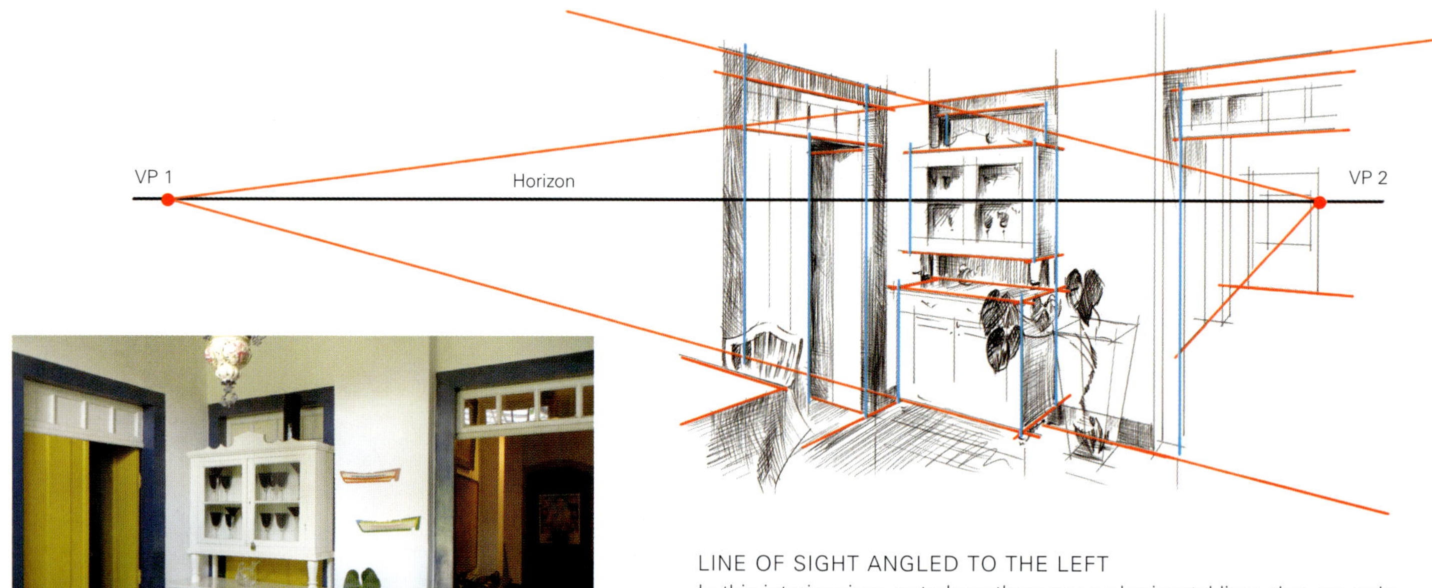

LINE OF SIGHT ANGLED TO THE LEFT

In this interior view, note how there are no horizontal lines that are truly perpendicular or parallel to the line of sight – unlike in a one-point perspective. All the vertical lines are perpendicular to the line of sight, so they will not appear to converge on a vanishing point, but all of the lines that are horizontal in space will converge on the two vanishing points. If we were to isolate our view of the hallway on the right, we'd be seeing something that approximates a one-point view, but because our line of sight is angled to the left, there will be two vanishing points.

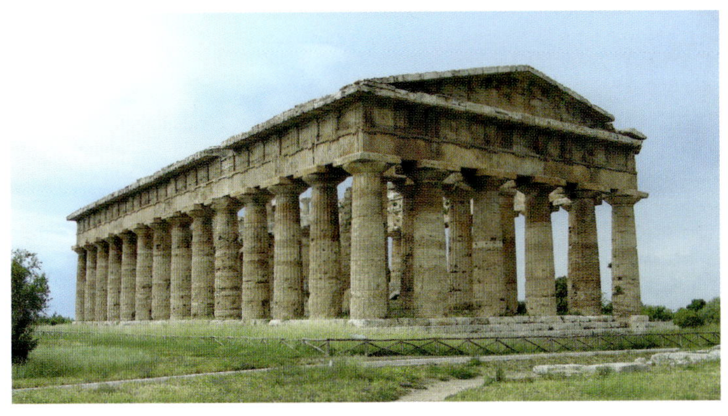

DISTANT VIEW, DISTANT VANISHING POINTS

Being further from the subject will mean that the vanishing points will tend to be further from one another. This is very evident with the vanishing point to the right of the temple. Note that the vertical lines in the view remain vertical in the drawing, just as they do in a one-point perspective.

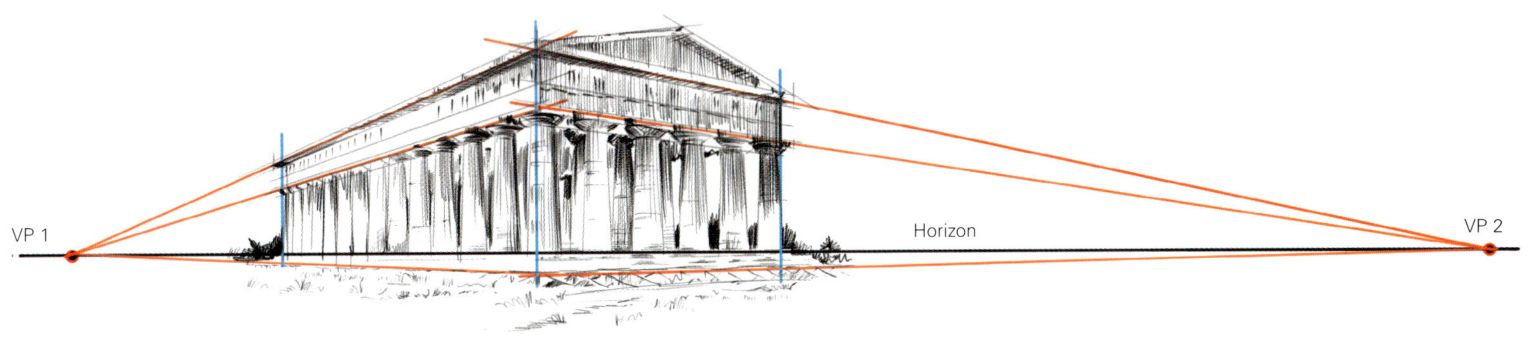

A ONE-POINT VIEW BECOMES TWO-POINT

Not all two-point perspectives have their vanishing points on the horizon line. In this photograph of 'Harlot's Hall' in Hot Springs, Arkansas (by Walter Arnold), all of the converging horizontal lines vanish to a point at eye level (which is up at the second floor, from where the photo was taken). But the lines of the sloping stair in the foreground converge on a point far below the eye level. Because the planes of the railings are aligned with the converging horizontal lines, this second vanishing point will be directly below the first (as indicated by the black dashed line). Another example of this phenomenon appears on page 47.

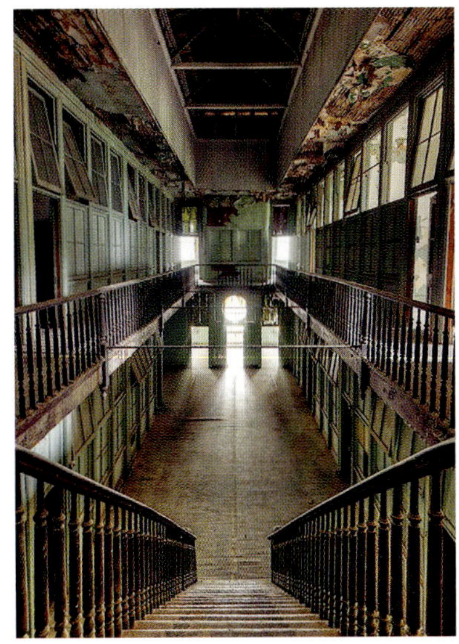

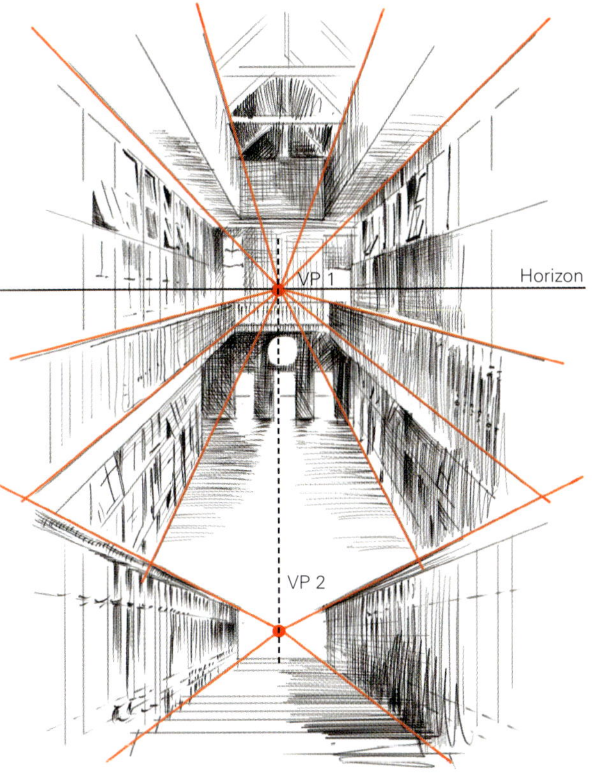

Understanding it

As in one-point perspective, thinking of your subject as a relatively simple geometric shape makes it easier to see where the vanishing points lie.

GO TO THE WORKBOOK

To help you understand two-point perspective read this section then turn to pages 116–125 and try the range of exercises shown in the grid chambers.

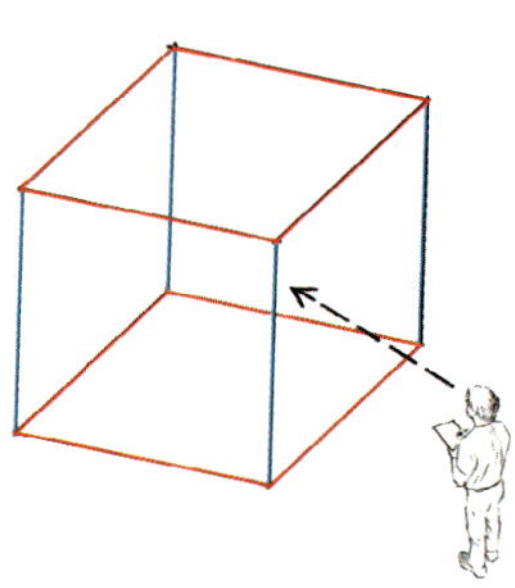

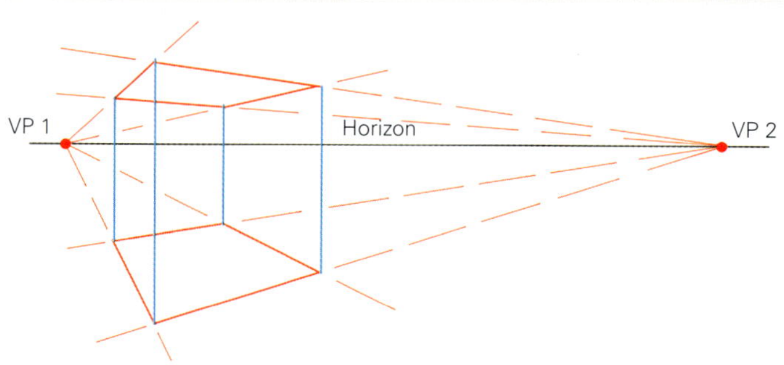

CUBE-SHAPED STRUCTURES
Let's imagine looking at the same cube discussed on page 24, but from a slightly different point of view, such that our line of sight is no longer parallel to any of the cube's edges.

Our line of sight is still perpendicular to the vertical lines, shown here in blue – and these will remain vertical in the perspective view, just as they did in the one-point example. The red lines in this case, however, are neither parallel nor perpendicular to our line of sight. In the

resulting perspective view, seen above, the set of red lines that move away from the viewer to the left will converge on the left vanishing point. The set of red lines that move away from the viewer to the right will converge on the right vanishing point.

RECTANGULAR BUILDINGS
When we look at a rectangular object or building from more or less the front, like this view of a temple in Paestum, Italy, we'll see one face more completely than the others. If we were standing directly in the centre in front of this temple, we'd be seeing a one-point perspective. But since the point of view is off to one side, and the line of vision is at an angle to the horizontal edges of the temple, it's a two-point view. In this case the eye level is below the bottom of the building, so it's effectively a 'worm's-eye' view. In constructing the drawing, it can help to draw very light guidelines that define the entire form of the object. Even though the bottom of the temple will not be visible in the finished drawing, you might begin by sketching the lines as part of the entire rectangular volume.

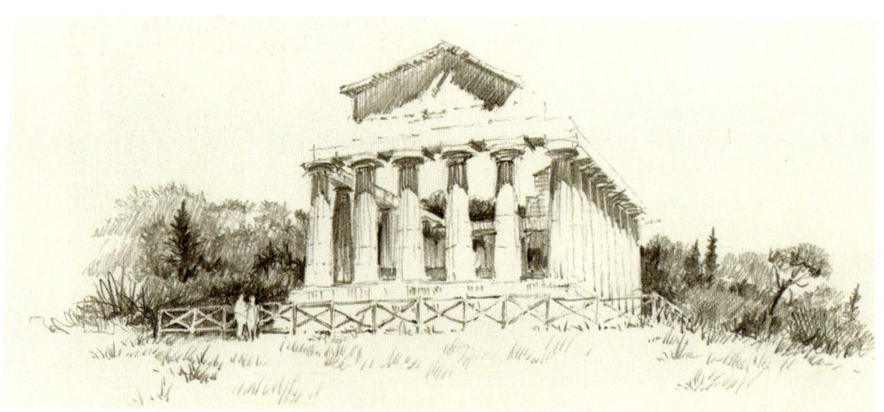

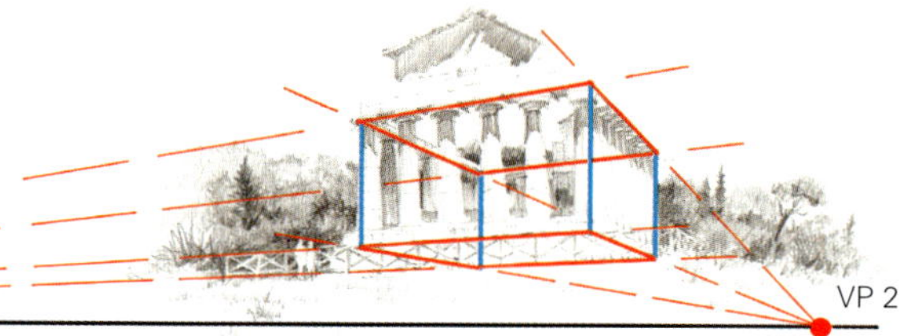

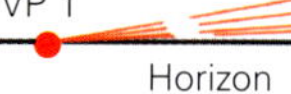

VAULTED AREAS

If we look at a space that's considerably more complex than a simple cube, we can see how the same basic rules still apply. Consider Arno Hartmann's drawing of a vaulted interior view as an example (right), and a diagram of roughly the same space (below). It's a challenging space to draw, but it can be made easier by breaking down the view into more manageable elements, and by using plenty of light guidelines in the initial layout of the drawing.

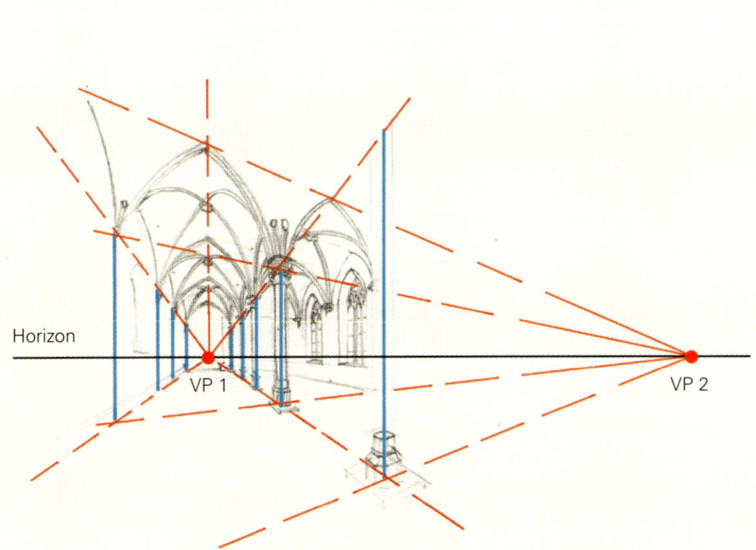

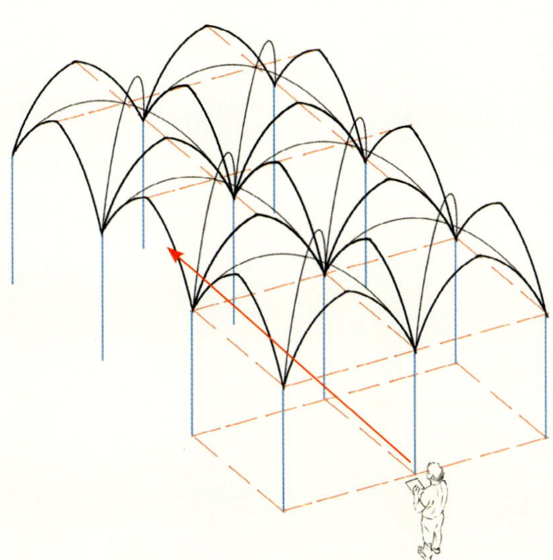

In the diagram, I've emphasised the cubes of space formed by the columns in the first two bays by outlining them in red dashed lines. In setting up a drawing of a space like this, it's wise to focus first on these sorts of simple, straightforward volumes, perhaps even to the point of ignoring for a time the complicated vaults of the ceiling above.

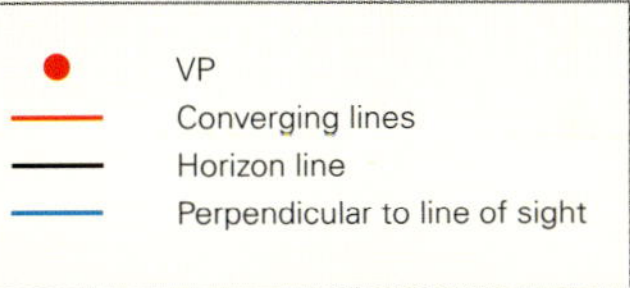

In the other four bays, however, the red dashed lines show how the peaks of the vaults also converge on the same two vanishing points. By establishing guidelines for both the cubic volumes and the peaks of the vaults, you can create a framework for the drawing, making it easier to accurately place the curves of the ceiling.

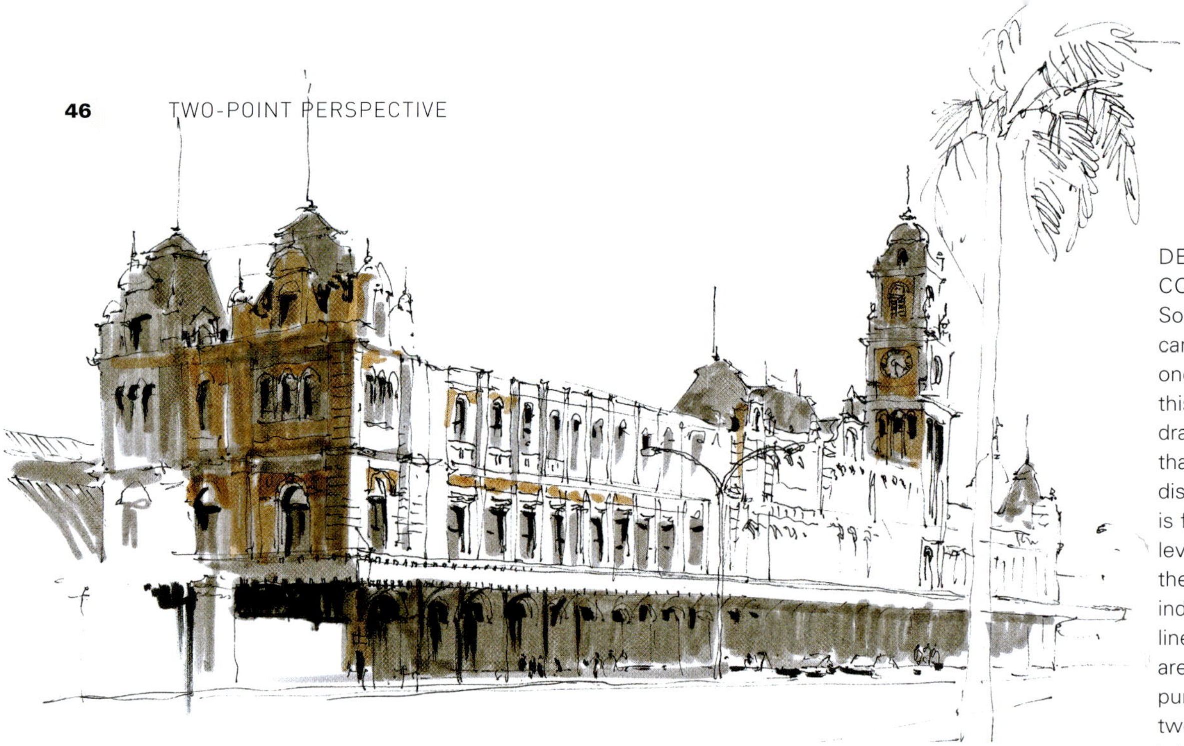

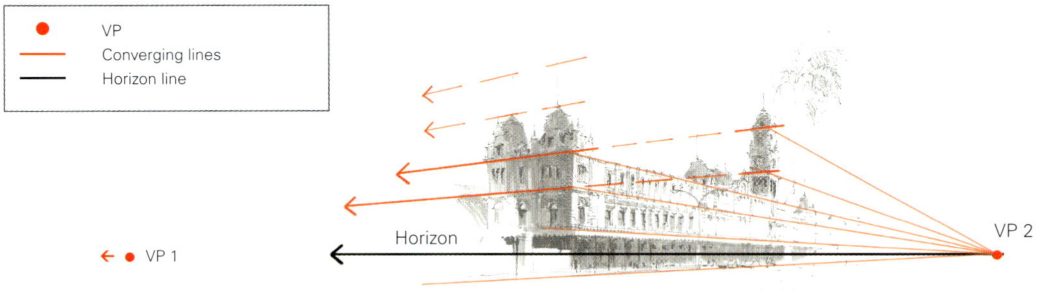

DEFINITION USING CONVERGING LINES

Sometimes, a converging line can be the basis for more than one element of the drawing. In this example, Eduardo Bajzek has drawn a long, narrow building that incorporates a tower in the distance. The left vanishing point is far off the page, where the eye level or horizon line would meet the red lines at the point indicated by the arrows. But the lines that radiate from this point are serving several important purposes. First, note how the two heavier converging lines at left help to define not only the near facade of the building, but if they were extended as guidelines, they would also help to define the levels of the tower in the distance. Also, note how the uppermost radiating or converging line helps to establish the very tops of the spires on the two towers in the foreground.

PEOPLE AND SHADOWS

It's not only drawings of buildings and other objects with well-defined lines and edges that can benefit from an understanding of two-point perspective. In this watercolour by Eduardo Bajzek, both the arrangement of the people in the view and the direction of their shadows have been established with the use of converging lines. While neither the people nor their shadows are precisely laid out according to these lines, their position and size is made much more believable because there's a consistent logic to their arrangement in the sketch – a logic based on the structure of two-point perspective. Note also how the eye level in this view is higher than the subject, because Eduardo was either standing or otherwise observing from a position above the people in the scene.

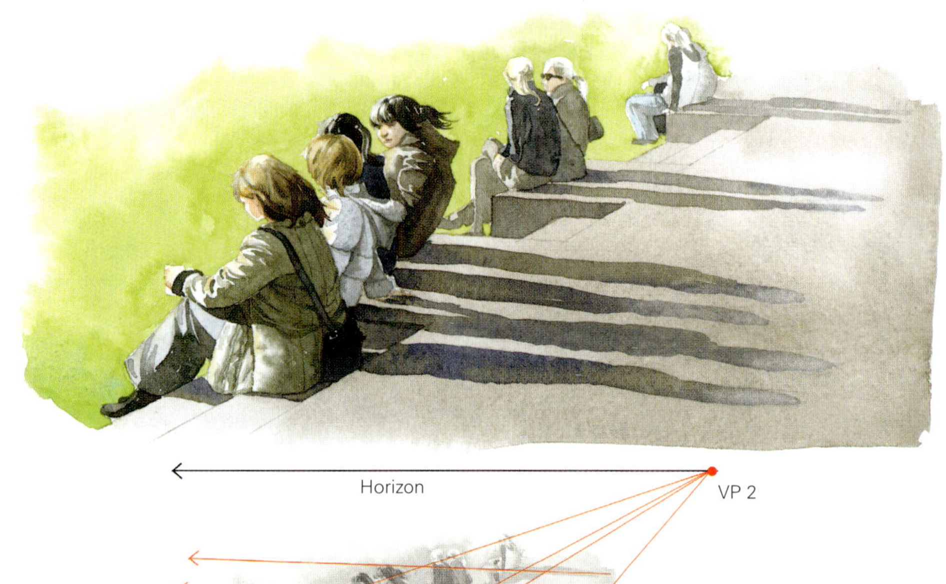

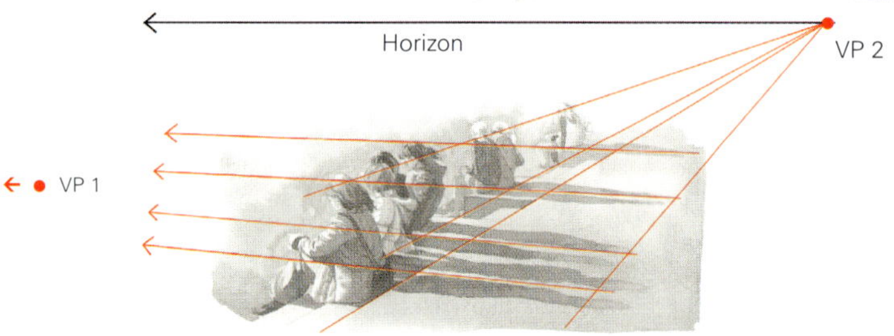

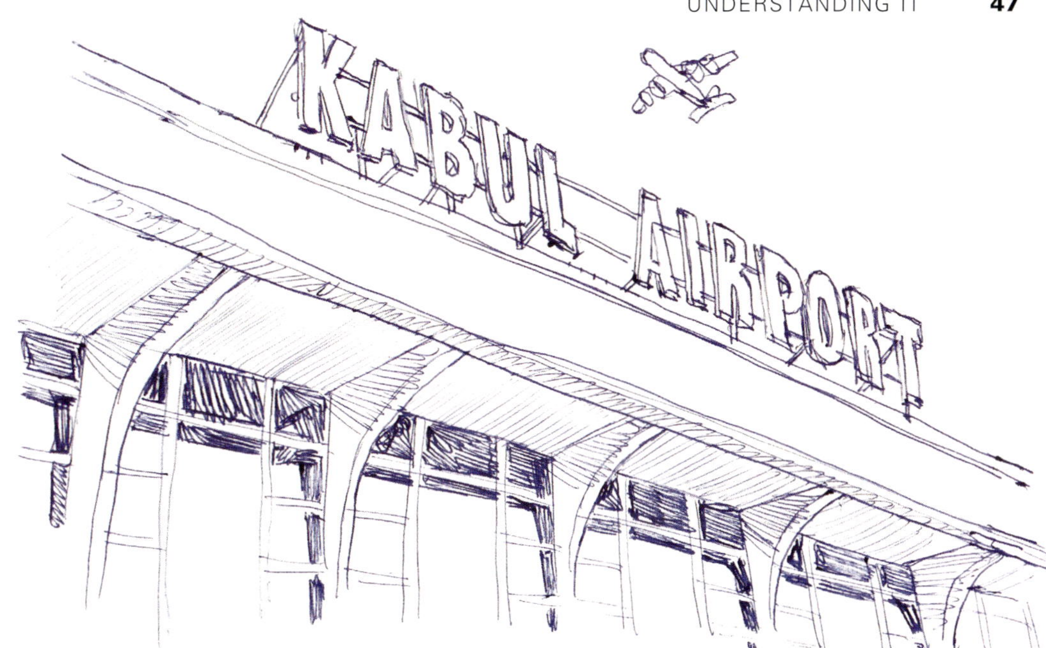

DISTANT VANISHING POINTS

In direct contrast to the watercolour of the people on the opposite page, the subject of this drawing by Richard Johnson is well above the eye level of the viewer. All of the lines that are horizontal in space will appear to angle downwards to the left and right, as shown in the diagram below.

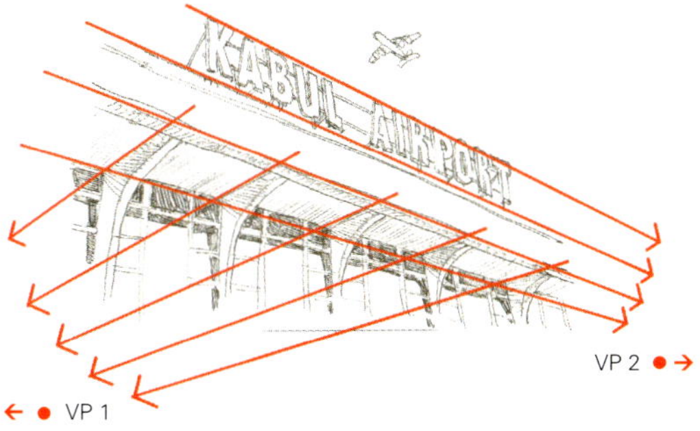

It's not uncommon to have one or even both of the two vanishing points off the page (see right), as was the case here. In these instances, some creative visualisation may be necessary in order for you to keep track of where your lines should be converging.

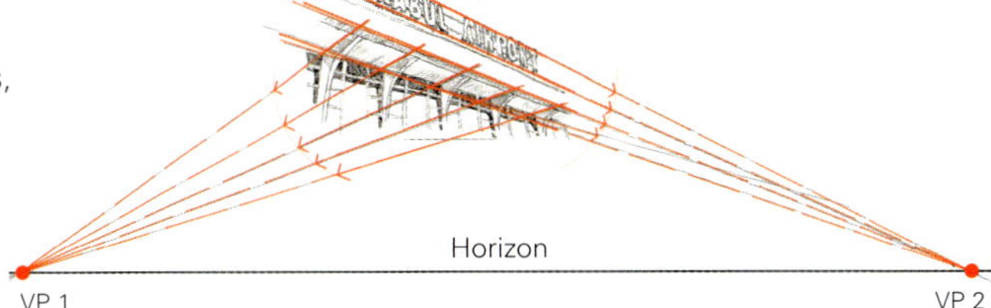

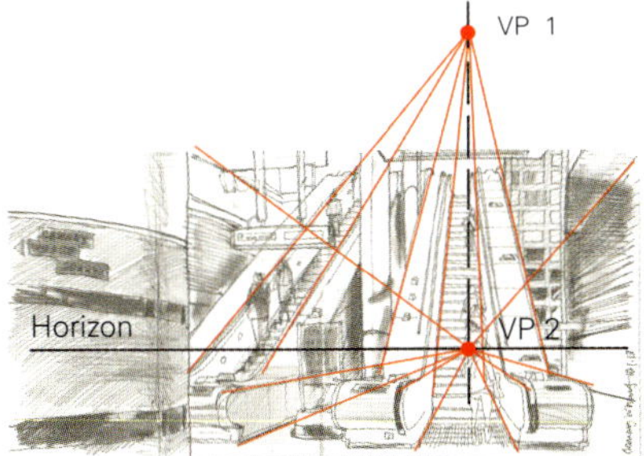

VERTICAL VANISHING POINT

In this sketch of the Canary Wharf tube station by Lis Watkins, the space might be considered a one-point perspective were it not for the dual escalator. Similar to the 'Harlot's Hall' photo on page 43, the presence of a sloping element means that there will be an additional vanishing point. In this case, that point is directly above the vanishing point at eye level (as indicated by the black dashed line), because the escalators are oriented along the same horizontal axis as the walls to their left and right.

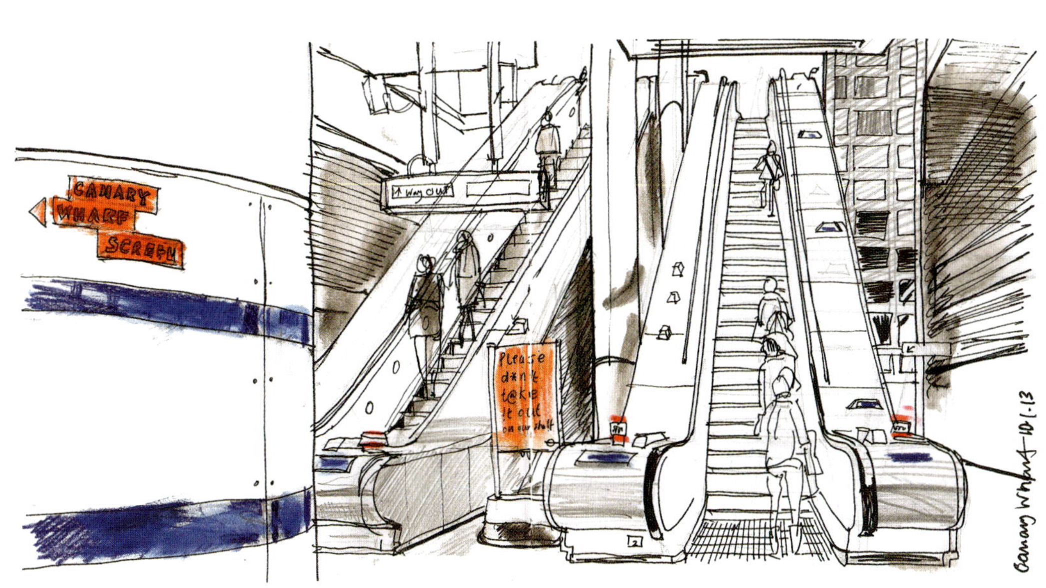

Applying it

Two-point perspective is useful any time you'd like to present a subject from 'off-centre', to visually describe its three-dimensional form more completely or in a more dynamic fashion than that afforded by one-point perspective.

45-DEGREE ANGLE

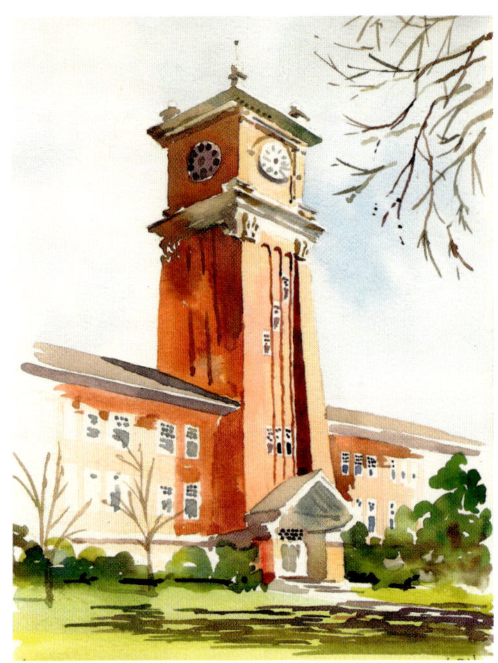

WSU CLOCK TOWER
◀ *Matthew Brehm*
Watercolour

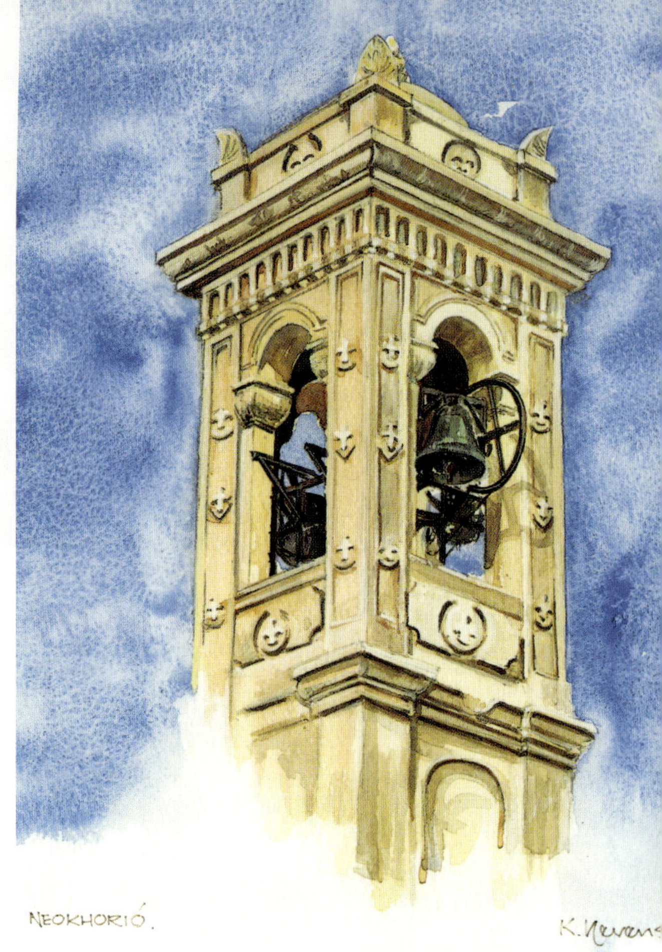

BELL TOWER
▶ *Keith Nevens* • Watercolour

Towers viewed from a fair distance, and from a roughly 45-degree angle, are perfect subjects for two-point perspective, even though their vanishing points are usually off the page. Both the drawing at right, and one of my sketches at left, show that the angles of convergence will be almost equal when a rectangular tower is drawn from this point of view.

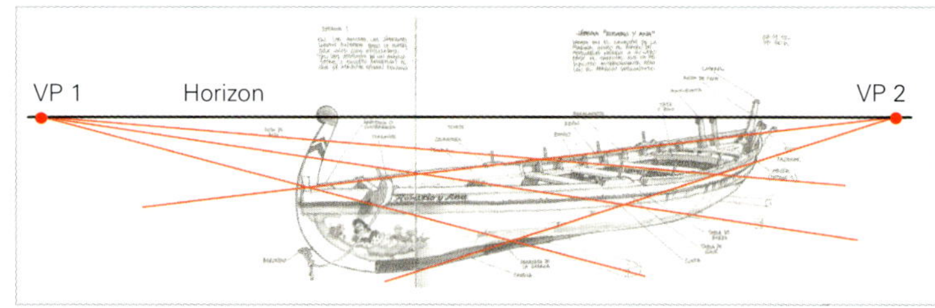

JABEGA BOAT
Luis Ruiz • Watercolour

▶ The boat in this sketch has very few straight edges. Nonetheless, a structure of converging lines can be a great help in mapping out the drawing. Note that the more distant gunwale appears to be an almost straight line radiating from the right vanishing point, while the near gunwale shows its curve more clearly from this angle such that the radiating line just touches it tangentially. The seats in the boat and the supporting boards below all appear to converge on the left vanishing point.

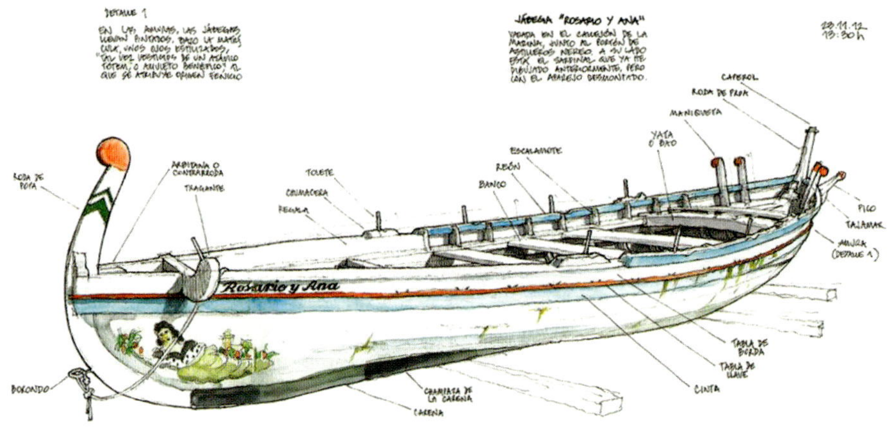

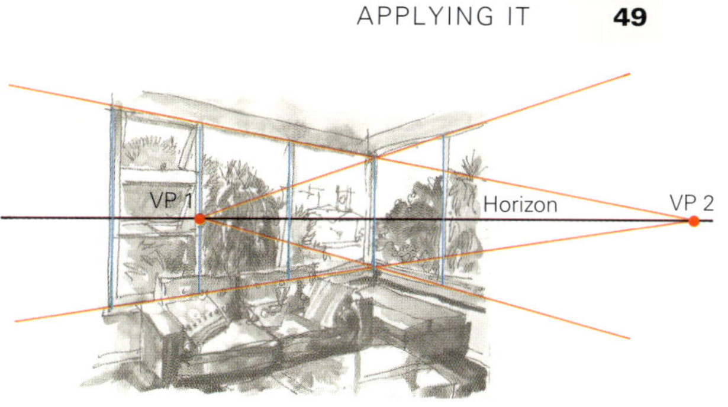

ROOM WITH A VIEW
Liz Steel • Ink and watercolour

◀ In this interior corner view, we see a simple construction of converging lines and the vertical mullions of the windows. It's a simple reversal of the typical two-point view of an outside corner. By letting the converging – or, in this case, radiating – lines extend towards your position as the viewer, the space is clearly framed by just four lines. These lines should cross each other above and below and fairly precisely at the vertical blue line where the windows turn the corner.

INTERIORS

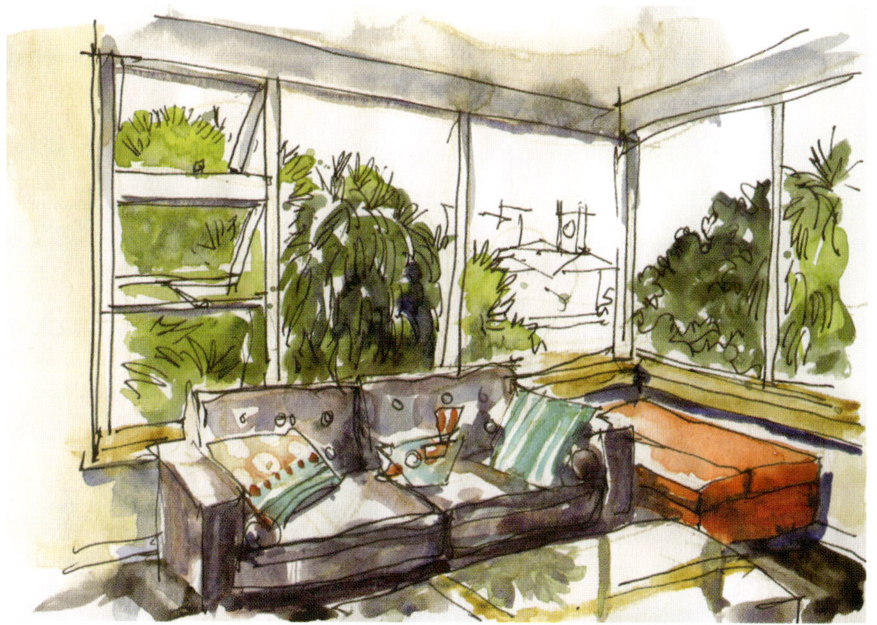

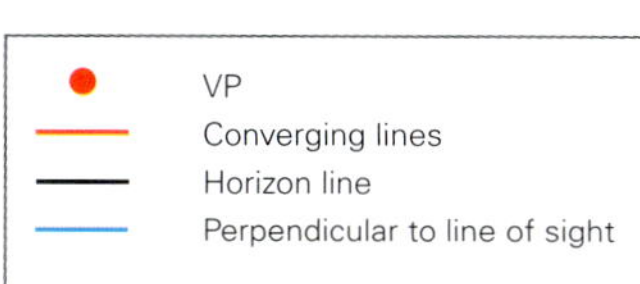

VIEWS THROUGH AN OPENING

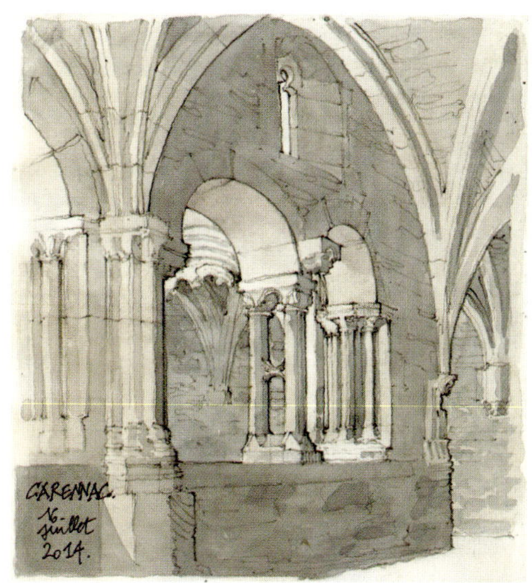

CATHEDRAL ARCH
▲ *Gérard Michel*
Watercolour

COURTYARD VIEW
▶ *Daniel Castro Alonso*
Watercolour

In drawings of openings from one space to another, the lines on the face of the wall will converge towards one vanishing point, while the lines that run through the wall (that is, in the direction of the wall's thickness) will converge on the other vanishing point.

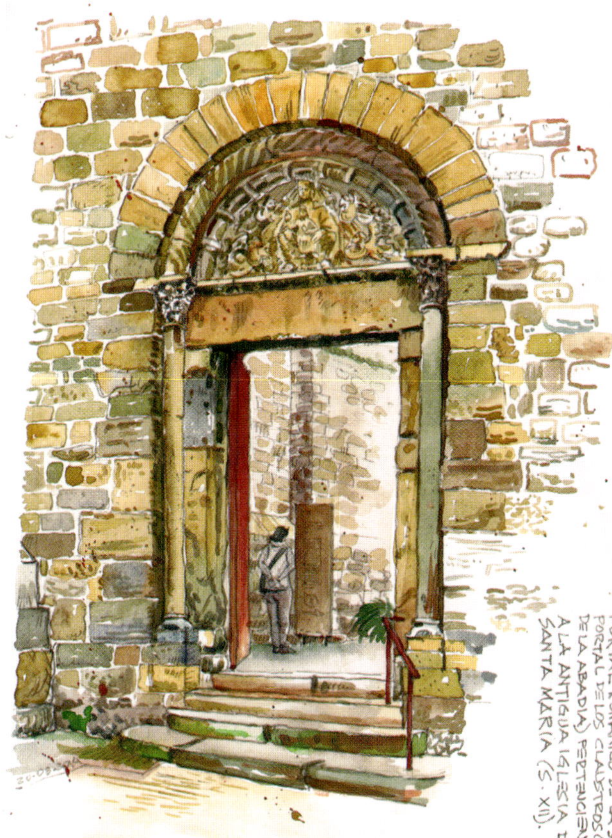

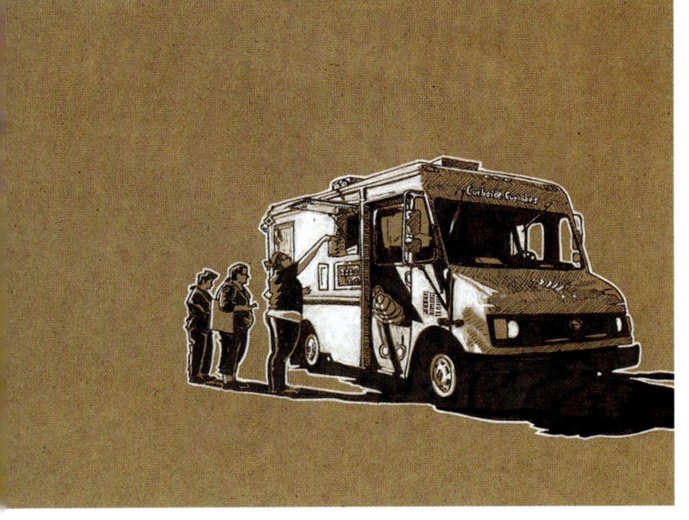

TRUCK AND GRAVE
Christian Tribastone • Ink

◀ ▶ Two-point perspective is used very effectively for these very different subjects – a food truck and gravestones. Even without any visible construction lines, it's clear how these images rely on lines that converge towards two vanishing points, right and left. The strong shadows and highlights add emphasis to the construction.

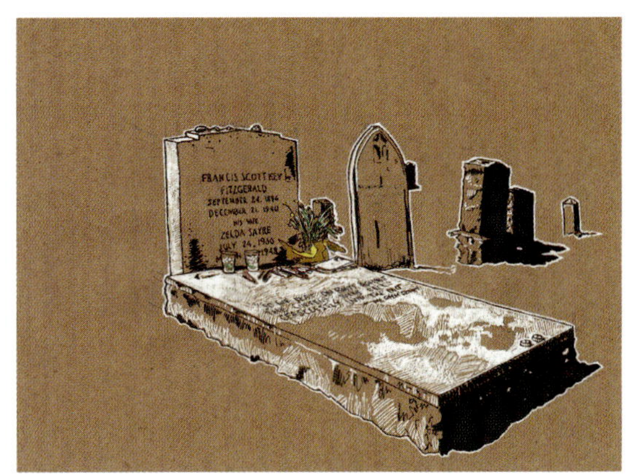

LIGHT & SHADE

CAPTURED MOVEMENT
Alexandre Veron • Watercolour

▶ In this comparatively loose sketch, the bold, almost horizontal line of the railing leads your eye directly to the right vanishing point, as does the shadow of the same railing along the lower right edge of the image. The shadows cast by the vertical stanchions of the railing contrast all of this rightwards movement. The arched bridge in the distance reinforces that the viewer's eye level is below the railing, almost even with the colourful cargo on the rear of the bicycle.

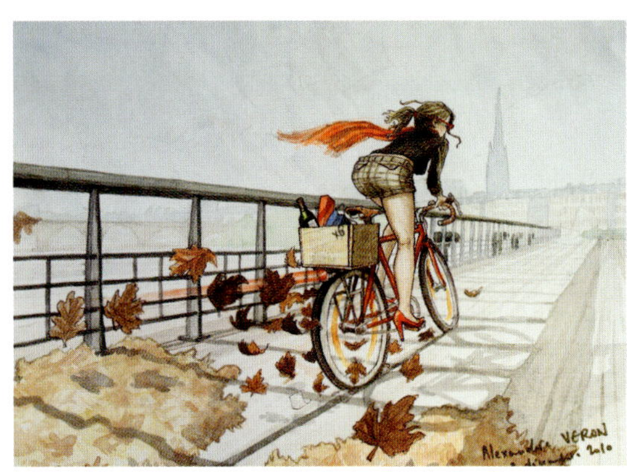

ELLIPSES

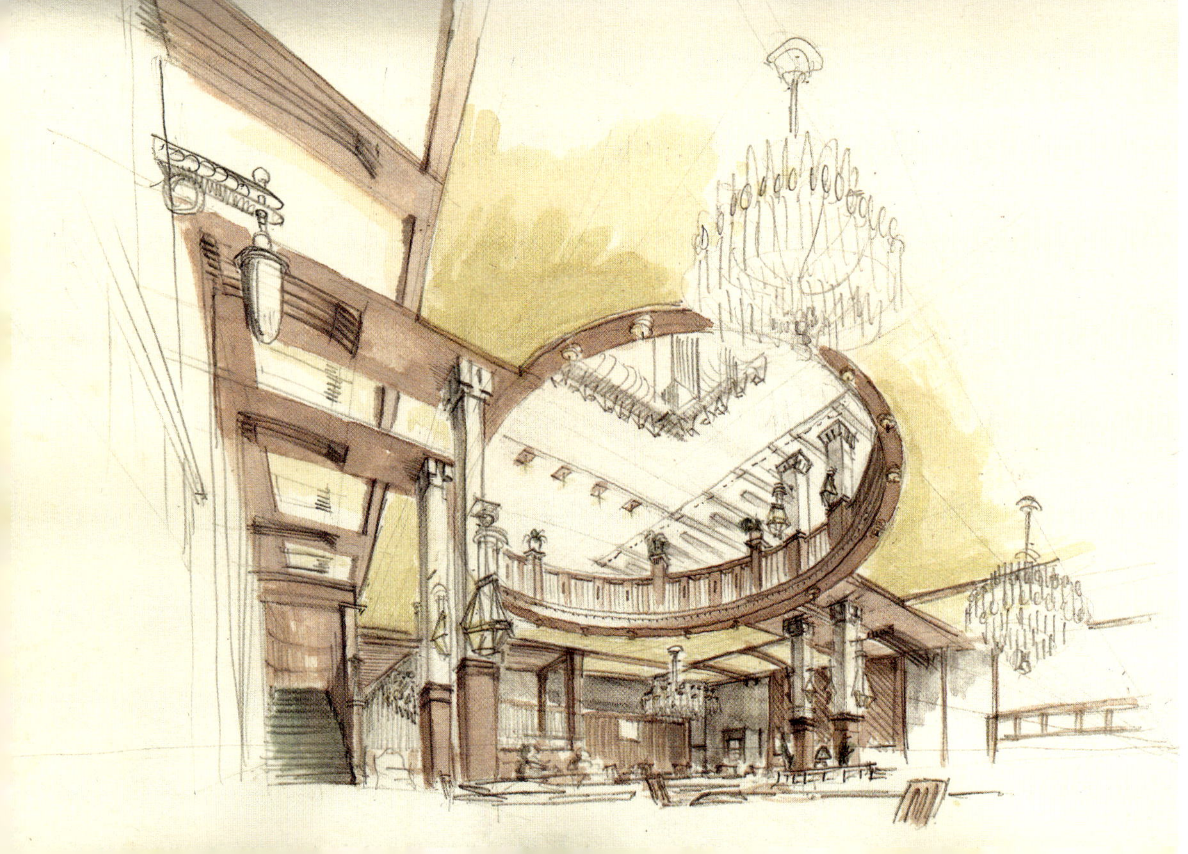

COMPLEX INTERIOR
Arno Hartmann • Pencil and watercolour

◀ The generous use of construction lines certainly helped create this rather spectacular interior view. When you're confronted with a subject like this, particularly when it involves substantial curves or a wealth of detail, it's always so important to look for the underlying structure of the perspective and to draw as many guidelines as needed before you even consider drawing any detail. If the overall composition is fairly accurate, and based on a strong sense of the converging lines of the perspective, things like curves and details will fall into place more quickly and easily.

STREET CORNERS

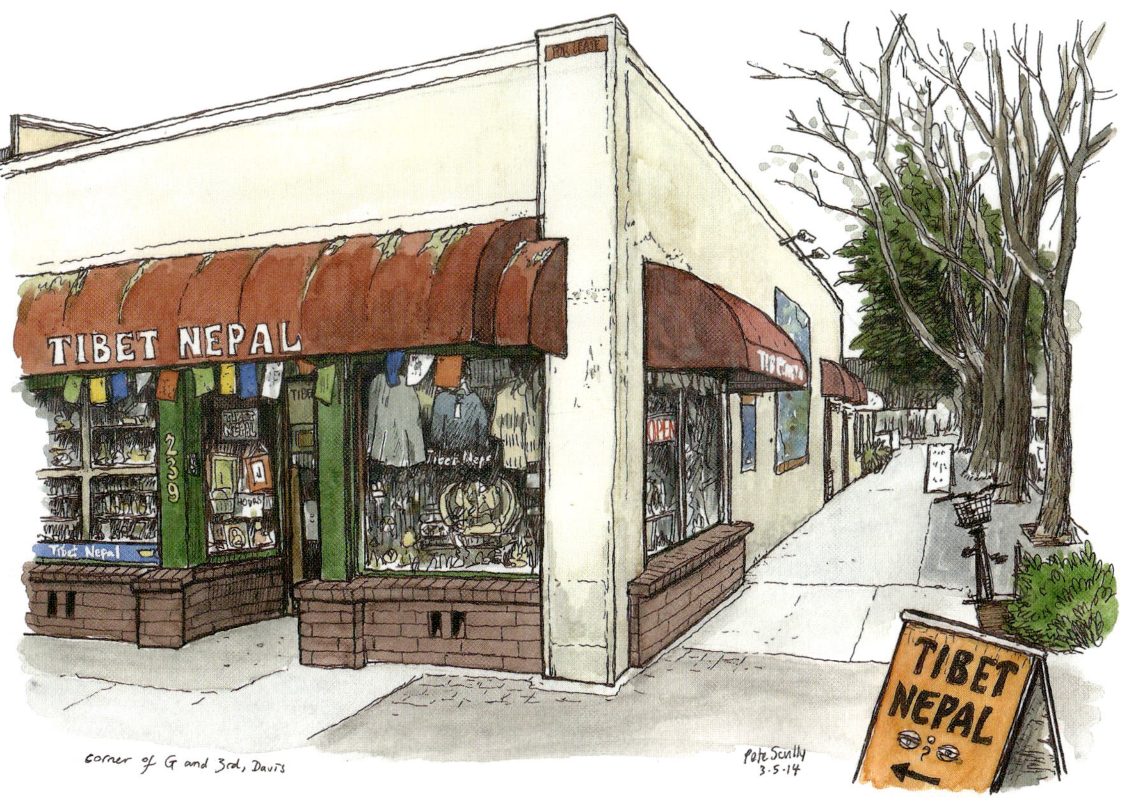

ANGLED STORE
Pete Scully • Watercolour

◄ The artist's point of view on this store in Davis, CA, places the left vanishing point well off the page, while the position of the right vanishing point helps to emphasise the long narrow space of the adjacent pavement. The sandwich sign in the foreground is obviously not parallel to the lines of the building, so even though its edges aren't long enough to indicate convergence, it still creates an interesting counterpoint to the rest of the image.

BUILDING AND VEHICLES
Florian Afflerbach • Watercolour

▼ In this line and watercolour drawing, the central subject of the building rises up to the highest point in somewhat dramatic fashion because the vanishing points are reasonably close together – in any case, they're both clearly visible on the page. If the vanishing points were placed further from one another, this would have the effect of 'calming' the perspective, thus making for a less dramatic view. It's great to see Florian's small thumbnail sketch at the top of the page – little drawings like this can be so important for developing your eye for perspective in general, or for working out particular issues regarding individual subjects. This sketch is also a good example of how vehicles can fall into line in a perspective view. The car at left is clearly framed by lines radiating from the left vanishing point, but note how the roof and undercarriage lines converge towards the right vanishing point.

How-to sequence

Although the main facade of this beautiful building is in the shade, light is hitting one side of it. Drawing it from a two-point perspective provides Eduardo Bajzek with a wonderful opportunity for a detailed tonal sketch.

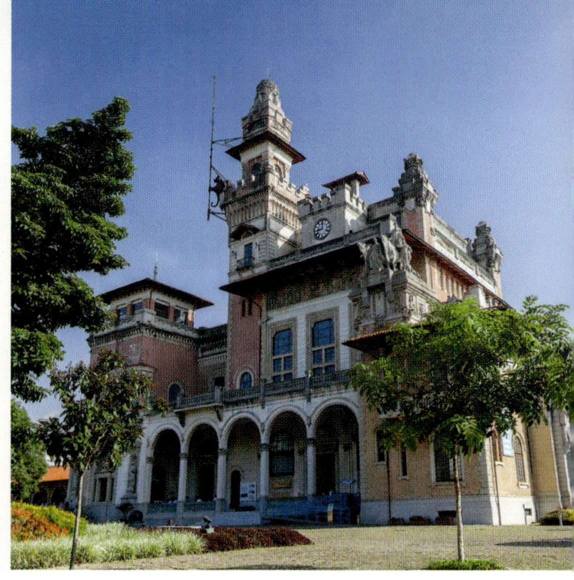

It's vital to establish the perspective with lightly drawn guidelines before you get into the detail of the architecture. Keep checking your measurements and angles throughout, and look for anything that will help you with the perspective lines – here, the roof overhangs the terrace above the loggia, and the arches are key to building up the perspective. Take note of the shadows, as they can change quickly when you are working en plein air.

STEP 1 ◀ Begin by making some very loose, light marks, seeking out the overall composition. Put in your eye level line – the line on which the vanishing points will occur – even though, in this case, the vanishing points will be off the paper.

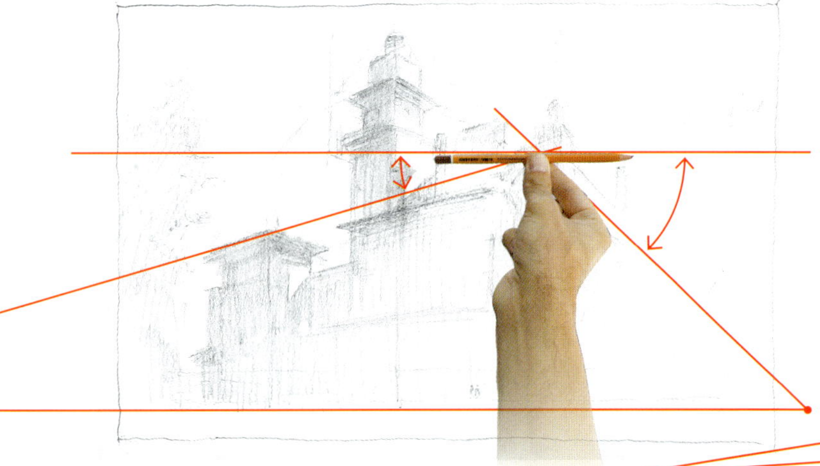

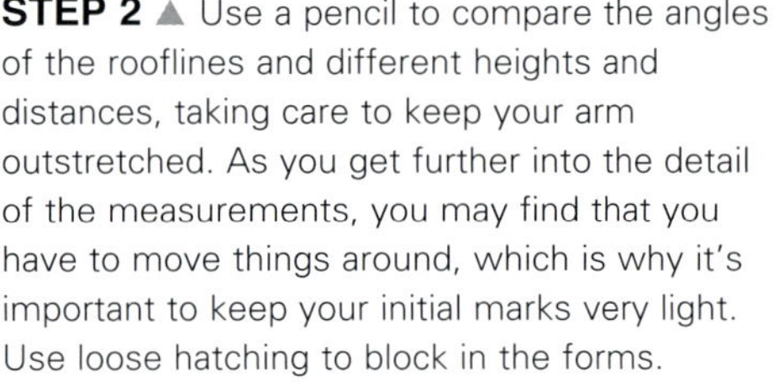

STEP 2 ▲ Use a pencil to compare the angles of the rooflines and different heights and distances, taking care to keep your arm outstretched. As you get further into the detail of the measurements, you may find that you have to move things around, which is why it's important to keep your initial marks very light. Use loose hatching to block in the forms.

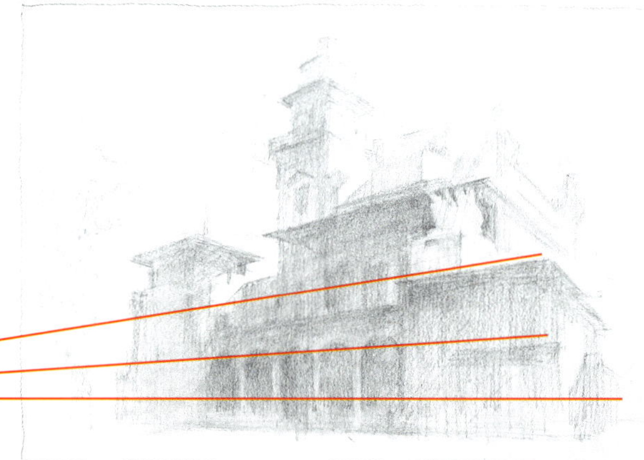

STEP 3 ▲ Continue building up the image, adding anything you can use to help verify the proportions, like windows, doors and the arches. Use a stump to blend the hatching, and a kneaded eraser to bring out bright areas on the side facade.

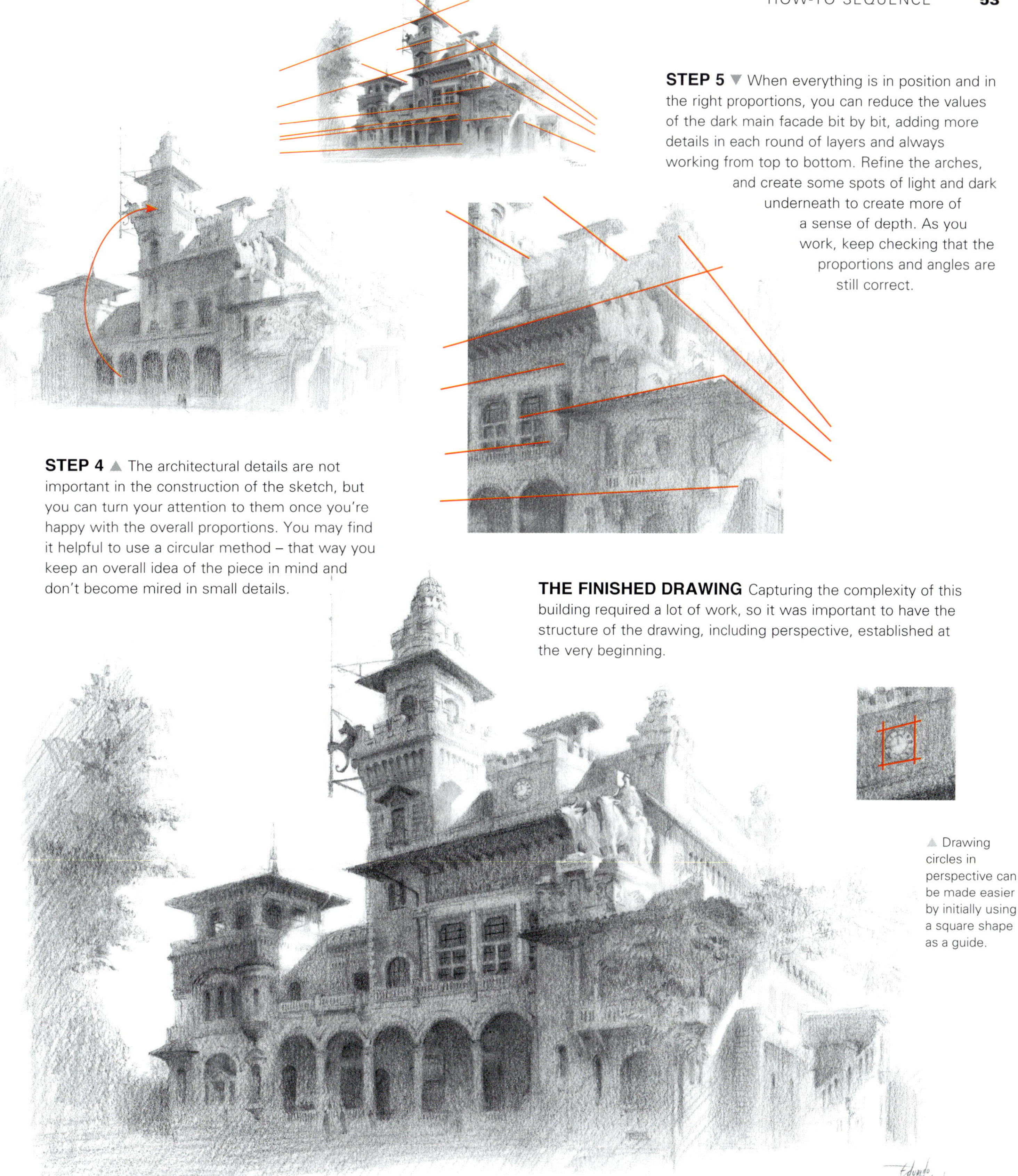

STEP 5 ▼ When everything is in position and in the right proportions, you can reduce the values of the dark main facade bit by bit, adding more details in each round of layers and always working from top to bottom. Refine the arches, and create some spots of light and dark underneath to create more of a sense of depth. As you work, keep checking that the proportions and angles are still correct.

STEP 4 ▲ The architectural details are not important in the construction of the sketch, but you can turn your attention to them once you're happy with the overall proportions. You may find it helpful to use a circular method – that way you keep an overall idea of the piece in mind and don't become mired in small details.

THE FINISHED DRAWING Capturing the complexity of this building required a lot of work, so it was important to have the structure of the drawing, including perspective, established at the very beginning.

▲ Drawing circles in perspective can be made easier by initially using a square shape as a guide.

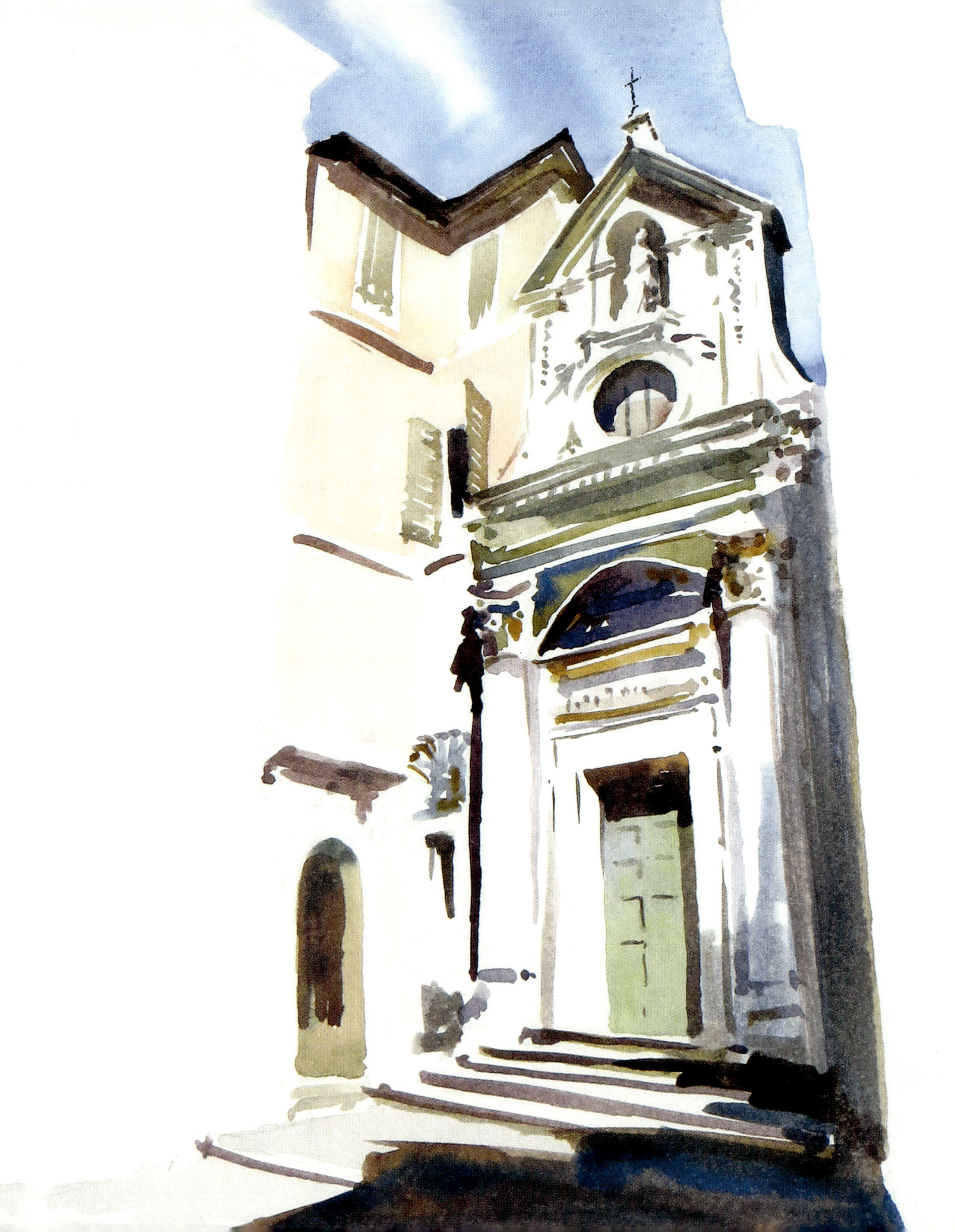

3 POINT PERSPECTIVE

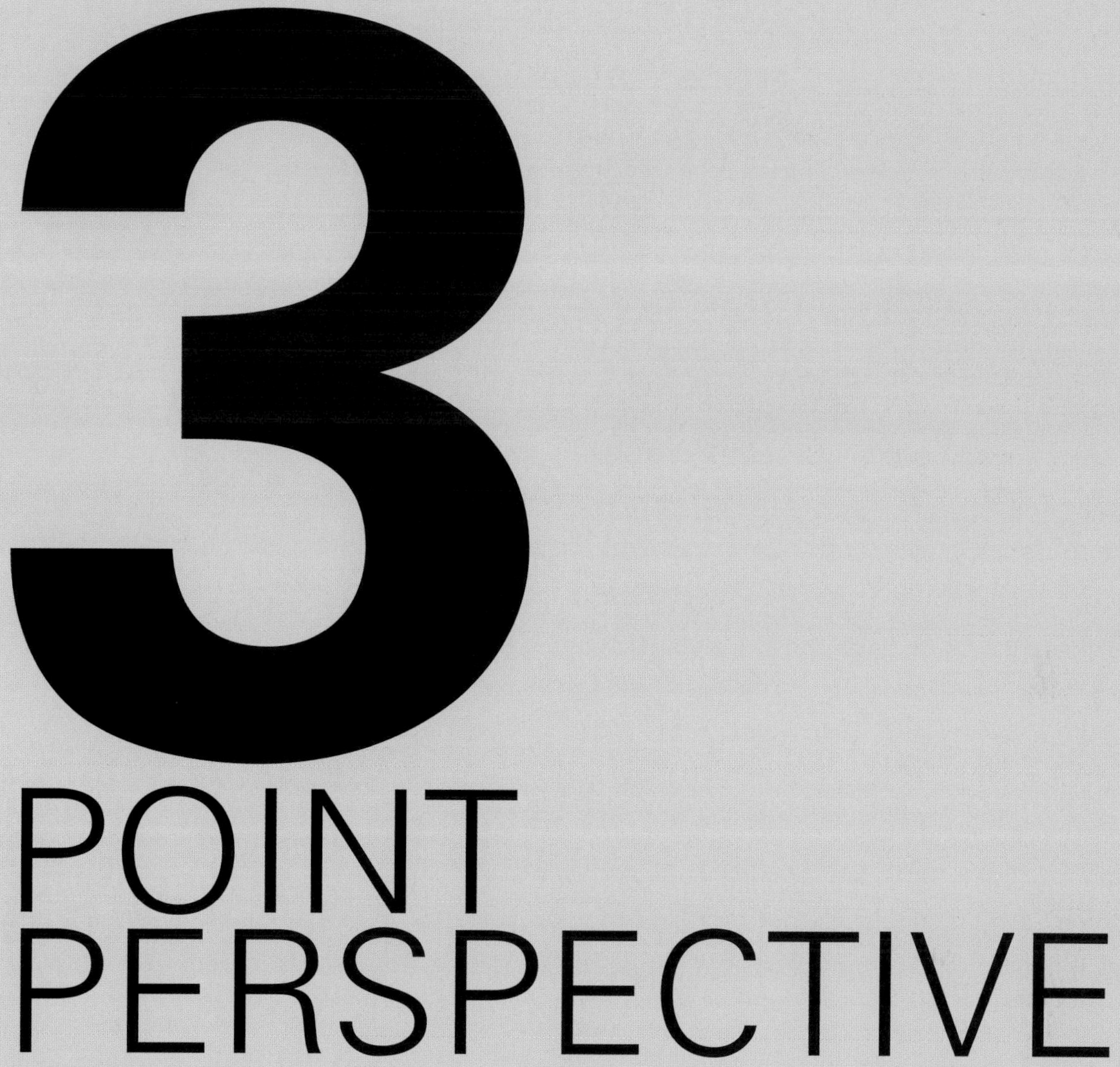

Three-point perspective allows us to represent what we see when we look upwards or downwards. It includes vanishing points on the horizon line, as is the case with one-point and two-point, but adds a third either directly above or directly below our position as the viewer.

◄ SANTA BARBARA DEI LIBRARI, ROME • *Matthew Brehm* • Watercolour

Introduction

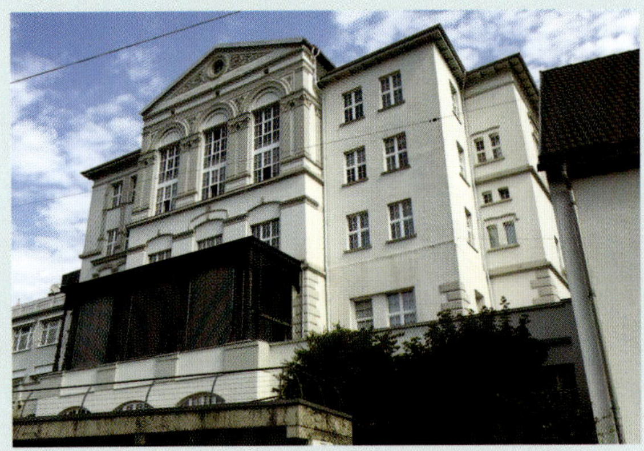

What is three-point perspective?

While two-point perspectives are often more dynamic than one-point drawings, three-point perspectives are more dynamic still. With three-point perspective, we can begin to convey increased drama – the height of a very tall building, for example, or the precarious feeling of being far above a cityscape.

In addition to the typical two vanishing points, left and right, we find a third, either directly overhead or directly below our vantage point. So a tall building will appear to diminish in size as it climbs towards the sky – or vice versa, as if we are above and looking down. Three-point perspectives can be more challenging to draw than one- or two-point, because it's common that at least one vanishing point – and sometimes all three – is some distance from the subject. This means that the point or points will be far off the page of your drawing. To compensate, you will need to visualise where the vanishing points are in relation to the composition. The added effort is often worthwhile, because three-point perspectives do begin to describe even more accurately how we view the three-dimensional world around us.

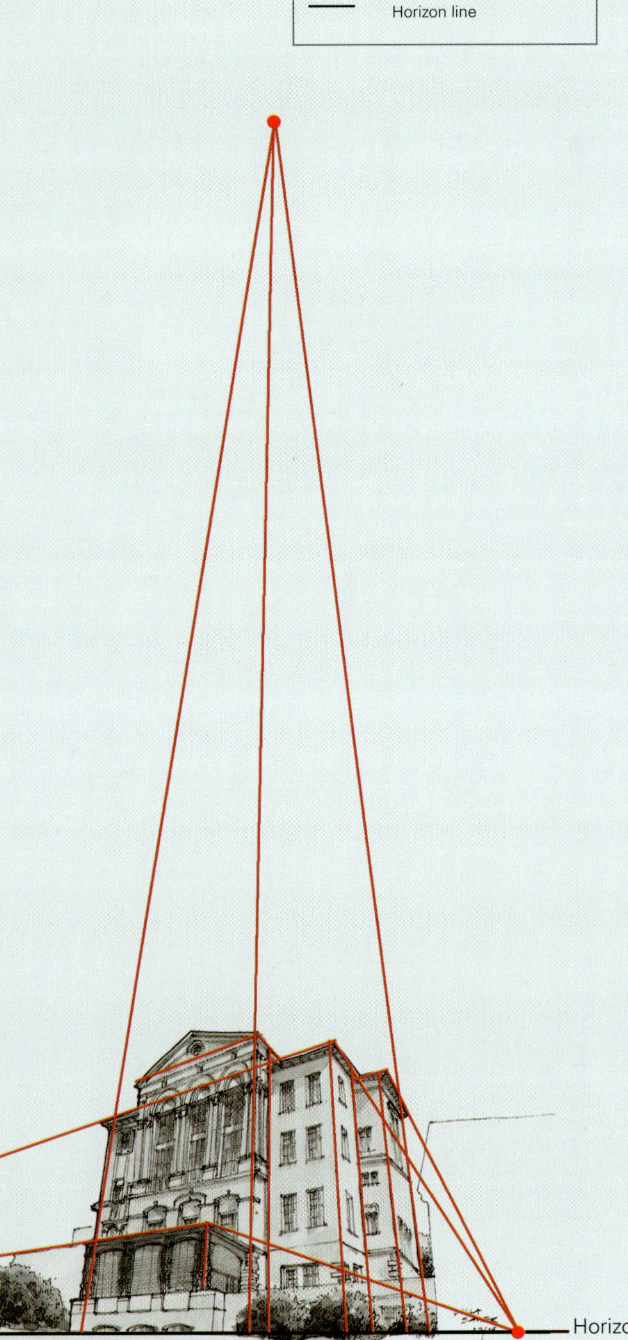

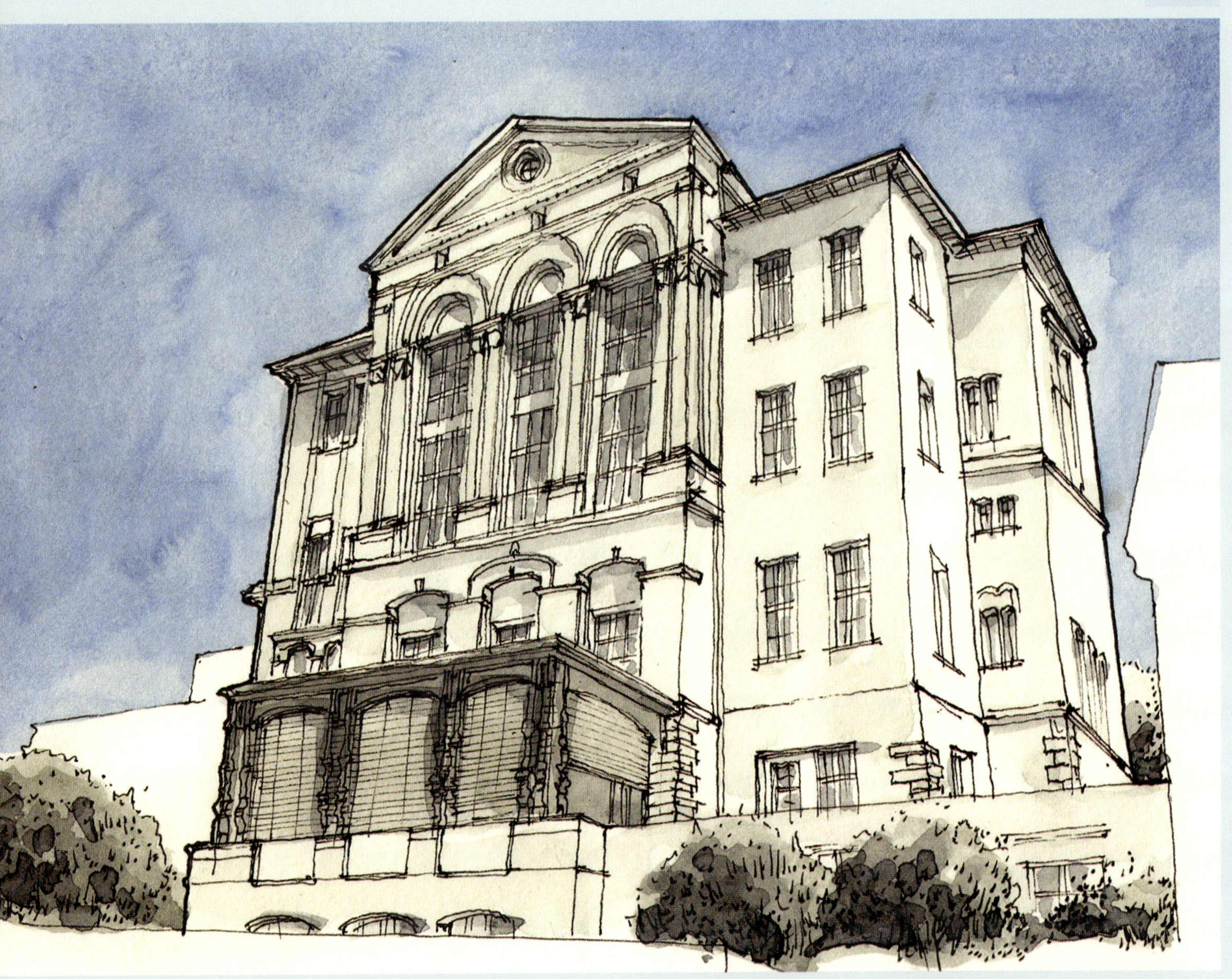

SIEGEN, GERMANY

Florian Afflerbach • Ink pen and watercolour

▲ Florian Afflerbach's drawing is a classic example of three-point perspective. The view is taken from one of the corners of the building, to see two flanks of it, and the line of sight is directed towards the top of this residential house. Lines that are horizontal in space recede towards left and right vanishing points, and the vertical edges converge on the third vanishing point overhead, emphasising the height of the building.

Seeing it

In a three-point perspective view, there will be the same left and right vanishing points found in a two-point view, with the addition of a third point either directly above or directly below the centre of the view. Lines that are oriented vertically in space will appear to converge on the third point in the drawing.

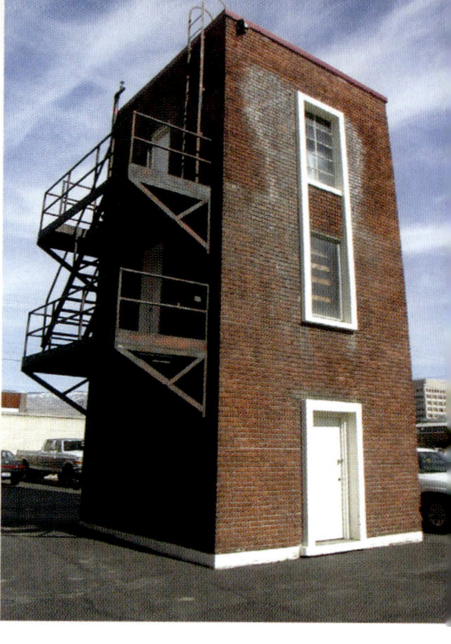

▲ When viewed at close range, even a simple tower like this will appear to converge on a point directly overhead.

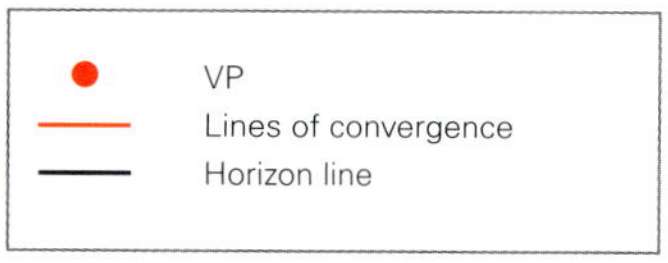

LOOKING UPWARDS

With three-point perspective, we still see lines converging on points to the right and left along the horizon line (as is the case with two-point perspective), but with the addition of a third vanishing point appearing either directly above or directly below the subject. If we look at the box below, we see that our eye level is relatively low and our line of sight is angled upwards towards the area above the box. This means that the top of the box is more distant from our point of view – even if the increased distance is slight – and therefore the top of the box should appear smaller than the bottom.

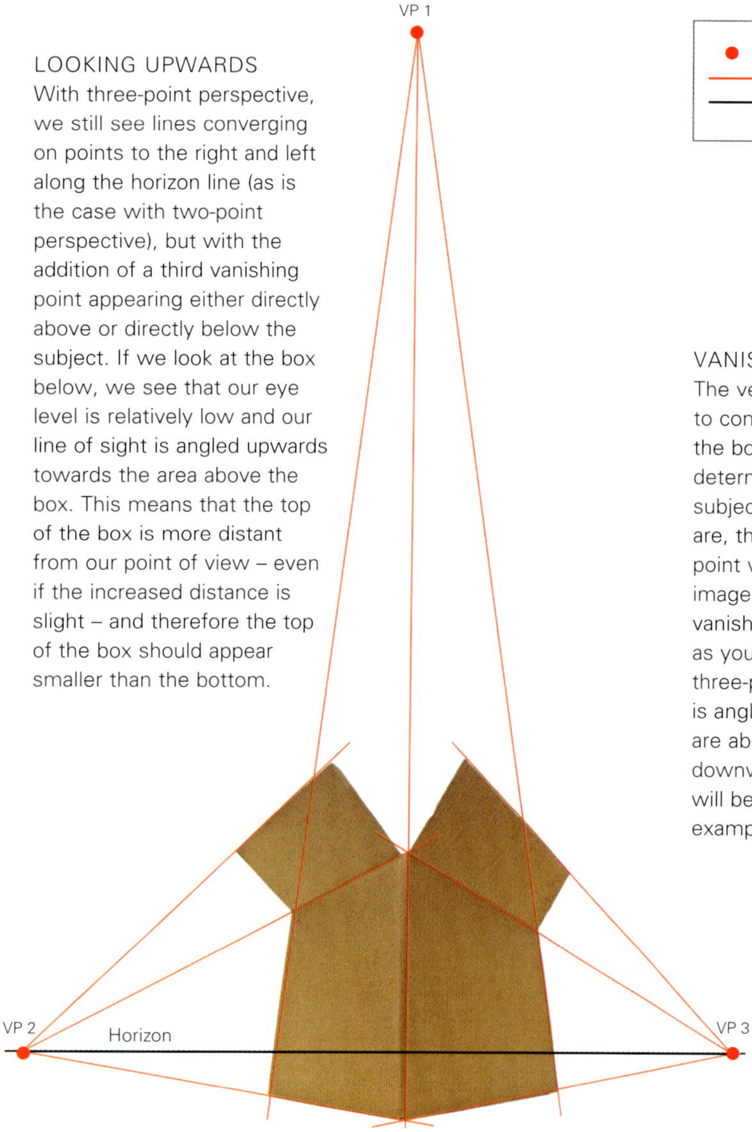

VANISHING POINT DISTANCE

The vertical edges of the box will appear to converge on a point directly above the box – just how far above will be determined by your distance from the subject in view. The further away you are, the higher the vertical vanishing point will be above the subject. The image at lower right shows how this vanishing point gets closer to the subject as your point of view gets closer. With three-point perspective, your line of sight is angled either up or down. When you are above a drawing subject and looking downwards, the vertical vanishing point will be below the subject, like the examples at the top of the next page.

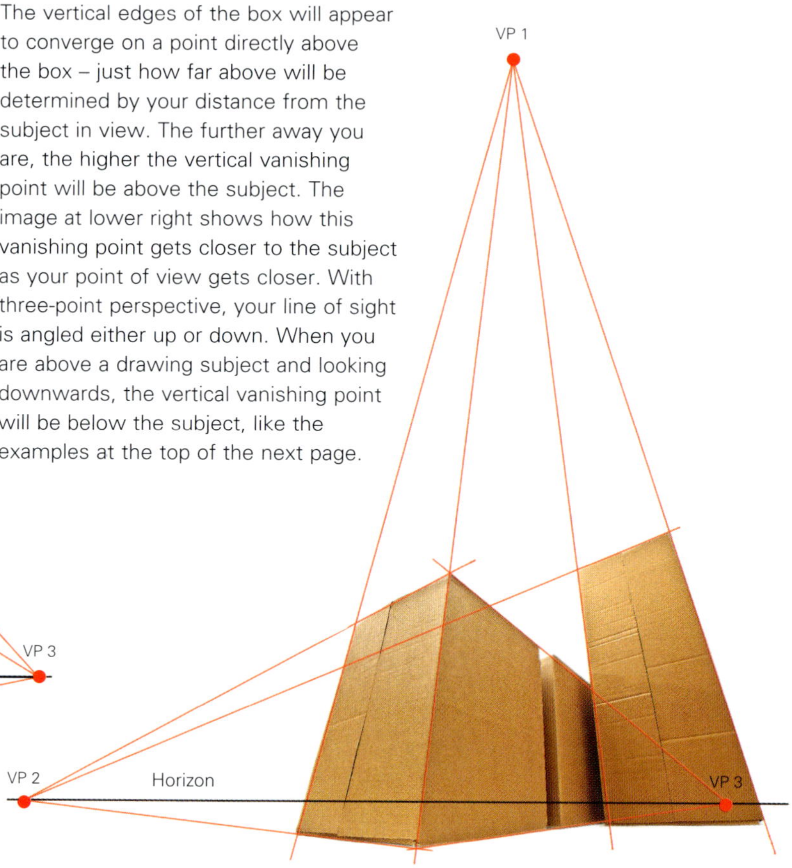

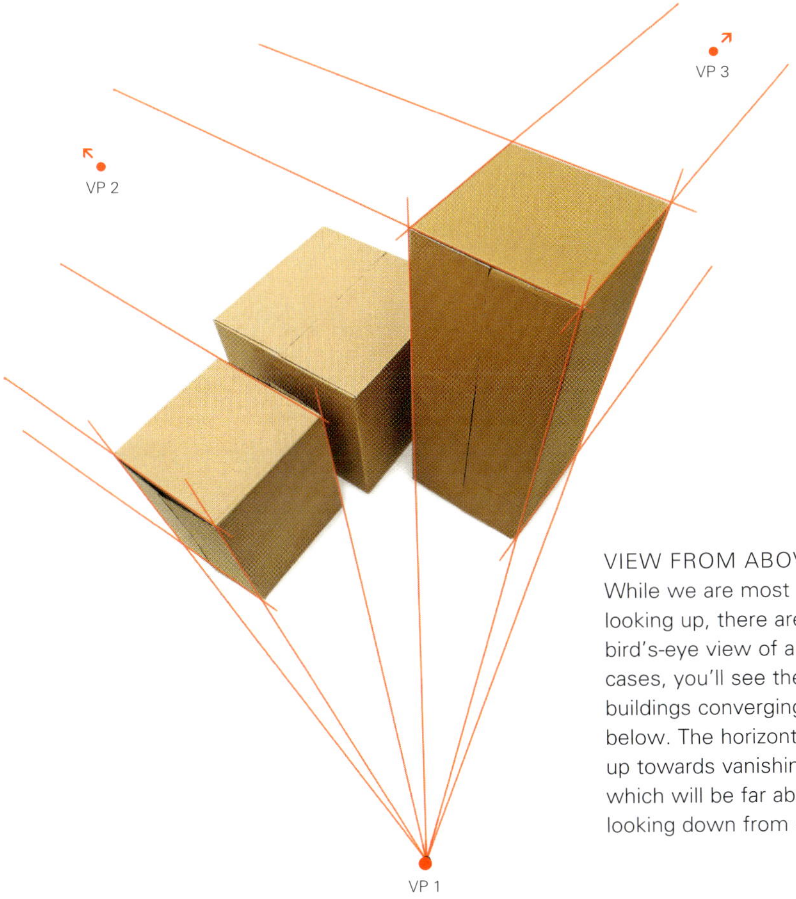

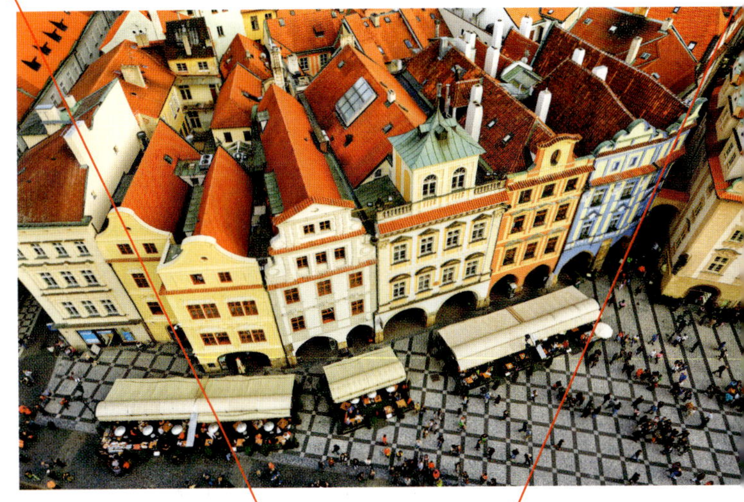

VIEW FROM ABOVE

While we are most commonly on the ground looking up, there are times when we have a bird's-eye view of a drawing subject. In these cases, you'll see the vertical edges of boxes or buildings converging on a vanishing point directly below. The horizontal edges will appear to rise up towards vanishing points on the horizon line, which will be far above the subject when you're looking down from above.

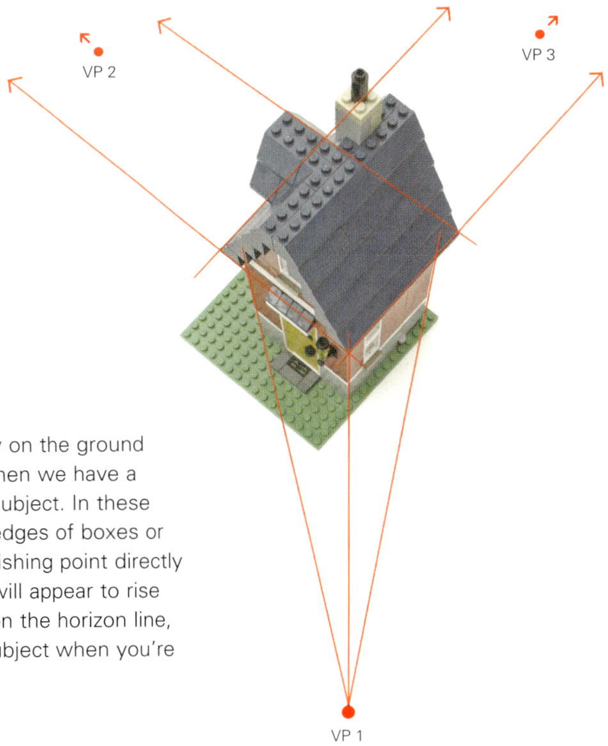

DRAMATIC VIEWS

Three-point perspective becomes very useful when we'd like to take a more extreme point of view on a subject – standing at the foot of a tall tower, for example, or looking down from the top of a tall tower.

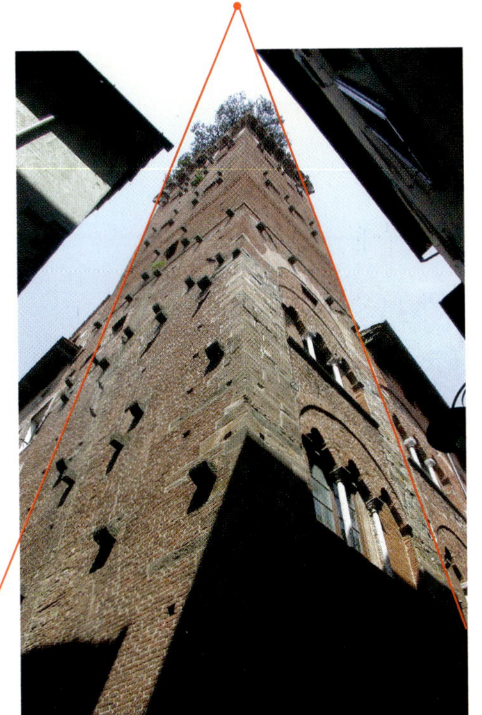

Notice that the horizon line is nowhere to be seen in these examples. If our line of sight is steeply angled, either upwards or downwards, the horizon line will be in our extreme peripheral vision – if it's visible at all. When we'd like to include what's in our peripheral vision, however, curvilinear perspective is usually necessary and will be covered on pages 92–109.

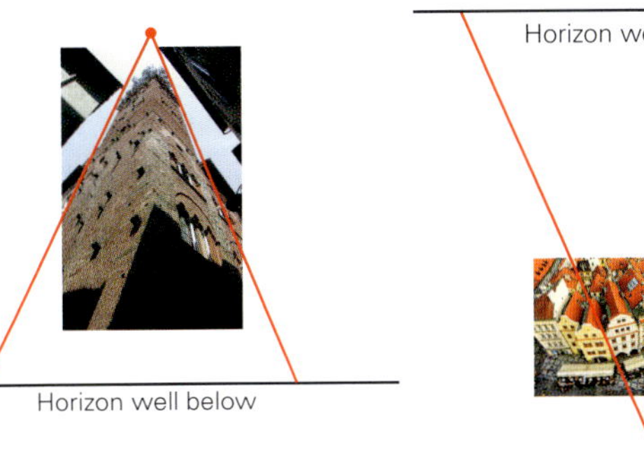

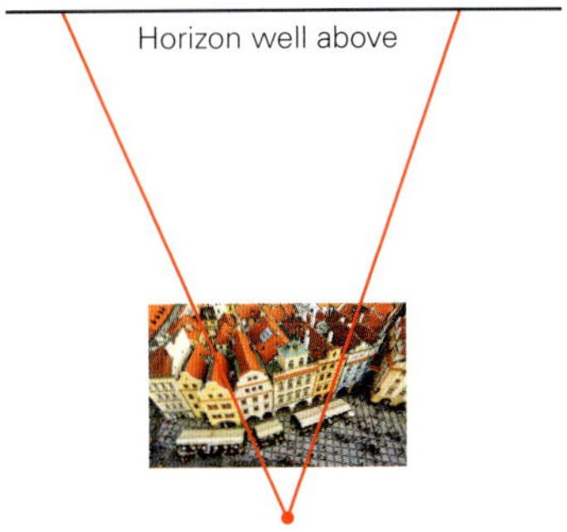

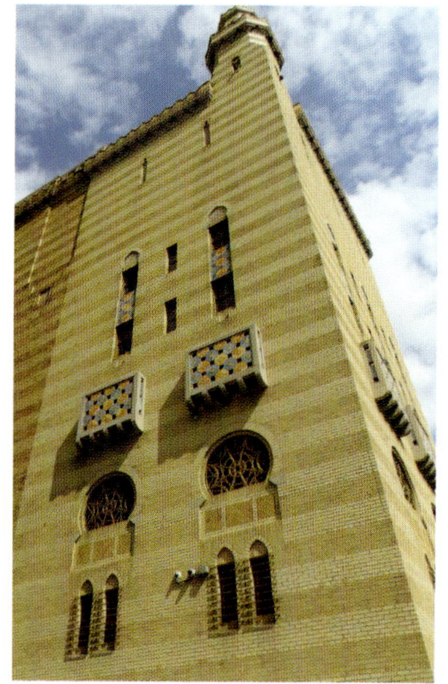

VERTICAL CENTRE LINE

The Fox Theatre in Atlanta, Georgia, has a very tall corner tower with a fascinating composition of openings and projections. The adjacent pavement, where the corner meets the street level, is not very interesting, so the subject is a perfect candidate for a three-point perspective view. The lines that are parallel to the ground converge on vanishing points left and right, as in a two-point perspective, but the vertical lines converge on a third point overhead, along a truly vertical line that's roughly centred in the composition. In this case, the line of sight is directed to the left of the corner of the building – note how the left and right vanishing points also move to the left along the horizon line, as compared to the view of the building below.

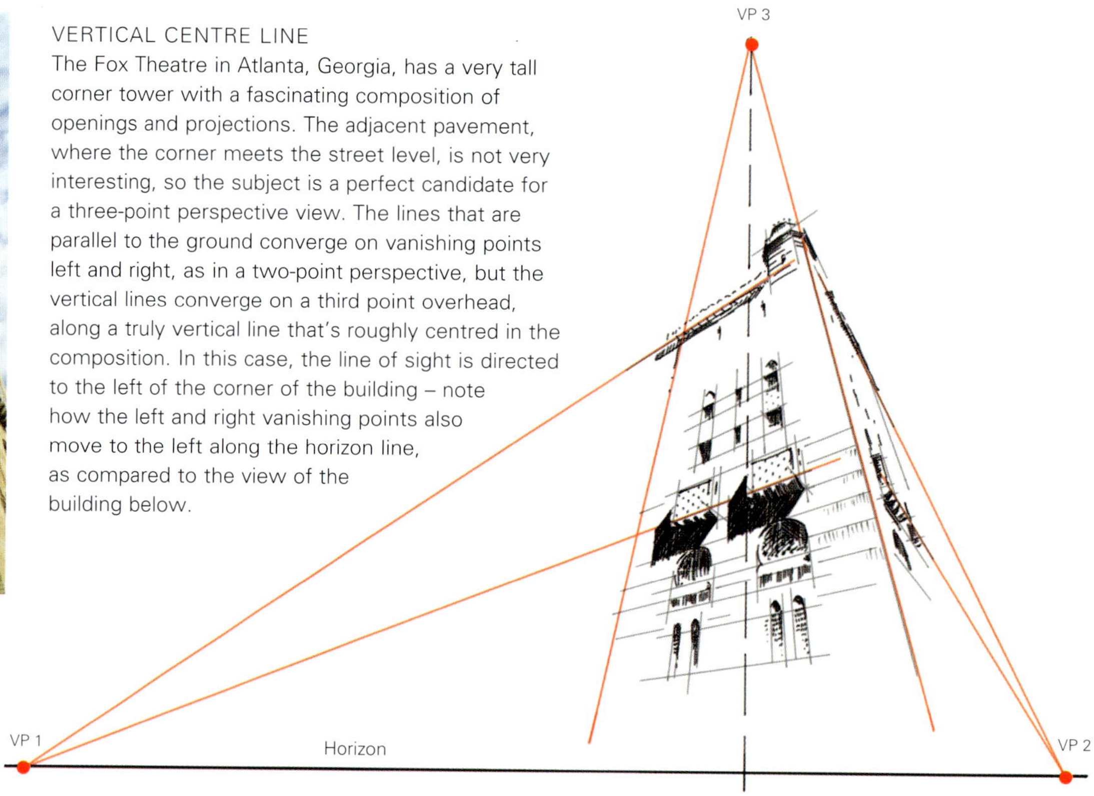

45-DEGREE ANGLE, LOOKING UP

Looking up at a tall structure from a 45-degree angle is perhaps the simplest example of three-point perspective. The near corner is almost in the very centre of the view, so it can effectively be drawn as a vertical line. All other lines that are vertical in space will appear to converge on a vanishing point directly above. The left and right vanishing points will be roughly equidistant from the centre of the composition.

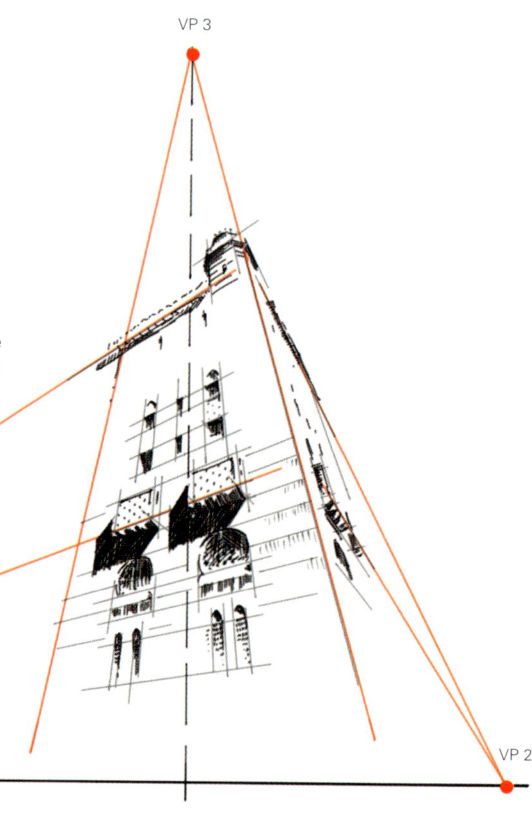

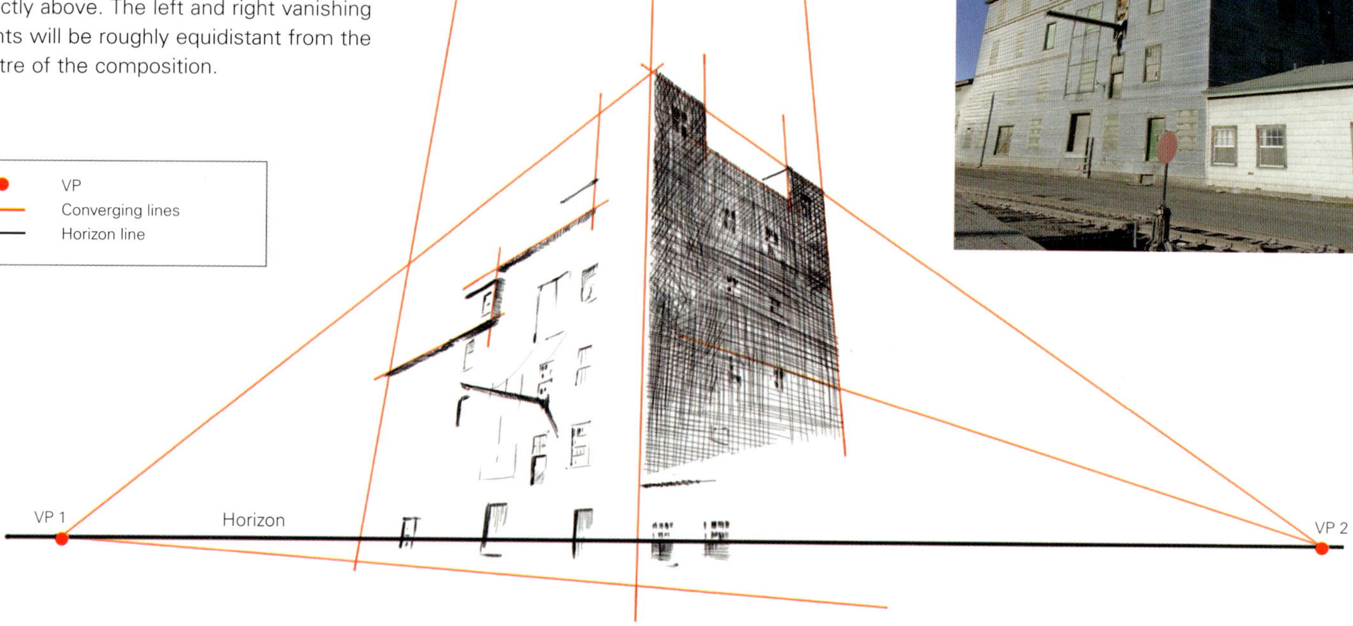

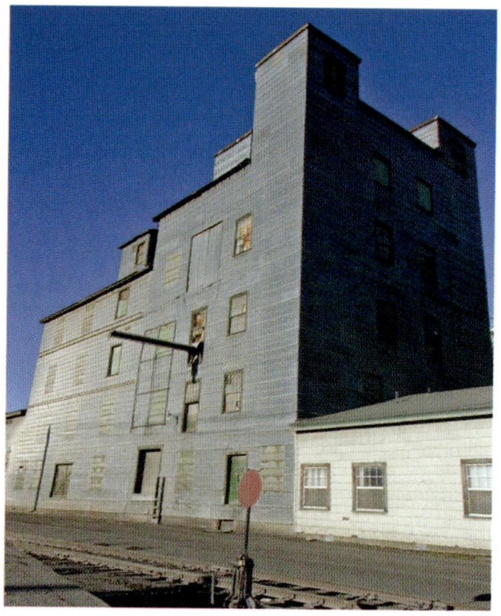

LOOKING DOWN

In this case, the eye level is above the composition, out of sight and off the page. Although the right vanishing point is not clear in this image, it remains a good example of what we see when we're above the subject and looking down. The floor line and the tops and bottoms of the frames on the wall all converge on a point far to the left. The sides of the frames – and the standing figures – converge on the third vanishing point far below the image. Even if the lines of convergence are not perfectly focused on the vanishing point, their angles will convey that your point of view is from above.

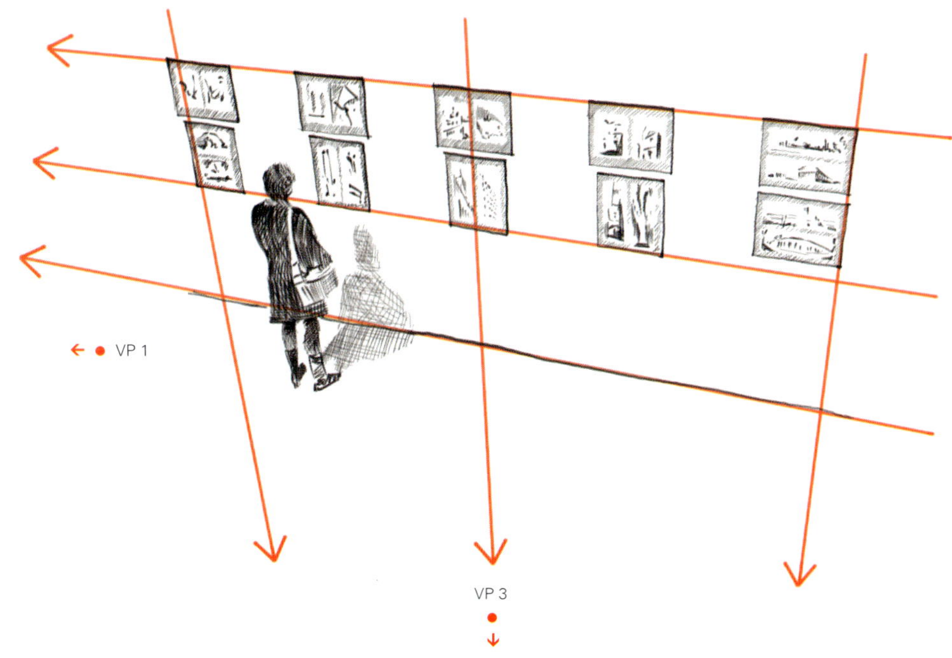

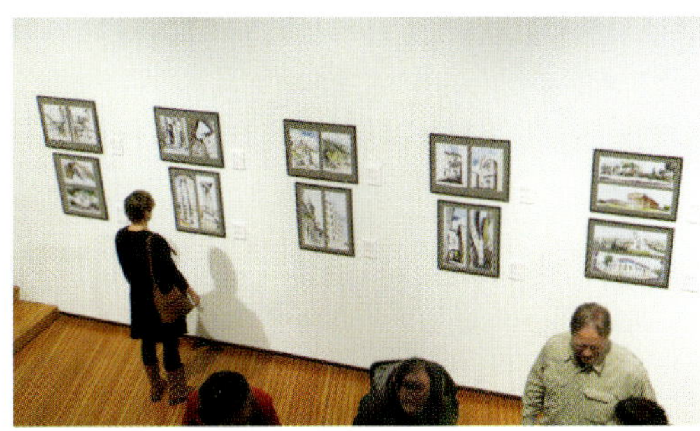

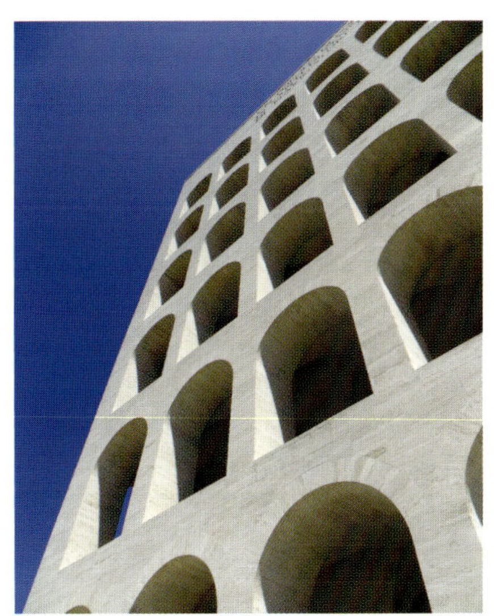

UP CLOSE

The closer you are to the subject, and the more you are looking straight up, almost directly overhead, the closer the vertical vanishing point will be to the subject in view. Your eye level will be well below and out of your view entirely, so you'll need to estimate the locations of the left and right vanishing points. In this image, there are no clear edges that converge on the right vanishing point, but it can be very effective to align the shaded hatch patterns as though they are converging, as shown with the two arrows bottom centre in the sketch below. This approach to shading will be discussed in greater detail in a later chapter.

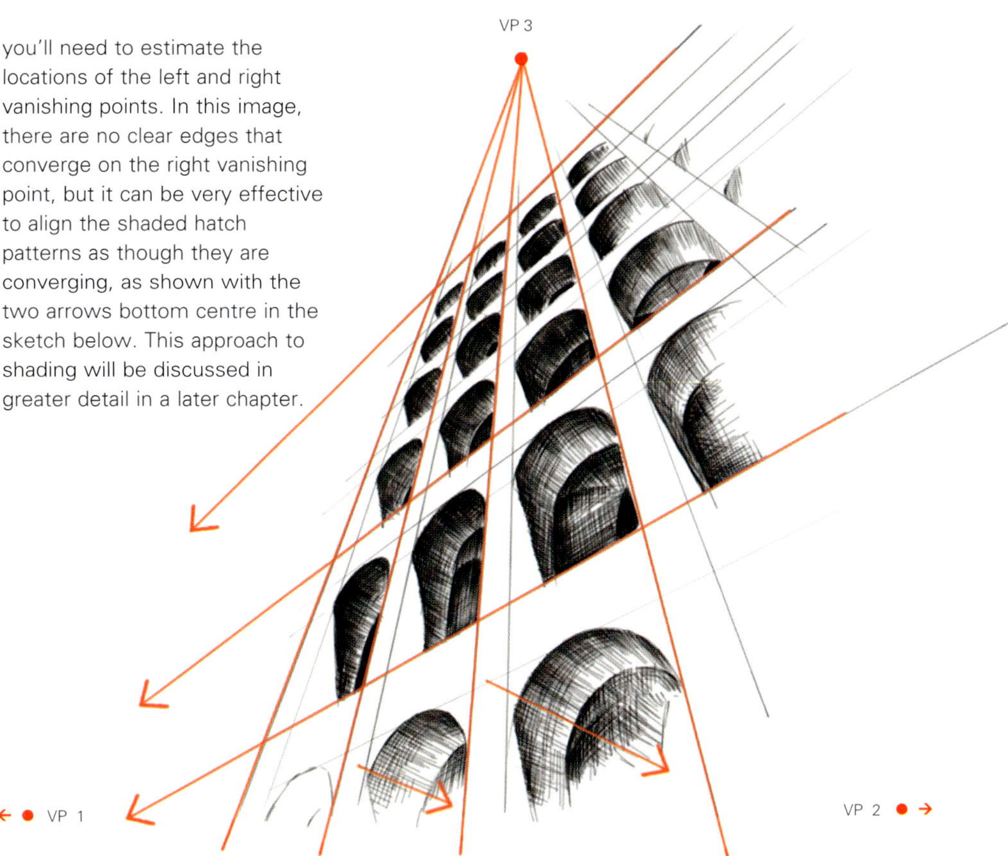

Understanding

If we add two levels to our basic cube, we can begin to illustrate how three-point perspective works. Most importantly, our line of sight is no longer perpendicular to the vertical edges of the stacked cubes. In other words, all of the lines visible from this point of view and along this line of sight will appear to converge on vanishing points.

GO TO THE WORKBOOK

To help you understand three-point perspective read this section then turn to pages 126–129 and try the range of exercises shown in the grid chambers.

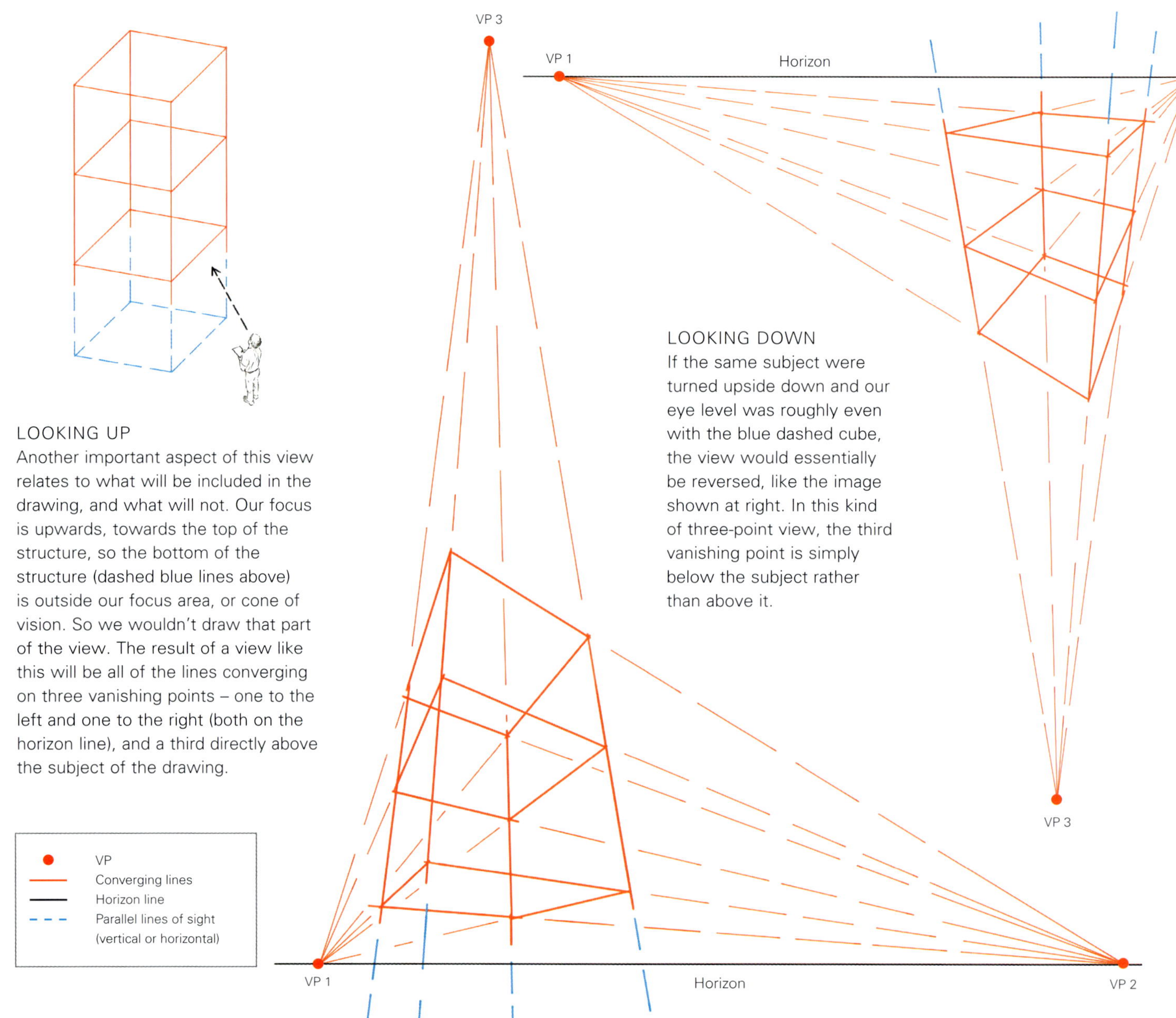

LOOKING UP
Another important aspect of this view relates to what will be included in the drawing, and what will not. Our focus is upwards, towards the top of the structure, so the bottom of the structure (dashed blue lines above) is outside our focus area, or cone of vision. So we wouldn't draw that part of the view. The result of a view like this will be all of the lines converging on three vanishing points – one to the left and one to the right (both on the horizon line), and a third directly above the subject of the drawing.

LOOKING DOWN
If the same subject were turned upside down and our eye level was roughly even with the blue dashed cube, the view would essentially be reversed, like the image shown at right. In this kind of three-point view, the third vanishing point is simply below the subject rather than above it.

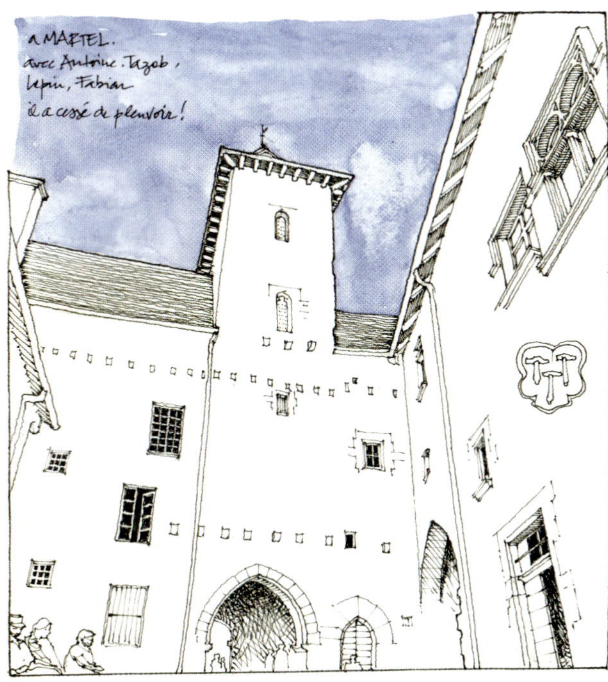

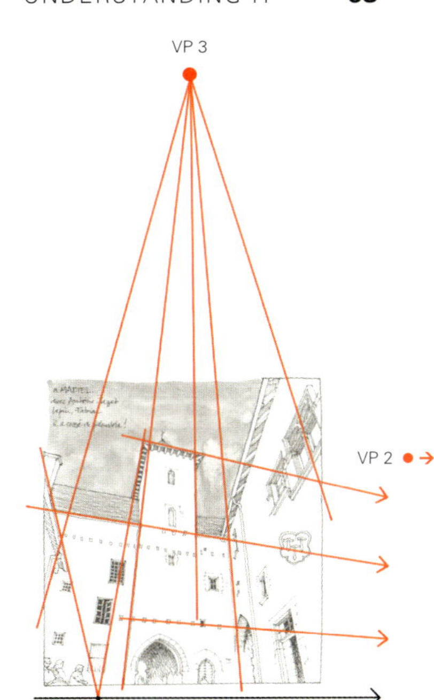

TOWER

In this piece by Gérard Michel (at left), the view is aimed upwards towards the tower. One set of lines recedes off towards the right vanishing point, well off the page in this case, and indicated by the arrows in the diagram at right. Another set of lines converges on the left vanishing point, near the group of figures at lower left. The wall on the right must have been at a different angle, not parallel to the left wall, because it doesn't converge on the left vanishing point (this situation will be covered in the chapter on multiple-point perspective). The third vanishing point, directly above the centre of the subject, governs the vertical lines of the courtyard.

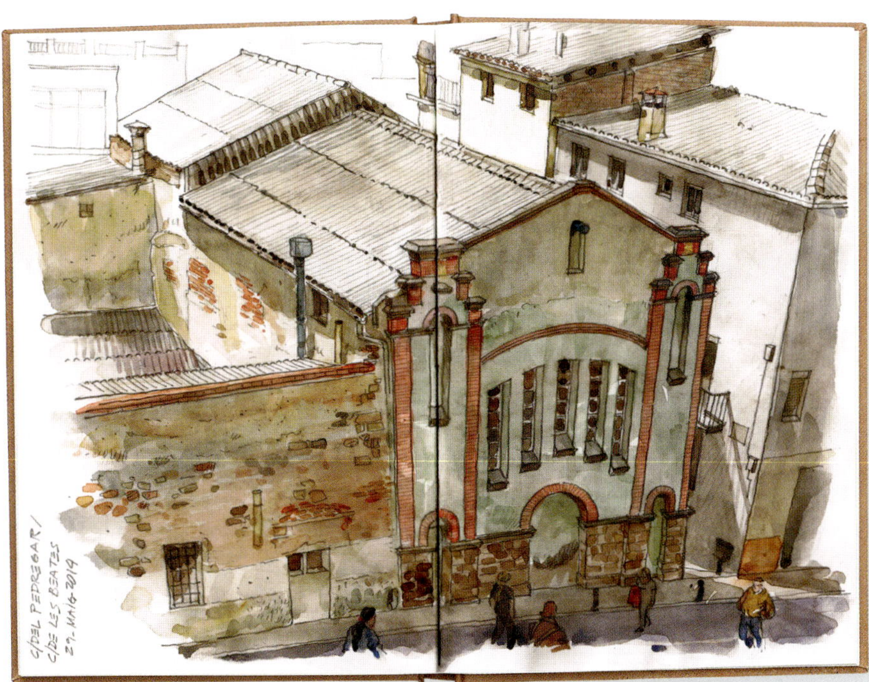

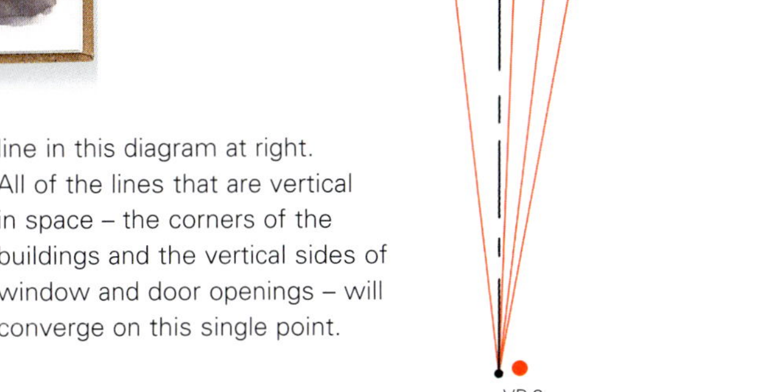

ROOFTOPS

Daniel Castro Alonso's view is from above and looking downwards. The horizon line is therefore above the subject, because that's where the viewer's eye level is located. Again, there is a vanishing point to the left and another to the right, with the third being directly below the centre of the subject, as shown with the black dashed line in this diagram at right. All of the lines that are vertical in space – the corners of the buildings and the vertical sides of window and door openings – will converge on this single point.

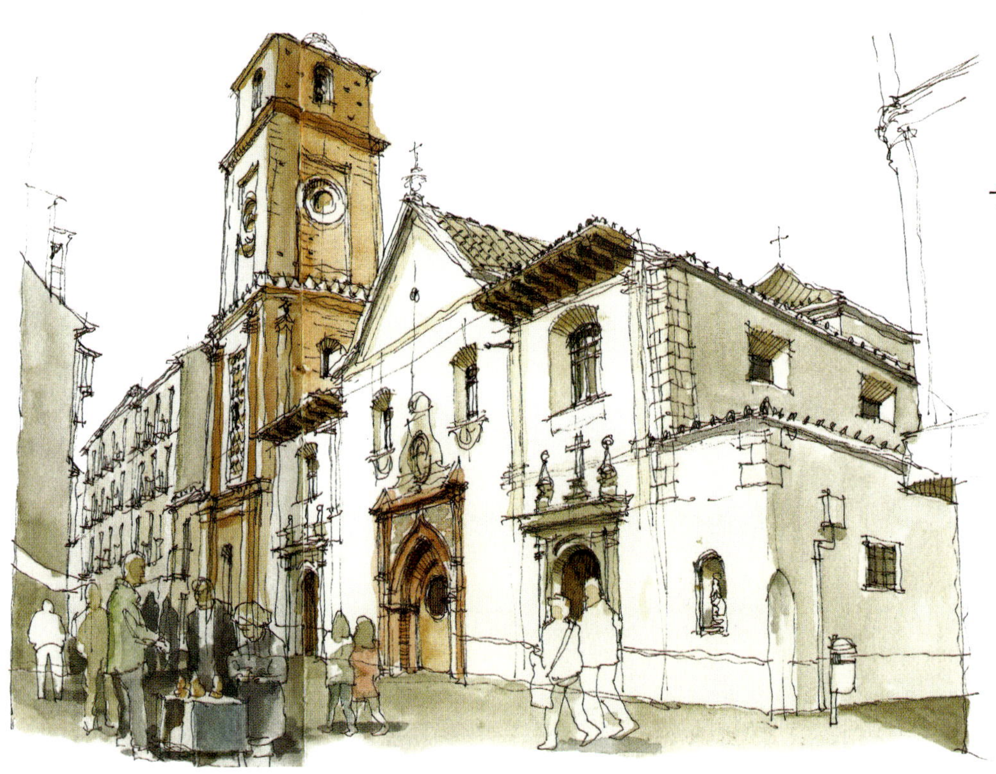

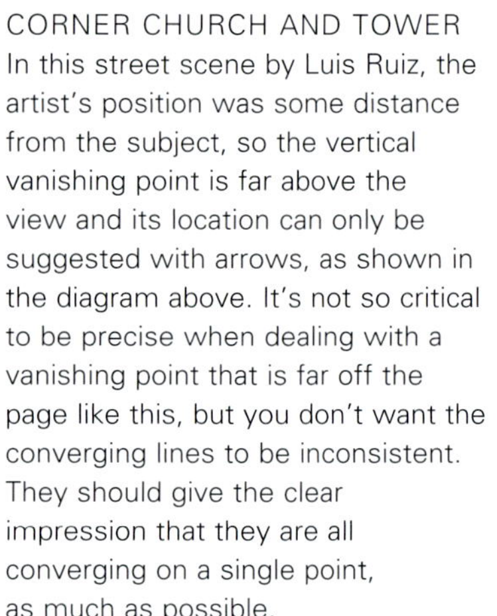

CORNER CHURCH AND TOWER

In this street scene by Luis Ruiz, the artist's position was some distance from the subject, so the vertical vanishing point is far above the view and its location can only be suggested with arrows, as shown in the diagram above. It's not so critical to be precise when dealing with a vanishing point that is far off the page like this, but you don't want the converging lines to be inconsistent. They should give the clear impression that they are all converging on a single point, as much as possible.

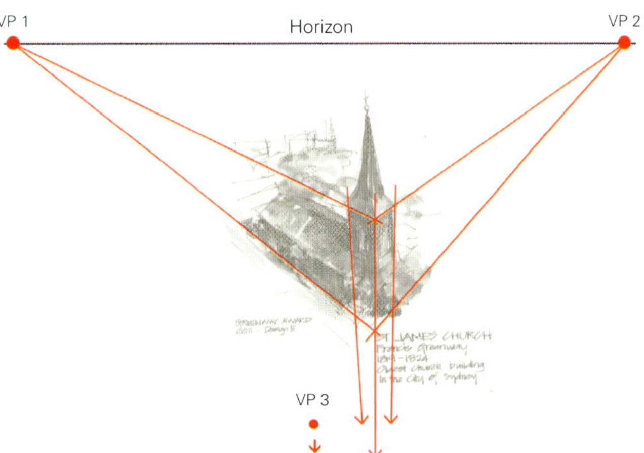

ABOVE THE STEEPLE

In Liz Steel's watercolour sketch of St James Church, the eye level and resulting horizon line are even higher than the tip of the church's steeple – so the horizon line and its associated vanishing points, right and left, were not on the page. Nonetheless, there is a clear sense of consistency regarding the lines that converge towards all three of the vanishing points, even in what appears to be a relatively 'loose' sketch. It can help to repeatedly visualise where the vanishing points are in relation to your drawing, perhaps by using a long ruler or other straight edge, or even by placing a small pebble or other object on the ground beyond your sketchbook, roughly in place of a particular vanishing point.

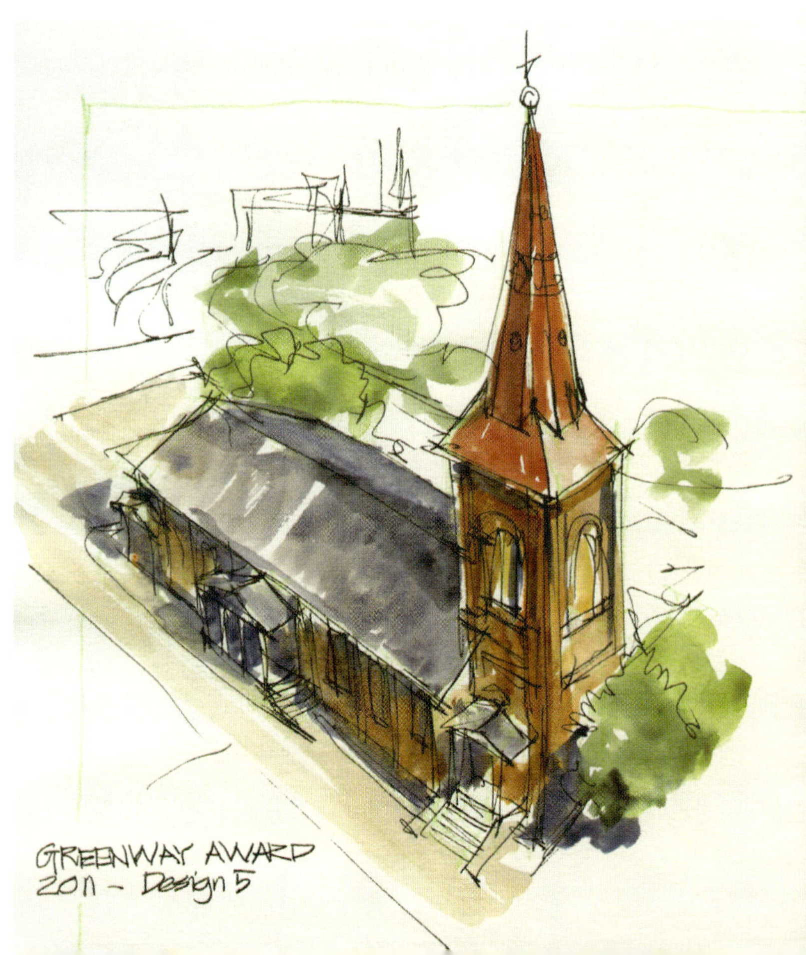

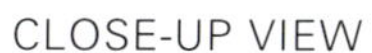

CLOSE-UP VIEW

In another example of a limited cone of vision, this beautiful drawing by Gérard Michel presents just one detail of a larger building. If we were to extend the lines of convergence to the right, left and vertical vanishing points, we begin to see something of what hasn't been drawn, and can imagine the windows above, below and perhaps to the left of this one. It becomes more apparent how this one window fits into its larger three-dimensional context. Note also how the projecting elements – the balcony and pediment – are defined in part by the lines converging on the left vanishing point. In fact, any lines that are perpendicular to the wall surface will converge on this point.

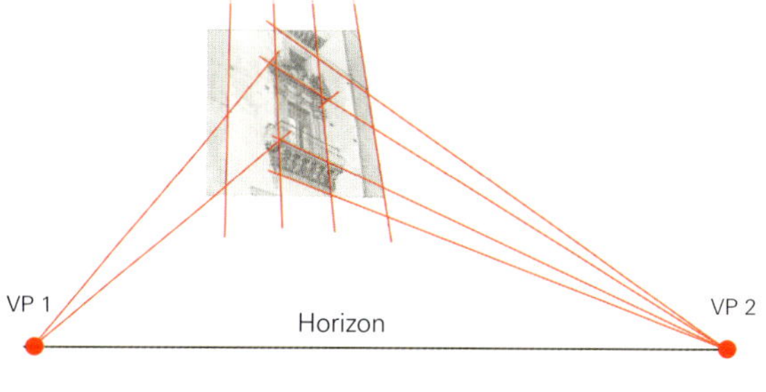

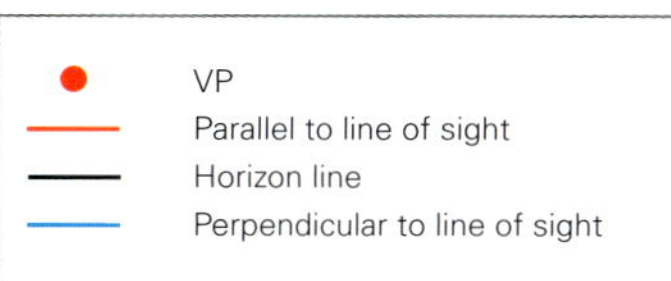

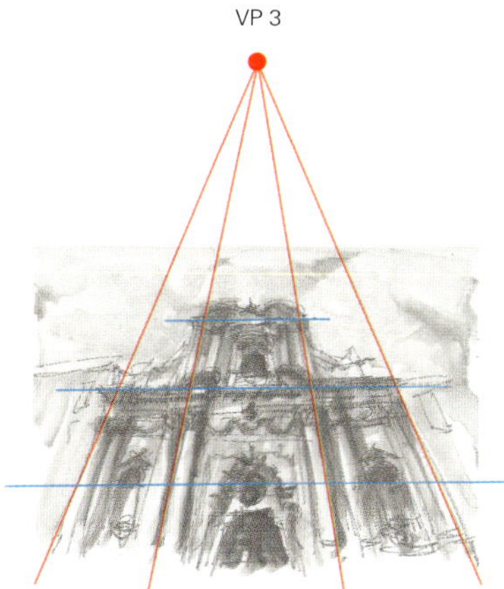

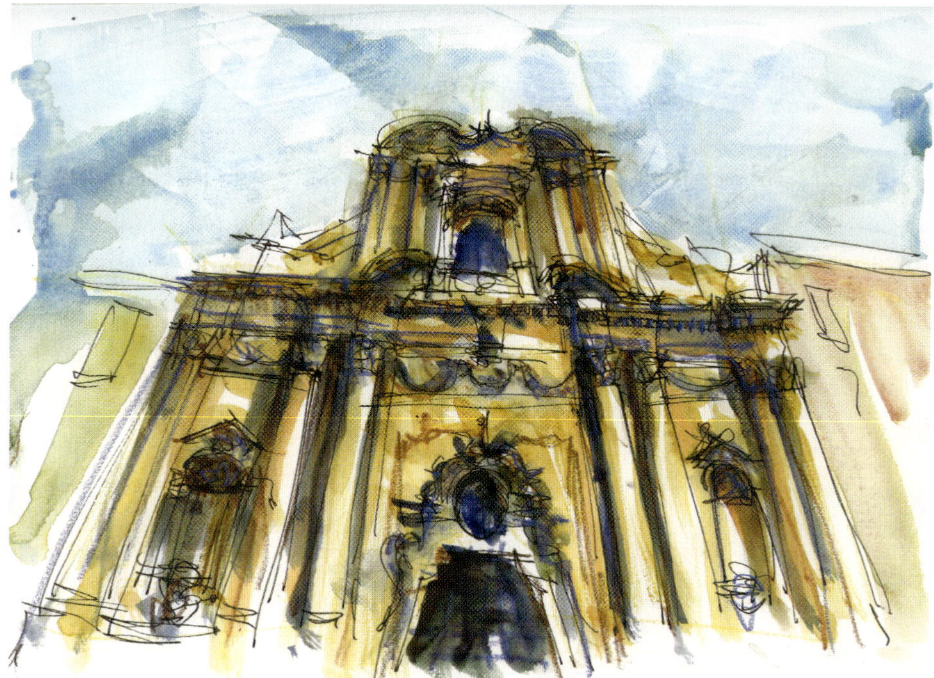

IMPOSING CHURCH

Liz Steel's watercolour of a Baroque church facade isn't technically a three-point perspective, though it certainly has some of the same elements. Because she was 'on axis' with the church (meaning that she was apparently on the centre line of the building), there are no strongly evident left or right vanishing points. There is only the vertical vanishing point directly above the subject. The result is actually more like a one-point perspective, but because her line of sight was aimed upwards, that one point is overhead rather than being on the horizon line.

three-point perspective

three-point perspective
Applying it

Applying three-point perspective requires finding a suitable subject that has an obvious vertical orientation, and then emphasising this orientation with the use of lines that converge on a vanishing point above or below.

BORDERED TOWER
Richard Johnson • Ink

▶ Richard Johnson has added a rectilinear border as if to accentuate the narrowing of the corner tower as it rises away from the viewer.

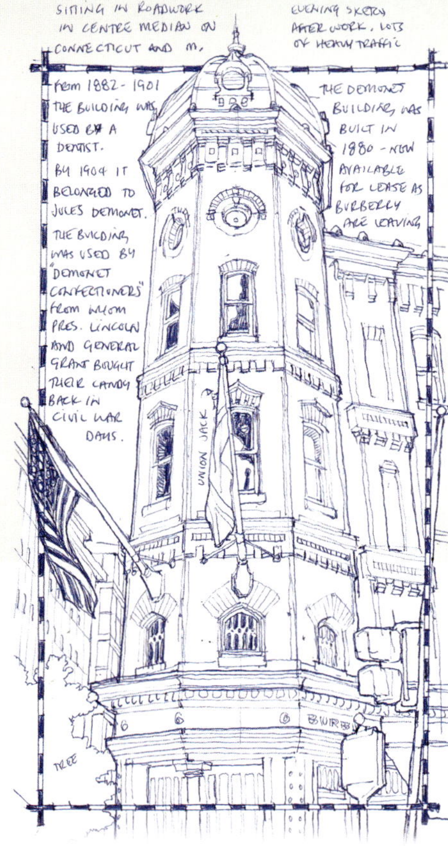

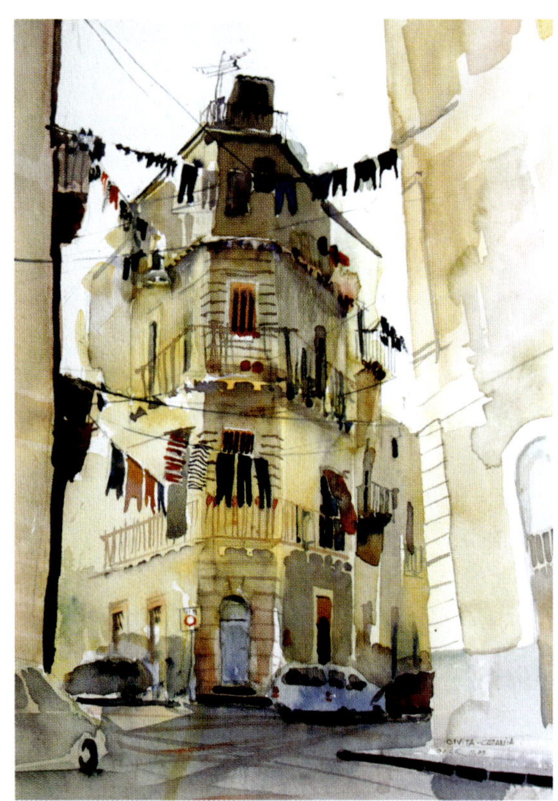

FESTOONED APARTMENTS
Omar Jaramillo • Watercolour

▲ Three-point perspective is one of the best approaches to depicting towers (and corners that are towerlike). Here, the adjacent walls have been brought in towards the centre, particularly on the right, and the artist has filled the space with criss-crossed laundry lines.

HEXAGONAL TOWER
Daniel Castro Alonso • Watercolour

▶ Castro emphasises the height of this Gothic tower and adjacent buttress, carefully placing a single, looming gargoyle that peers down from high above.

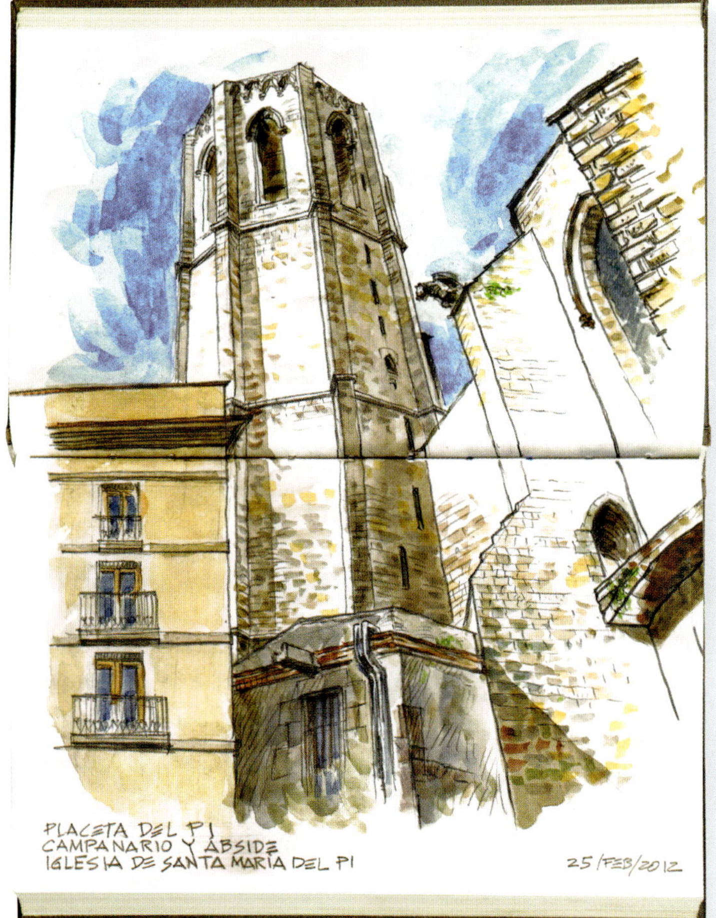

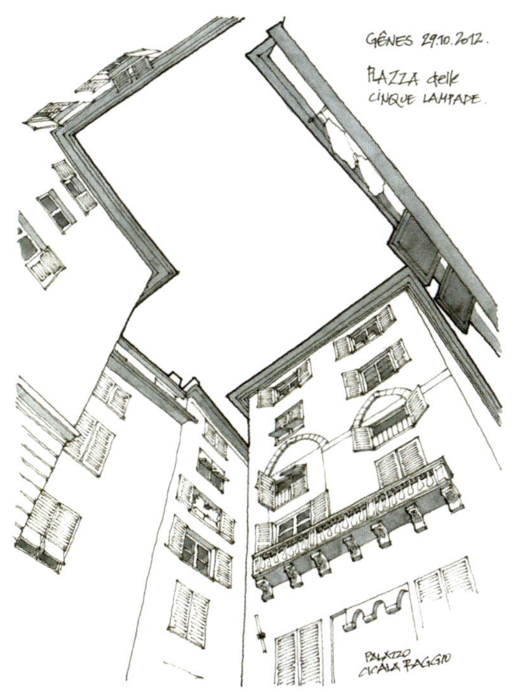

ENCLOSED SPACES

LOOKING SKYWARD
◄ *Gérard Michel* • Watercolour

COURTYARD VIEW
▶ *Matthew Brehm* • Watercolour

Tight courtyard spaces like these immediately carry our gaze upwards toward the sky, and this sort of view makes for a wonderful sketching challenge. In fact, there are more than just three vanishing points in each of these images, and even a touch of curvilinear perspective in the drawing on the right. But the fundamentals of both views are based on a single vanishing point overhead, and two major sets of converging lines moving to the right and left towards vanishing points on horizon lines far below the images.

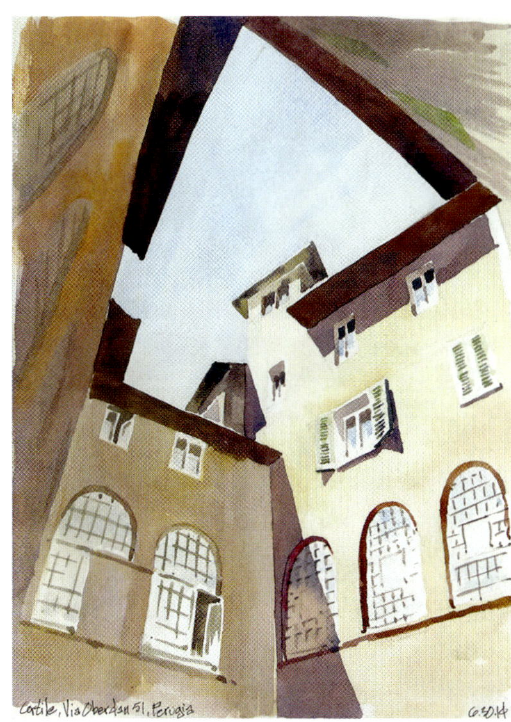

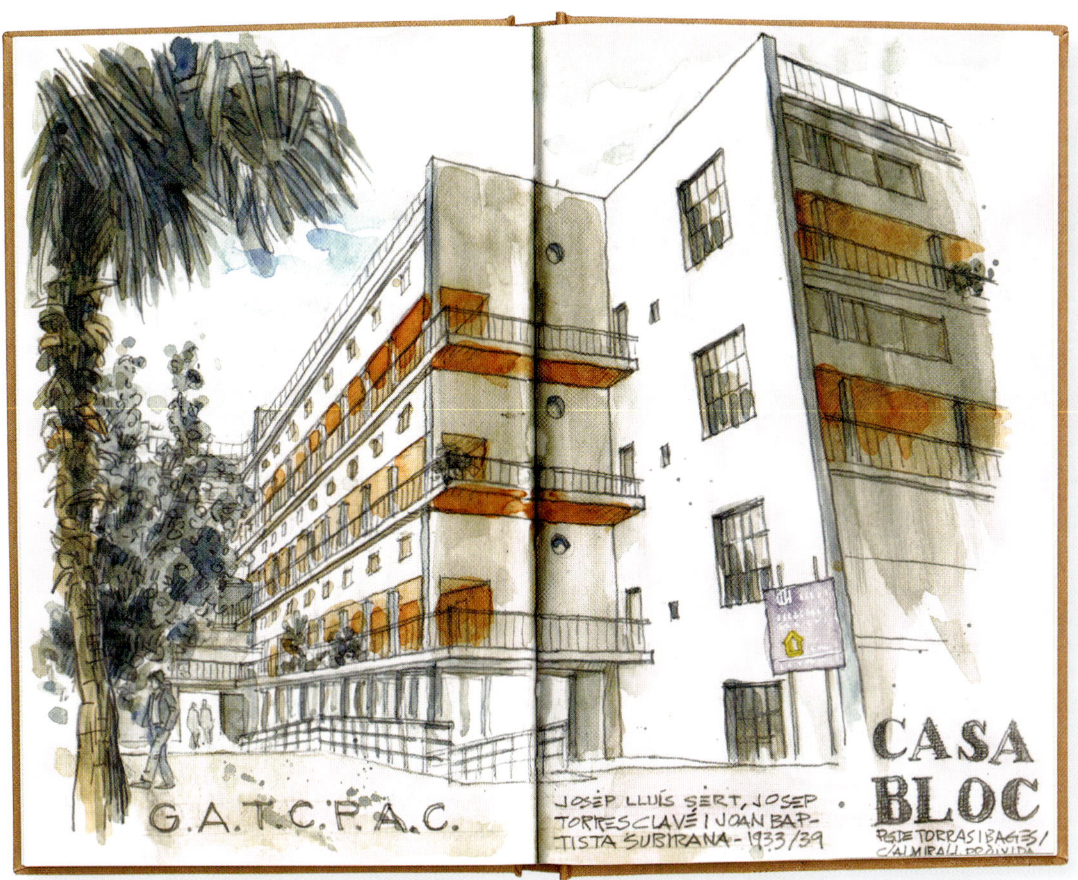

LIVENING UP A COMPOSITION
Daniel Castro Alonso • Watercolour

◄ This image shows how an otherwise ordinary two-point perspective can be made considerably more dramatic with a strong hint of three-point convergence. While the bulk of the view on the left side of the drawing is constructed with only the left and right vanishing points, the corner at near right in this view angles upwards towards the centre. As you set up the sketch, it doesn't require too much planning to consider applying three-point perspective to further enliven a view, especially if the subject soars over your head or if you happen to be positioned above the subject. Just a few strategic lines converging on a point far above or far below will accentuate the vertical dimension.

TOWERING INTERIORS

CATHEDRAL INTERIOR
◄ *Maarten Ruijters*
Pencil and watercolour

CATHEDRAL CEILING
▼ *Luis Ruiz*
Pencil and watercolour

Three-point perspective is an effective means of rendering height and complexity when drawing grand interior spaces, such as these two cathedrals. Maarten Ruijters (left) and Luis Ruiz (below) have employed a similar strategy by looking upwards into the domed and vaulted spaces, with the many vertical lines of the piers converging on a single point far above. In both drawings, the bones of the architecture are clear. It always helps to focus on the most basic forms when constructing drawings of spaces such as these. Use a relatively hard graphite pencil to lay things out first, and only then begin to add detail in ink or softer graphite.

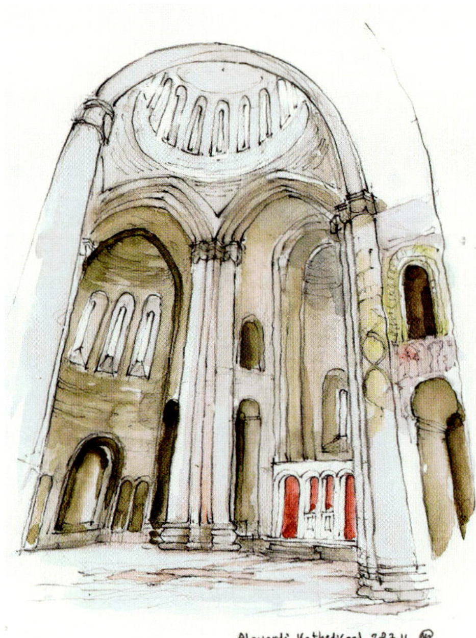

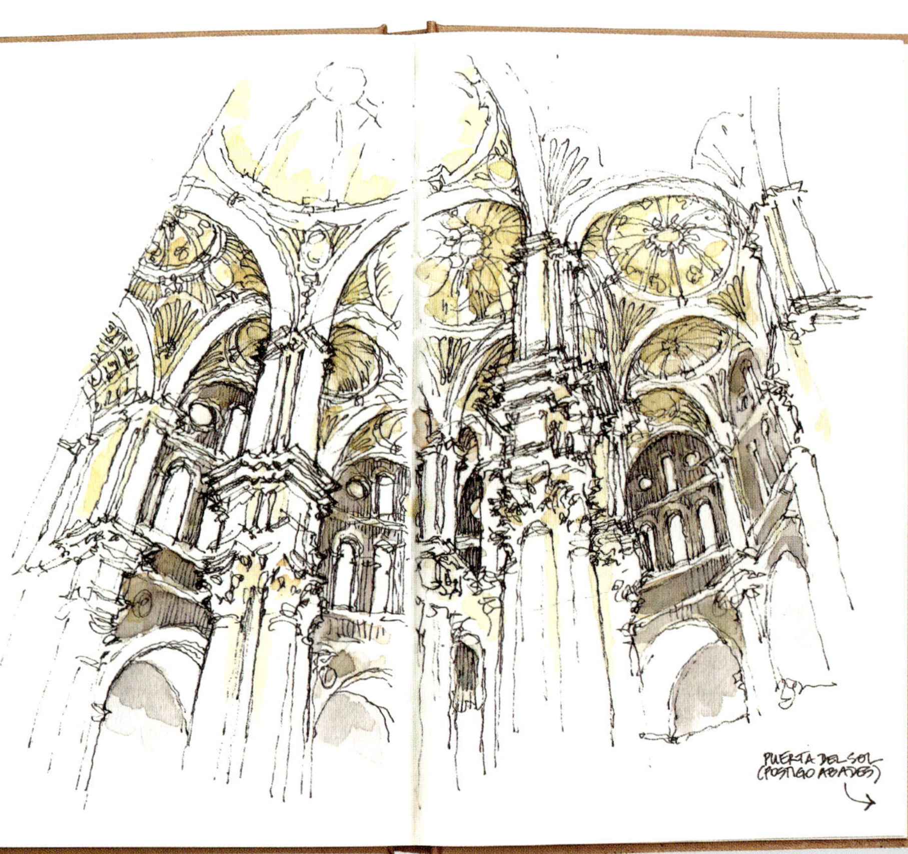

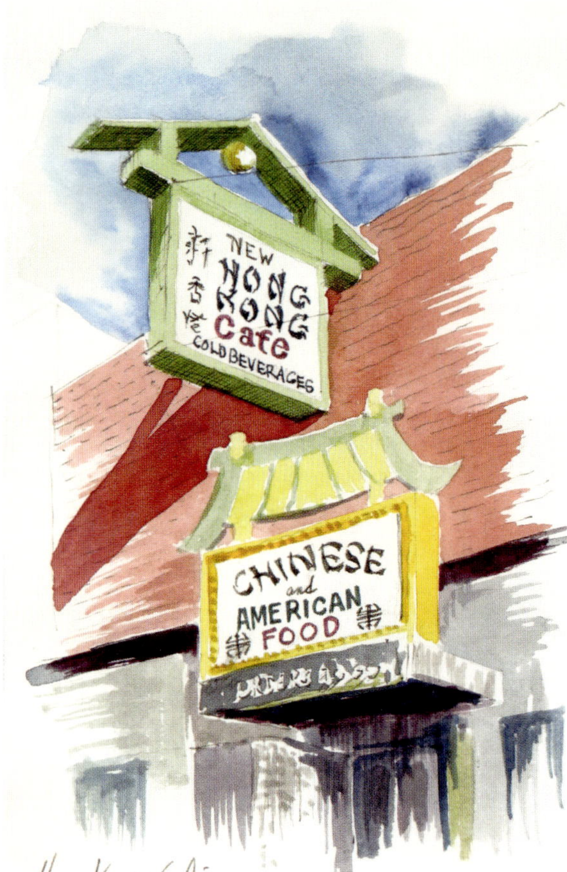

HONG KONG CAFE
Matthew Brehm • Pencil and watercolour

▲ I sketched these marquee signs in Moscow, Idaho, trying to capture some of the specific character of my little town. While the supporting building was necessary as context for these signs, it is not the primary focus. And even though the drawing doesn't present a very dramatic three-point view, the signs do converge slightly towards a vertical vanishing point. The effect of a three-point perspective can be subtle when you're not viewing the subject from very close and looking straight up into the sky, but even a small amount of vertical convergence will convey the sense of height. It's also a good strategy when the ground plane is less interesting – note how I've simply faded things out as they come down to street level.

BIRD'S-EYE VIEW

OVERLOOKING ONTARIO
Brenda Murray • Pen and watercolour

▼ It might help to imagine a single vanishing point at the centre of the Earth, as appears to be the case in this aerial view of Kitchener, Ontario, by Brenda Murray. This drawing is perhaps more technically a curvilinear perspective, with the left and right vanishing points aligned along the sweeping curve of the horizon. But the operative vanishing point, the one that really sets up the vertical diminishment of the buildings, is far below the subject.

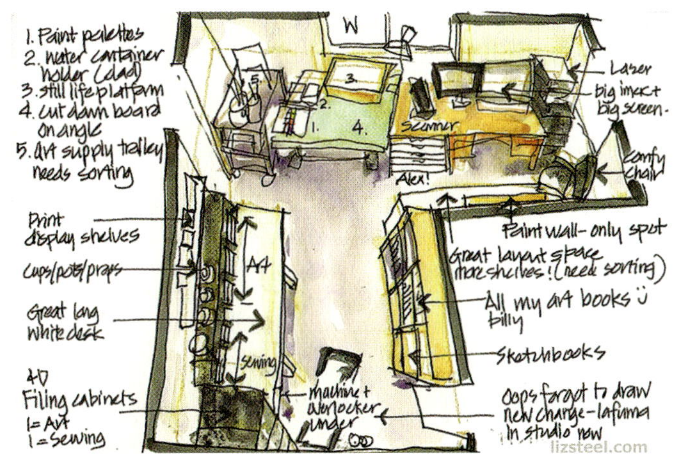

STUDIO PLAN
Liz Steel
Ink and watercolour

◀ Liz Steel puts three-point perspective to good use in this sketch of her studio (left). By bringing the corners and walls towards the vanishing point directly below the space, we can see more of the room and its contents; the space effectively opens up in the viewer's direction. Applying perspective in this way can be far more effective than using a more static two-dimensional plan drawing. The size and character of the space is immediately more evident, and the sketch as a whole is simply much more engaging as an image.

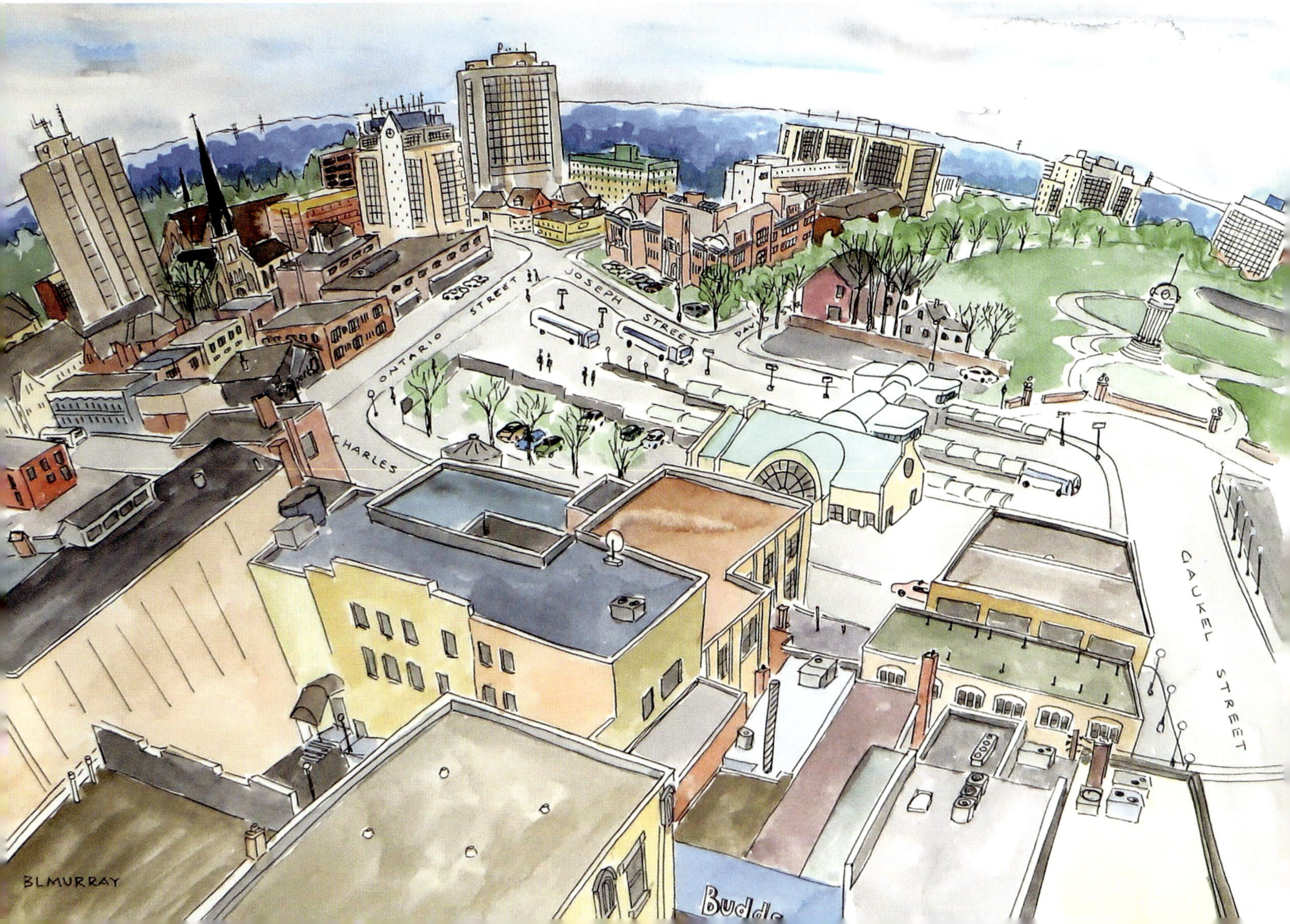

How-to sequence

This old German town is situated on a hill – an ideal position for Florian Afflerbach's demonstration of three-point perspective. If you look up (or down), vertical lines like building edges don't stay vertical, but recede towards a third vanishing point. The vanishing point for vertical lines is above the sketcher's head – under the roof overhang.

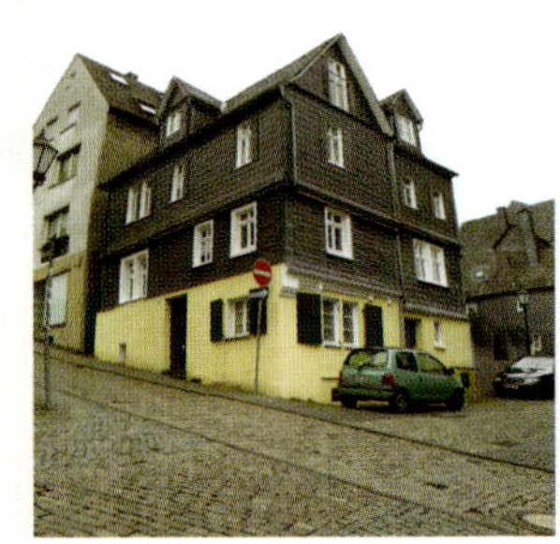

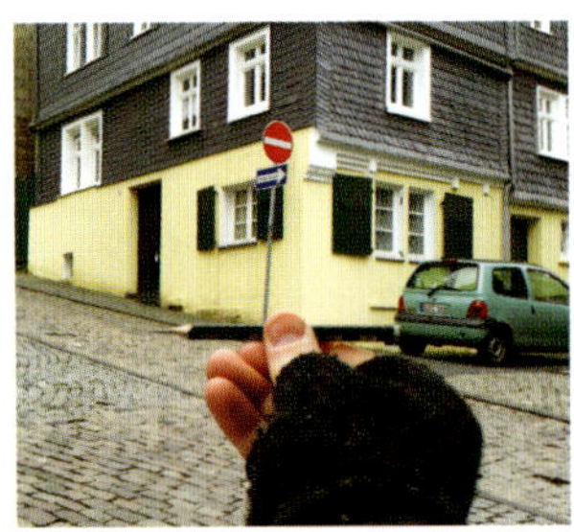

▶ The preparatory drawing shows the main information of the final drawing, including the construction of the perspective.

The frame is a scaled copy of the drawing sheet (see final drawing) the sketcher uses, and it helps to place the scene on the paper. The position of the horizon and the vanishing point should also be fixed here. For the correct construction of the perspective, it is useful to place all the vanishing points on to the paper.

Don't make the preparatory drawing bigger than the back of your hand.

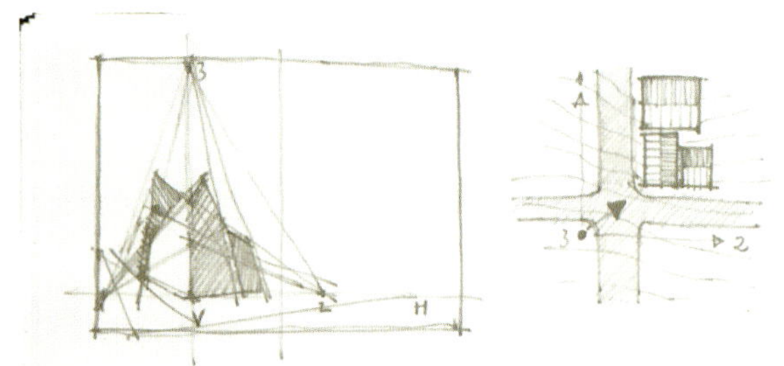

This explanation sketch (above right) should be done before the actual perspective drawing. It is a little sketch of the location and the sketcher's line of sight (see arrow) as an abstract floor plan. In this case, the viewpoint is across the road to the corner of the building. That's why the perspective will have two vanishing points (1 and 2).The sketcher must also look up to see the building. For this reason, a third vanishing point (3) appears. It is exactly above the sketcher's station point.

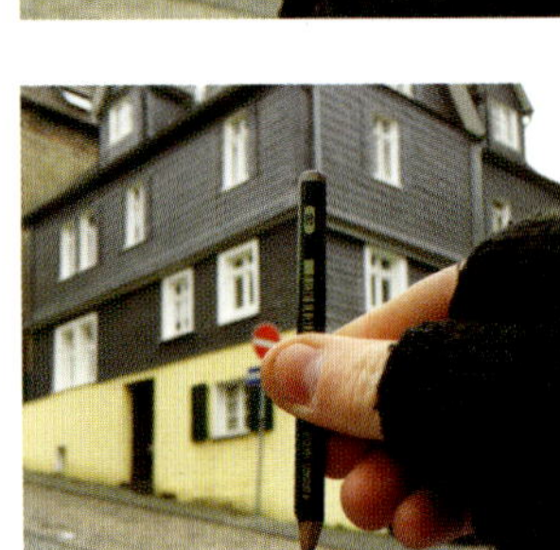

▲ The drawing instrument is an ideal tool for measuring lengths, angles and proportions of a building. It can be placed directly against the lines of streets, building edges or sloping roofs. Remember to always measure with your arm outstretched. The measured results can be compared for fundamental proportions.

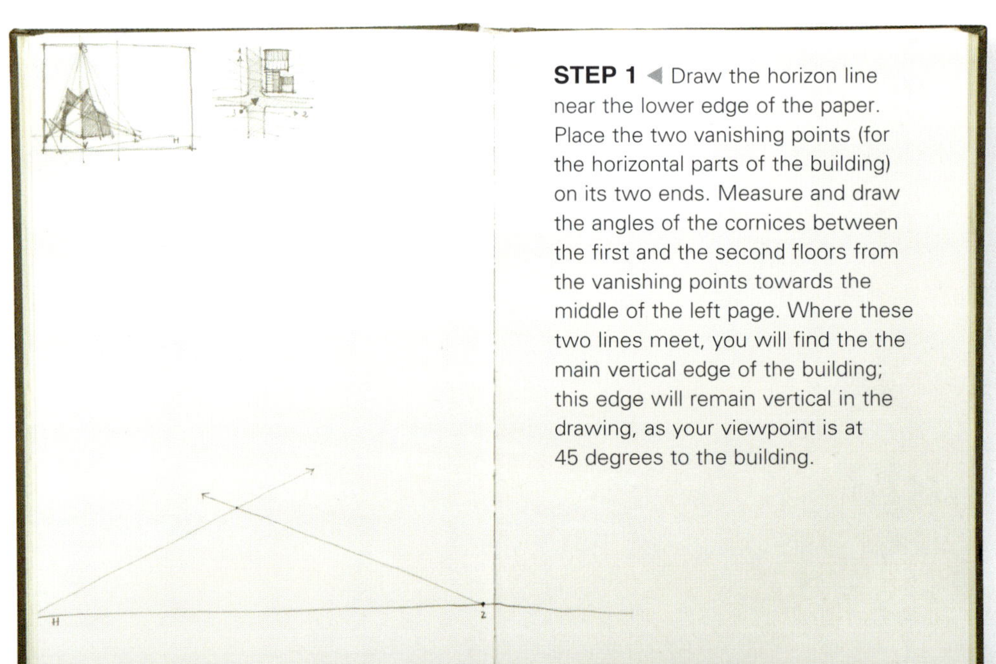

STEP 1 ◀ Draw the horizon line near the lower edge of the paper. Place the two vanishing points (for the horizontal parts of the building) on its two ends. Measure and draw the angles of the cornices between the first and the second floors from the vanishing points towards the middle of the left page. Where these two lines meet, you will find the the main vertical edge of the building; this edge will remain vertical in the drawing, as your viewpoint is at 45 degrees to the building.

STEP 2 ▶ Add some more angles of other cornices to create the structure of the house. As the street on the left is ascending, the edge line (where the house meets the street) will not vanish towards the left vanishing point. The distance of the third vanishing point from the horizon line can also be measured (see photo of the location). Just compare the height of the building and the distance from the top of the building to the roof overhang.

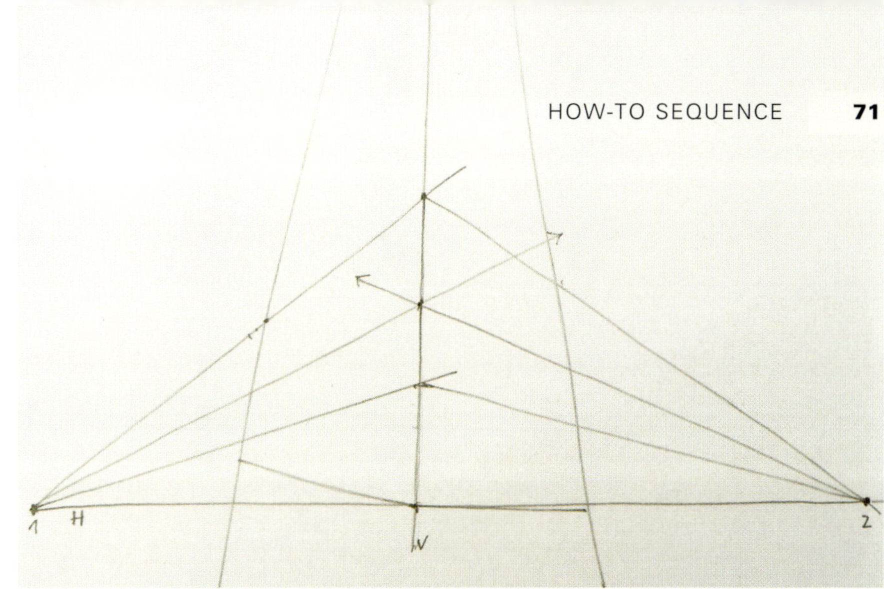

STEP 3 ▶ Accentuate the main structure of the building. Add the gabled roof – its ridge can be found if you draw two diagonals through the lower rectangle and then another line from the crossing point towards the third vanishing point. The gable will lie on this line – just measure the slope of the roof. The left dormer is also in the middle of the left house side. Try to place it above the crossing point.

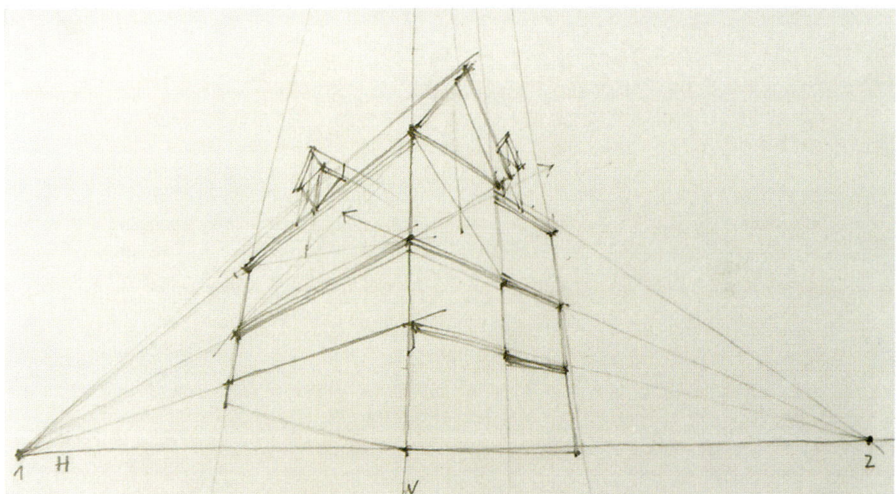

STEP 4 ◀ Now add all the building's doors and windows. Make sure to give all the reveals a certain depth – the actual window is placed in the middle of the walls. That is why you have to take care of all your three vanishing points when you draw the windows.

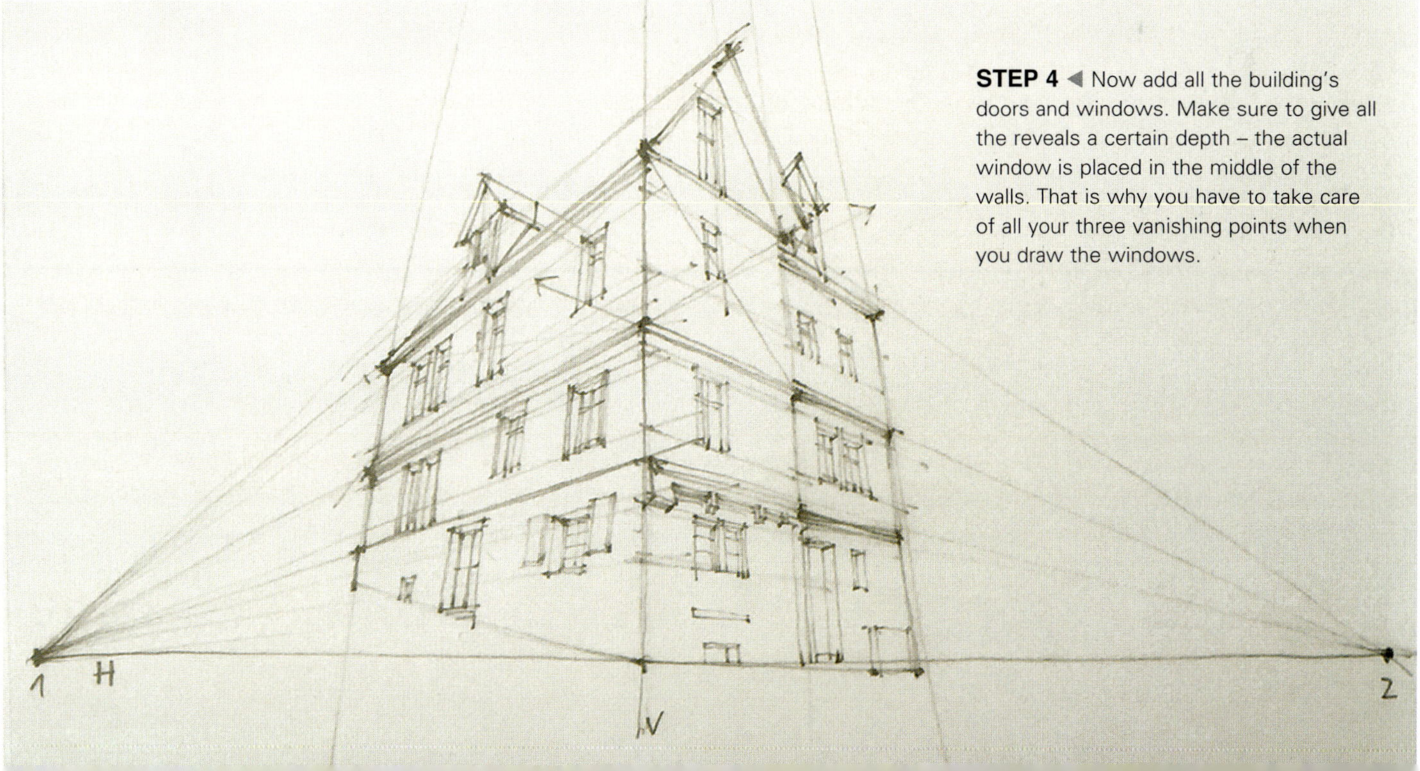

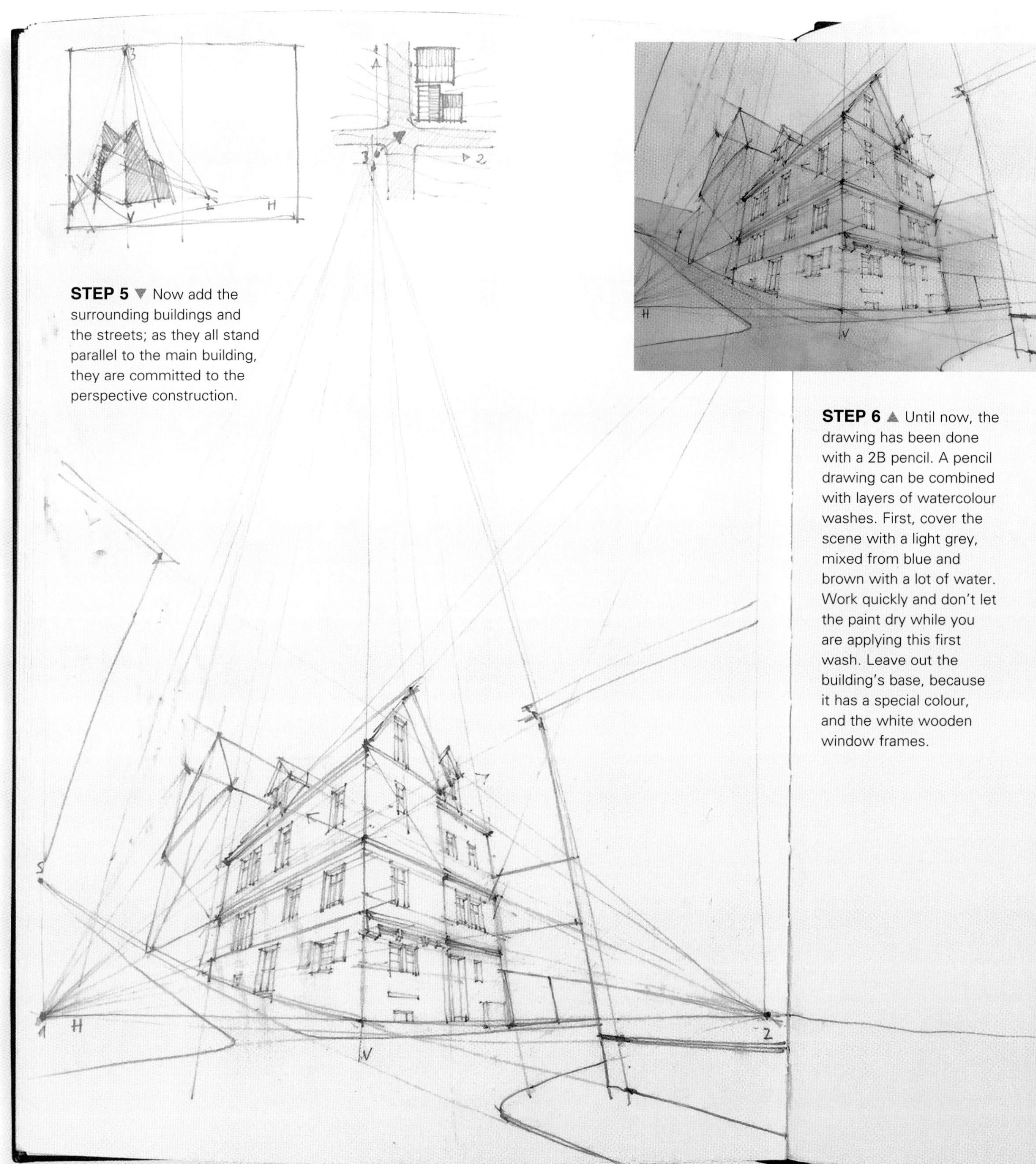

STEP 5 ▼ Now add the surrounding buildings and the streets; as they all stand parallel to the main building, they are committed to the perspective construction.

STEP 6 ▲ Until now, the drawing has been done with a 2B pencil. A pencil drawing can be combined with layers of watercolour washes. First, cover the scene with a light grey, mixed from blue and brown with a lot of water. Work quickly and don't let the paint dry while you are applying this first wash. Leave out the building's base, because it has a special colour, and the white wooden window frames.

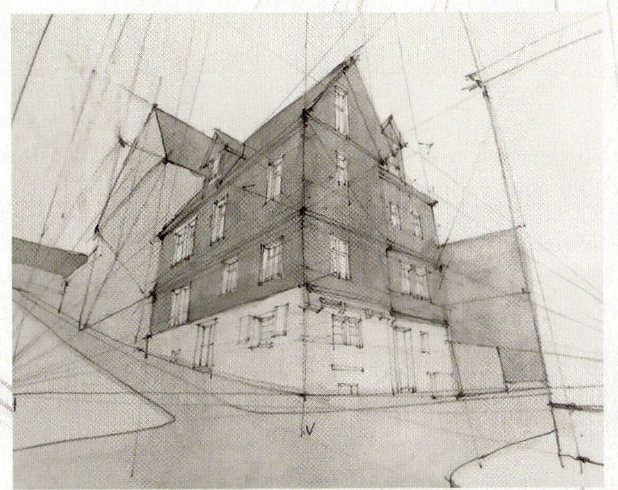

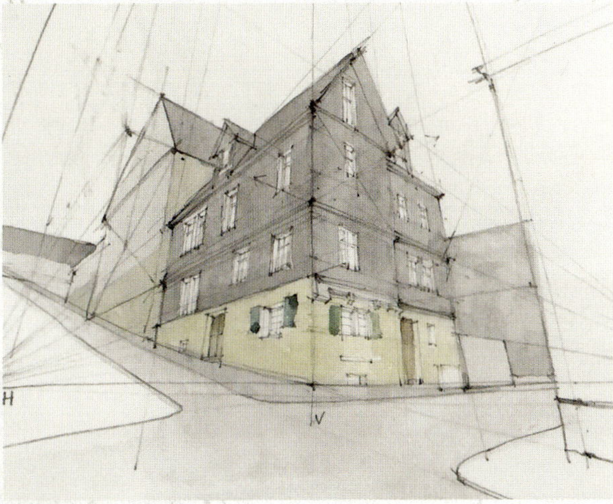

STEP 7 ▲ When the first wash is dry, add a layer of darker grey watercolour to all the slate-covered walls and roofs.

STEP 8 ▲ Finally, add special colours like the base of the centre building, the doors and the shutters.

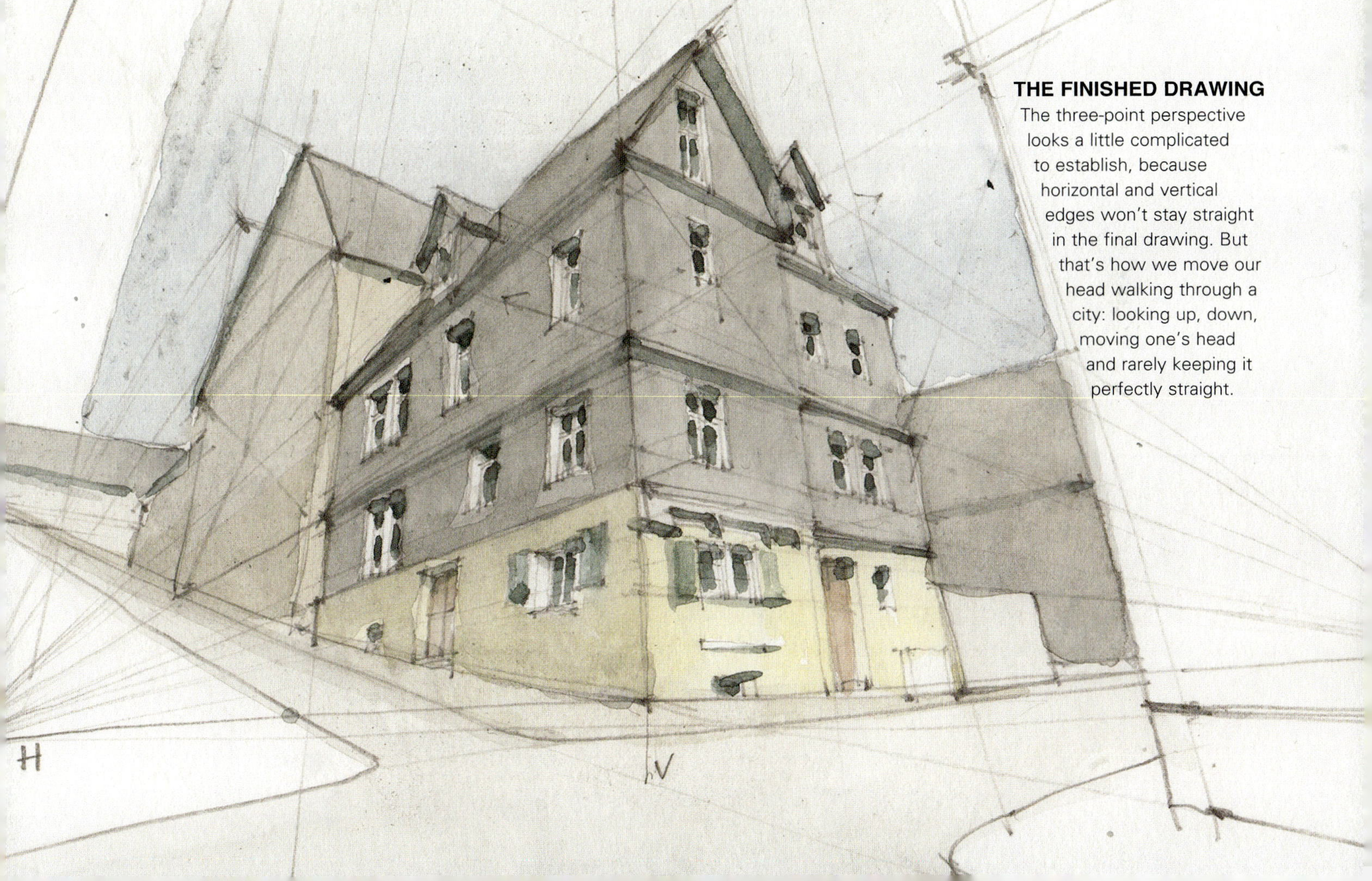

THE FINISHED DRAWING

The three-point perspective looks a little complicated to establish, because horizontal and vertical edges won't stay straight in the final drawing. But that's how we move our head walking through a city: looking up, down, moving one's head and rarely keeping it perfectly straight.

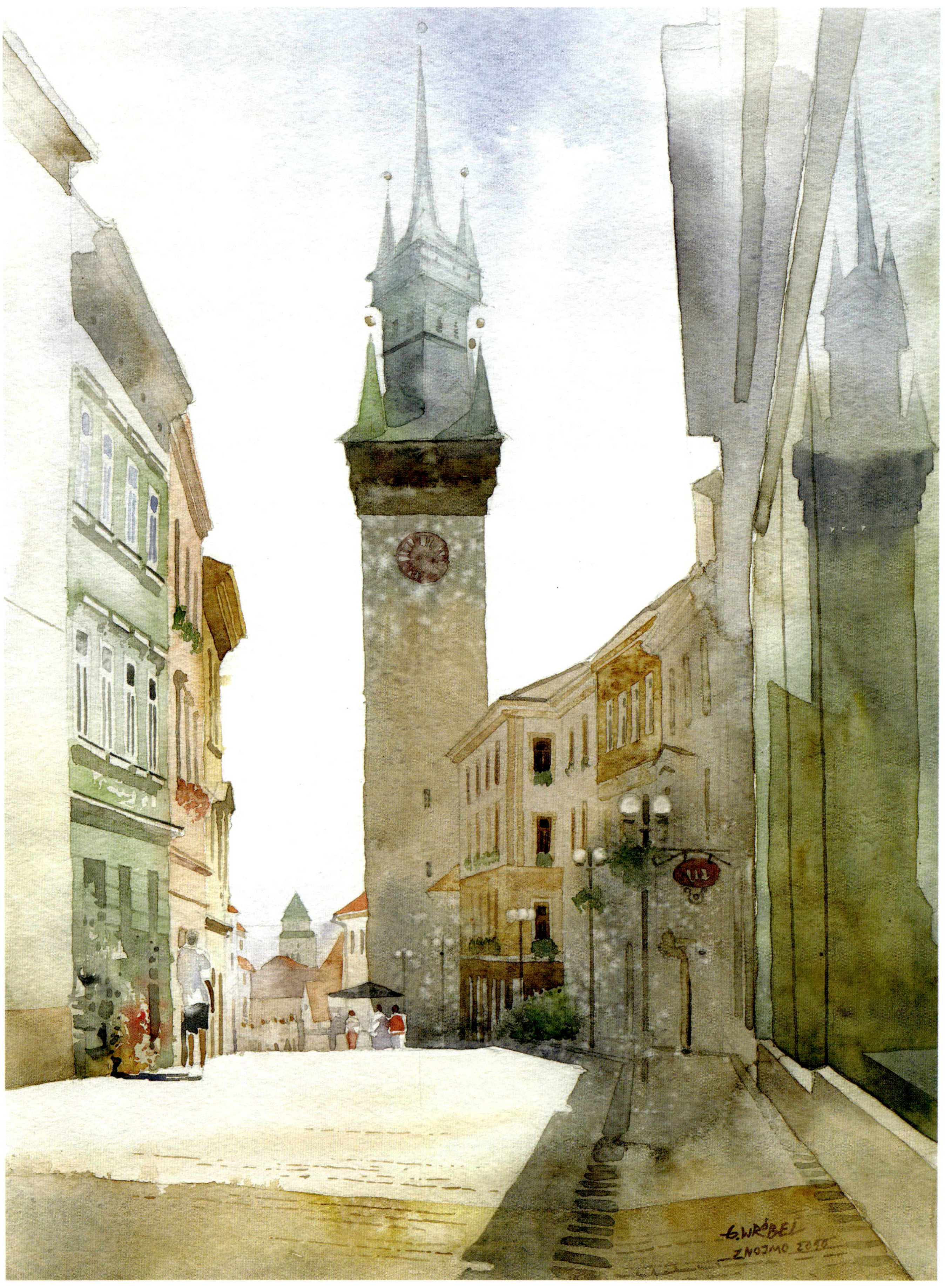

G. WRÓBEL
ZNOJMO 2020

MULTI-POINT PERSPECTIVE

When dealing with places that are not arranged purely on a grid, it's likely that we'll see multiple vanishing points, rather than only one, two, or three. This is especially true in medieval towns and cities, where streets tend to meander and the arrangement of buildings is typically somewhat random.

ZNOJMO, CZECH REPUBLIC • *Grzegorz Wróbel* • Watercolour

Introduction

▶ VIA DEL SEMINARIO, ASSISI, ITALY
Matthew Brehm • Graphite and watercolour

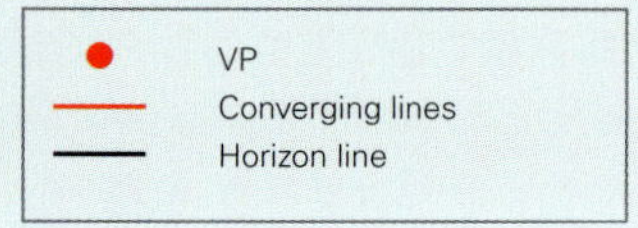

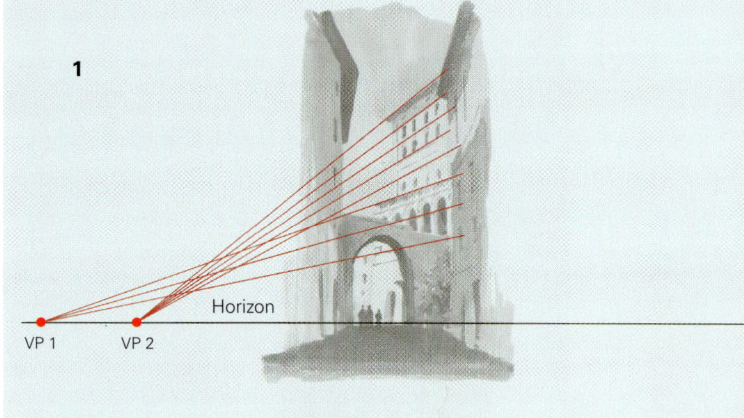

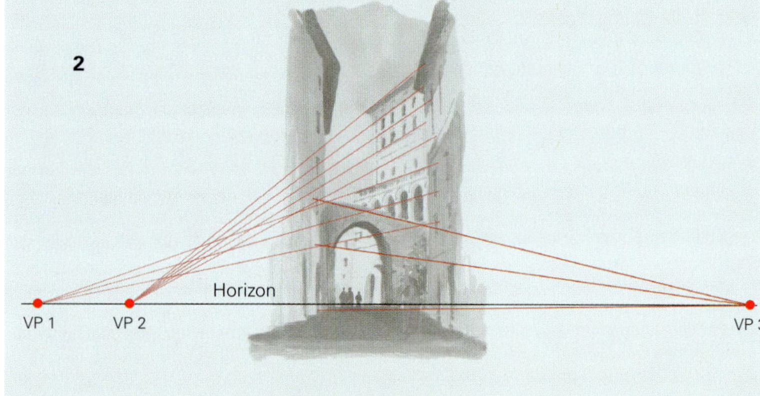

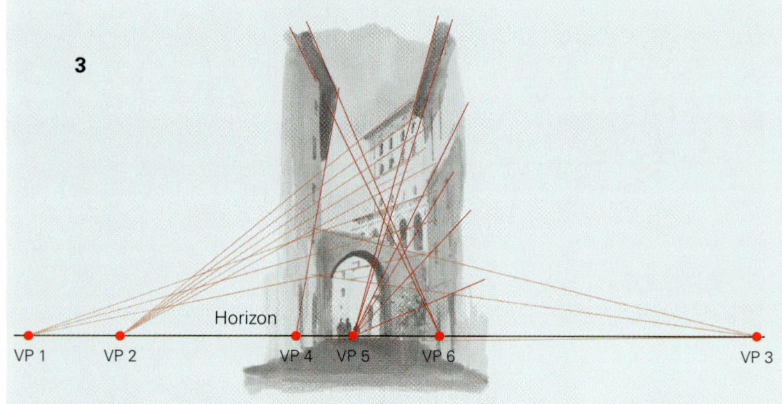

What is multi-point perspective?

Most perspective instruction focuses only on one-point, two-point and three-point, and it's extremely useful to understand how to apply these in a drawing. But in many circumstances, especially in places that are not perfectly rectilinear, what we actually see are numerous vanishing points. Depending on the arrangement of the buildings, spaces and objects in our view, there may in fact be any number of vanishing points.

When buildings or objects are not arranged on a rectilinear grid – in other words, when they are at odd angles to one another – each plane or facade will probably have its own vanishing point. Presented over the next several pages are many examples of this visual phenomenon in photos and drawings, but the multitude of converging lines can become a bit confusing. In order to keep the diagrams as clear as possible, the most prominent sets of lines are the focus, but try to look for other sets that may not be shown.

◀ ▶ In this street view, there are actually six distinct vanishing points that helped me lay out the watercolour. The arcade and building above it (beyond the arch) are actually not perfectly aligned with one another, so each has its own vanishing point (diagram 1). The archway at centre has another prominent vanishing point off to the right (diagram 2), and the roof eaves are defined by a few more points towards the centre (diagram 3). If my line of sight were aimed upwards rather than remaining horizontal, there would be yet another vanishing point overhead (diagram 3), as we saw in the chapter on three-point perspective.

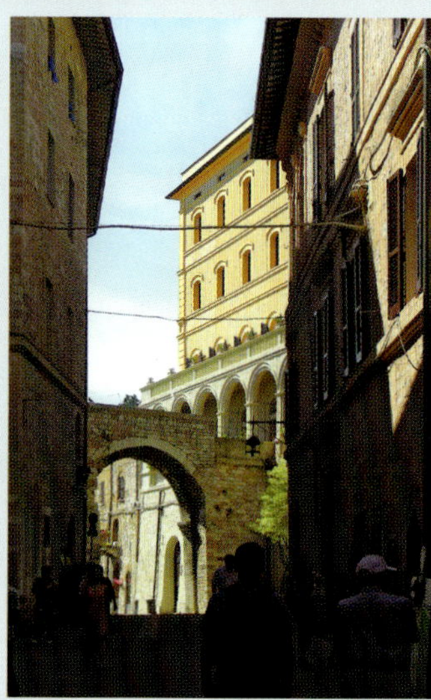

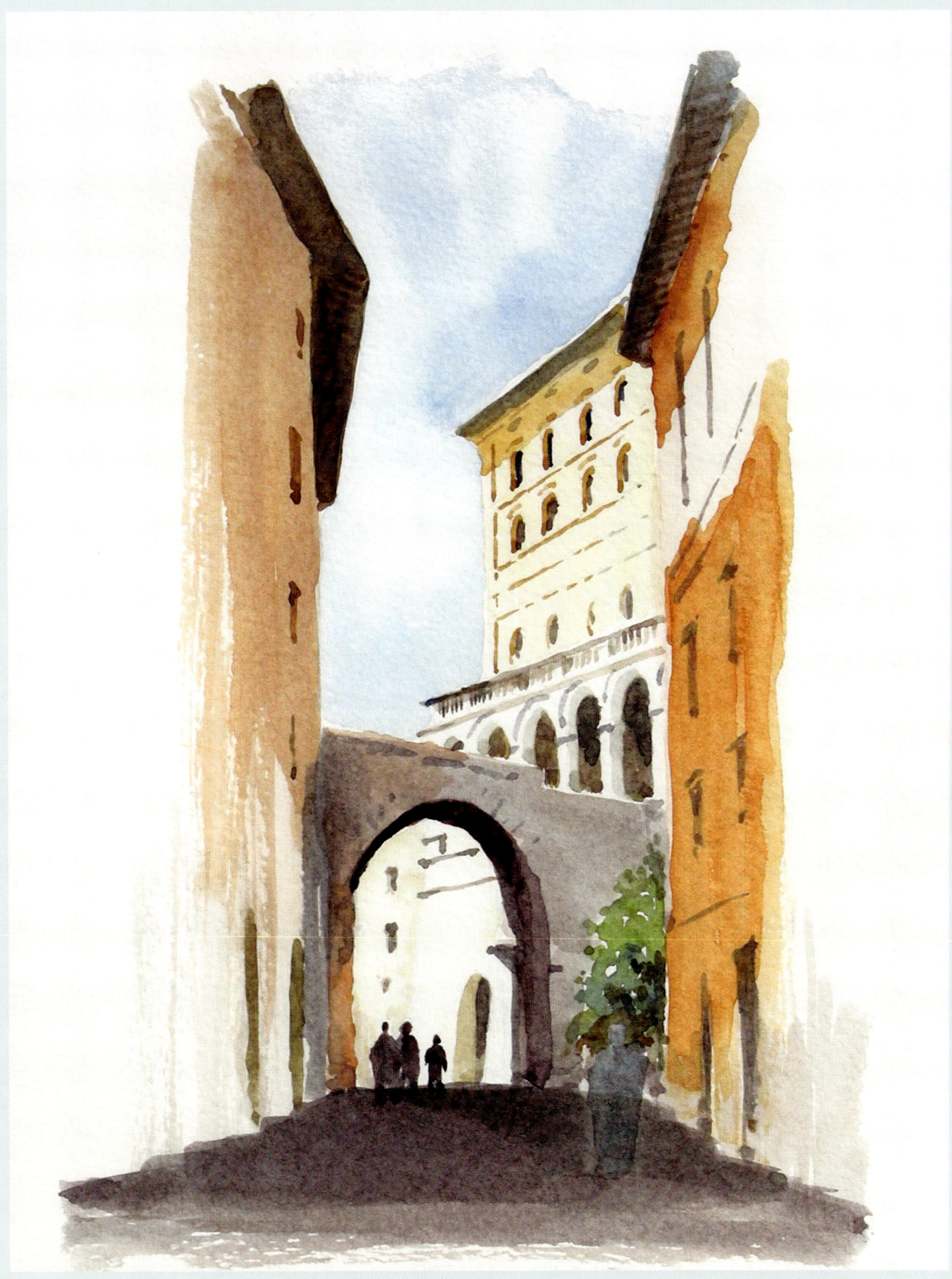

Seeing it

Multi-point perspective takes into account objects and spaces that are not arranged solely on a two-dimensional grid. Many views include walls or other planes that are oriented at some other angle, requiring additional vanishing points to establish how they would appear to converge.

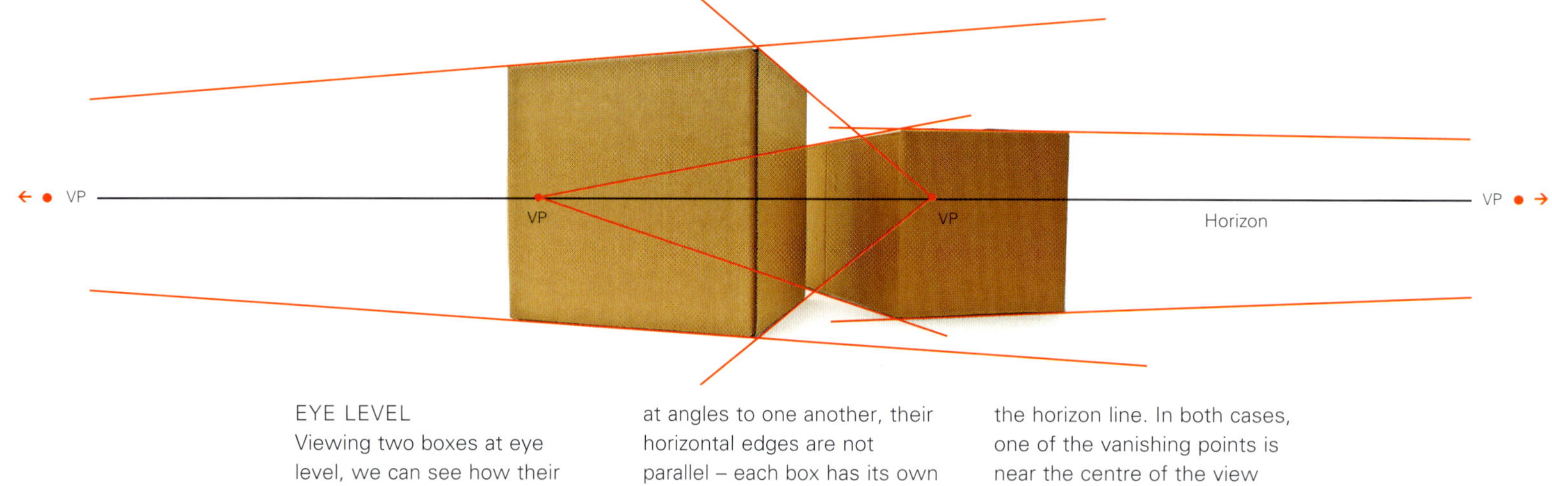

EYE LEVEL
Viewing two boxes at eye level, we can see how their horizontal edges recede to vanishing points on the horizon line. But because the boxes are at angles to one another, their horizontal edges are not parallel – each box has its own two sets of parallel horizontal lines, so each box will have its own pair of vanishing points on the horizon line. In both cases, one of the vanishing points is near the centre of the view while the other is far off to the left or right, but still on the horizon line.

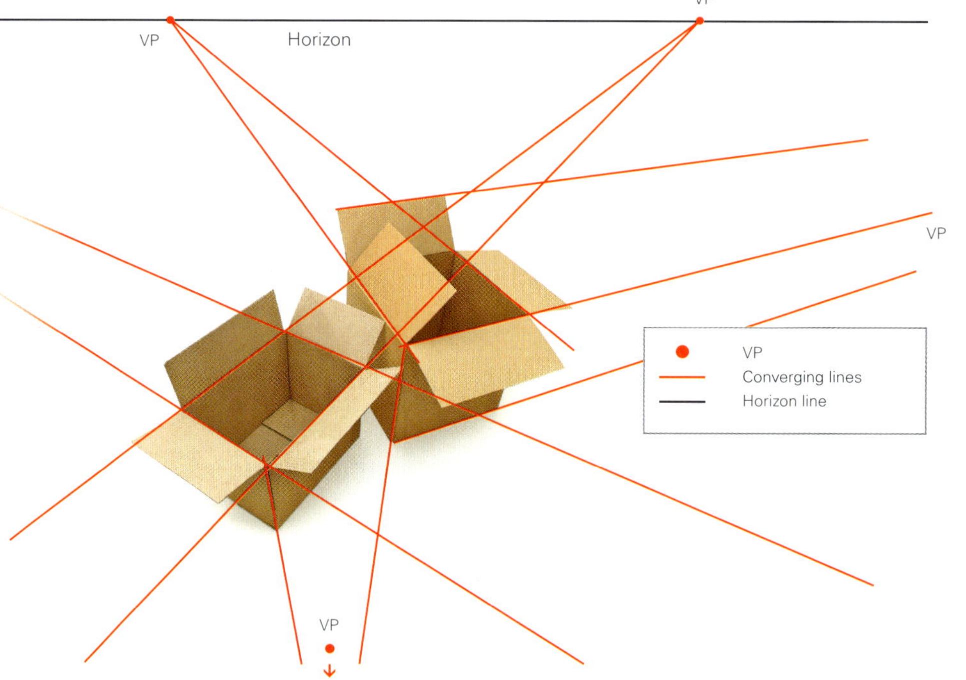

FROM ABOVE
When the boxes are viewed from above, and when their flaps are open at random angles, the number of vanishing points increases. Again, each box will have its own pair of vanishing points defining its horizontal edges, with a third point directly below, as discussed in the chapter on three-point perspective (pages 54–73).

There are still more converging lines along the side edges of the open flaps – these will converge on points above and below the horizon line. For the sake of clarity, I haven't indicated these lines – in multiple-point perspective, it can become a bit confusing to keep track of all the various sets of converging lines.

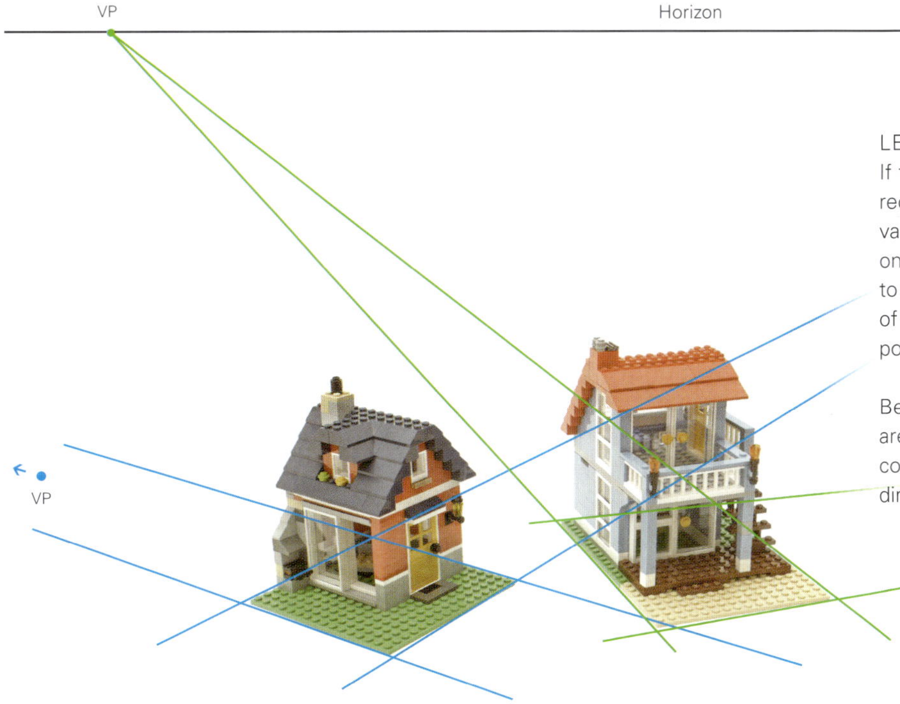

LEGO HOUSES

If the houses do not both align to the same rectilinear grid, each will have its own set of vanishing points. The house on the left has one vanishing point to the right and another to the left (blue lines). The horizontal edges of the house on the right converge towards points indicated by the green lines.

Because the vertical edges of both houses are parallel to each other, they will all converge on the same point, in this case directly below.

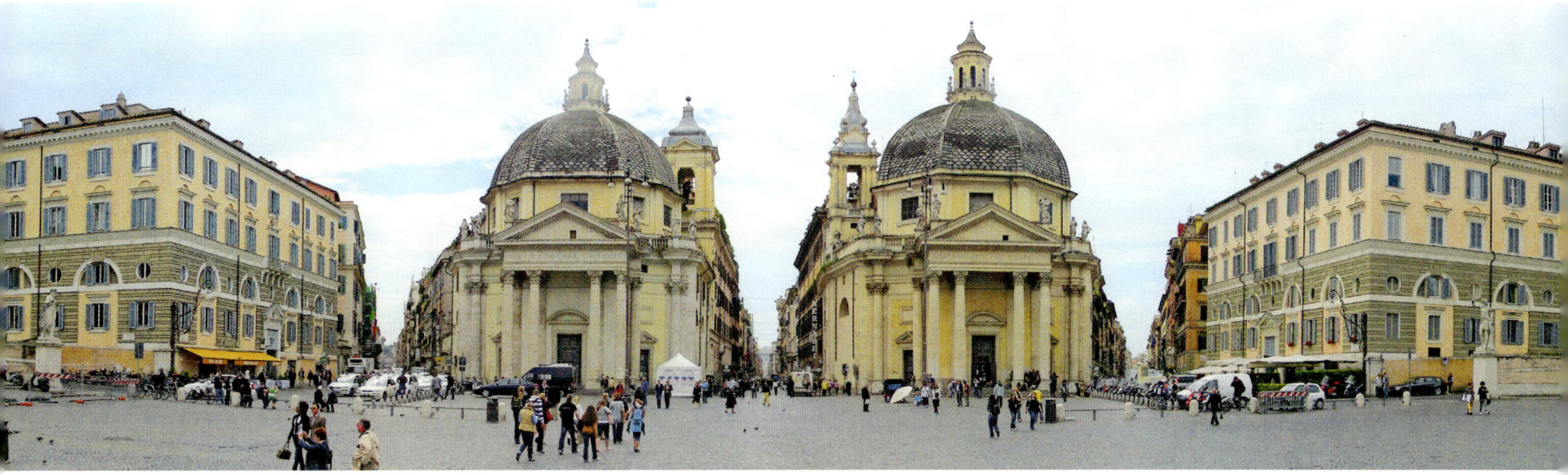

VP

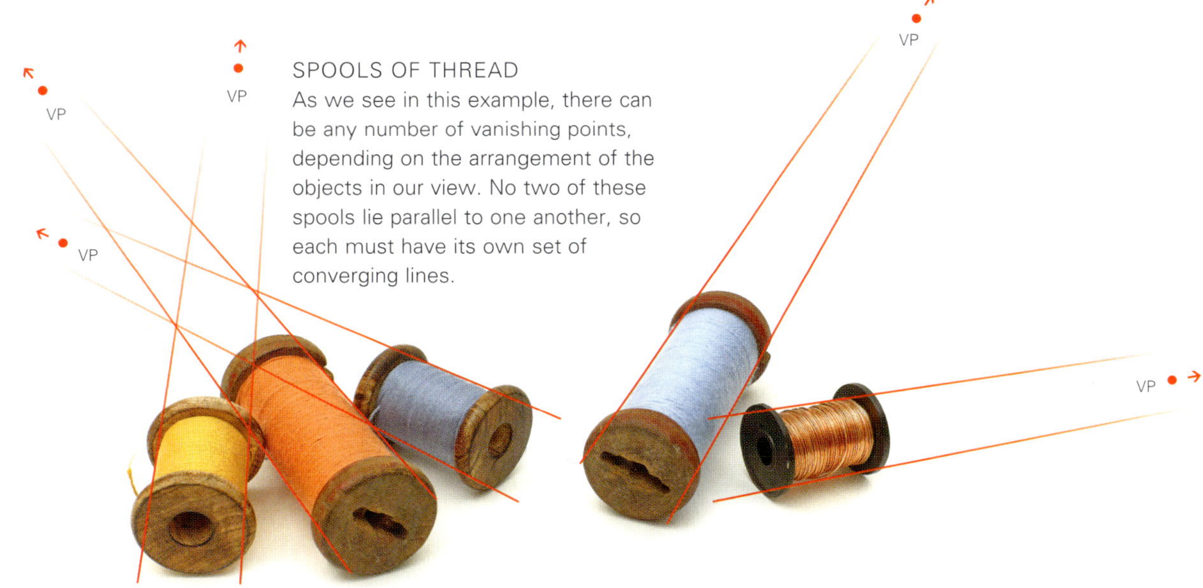

ENTERING ROME

In one of the most famous perspective views in the world, three streets radiate from the Piazza del Popolo. It can be plainly seen that each street converges on its own vanishing point in the distance, while the angled buildings at left and right have their own sets of vanishing points.

SPOOLS OF THREAD

As we see in this example, there can be any number of vanishing points, depending on the arrangement of the objects in our view. No two of these spools lie parallel to one another, so each must have its own set of converging lines.

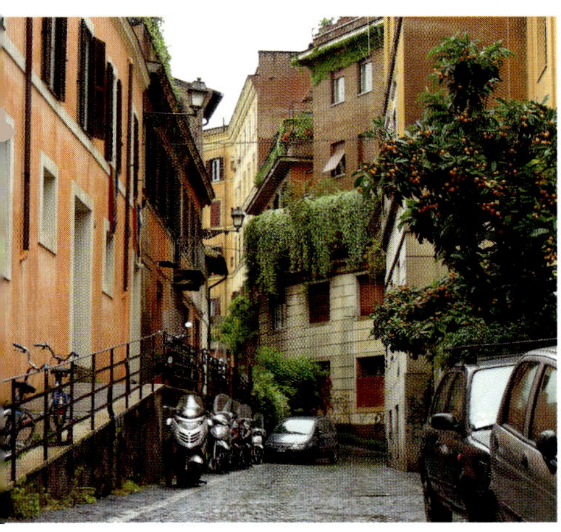

BREAKING THE GRID

Vicolo dell'Atleta in Rome is a street that has evolved over many centuries of development, and the buildings and pathways are decidedly non-rectilinear in their arrangement. In these diagrams and the image at left, look for all the different sets of converging lines. This first image identifies four sets, but see if you can find more.

When you're dealing with sloping elements like the ramp and railing here, remember that there will be two vanishing points – one for the horizontal and vertical planes, and the other for the slope. The vanishing point for the slope will be either directly above or below the one for the other planes (right).

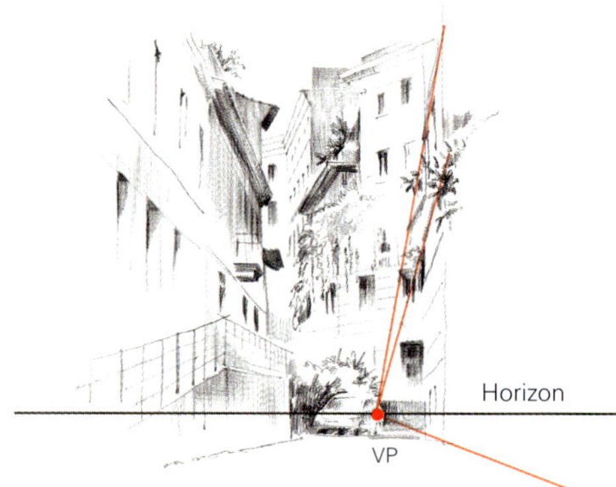

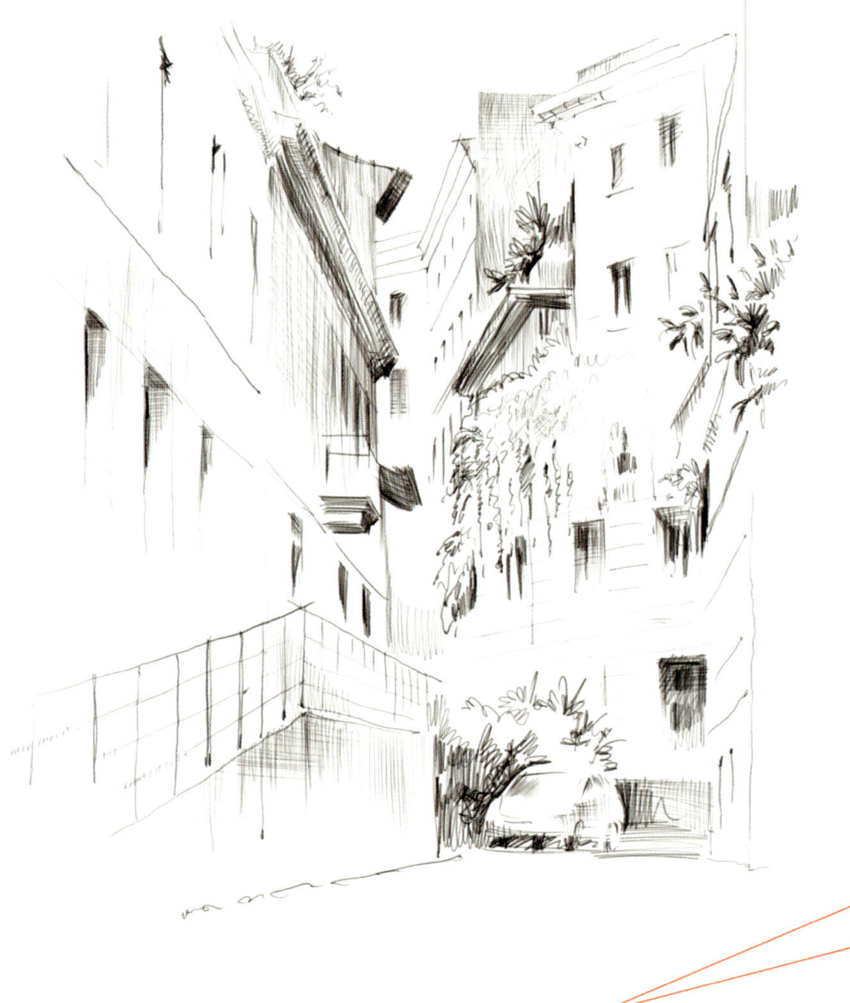

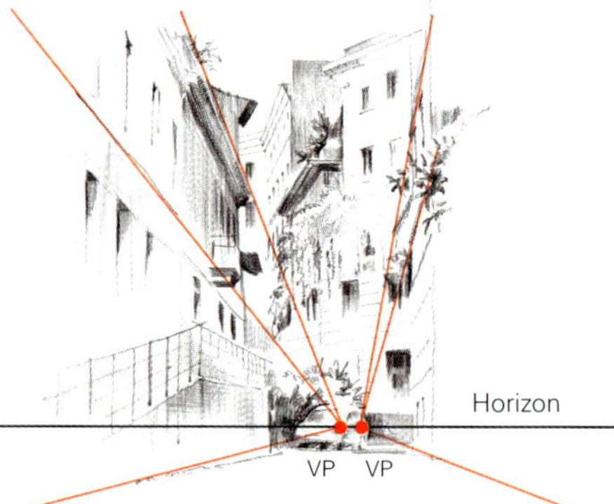

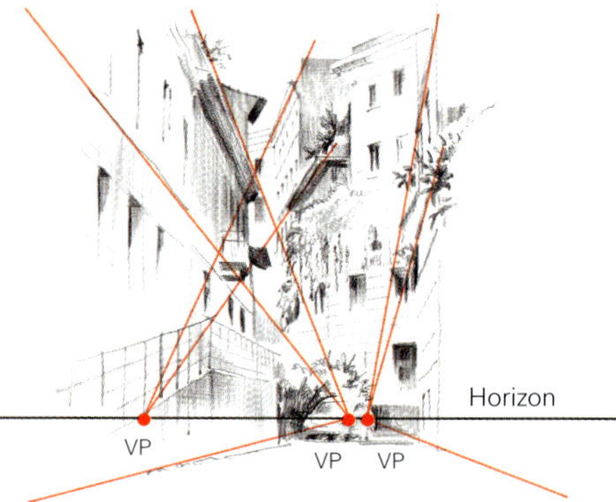

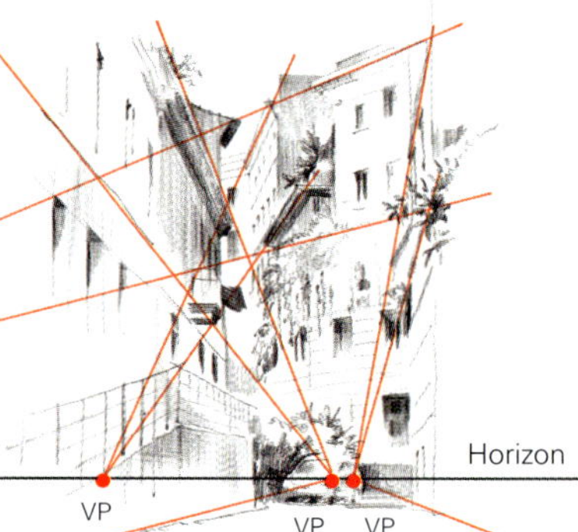

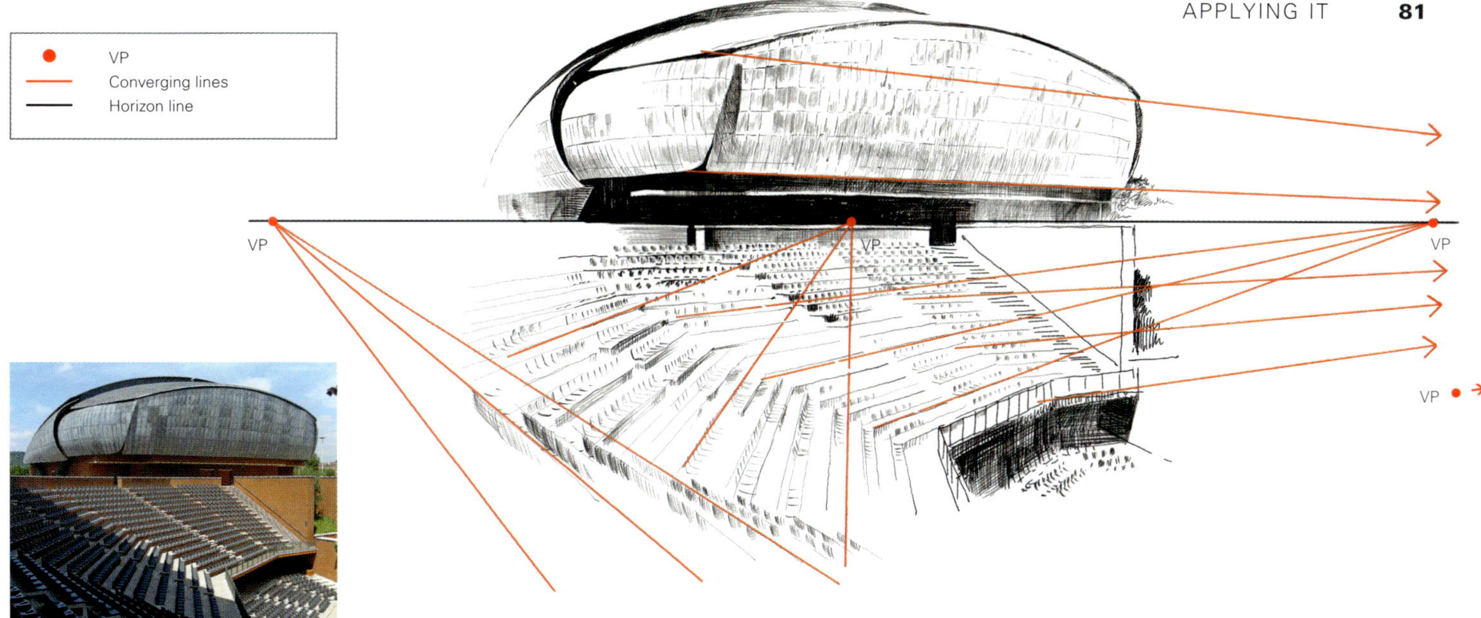

AUDITORIUM SEATING

At this outdoor performance venue in Rome, it's quite easy to see the multiple vanishing points at work because the many rows of seats create very apparent sets of converging lines. Each bank of seats is at a different angle to the others, resulting in at least four vanishing points in this image. Since our line of vision is level with the ground rather than looking upwards or downwards, all the vanishing points are on the horizon line. The nearest seats converge on a point off to the left, the next group of them converge on a point at the centre of the image, the third group converge on a point to the right and the final group (along with the nearest part of the building above), on a point far off to the right.

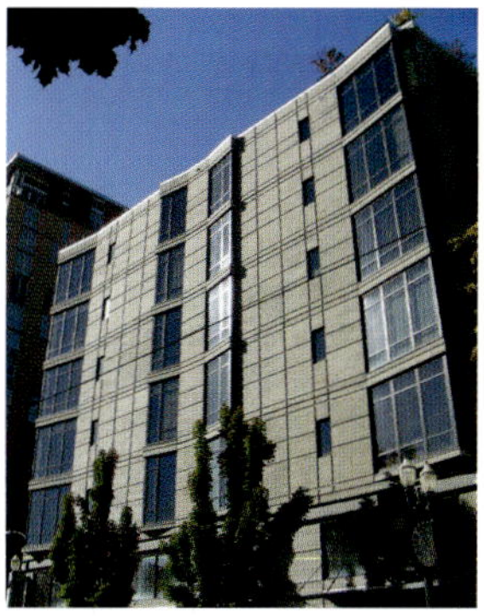

A SHIFTING FACADE

This building in Portland, Oregon, has a facade that breaks from the typical straight street front. The four vertical window elements project slightly to create enhanced views and a more interesting elevation. In this image, there are at least five vanishing points, including one that's not shown in the diagram, but is off to the right. Because the line of vision is directed upwards, there's also a vertical vanishing point, indicated by the arrows.

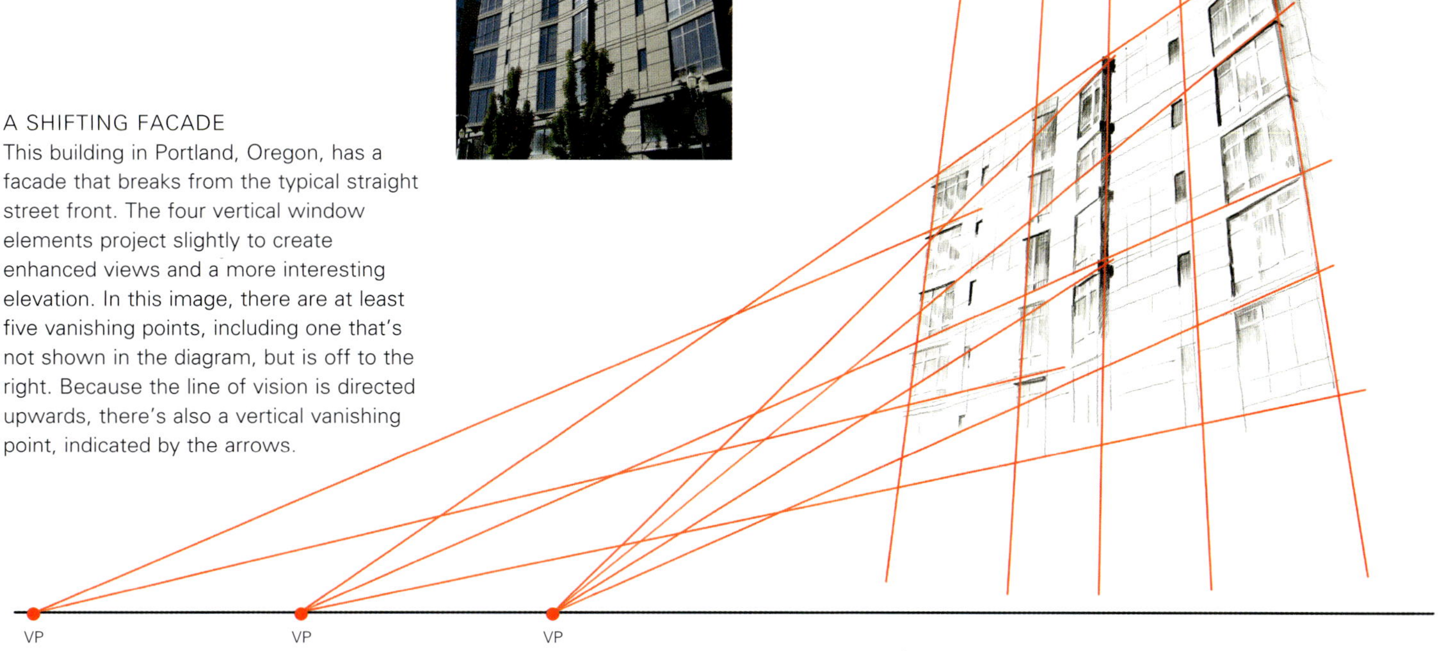

Understanding it

When flat planes are at odd angles, rather than being perpendicular to one another, there will be multiple vanishing points in the view. The diagrams and examples in this section will help you understand these points in a wide variety of circumstances.

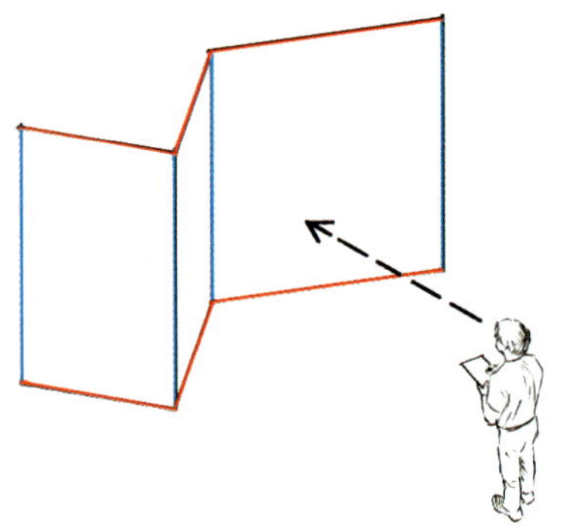

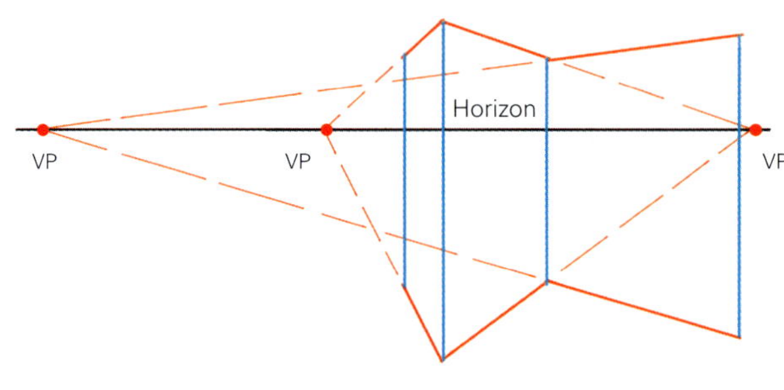

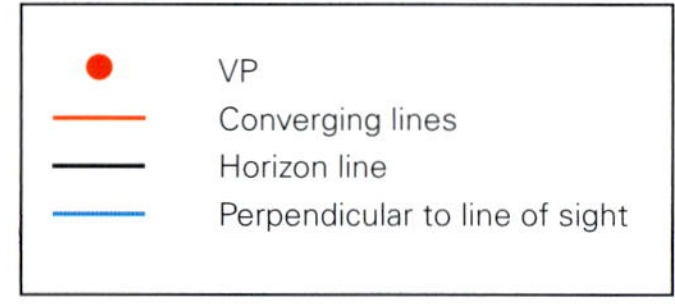

MULTIPLE PLANES
Let's consider another diagram similar to those in earlier chapters. Our line of sight is parallel to the ground, so the blue lines are perpendicular to our line of sight, and they will appear to be truly vertical in our view. But this time the subject in view is not a simple rectilinear cube or tower. Instead, we see three vertical planes at odd angles to one another, and not arranged on a two-dimensional grid like the previous examples. This means that each plane will have its own vanishing point. Since the red converging lines are parallel to the ground, the vanishing points will all occur on the horizon line, but each set of parallel lines (the top and bottom edge of each plane) will converge on its own point, as seen in the perspective diagram above.

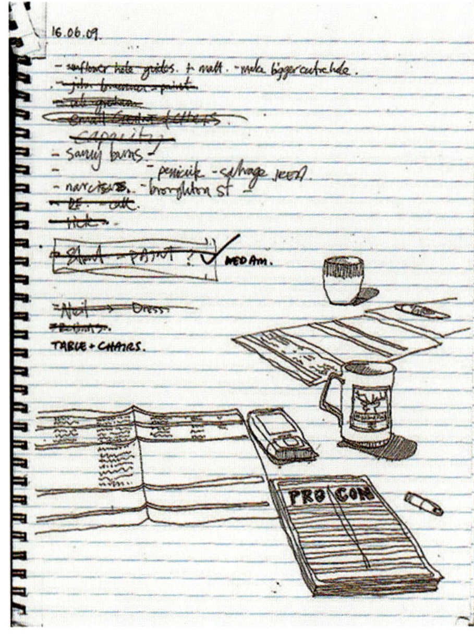

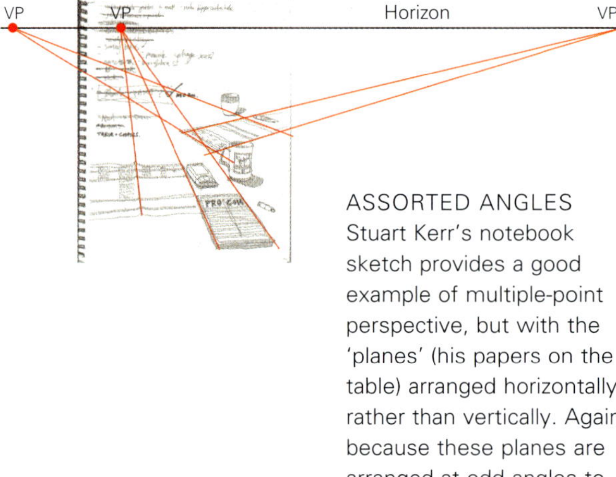

ASSORTED ANGLES
Stuart Kerr's notebook sketch provides a good example of multiple-point perspective, but with the 'planes' (his papers on the table) arranged horizontally rather than vertically. Again, because these planes are arranged at odd angles to one another, and not arranged on a grid, each will have its own set of converging lines. The papers at upper right appear as a simple two-point perspective, with one vanishing point to the right and the other to the left. But the papers in the foreground are at a different angle, so they get their own vanishing point. Because all the papers are lying flat on a table, parallel to the ground and our line of sight, all their vanishing points occur on the horizon line.

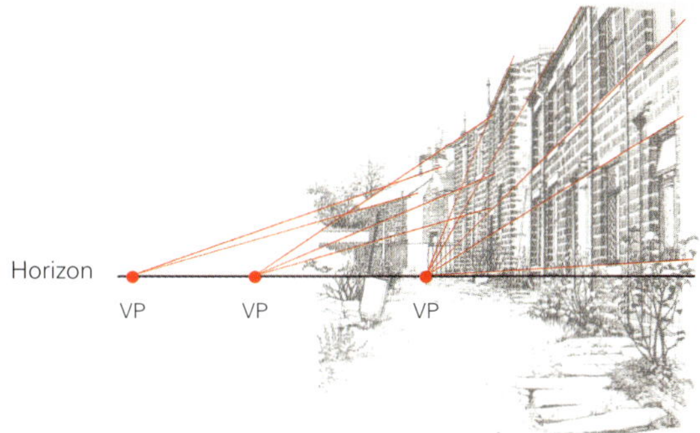

FACETED FACADES

This drawing by Pat Southern-Pearce presents a fairly common situation that lends itself to an understanding of multiple-point perspective. What happens when we view a slightly bending lane, where the building facades don't curve along the bend but instead are faceted – each one shifting its angle slightly from the ones immediately adjacent? Here, the two facades at right are parallel to one another, so their horizontal lines (the roof eaves, the tops and bottoms of windows and doors) will converge on the same vanishing point. But the two buildings at left are not parallel to one another or to the two buildings at right, so each of these facades has its own vanishing point. Notice how, as the angle of each building shifts towards our point of view, its vanishing point slides leftwards along the horizon line. Try to visualise what would happen if there were another building in the distance that was shifted still further – where would its vanishing point be? Can you visualise it even further out to the left along the horizon line?

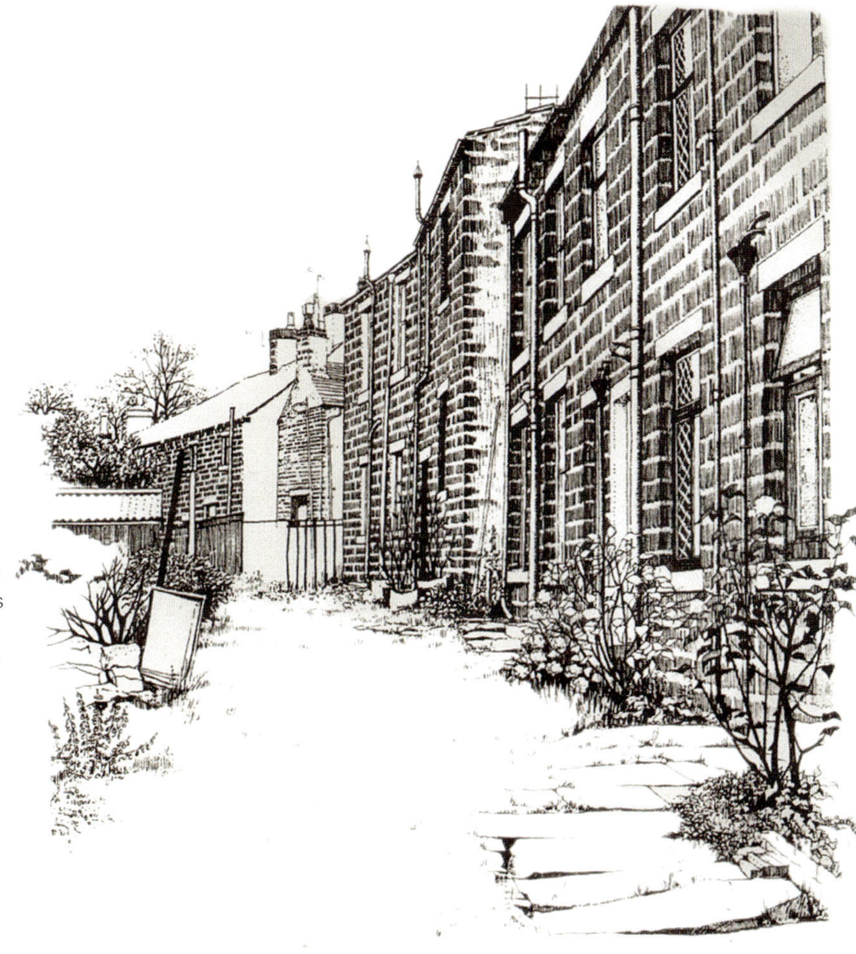

IDENTIFYING VANISHING POINTS

As the buildings move into the distance, their facades begin to shift their angles slightly. But there is also a bell tower in the distance that is at yet another angle. Gérard Michel made this clear in his drawing by establishing vanishing points for each of the building facades. Those that are parallel to one another – at near left and near right – can be handled with a simple one-point perspective, using the vanishing point shown at the centre of the diagram below. But the buildings at the far end of the street, and the bell tower beyond, require additional vanishing points. There are at least a few more vanishing points in this image; can you identify additional sets of lines that are parallel in space, and that would converge on these other vanishing points?

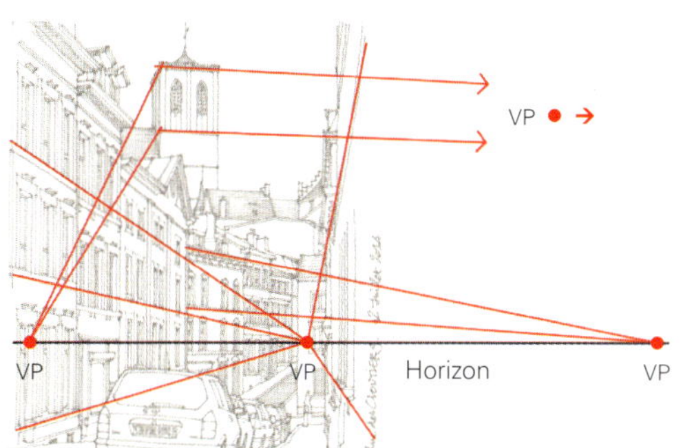

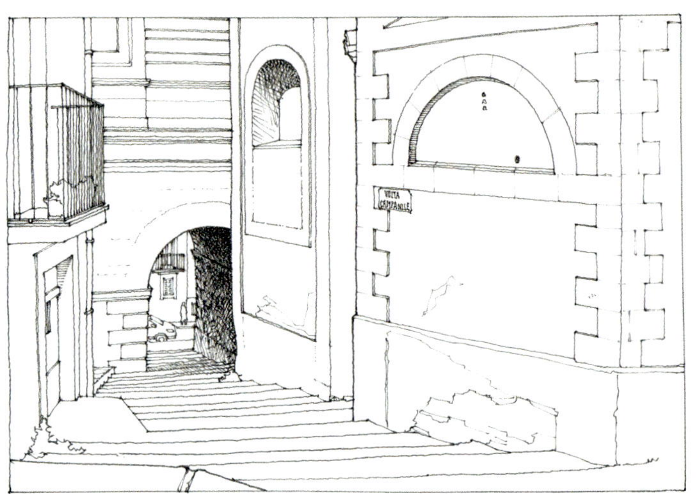

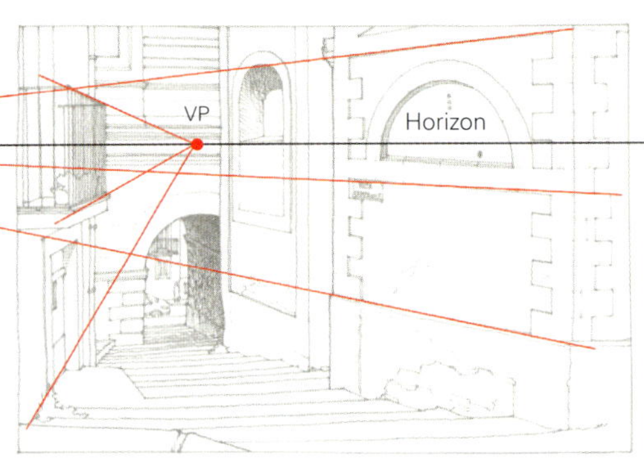

AN INTRIGUING VIEW

In this drawing by Gérard Michel, we're seeing down an interesting path of stairs through an arch, with our eye level near the top of the view. The small balcony at left and the wall at right angle towards one another, each with its own vanishing point. Because the flat part of each stair (the 'tread', as opposed to the 'riser') is parallel to our line of sight and horizontal in space, the lines along the edge of each stair would converge on vanishing points on the horizon line.

WORKING OUTSIDE OF A GRID

In this street scene by Daniel Castro Alonso, we can spot at least five different vanishing points along the horizon line, and at least one more above the horizon line. The numerous varying angles of the building facades each set up their own points of convergence; this is clearly not a rectilinear, gridded street network. Also, the street at left slopes upwards into the distance, so there would be another vanishing point up and to the left of this view, well above the horizon line.

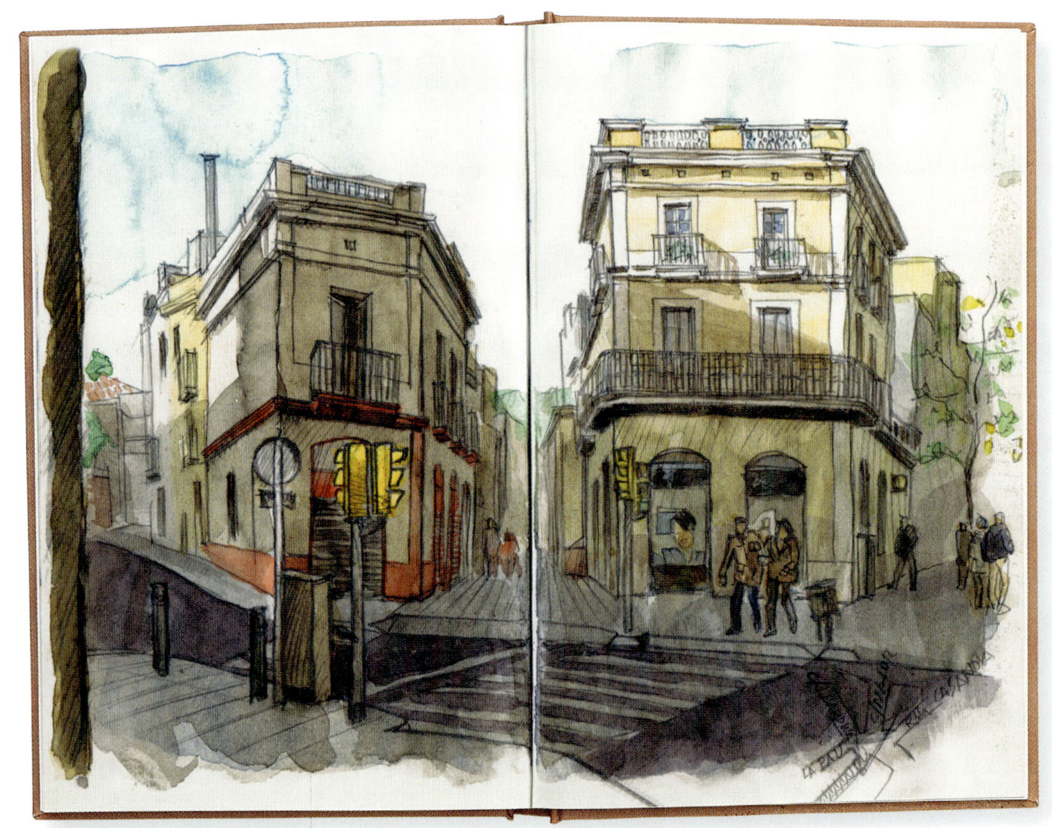

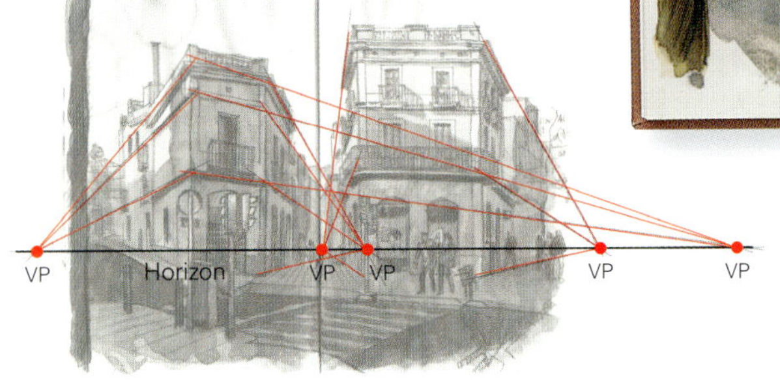

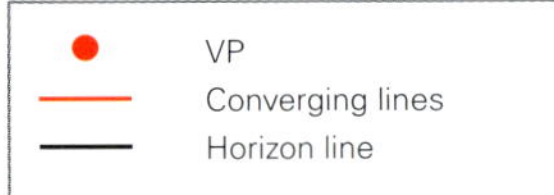

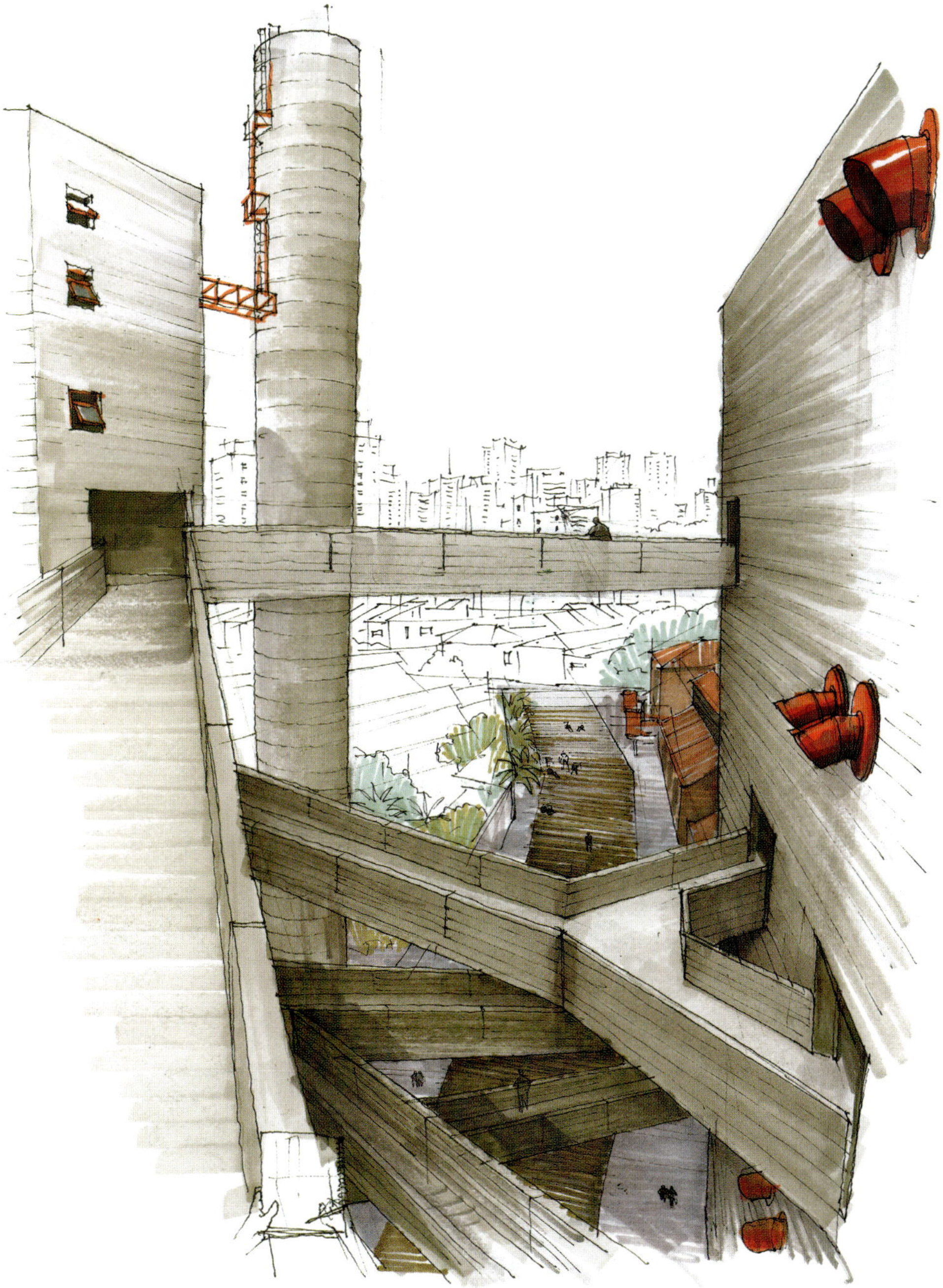

UNLIMITED VANISHING POINTS

In certain circumstances, there's really no limit to the number of different vanishing points necessary to establish the perspective. In Eduardo Bajzek's drawing at left, the buildings and connecting walkways are all at varying angles to one another. With every shift in angle, there needs to be a new vanishing point – only seven of them are identified in the diagram, but there are more.

WHEN VANISHING POINTS DO NOT OCCUR ON THE HORIZON LINE

When the ground plane is not perfectly flat, as in Maarten Ruijters' drawing below, there will also be a series of vanishing points that help establish lines of convergence for stairs and slopes. As these lines turn and twist, the vanishing points will move accordingly, and since these lines are not parallel to our horizontal line of sight (because the ground is not flat), the vanishing points will not occur on the horizon line. See how many vanishing points you can identify in this drawing – some are to the left or right, and some are above or below the horizon line.

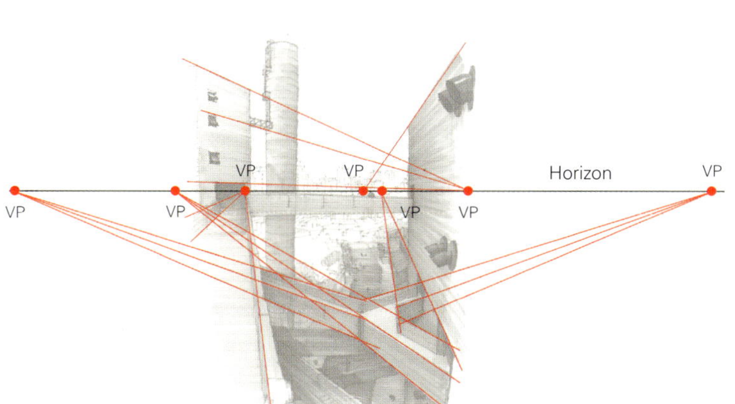

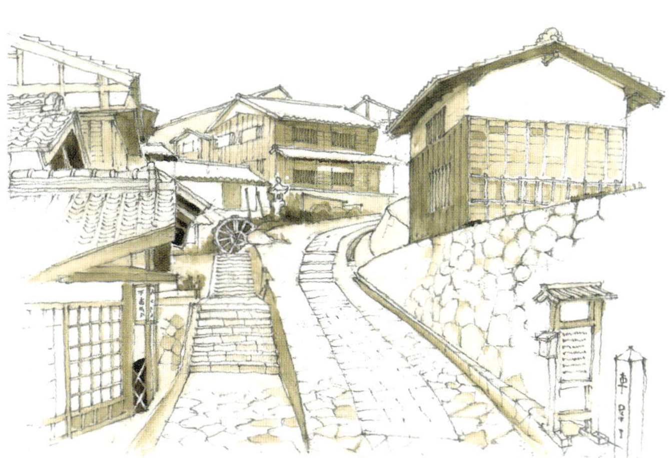

Applying it

Applying multiple-point perspective often requires us to identify and draw several sets of converging lines, and to keep these sets of lines distinct from one another as the drawing develops.

CONTRASTING POSITION
Eduardo Bajzek • Watercolour

▼ Eduardo Bajzek's quiet street scene, below, creates a simple but highly effective focal point in the distance. The lone angled building at the end of the space creates a nice contrast to the flanking buildings. When you are searching for suitable sketching subjects, it can help to be on the lookout for slightly out-of-the-ordinary spatial situations exactly like this.

CITY STREETS
Sharon Smart • Watercolour

▶ This watercolour of Colliers Wood High Street creates an interesting juxtaposition of scales that is augmented by the opposing vanishing points of the foreground and background. The building in the distance is only slightly in perspective, while the row of houses angles more dramatically away from our point of view.

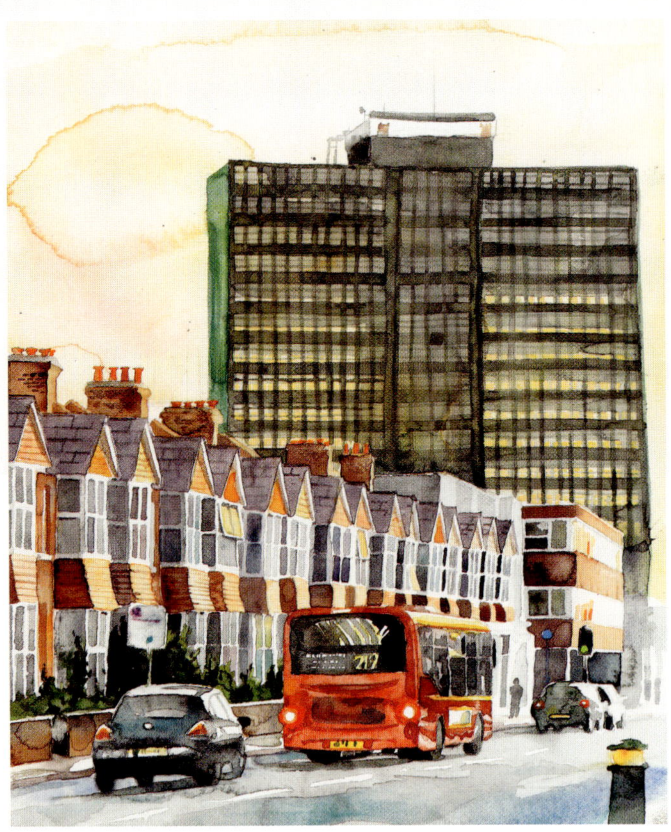

CITY SCENES

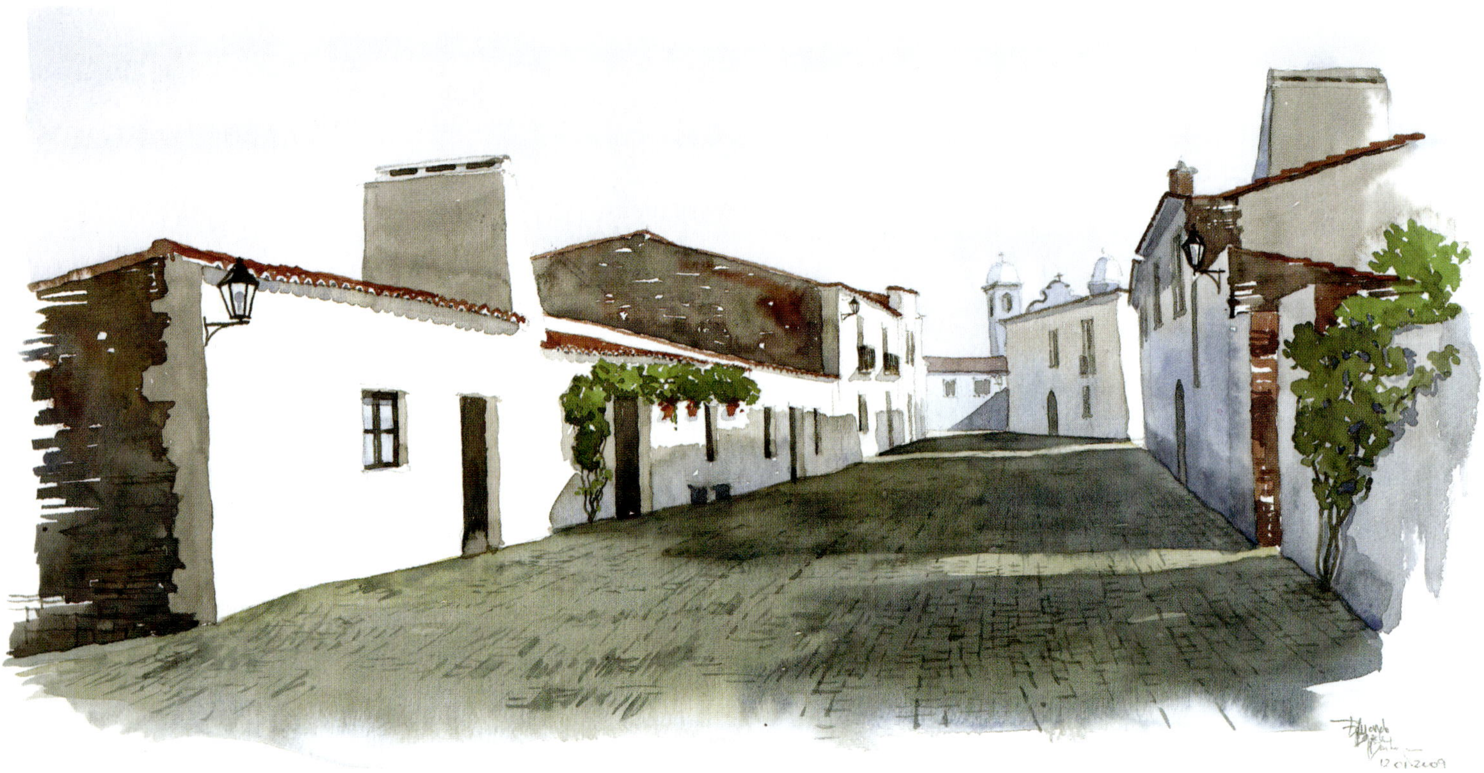

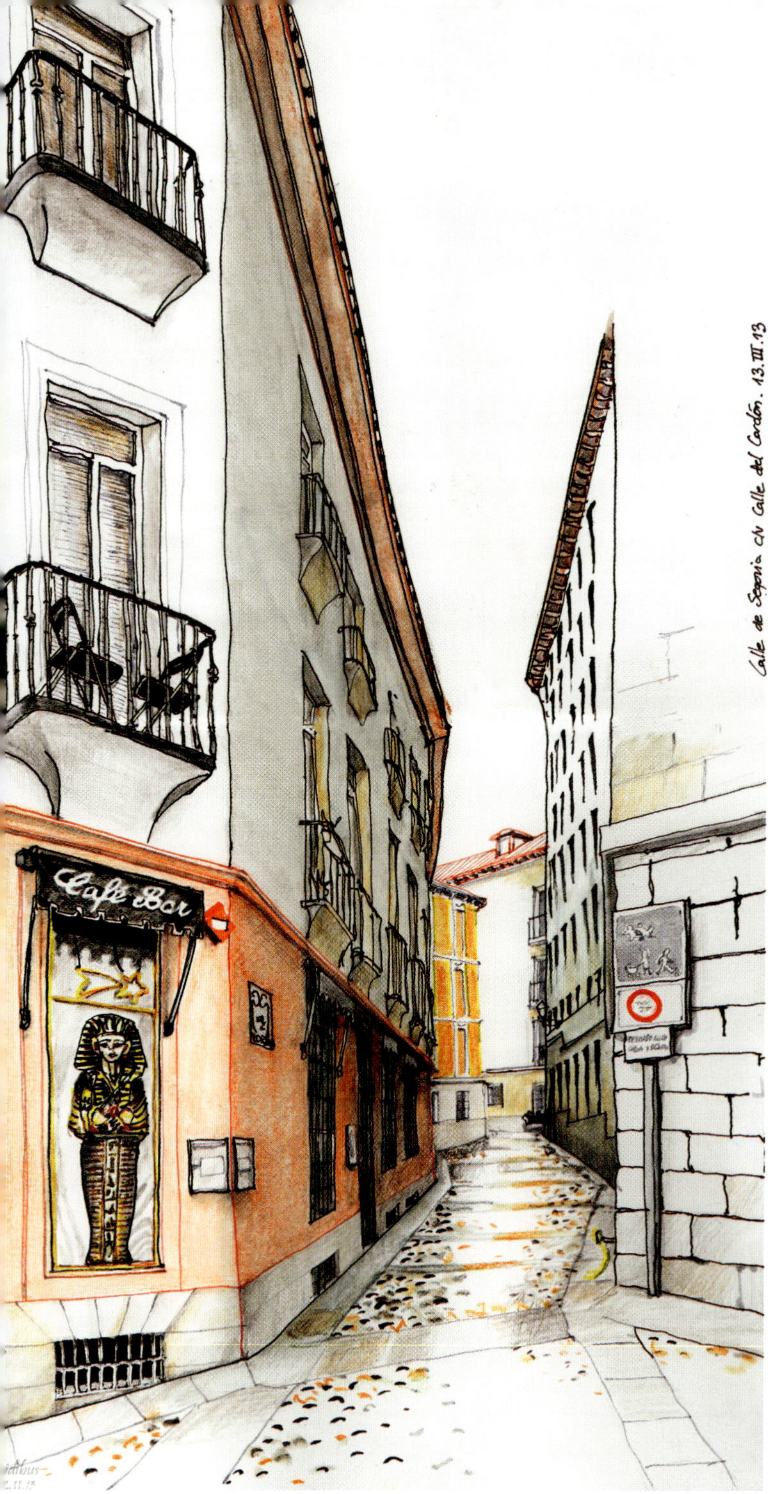

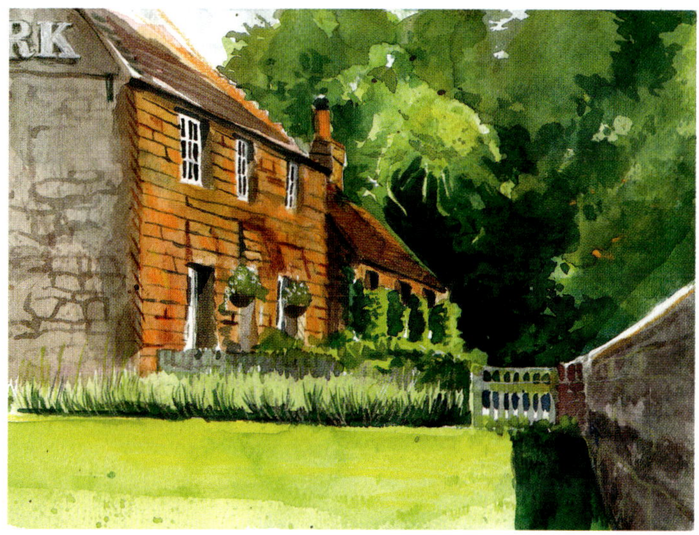

CHÂTEAU ELEVATION
Maarten Ruijters • Watercolour

▼ In the drawing of this château, we have a fascinating study in multiple vanishing points. The château itself is effectively seen in elevation, with very little perspective convergence visible. But the series of walls and stairs that lead us to the building in the distance shift and turn along the hillside, with several vanishing points needed to help establish consistency among the sets of parallel lines.

COUNTRY LIVING
Sharon Smart • Watercolour

▲ In this watercolour, we can easily understand that the garden wall at right and the building at left are not parallel to one another because they obviously have different vanishing points. It's a subtle distinction, but important to conveying an accurate sense of place.

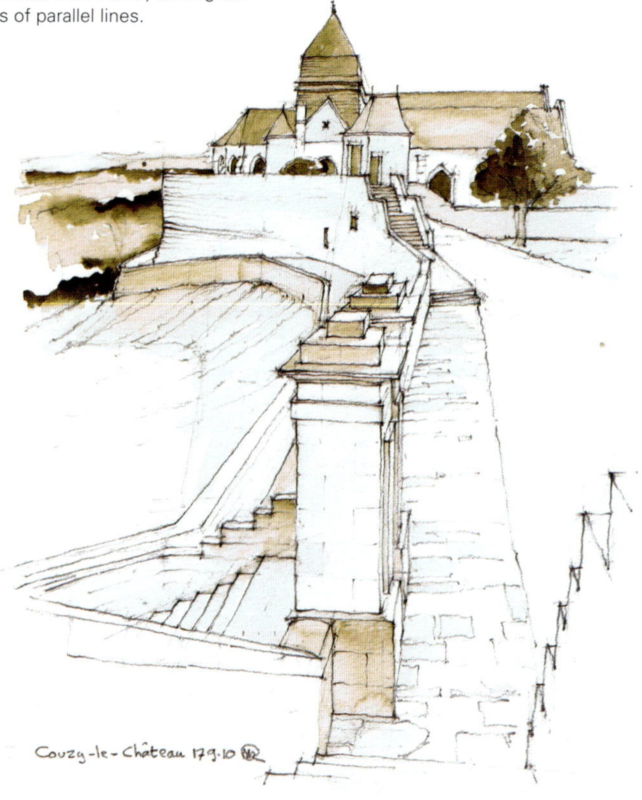

A NARROW VIEW
Ana Rojo • Watercolour

▲ This fascinating street scene demonstrates the usefulness of multi-point perspective. As the little lane rises up slightly into the distance, the lines that are horizontal in space recede to the horizon line – in this case a bit below the far end of the street. The roof eaves at left and right almost approach being vertical lines because the lane is so narrow and the buildings so tall. It's a common mistake with subjects like this to make these roof lines flatter and less dramatically vertical than they actually appear. Always strive to be as consistent as possible with every element of the drawing.

SANTA CHIARA BELL TOWER
Matthew Brehm • Watercolour

▶ Small medieval towns are wonderful places to observe and draw using multi-point perspective. These places were developed over great lengths of time – often over many centuries – and they rarely benefited from a cohesive plan for their layout, unlike modern cities that are almost invariably based on a grid arrangement. The resulting streets and spaces are often a dizzying array of opposing angles that we now see as the epitome of charm. This street in Assisi, Italy, creates a perfect framework for the bell tower. As the street drops down the hill, the flanking walls turn and twist in relation to one another. While relatively little of the vertical surfaces are in view – especially on the left – the projecting roof eaves give strong clues as to their orientation.

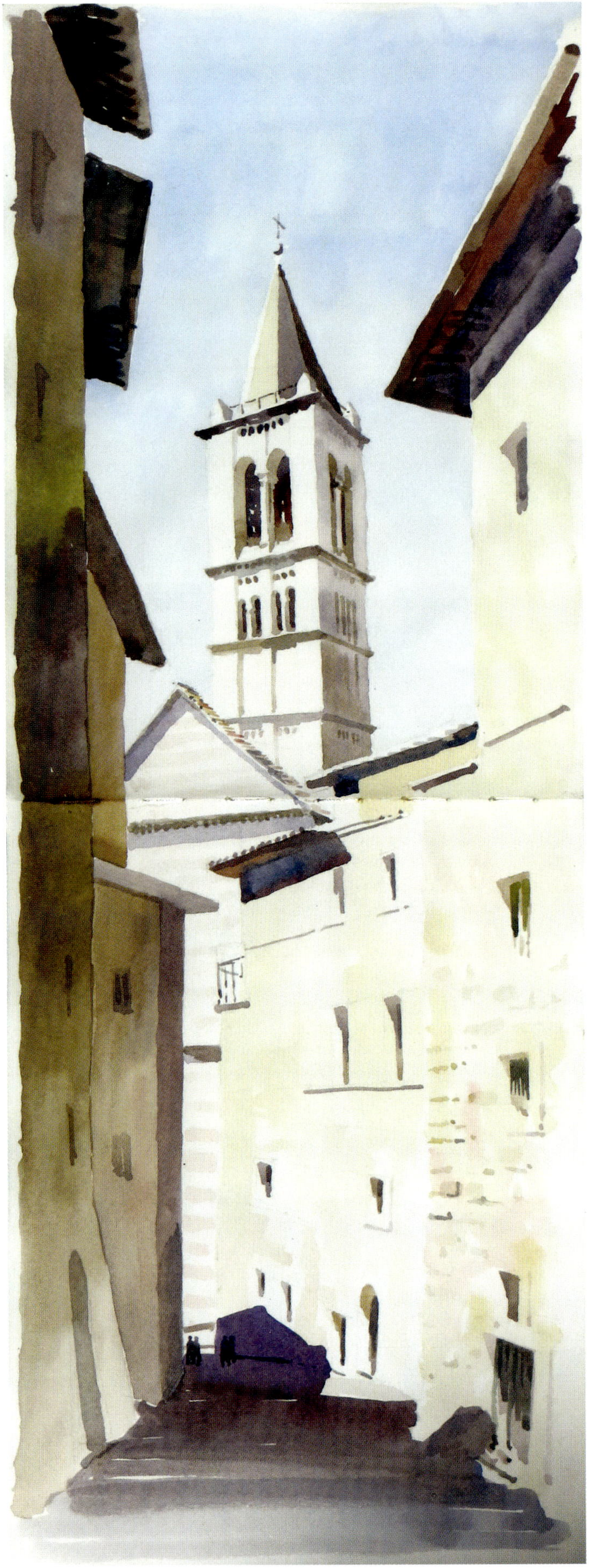

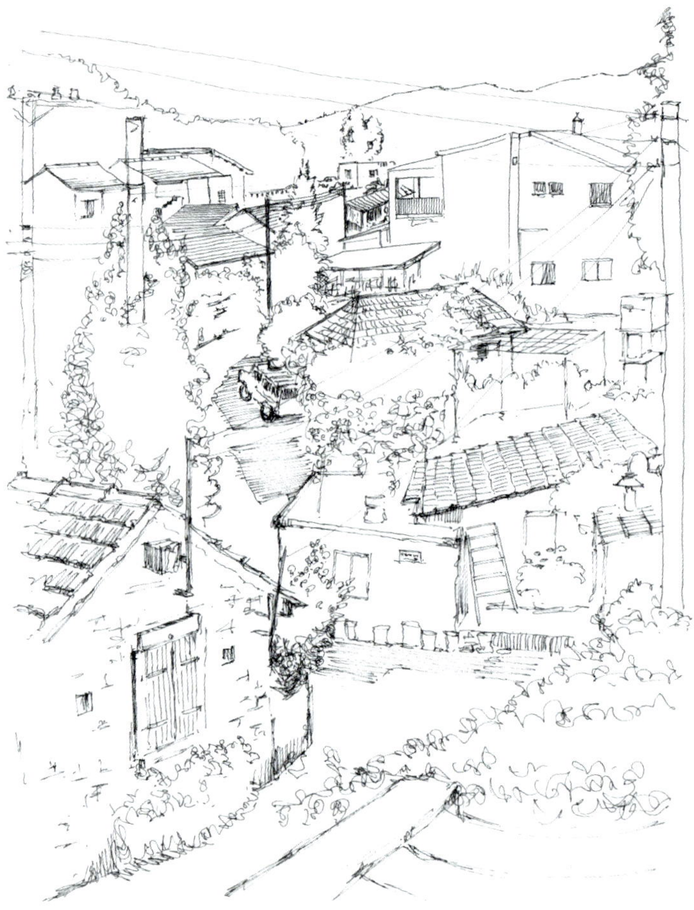

LANIA VILLAGE
Keith Nevens • Pen and ink

▲ In this drawing of a village in Cyprus, almost none of the buildings align with any of the others. This randomness of arrangement creates an interesting subject and a significant challenge for observing and drawing. An understanding of multi-point perspective will have you seeking out subjects like these for the wonderful sketching opportunities they present, and you'll begin to see just how frequently this understanding will be put to the test. But with regular practice, you'll relish chances to tackle complex subjects that go far beyond the more typical one-point, two-point and three-point views.

KASSEL SKYLINE
Omar Jaramillo • Watercolour

▼ The view in this sketch is looking across rooftops, with the ridges and eaves creating the sense of space and distance that recedes towards the horizon. The angles of the two foreground buildings in particular contribute to the central focus of the image, with the cool shaded area between them contrasting with the warm sunlight above.

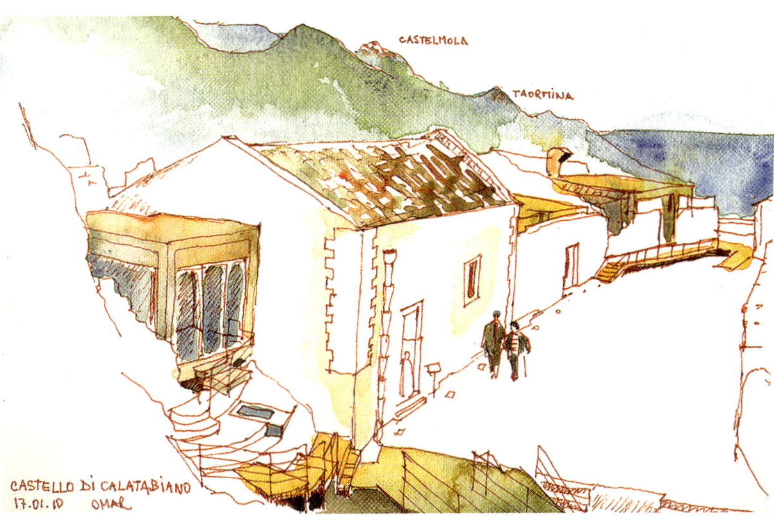

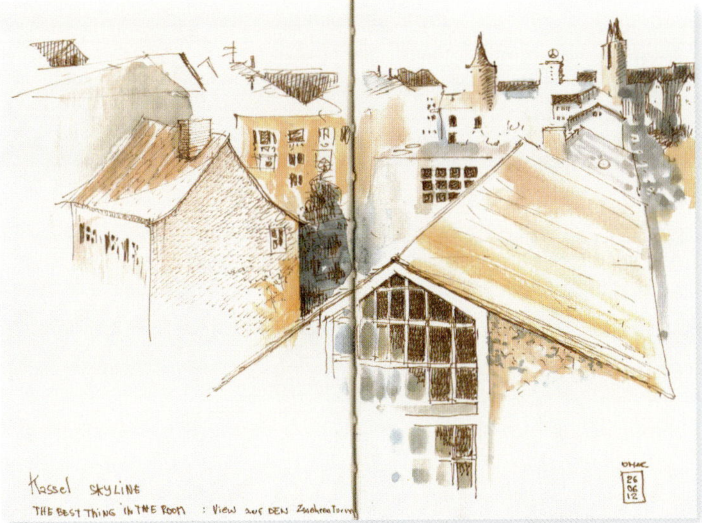

CALATABIANO
Omar Jaramillo • Ink and watercolour

▲ This ink and watercolour drawing is a simple, but very effective display of multi-point perspective, with the most distant building angling just slightly to the right and outwards towards the sea. The elevated point of view is reinforced by the relationship to the distant horizon and its position well above the two figures in the foreground. Try to visualise how the lines of convergence would arrive at the horizon line as defined by the upper edge of the water.

ROOFTOPS

XAUS SERRA HOUSE
Daniel Castro Alonso
Watercolour

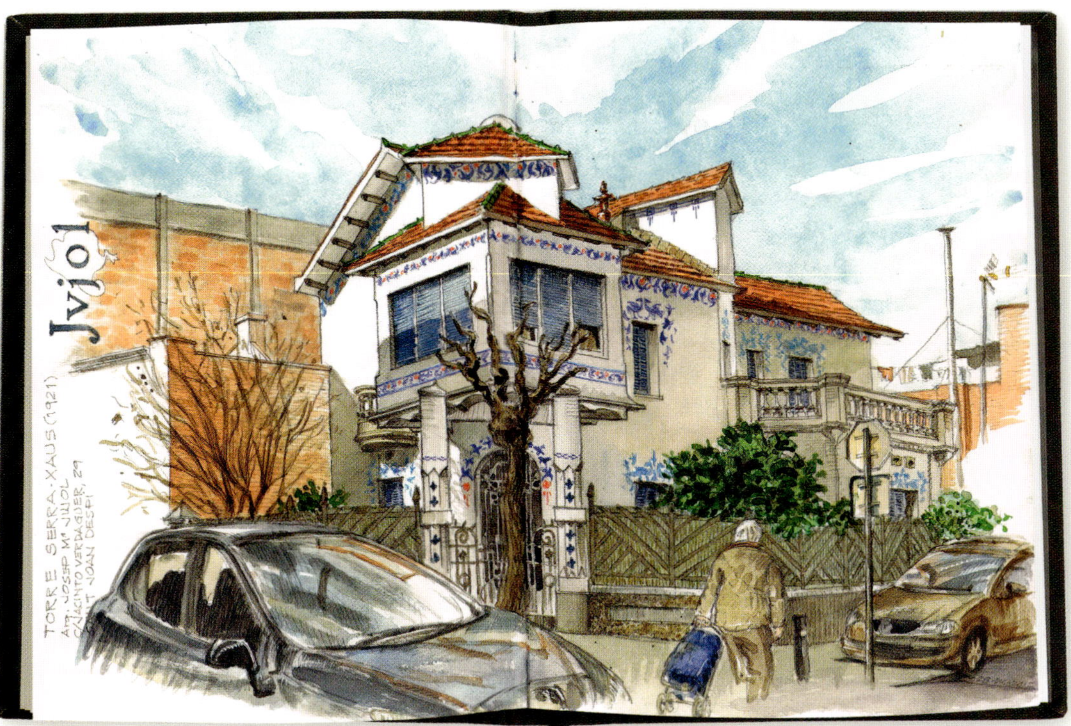

◄ This curious building has at least seven or eight sets of lines that are parallel in space. Each volume of the house, and its associated roof lines, will be defined by two vanishing points, so it's a bit like combining several two-point perspective views into a single composition. In developing a multi-point perspective, it can often help to focus on one volume at a time – essentially breaking the overall composition into as many one- or two-point perspectives as necessary. It remains important that all smaller units relate to each other in the end, and the composition as a whole is accurate and makes visual sense.

multi-point perspective
How-to sequence

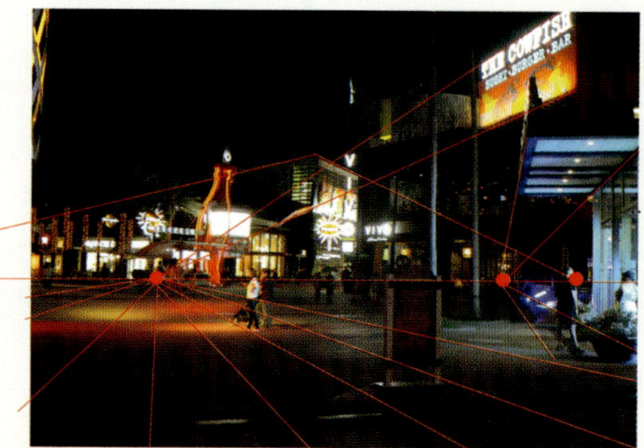

Thomas Thorspecken's *City Walk*, a sketch of one of the main avenues in Universal Studios Theme Park, is full of life and glowing neon colours against the night sky. The buildings are not square to each other, so each has its own vanishing point.

STARTING OUT

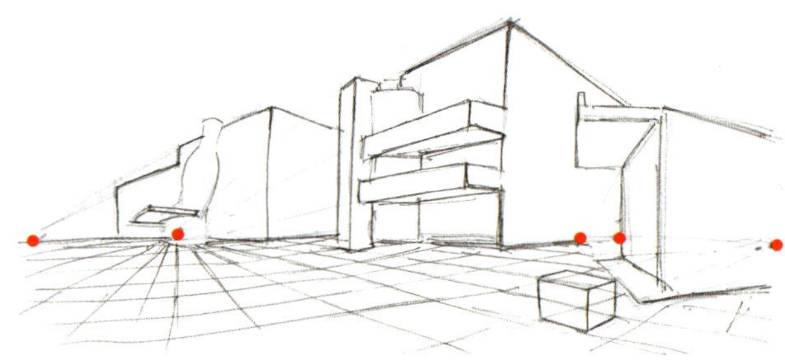

This thumbnail sketch shows five vanishing points. A sixth vanishing point would exist far off the sketch page to the right for the walls of the right-hand building. I considered the second vanishing point from the left to be the primary vanishing point of the scene.

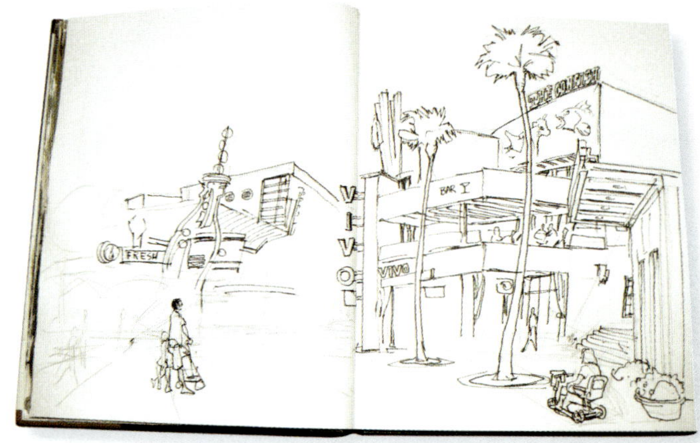

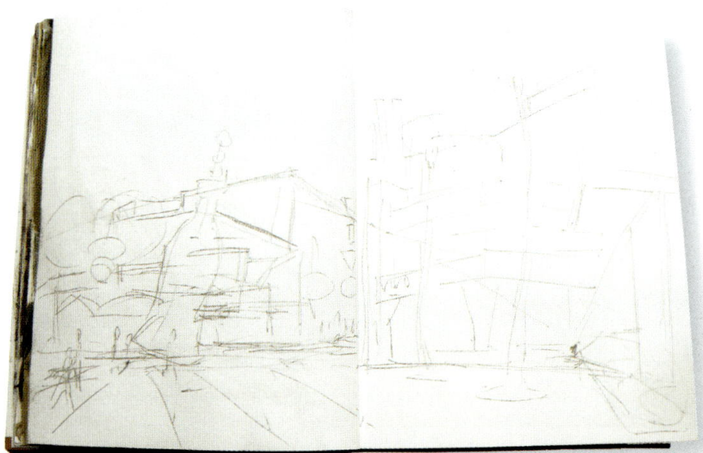

STEP 1 ▲ Begin by putting in the horizon line and then finding the two primary vanishing points of the large neon bar sign and the building towards the back of the square. Also put in the awning on the right; you can use it to frame the right-hand side of the sketch. The highest object was the palm tree, so that was added next.

STEP 2 ▲ Ink the sketch with a fine-nib pen, working either from right to left or from foreground to background. The woman in the scooter was built from the ground up and that base has its own vanishing point. I just needed a couple of people in the foreground; the rest will be sketched in as a group later.

STEP 3 ▼ Add a spotlight oval on the ground plane to indicate that the father and daughter will be at its centre. The pavement lines in the square were curved, but I made them straight to lead the eye back to the vanishing point behind the father and daughter. Add the crowd of people in the background.

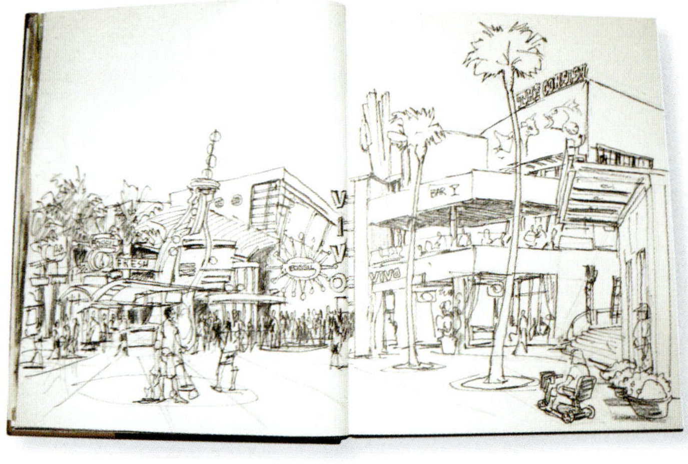

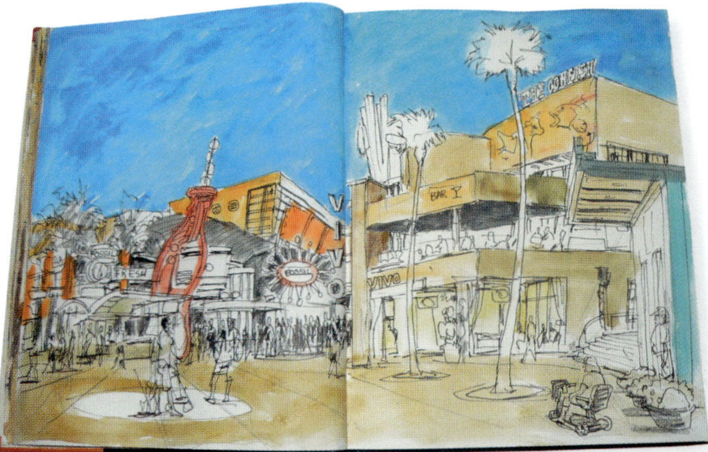

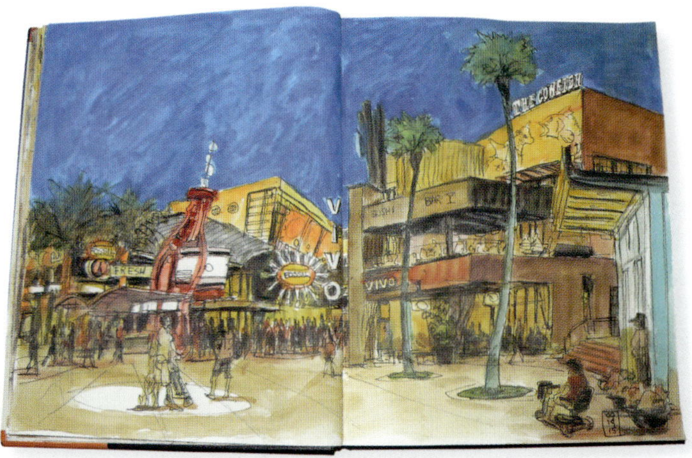

STEP 4 ▲ By this time all the neon lights are on, so it is time to paint. The setting sun lights up one face of the buildings, so catch that orange surface first, followed by the blue sky. Try to cover as much of the sketch as you can while painting around the artificial lights. Put in the reds of the Coke sculpture and then use yellow ochre to darken more of the sketch.

STEP 5 ▶ Add green foliage and darken the shadow sides of the buildings by adding purple to the yellow ochre. At this point in the process, pay careful attention to colour temperature and value: keep asking yourself whether the area you're working on is warm or cool, light or dark. Keep building up the darks with every stroke.

FINISHED DRAWING ▼ The pure blacks and pure whites, and the warmth of the artificial lights contrasts with the cool night sky. With watercolour, it is hard to achieve pure points of light. I decided to give a general impression of the lights' effects instead.

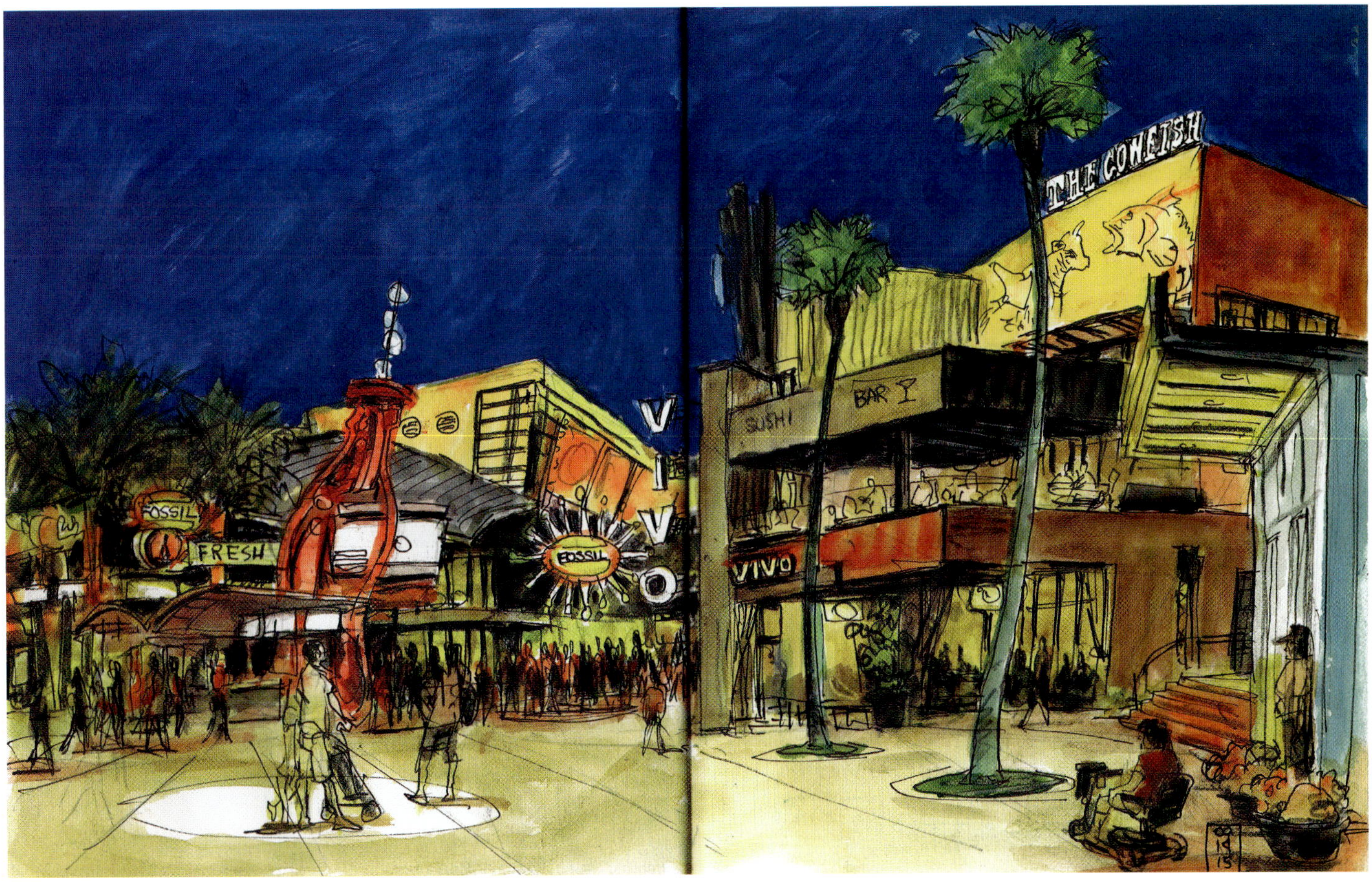

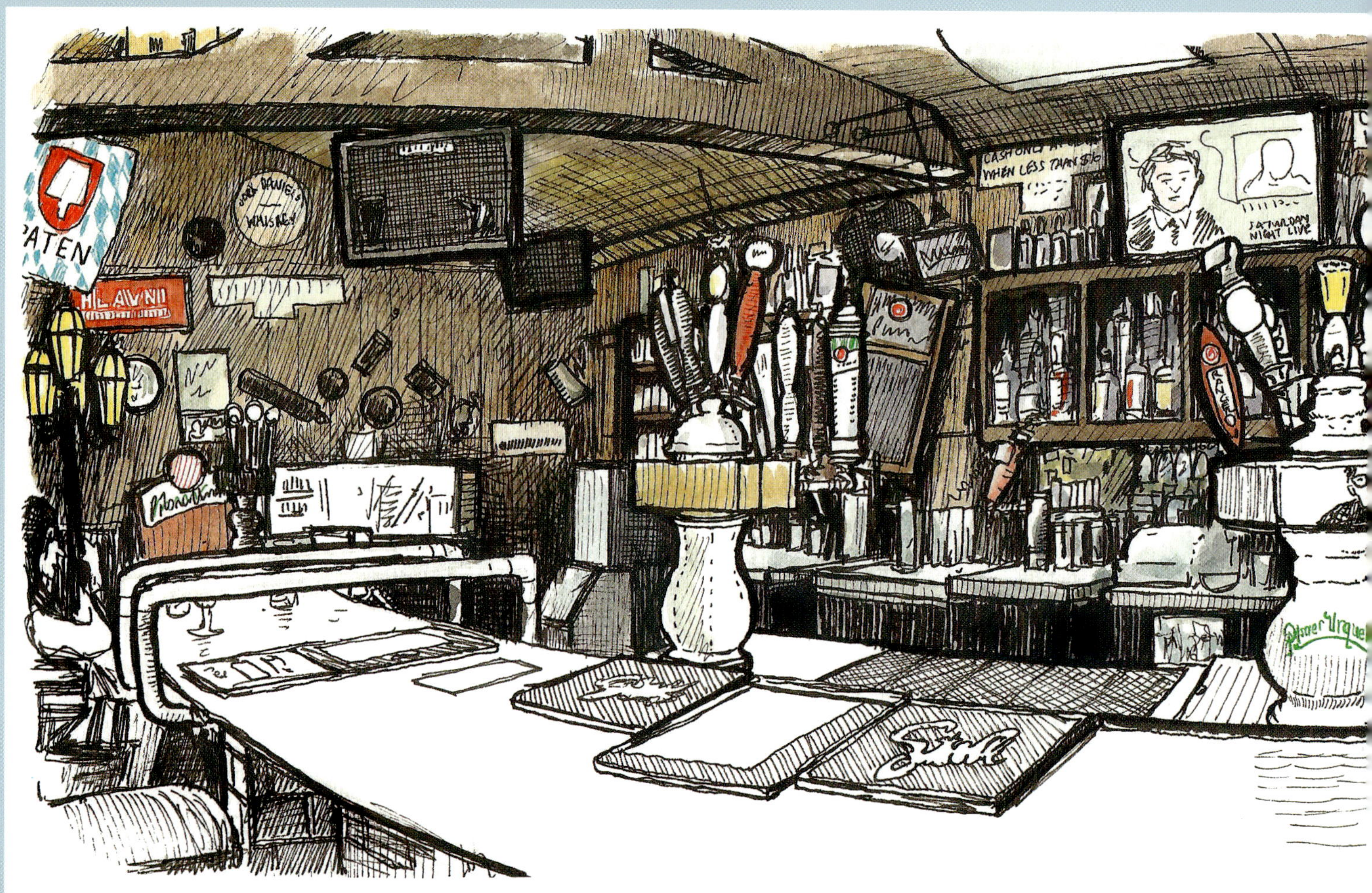

CURVILINEAR

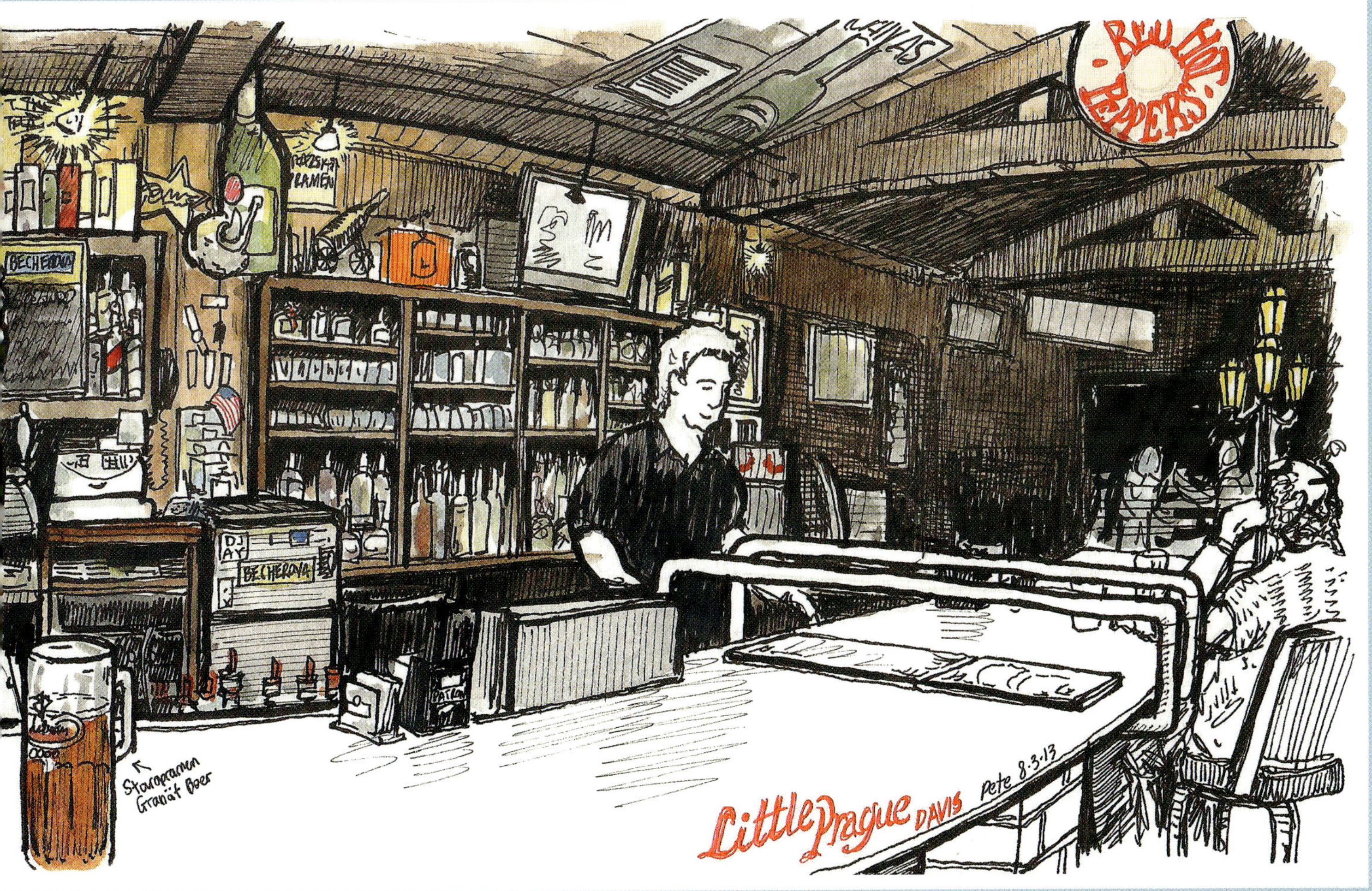

PERSPECTIVE

Curvilinear perspective allows us to dramatically expand our view and include what we see in our peripheral vision. At first glance, the resulting drawings appear to be distorted and even a bit confusing, but they might be even more faithful to what we actually see than linear perspective drawings.

▲ LITTLE PRAGUE • *Pete Scully* • Ink and watercolour

Introduction

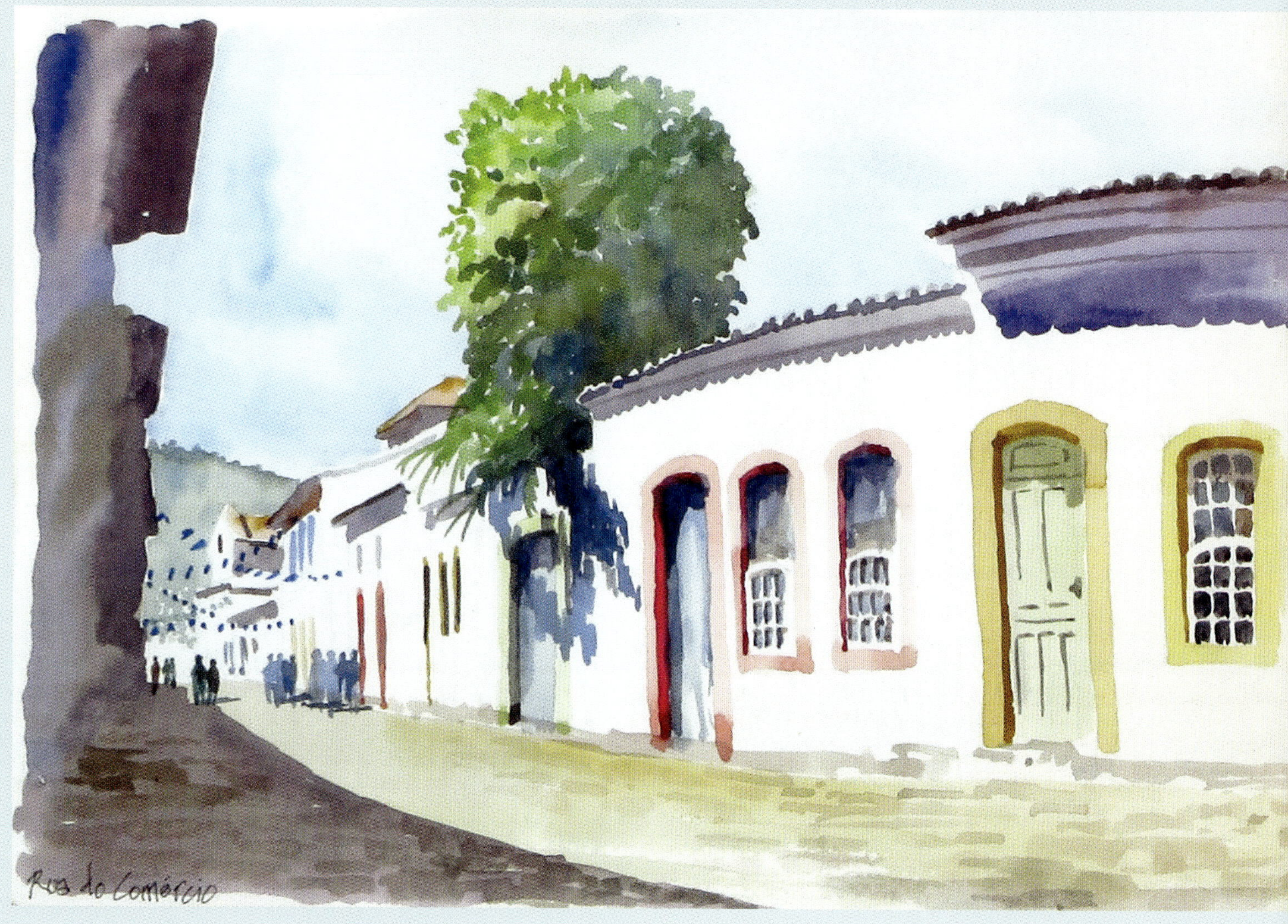

What is curvilinear perspective?

Peripheral vision allows us to see quite a lot – above, below, to the left and right – and not only the space and objects directly in front of our noses. Curvilinear perspective is a way to represent what we can see out of the corners of our eyes. To make this type of drawing, we need to collapse a wide-angle view on to the sketchbook page by distorting the ordinarily straight lines of other types of perspective.

'Linear' perspective encompasses one-point, two-point, three-point and multiple-point drawings because lines that are straight in space remain straight when applied in a drawing. This type of perspective relies on a limited 'cone of vision', which is the amount we see within about 60 degrees of our line of sight.

With curvilinear perspective, we can show what we see outside this central cone, in what we call our peripheral vision. You'll sometimes see reference to 'cylindrical' or 'spherical' perspective, and both approaches are useful in certain contexts. I use the term 'curvilinear' as a general expression that would include these other types of drawing because the perspective construction requires the use of curves rather than just straight lines.

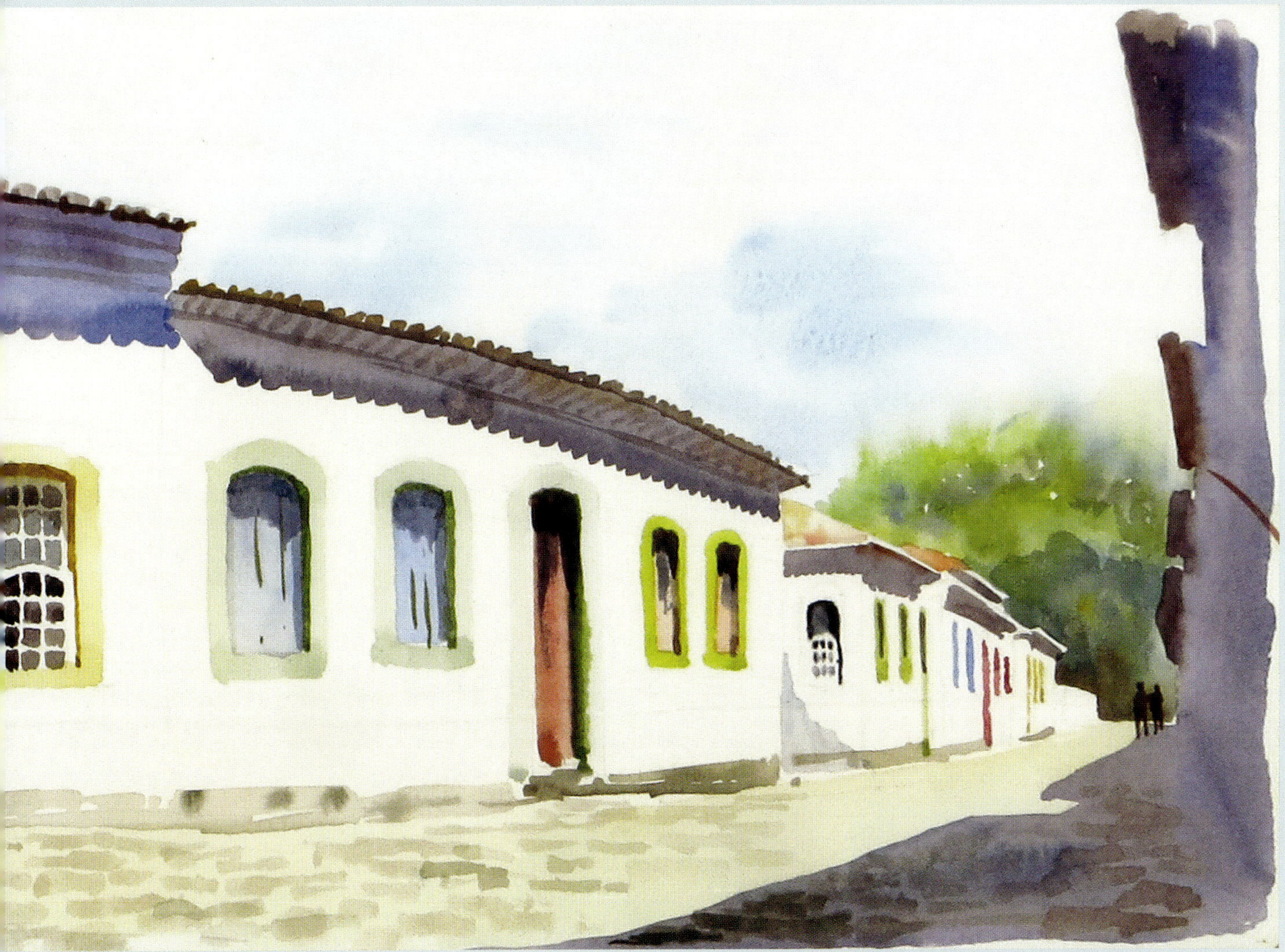

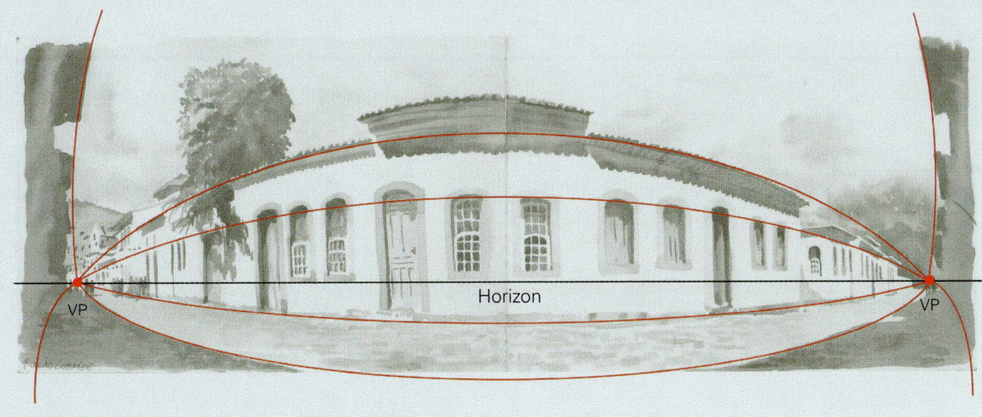

▲ RUA DO COMÉRCIO
Matthew Brehm • Graphite and watercolour

▲ ◀ In this street view from Paraty, Brazil, I was looking straight across the street while trying to include my peripheral view to the left and right. The diagram at left shows how the horizontal lines of the buildings were made to curve in the drawing, meeting at one vanishing point to the left and another to the right.

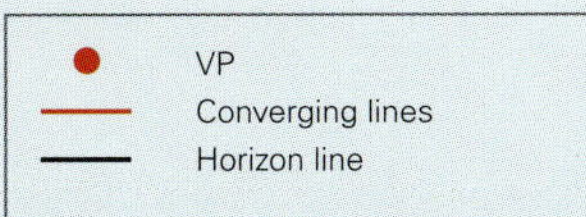

Seeing it

Curvilinear perspective can be challenging to see, because the phenomenon of curving lines of convergence occurs outside of our central field of view – we see it only when we include our peripheral vision. Curvilinear perspective is a way to bring a much wider angle into the view, by warping lines that would otherwise be straight in a typical perspective drawing.

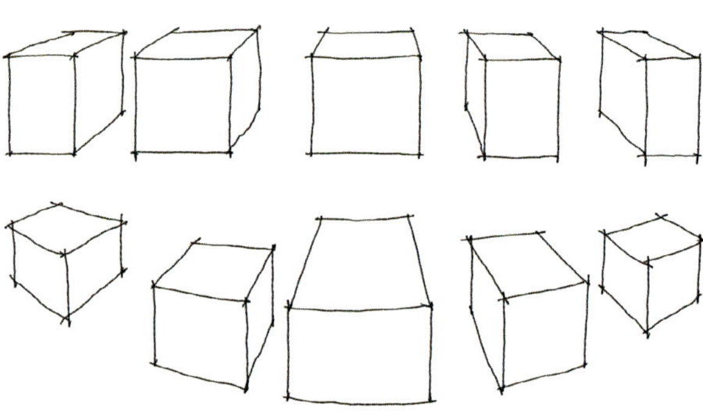

AT ITS SIMPLEST
In a linear perspective drawing, lines that are straight in space are drawn as being straight, like the top row of boxes above. But this ignores the fact that the boxes on the left and right are further away from our point of view, and should therefore appear to be smaller than the boxes in the centre. Curvilinear perspective allows for this visual phenomenon by bending lines in the drawing, like the bottom row of boxes in the sketch.

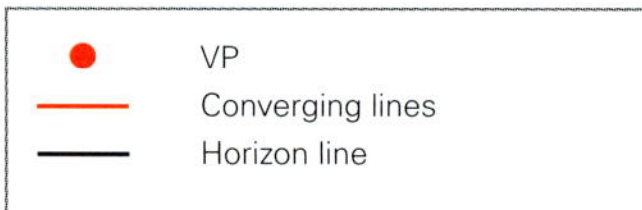

HORIZONTAL AND VERTICAL LINES
In curvilinear perspective, whether the lines in space are vertical or horizontal, they will appear to bend as they get further away from your position as the viewer. So horizontal lines will bend towards the horizon line as they move away from your line of sight and into your peripheral vision left and right – like the diagram below. Vertical lines will bend towards the centre of the view as they move away from your line of sight and into your peripheral vision up and down – like the diagram at right. In both cases, the lines nearest to your line of sight (that is, nearest to the centre of the view) will appear to be truly horizontal or vertical.

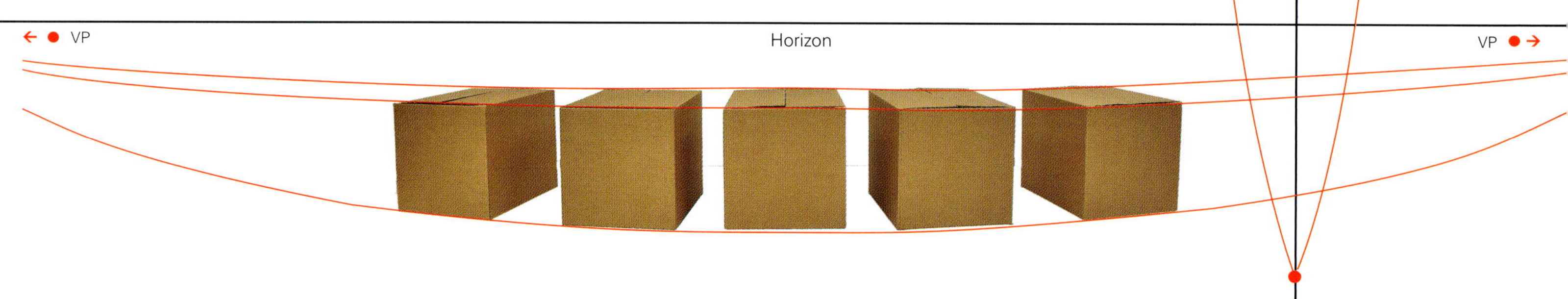

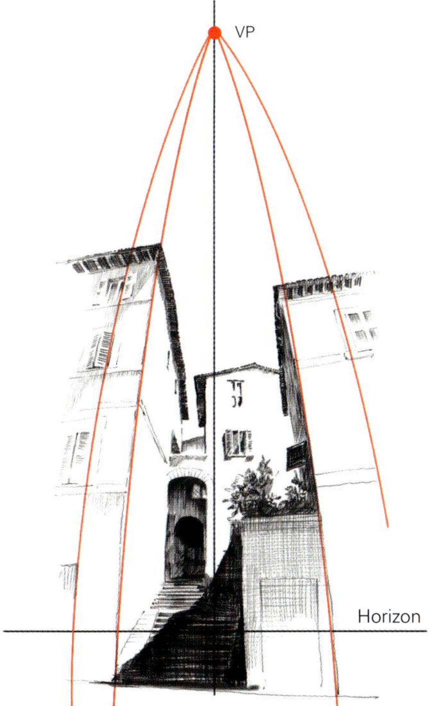

BASIC VERTICAL CURVATURE

If we include in our view both the eye level and what appears in our peripheral vison above, we begin to see curvature of vertical lines. At our eye level, lines that are vertical in space will appear to be truly vertical. But as the subject in view gets further away from our position, the lines will bend inwards as the subject appears to get smaller in the vertical distance.

BASIC HORIZONTAL CURVATURE

When our line of sight is effectively parallel to the ground, focused on a horizontally-oriented, wide-angle field of view, the majority of the curvature will occur along horizontal lines. This view demonstrates the way buildings will appear to curve as they recede into the distance, away from our point of view. The portion of the building at right is closest to our point of view, and the facade is perpendicular to our line of sight. So it appears to be in elevation rather than in perspective. But the left portion of the building is clearly further from our point of view and receding into the distance – it therefore appears in perspective, with the horizontal lines converging on a vanishing point off to the left, out of the view. Instead of appearing as perfectly straight lines, the roof eaves, balusters and other horizontals appear to curve – from being horizontal in the right portion of the view to being angled downwards at left.

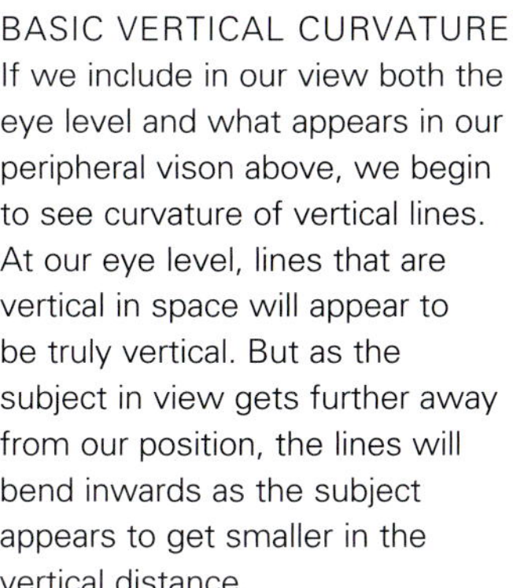

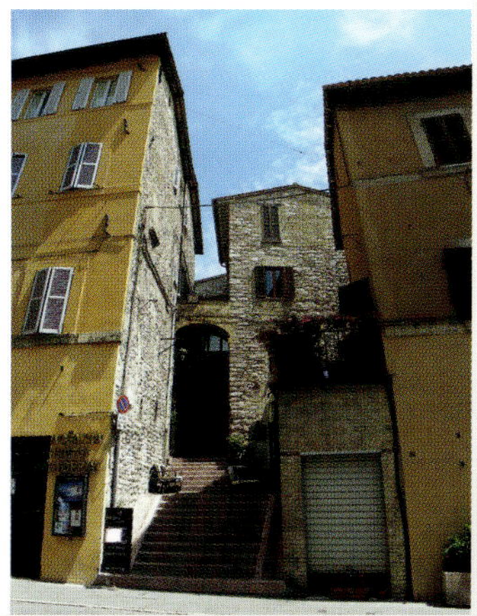

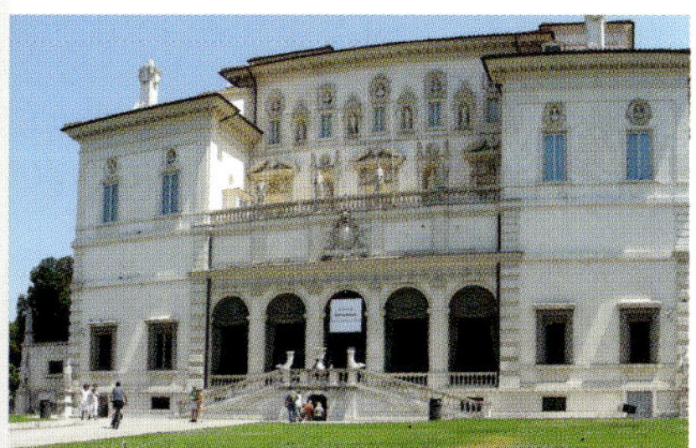

COMBINING HORIZONTAL AND VERTICAL CURVATURE

This view of a little agricultural building might not call for curvilinear perspective. I might ordinarily straighten out the curving lines, to sort of wrestle the curvilinear into a more linear approach, if only for the sake of simplicity. But showing the subtle curvature both horizontally and vertically does begin to emphasise our proximity to the subject, making the near corner appear much closer than the rest of the building. This is one of the pleasures of curvilinear perspective – it literally allows you to bend the otherwise stringent 'rules' of linear perspective to create a more dynamic view – one that begins to more accurately depict the way we perceive the world around us.

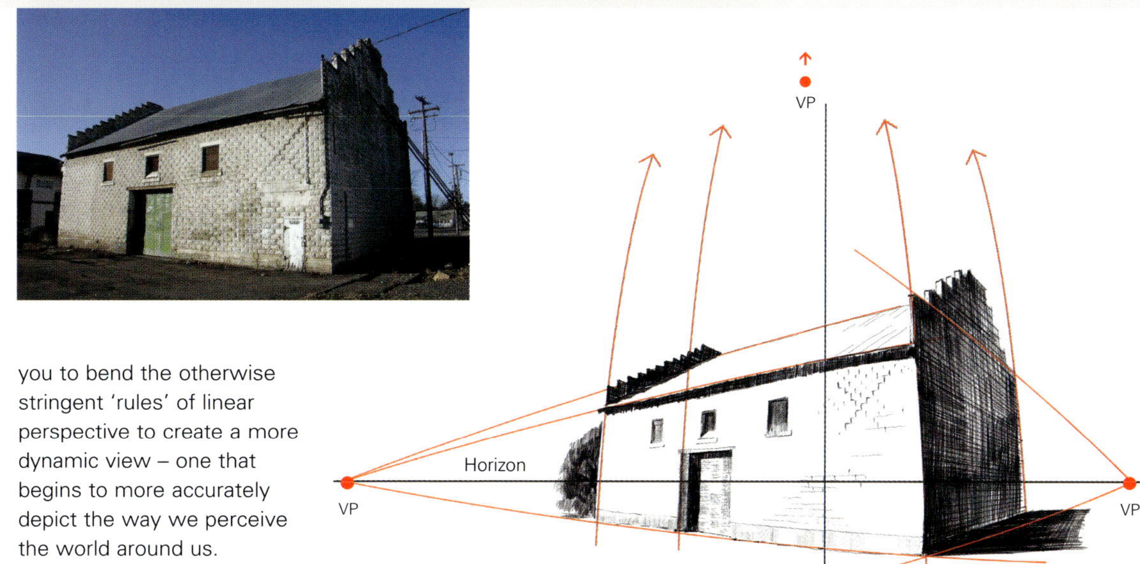

Understanding it

To understand curvilinear perspective, always remember that objects appear to get smaller as they get further away from our point of view, and that even when we know a line is straight in space, it might appear to bend as it moves into our peripheral vision.

GO TO THE WORKBOOK
To help you understand curvilinear perspective read this section, then turn to pages 130–137 and try the range of exercises shown in the grid chambers.

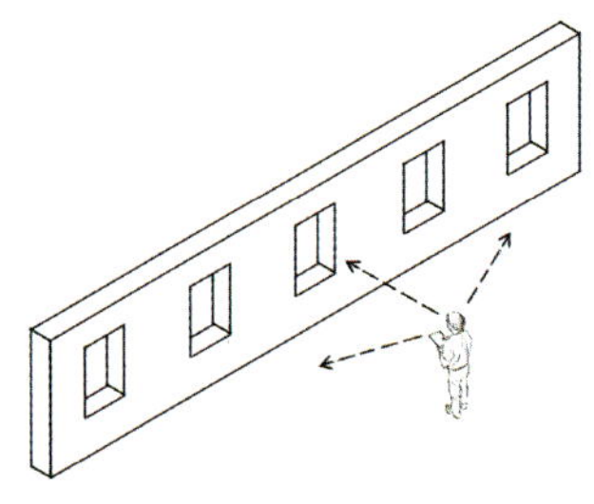

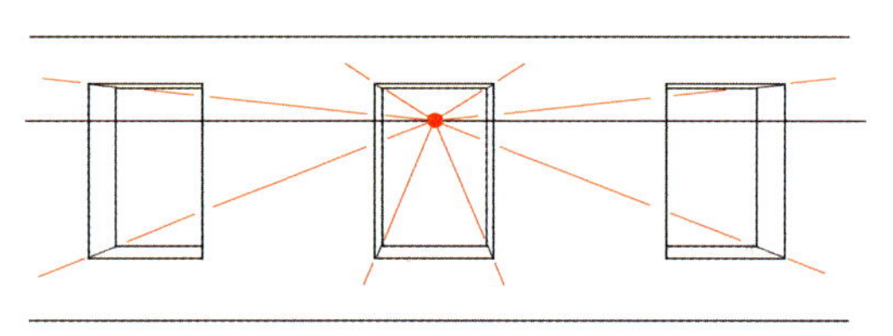

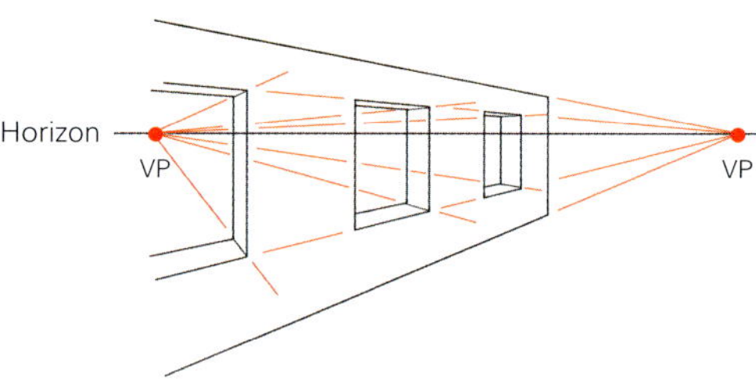

UNDERSTANDING WIDE VIEWPOINTS
If we were looking at the wall in the diagram above, the resulting drawing would depend on our line of sight and our field of view. Looking straight at the central opening with a limited field of view would give us a one-point perspective, like the centre image above.

Looking to the right end of the wall, again with a limited field of view, we'd see something more like the two-point perspective above right (and the same would be true if we were to look towards the left end). But if we were looking straight at the wall with a wide field of view – thus including

our peripheral vision – we'd see something like the drawing below, which combines the one-point perspective at the centre with the two-point views to the left and right. Curvilinear perspective reconciles the different angles of the horizontal lines by bending them across a wide field of vision.

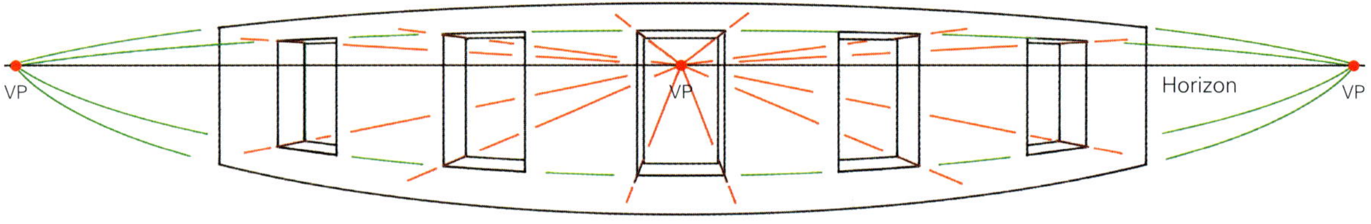

●	VP
red line	Converging lines
black line	Horizon line
green line	Curving lines of convergence

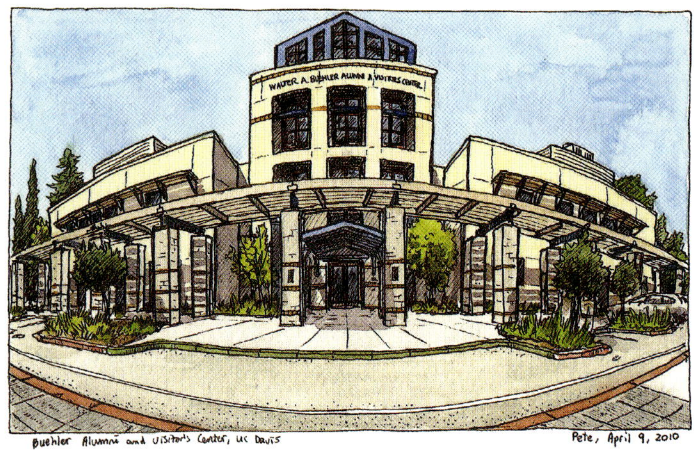

FISH-EYE VIEWS
The amount of curvature applied to the drawing doesn't need to be terribly precise, but the closer you are to the subject, the more dramatically the lines will appear to bend. A good example is this drawing by Pete Scully, which gives the sense of a fish-eye lens. If your line of sight is parallel to the ground, the horizon

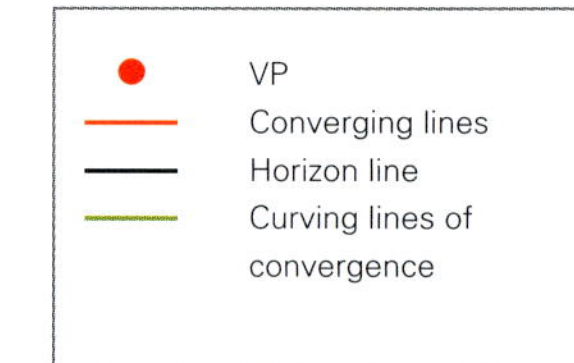

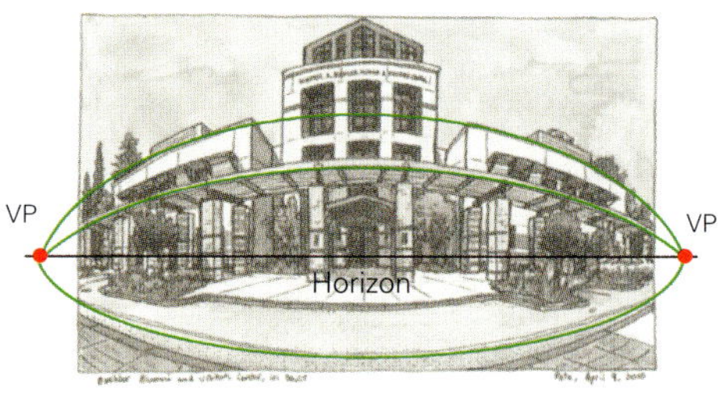

line will be flat, with curves rising above and falling below your eye level.

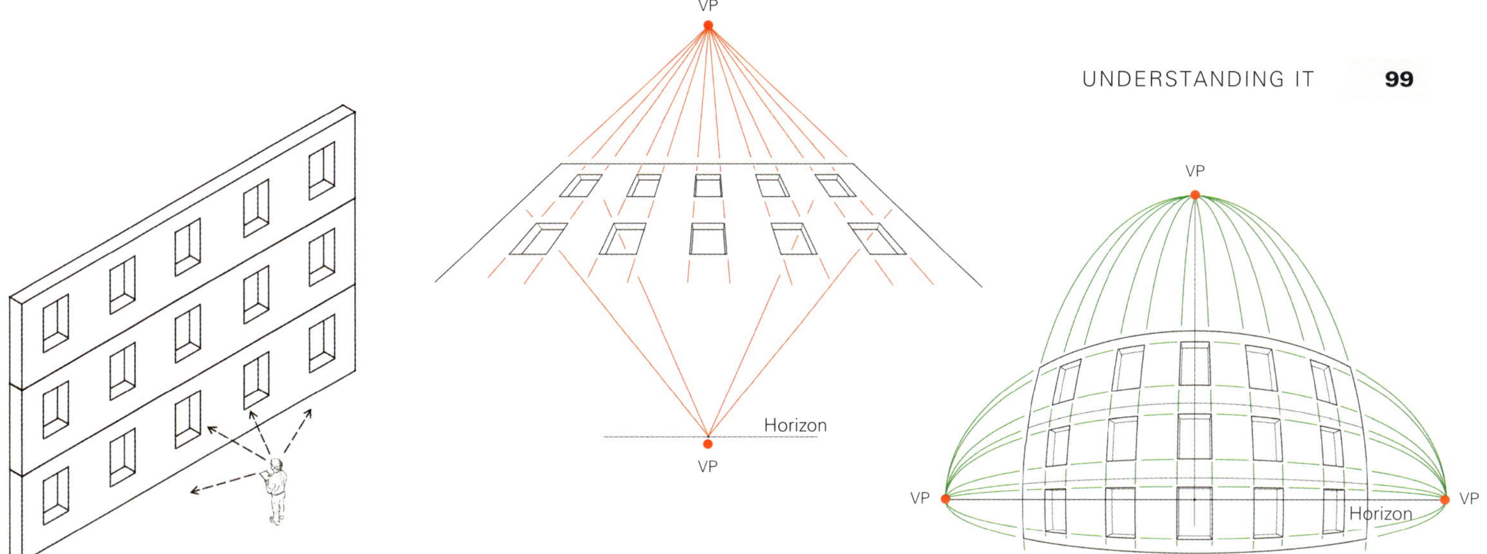

APPROACHING WIDE AND TALL SUBJECTS

If the subject in our view is also tall in addition to being wide, we'll need to approach the upper portion of the view as a three-point perspective, like the diagram above. To include the entire view, we'd effectively combine one-point (straight ahead), two-point (to the left and right) and three-point (above) into a single drawing, with curving lines connecting everything. Since the line of sight is still parallel to the ground, the horizon line remains horizontal in the drawing.

CURVING SKYWARD

In this drawing by Gérard Michel, the very tall towers of the cathedral are shown to converge on a point directly above the centre of the view. However, because the line of sight is directed upwards, the horizon line begins to curve, as shown in the diagram below.

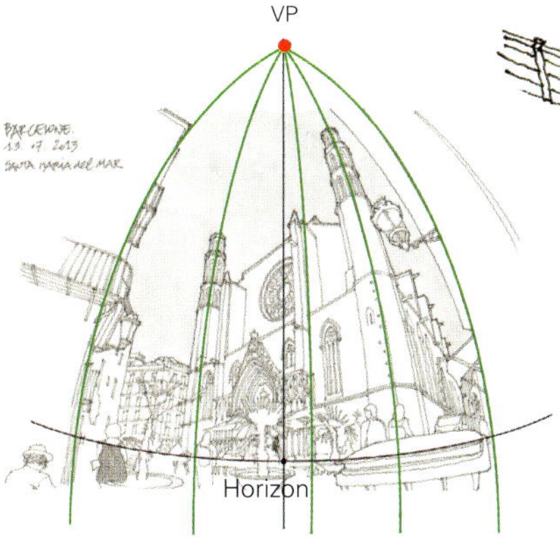

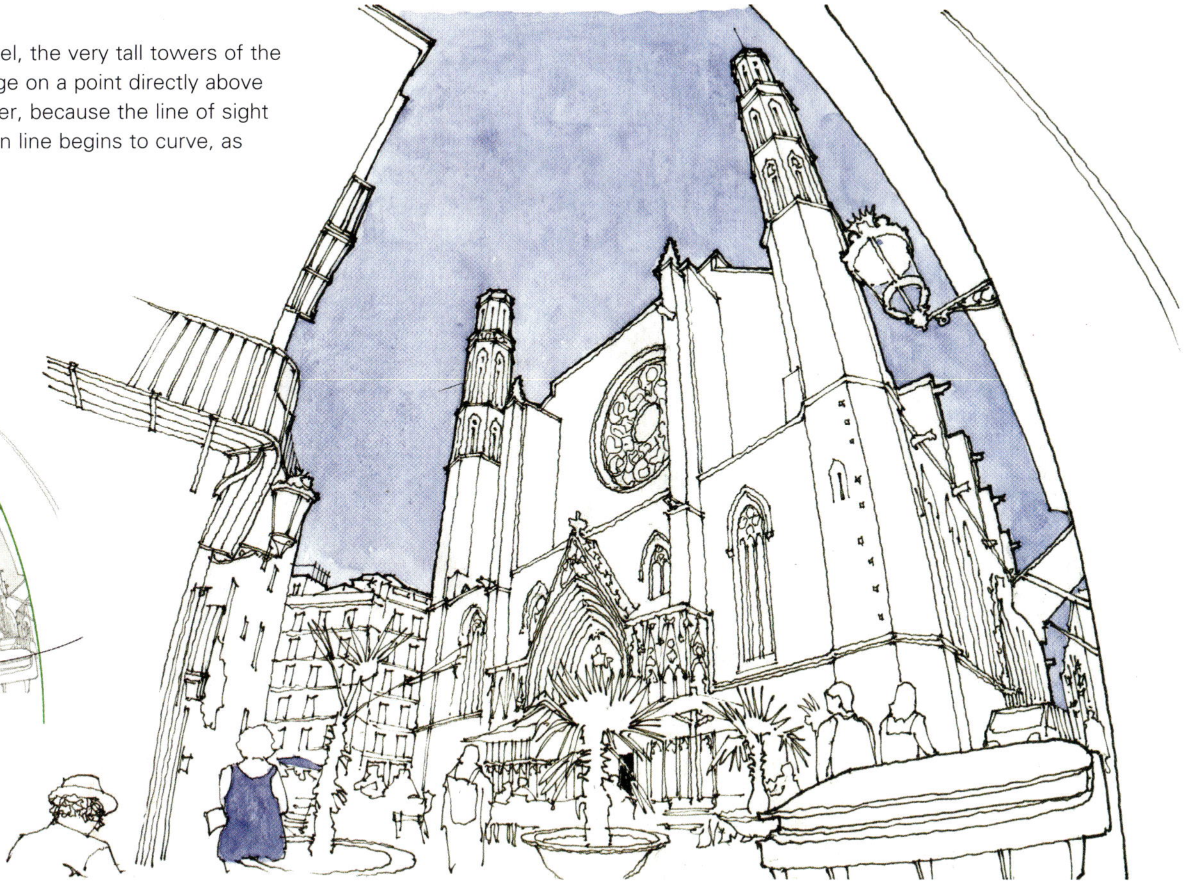

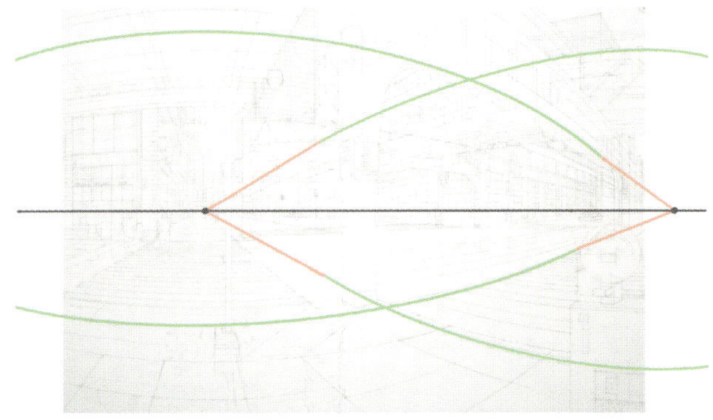

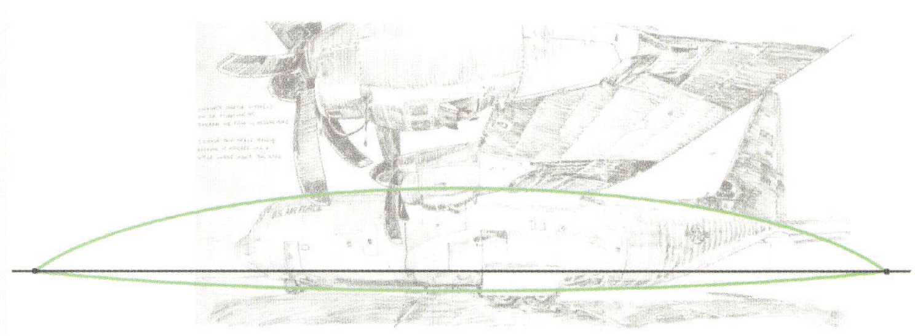

DRAWING THE VIEWER IN

In the set-up drawing for Nathan Walsh's *Chicago in the Rain* (129 x 183 cm [51 x 72 in]), we can see the underlying construction lines – most of them curving between two vanishing points – one out of view to the left and the other just barely out of view to the right. The third vanishing point, left of centre and at the end of the pavement, creates the primary focus of the composition. Notice how the lines radiating from this point only begin to curve as they move into the peripheral view, most evident at the right side of the image. Around the focal area, they remain straight – if we were to isolate this area we'd see a relatively simple one-point perspective. But by curving these lines as they move off to the right, Walsh creates a more complete understanding of the urban space.

ON THE WING

This drawing by Richard Johnson uses a very subtle amount of curvature to make clear the size of the aircraft. The engine, propeller and wing closest to our point of view are enormous compared to the fuselage, emphasising the distance, and the slight curvature of the fuselage reinforces this spatial dynamic. Notice how the nose and tail sections are in perspective, with their horizontals beginning to converge on points to the left and right, respectively. The centre of the plane appears to swell slightly, because it's closer to our point of view and therefore should appear to be larger than the nose and the tail. Even this small amount of curvature can have a significant effect.

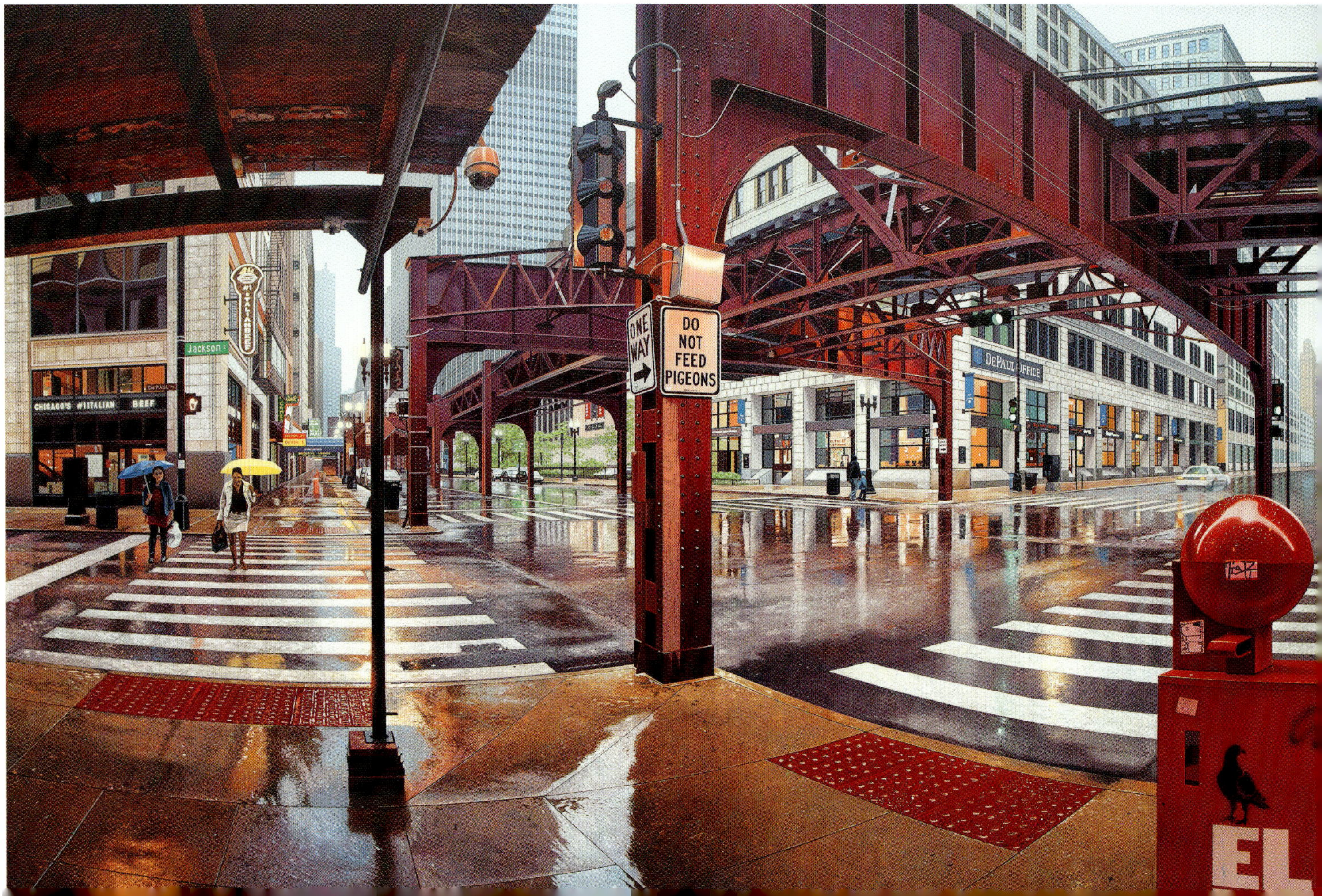

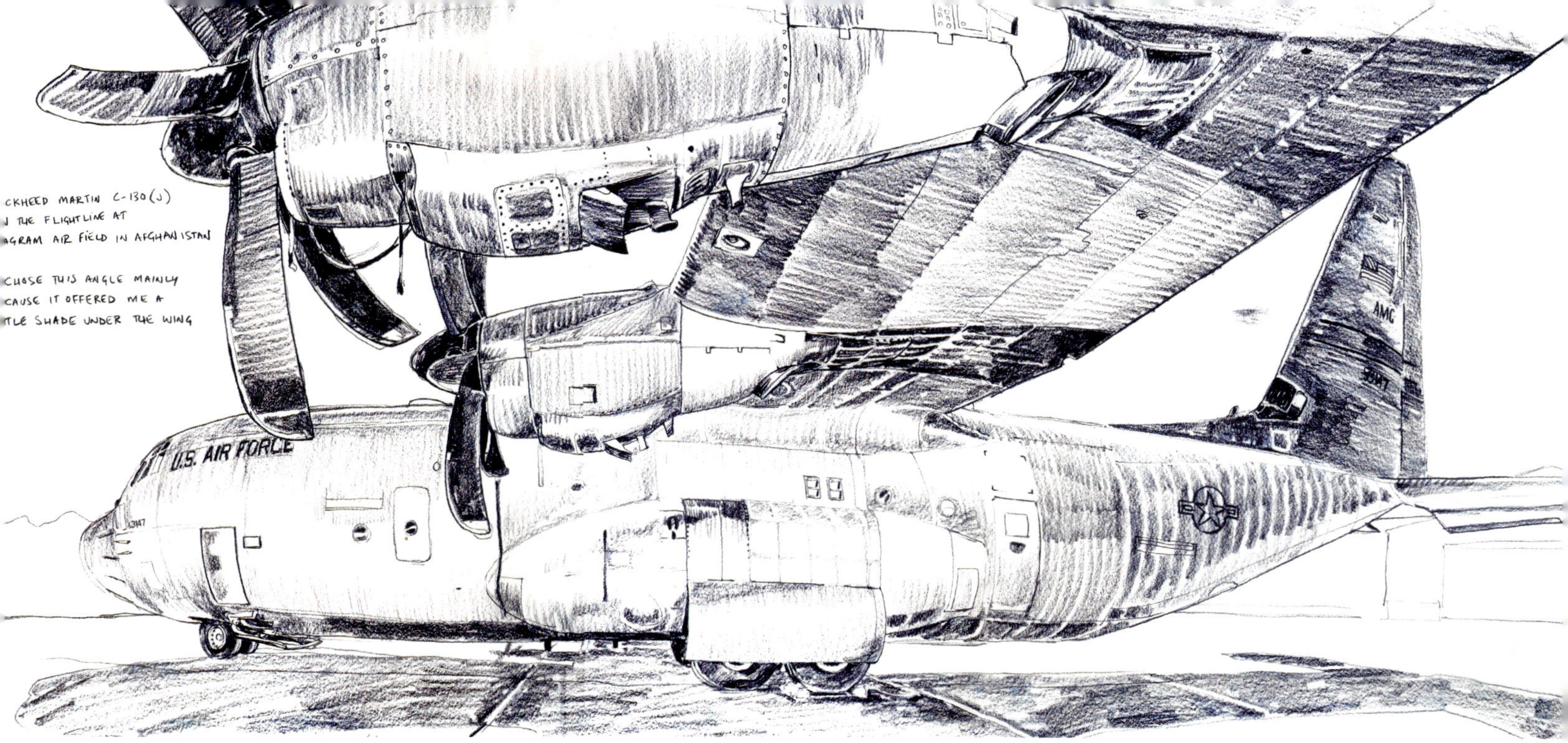

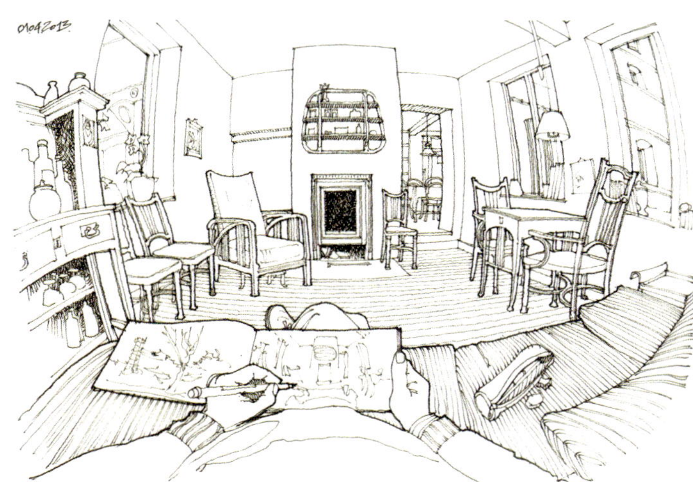

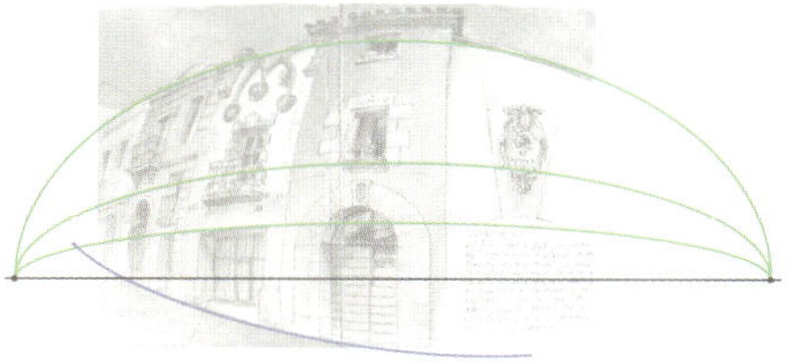

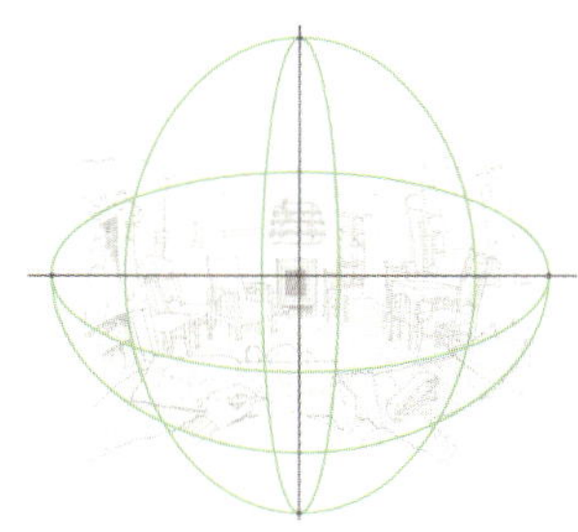

CURVED INTERIOR

This interior view by Gérard Michel is an excellent example of just how much you can see out of the corners of your eyes, and how curvilinear perspective can be used to give a sense of being inside a space rather than apart from it. There is very little distortion at the centre of the view – again, this is because the small field of view at the centre is essentially a one-point perspective. But as the field of view expands, the lines need to bend as the perspective changes and becomes increasingly distorted.

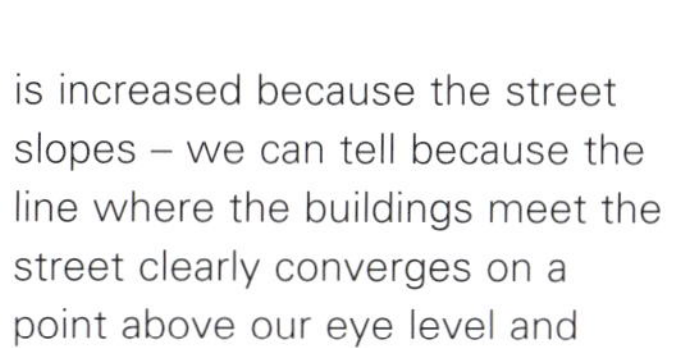

BULGING BUILDINGS

Curvilinear perspective can be used to emphasise portions of a view by bringing them much closer to the viewer. In this watercolour by Daniel Castro Alonso, the buildings at the centre of the image bulge outwards while the adjacent buildings diminish into the distance. In addition to the dramatically curved roofline, the sense of distortion here is increased because the street slopes – we can tell because the line where the buildings meet the street clearly converges on a point above our eye level and the horizon line.

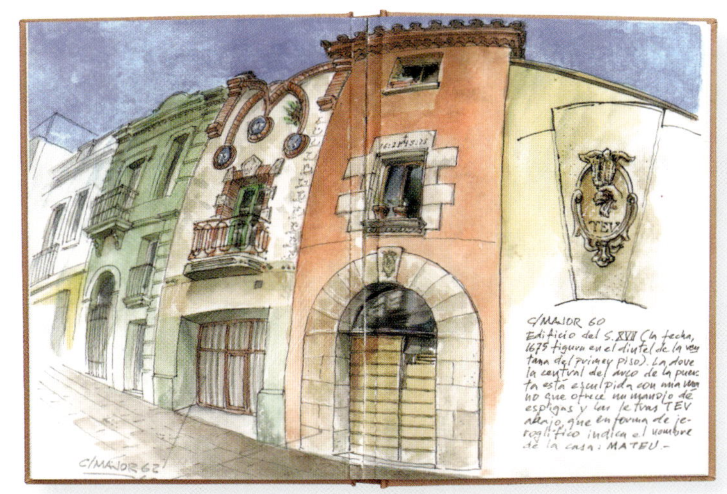

Applying it

Curvilinear perspective may be applied to a wide variety of subjects, from objects close at hand and tight interior spaces to much more expansive and dramatic wide-angle views.

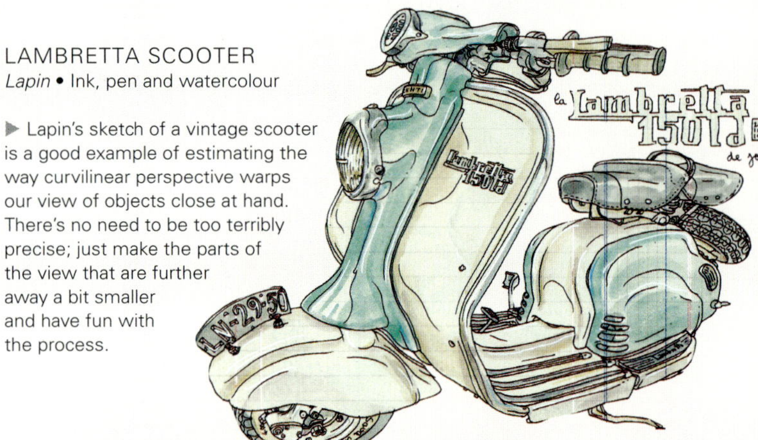

LAMBRETTA SCOOTER
Lapin • Ink, pen and watercolour

▶ Lapin's sketch of a vintage scooter is a good example of estimating the way curvilinear perspective warps our view of objects close at hand. There's no need to be too terribly precise; just make the parts of the view that are further away a bit smaller and have fun with the process.

URBAN SCENES

MATRIZ SQUARE, PARATY, BRAZIL
Matthew Brehm • Fountain pen

▼ I made this fountain pen drawing during a workshop on curvilinear perspective that was taught by Paul Heaston in Brazil. One of Paul's tips was to draw your sketchbook as part of the view – this will help force you to include much more of your peripheral vision than you ordinarily would. Also, don't be afraid to really warp the curving lines as you attempt to capture as much visual information as possible.

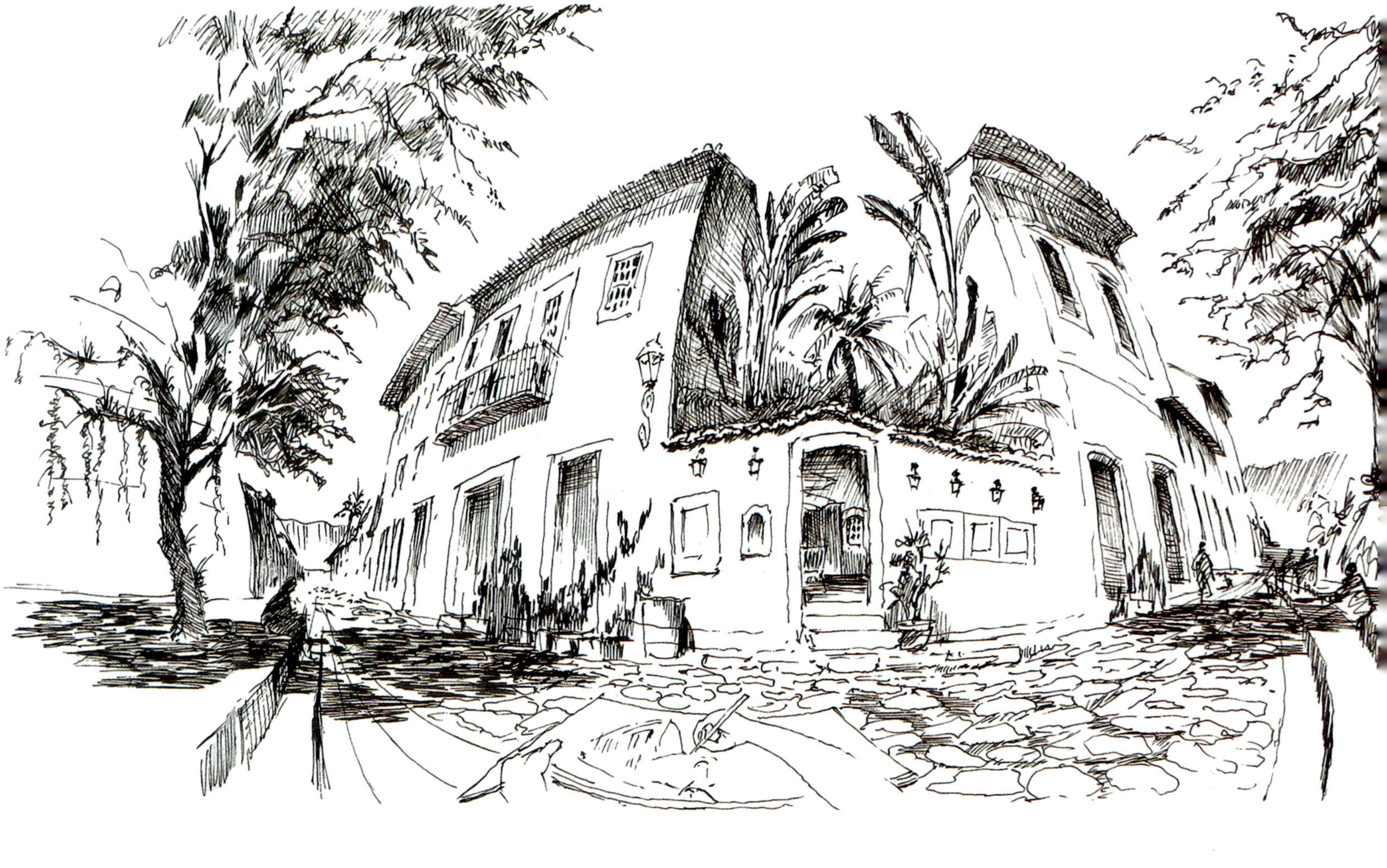

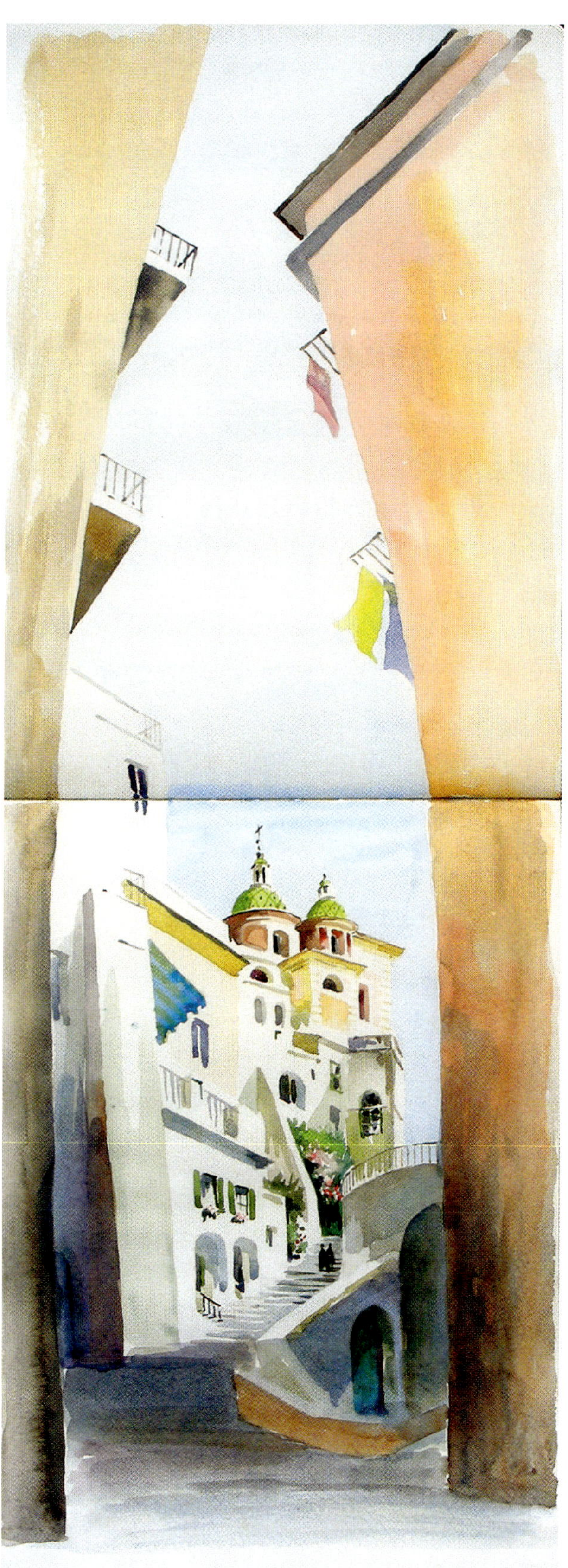

◀ CHURCH IN ATRANI
Matthew Brehm
Watercolour

In this Italian coastal town, I sketched the major church, Santa Maria Maddelena, trying to include the dramatic way it fits into its surroundings. The church and its characteristic tiled dome rise overhead and suddenly appear as you round the corner between two extraordinarily tall buildings. Curvilinear perspective allowed me to stress the close proximity and the height of these edges and to capture this sense of space in the view. Because my line of sight was aimed slightly upwards, and not level with the ground, I also brought the bottoms of the corners in a bit towards the bottom of the drawing, if only as an experiment.

▶ VIA DEL'ARCO DI SAN CALLISTO
Matthew Brehm
Watercolour

In this watercolour I tried to emphasise the great height of these buildings in Rome, and how close they are to one another. Without using curvilinear perspective – if all the verticals in this image were drawn as being truly vertical – I might have given the impression that my viewpoint was quite distant from the subject. Again, the curving lines were not precisely calculated for the drawing – I really just took some guesses after trying to sight the angles of the tops of the buildings above and connecting them through gently curving lines to meet the roughly vertical edges of the buildings as they met the ground. Because I was standing under the roof eaves at upper left, it did appear that the eave sloped up, slightly towards the right.

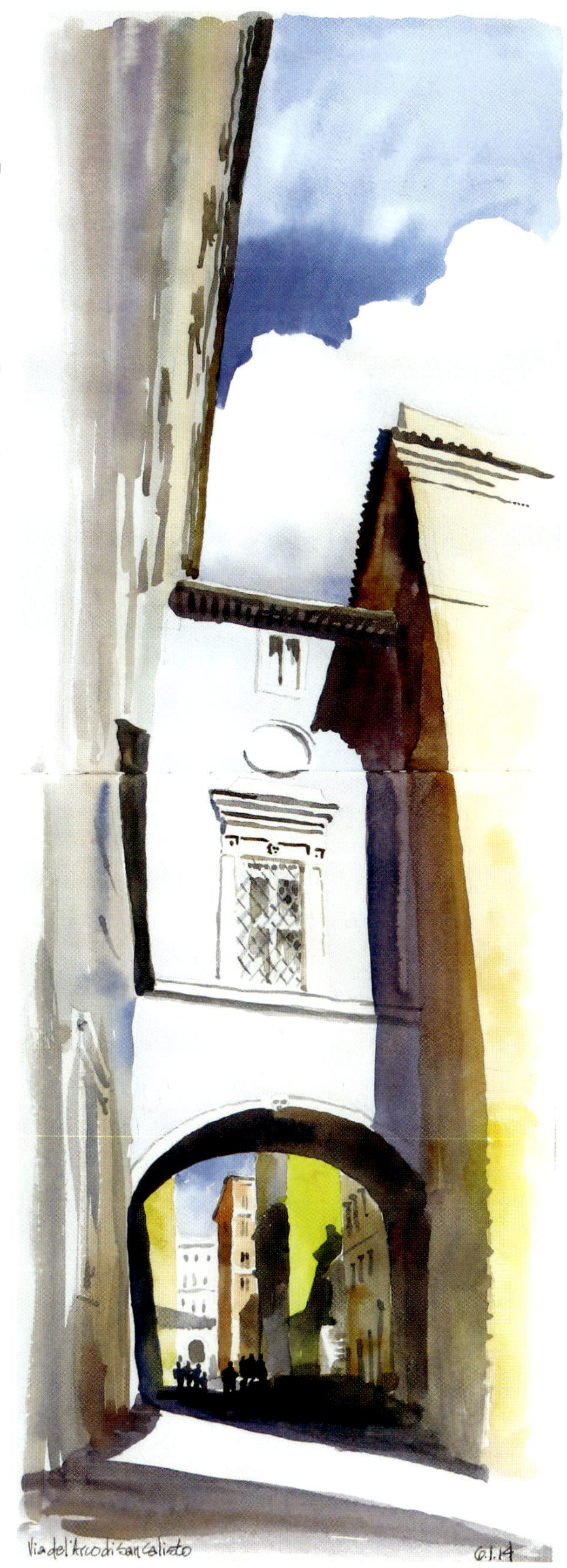

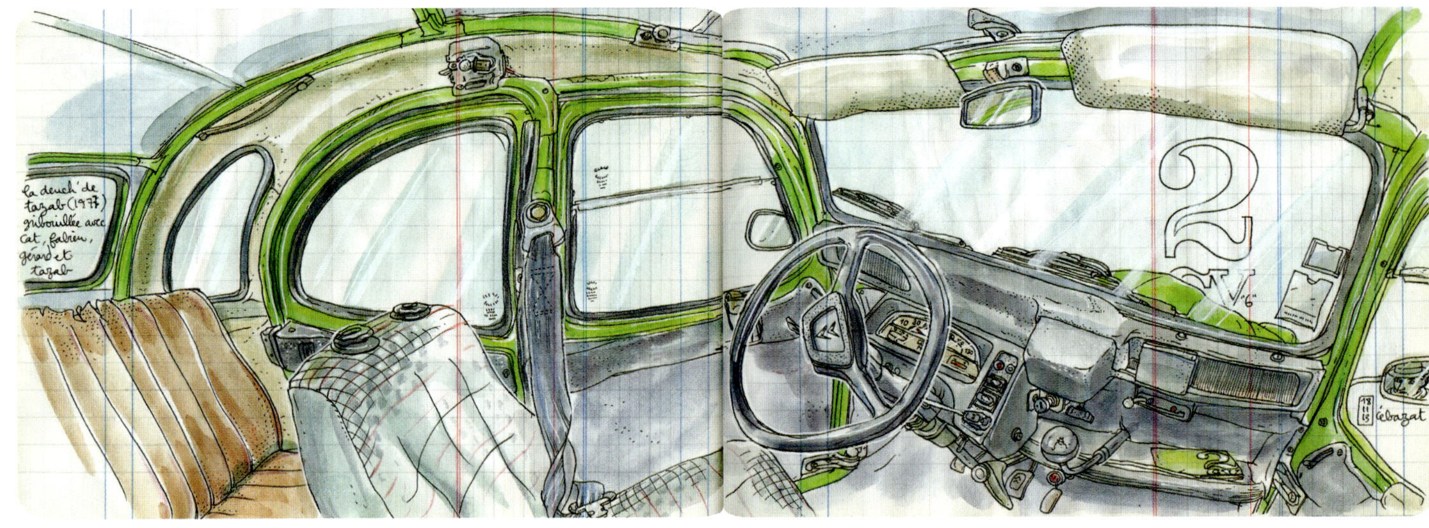

▲ DEUX CHEVAUX-VAPEUR
Lapin • Watercolour

▶ ROLLS ROYCE
Gérard Michel • Watercolour

▼ AIR TIME
Maarten Ruijters • Watercolour

Curvilinear perspective is often the only way to depict small, enclosed spaces, and is commonly applied in drawings of aeroplane and car interiors. In order to represent the edges of our peripheral vision, the drawing must be warped and distorted – taking a wide-angle view of three-dimensional space and translating it on to the two-dimensional surface of the page. So curvilinear perspective is most typically applied to views that stretch out left and right, like the aeroplane sketch by Maarten Ruijters (below).

Another way to think about drawing views of tight interior spaces is to lay them out, as though they've been cracked open, like this car interior by Lapin (above). Again, it's not so important to be precise; it's more the challenge of including as much as possible from everything you can see around you while trying to look straight ahead.

Gérard Michel has taken a more structured approach with the set-up of his drawing of a vintage Rolls-Royce (right). It can be extremely helpful to do small thumbnail sketches first, as he's done here, to figure out the underlying nature of the view, and how the lines would curve towards their vanishing points.

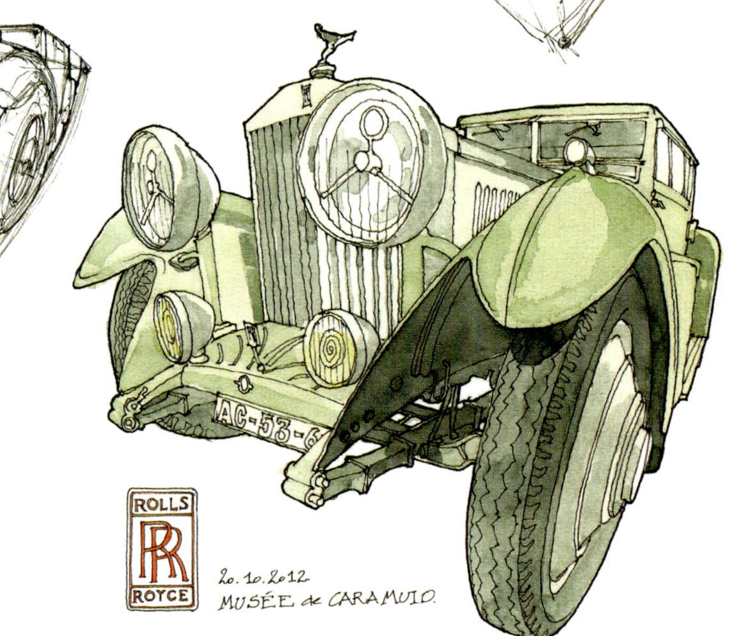

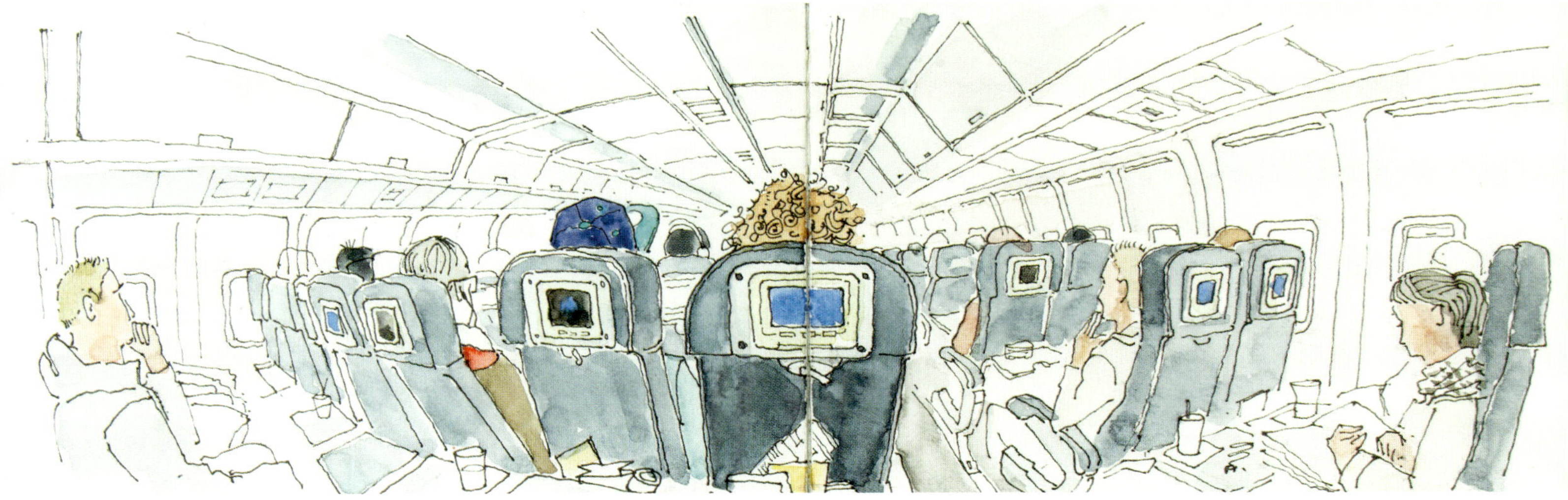

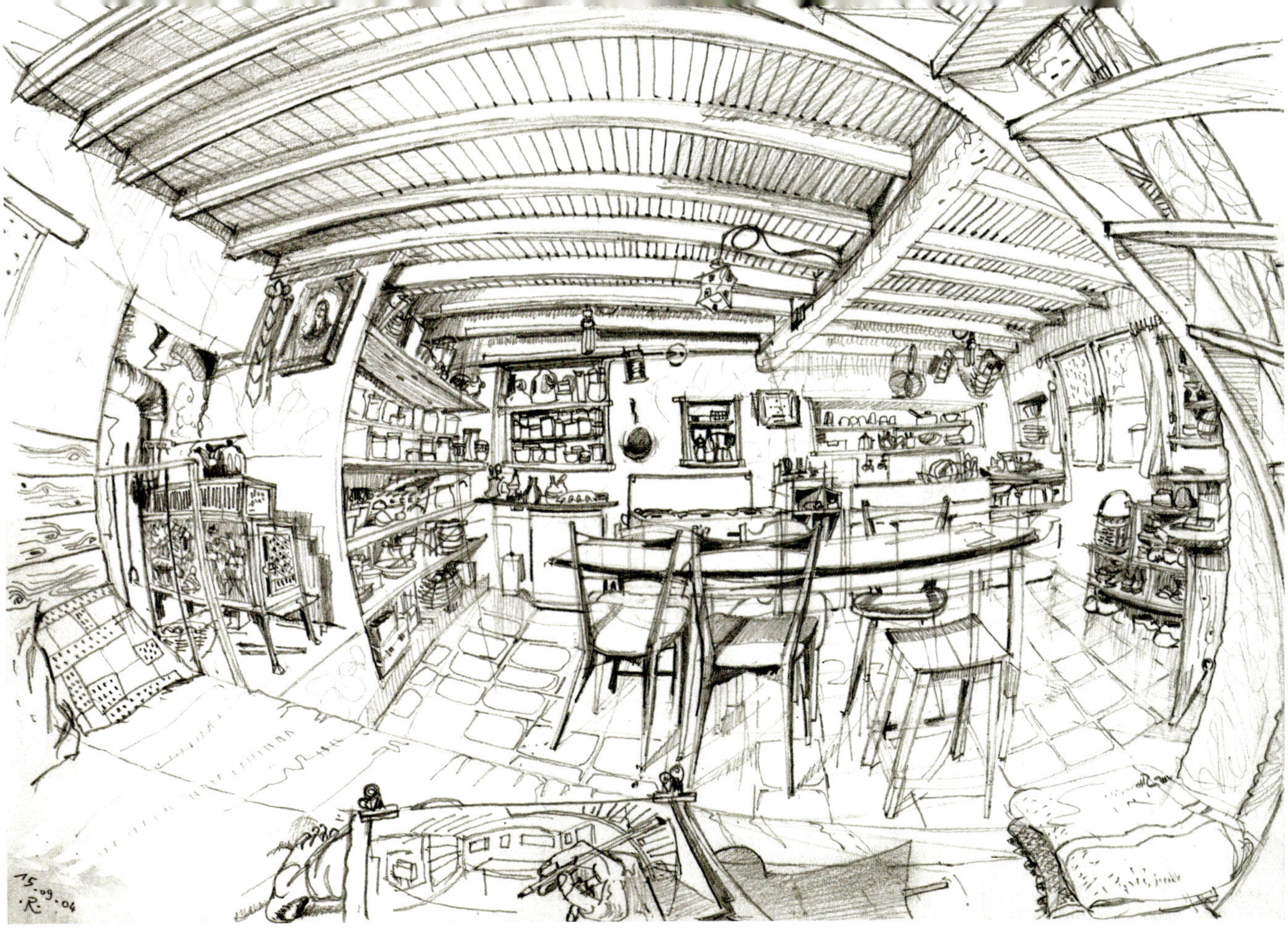

▲ **MOUNTAIN HOUSE**
A. Rmyth • Pencil

In A. Rmyth's wonderful sketch, we get the sense of concentric circles or ellipses that define the underlying structure of the view. It's almost essential to begin a drawing like this with a good amount of set-up lines – sketch them in lightly with a relatively hard graphite before adding ink or colour. If the overall structure of the view is carefully constructed, as it certainly is here, it will be much easier to add the multitude of smaller detail elements.

▶ **MARKET SCENE**
Luis Ruiz • Watercolour

Both the horizontal and vertical dimensions of this view are included, which helps to emphasise both the architectural character of the space and the lively, populous atmosphere of the market it contains. Only a bit of curve is needed to indicate the broader perspective.

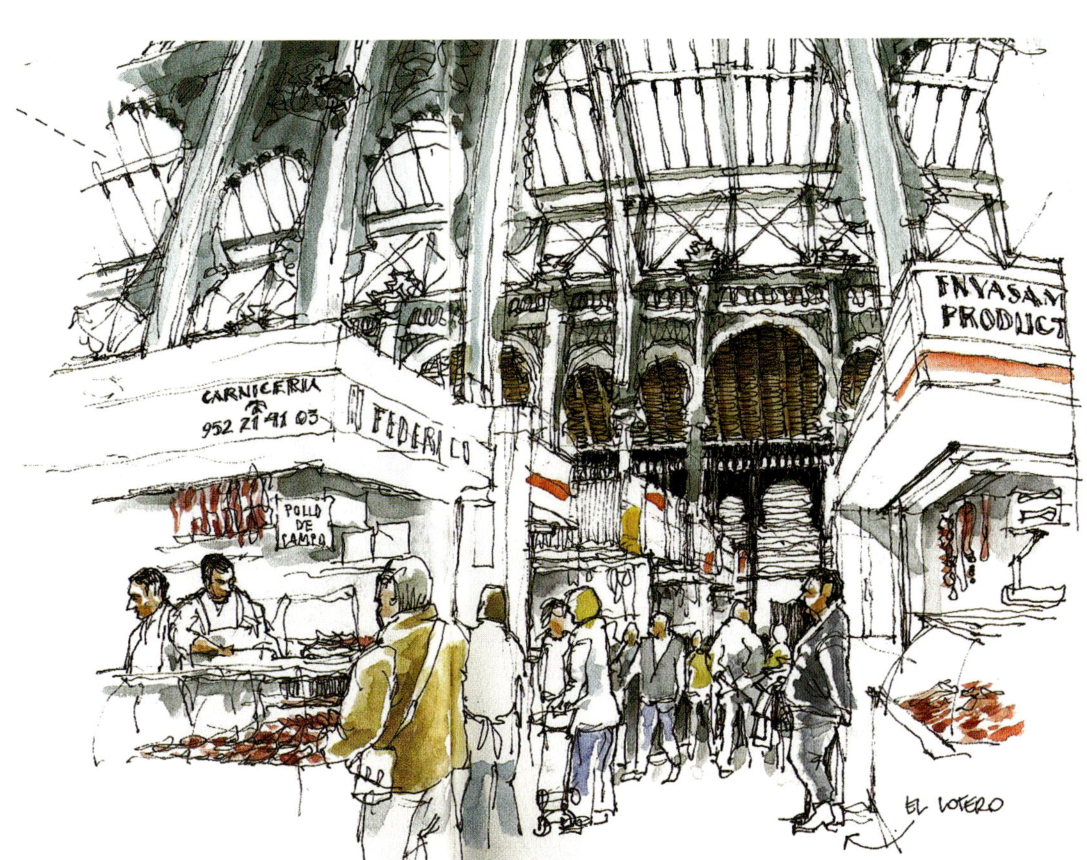

How-to sequence

Nathan Walsh wanted his work to wrap around the viewer, presenting an immersive space they felt they could enter into. The challenge here was to construct a drawing of the cable car station looking out towards the Queensborough Bridge in New York, which flowed easily from one space to another without an awkward or disjointed transition.

▶ The drawing combines interior and exterior spaces as well as a very wide angle of view. To connect these spaces together in a coherent way I used a form of curvilinear perspective which bends both horizontal and vertical lines. Working in this way suggests not just a view in front of the spectator but a space which exists around them. As they look up into the station roof vertical lines begin to converge subtly inwards towards a zenith point; conversely as they look down they begin to arc towards the nadir.

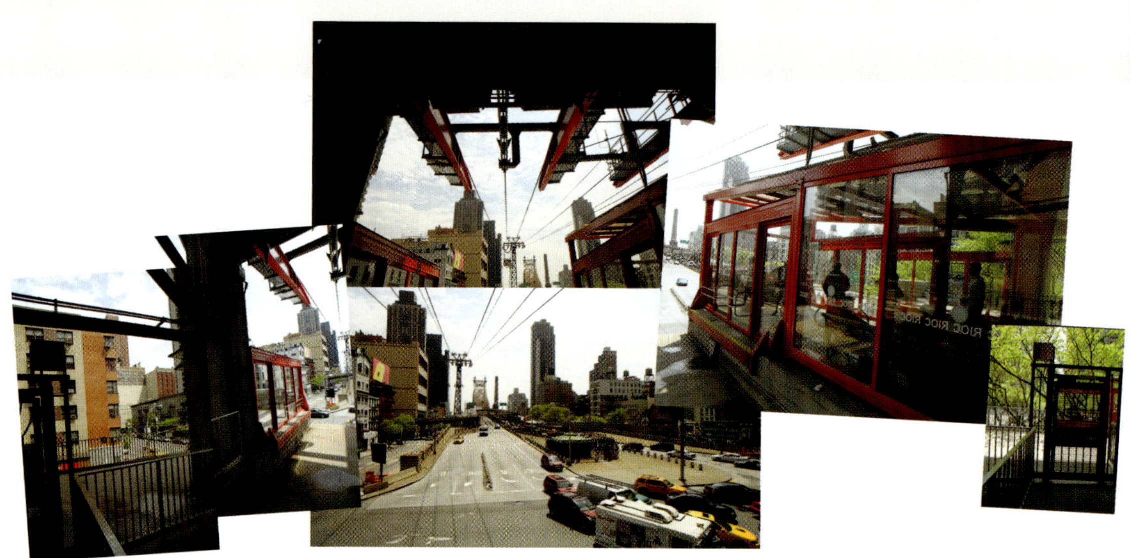

STEP 1 ▶ GRID

To begin with I decide on the general height and width of my drawing then place a perspectival grid over the top using Mark McKay's plug-in for Adobe Photoshop. This helps to generate a series of guidelines suggesting how much I want the vertical lines of the scene to bend towards their respective zenith and nadir vanishing points. I then draw in a prospective horizon line which runs across the full sheet of paper, not just the size of the image.

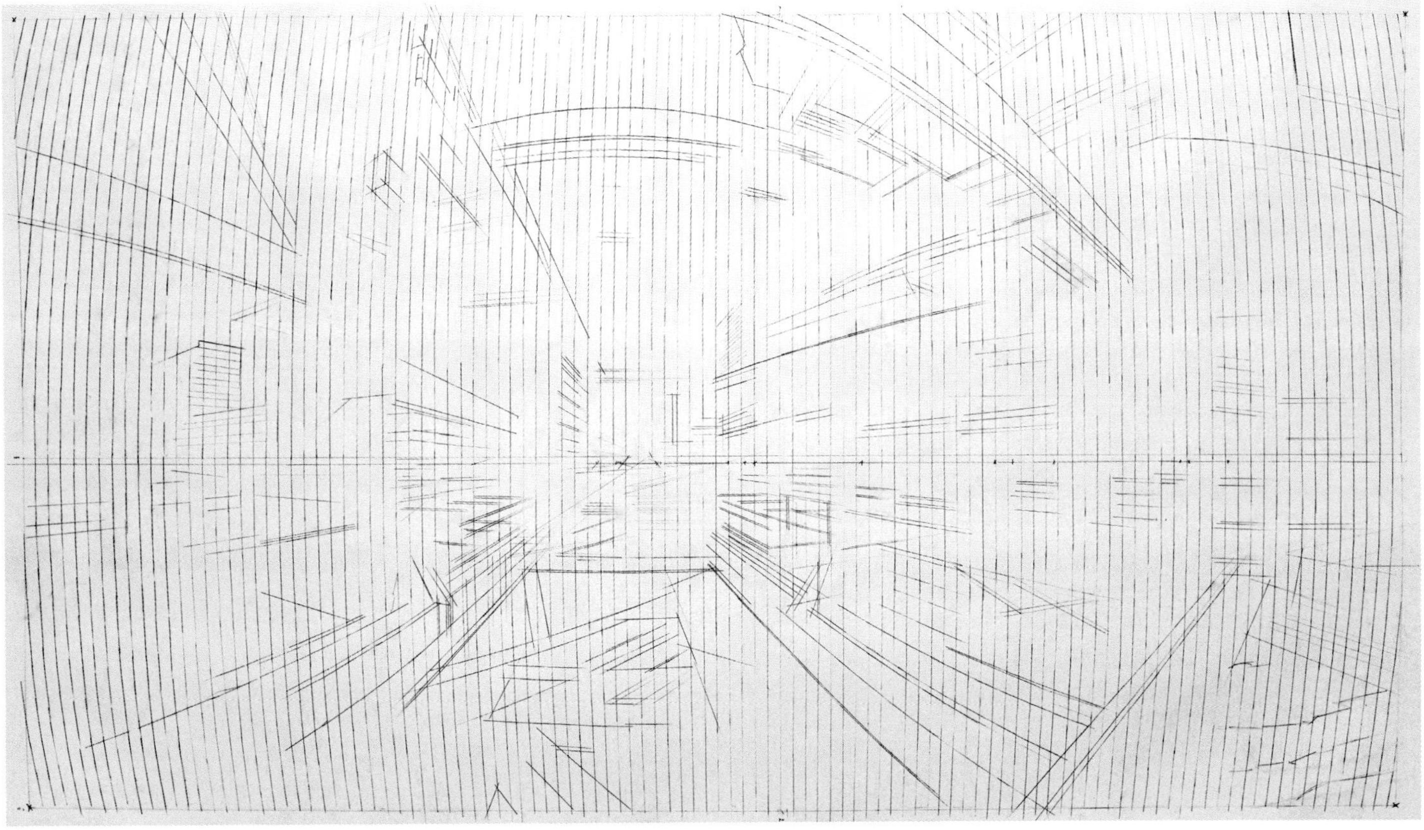

STEP 2 ▲ SIMPLE SHAPES
At this stage I will lightly begin to place objects in the scene, with each pictorial element – whether it be building, gate or tree – having its own separate vanishing point placed along the horizon line. Nothing is fixed at this time, all the information can be moved around and the height and position of elements are subject to considerable change. Initially I keep the drawing to a series of large, simple shapes and try to assess how they relate to each other and the composition as a whole. Working from the general to the specific allows me to not get too concerned with areas of complexity and detail too early on in the process.

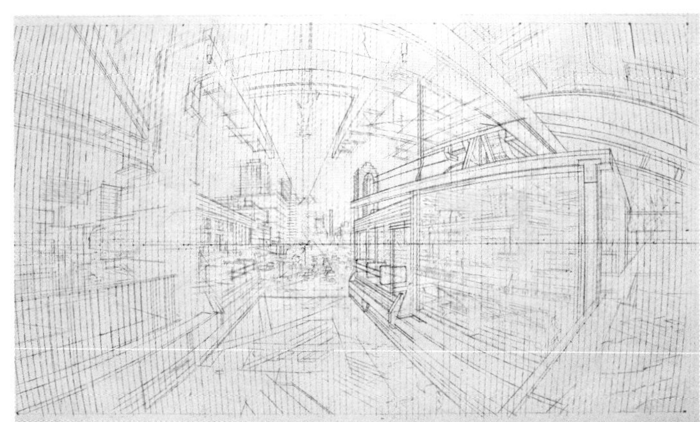

DRAWING METHODOLOGY
The drawing was made on large sheet of smooth Fabriano paper pinned to my studio wall. I work with HB pencils and a box of soft putty erasers. This allows me to move pictorial elements around and make changes quickly. This process of revision and change leads to a position where the work hangs together as a dynamic yet readable scene.

STEP 3 ▲ SPATIAL RECESSION
As my confidence in the drawing grows these simple shapes become more fixed in their relative positions and subdivided into smaller and smaller elements. Using simple mathematical ratios allows me to suggest the spatial recession of objects from the foreground to the background. As long as the information remains convincing I'm happy to make compositional changes which alter the reality of the location but offer an alternative view which obeys my own logic.

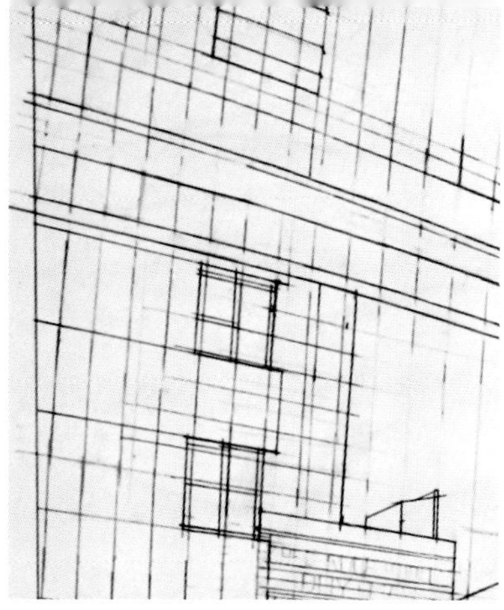

◀ The curved nature of the space reaches an extreme on the right-hand side of the station's ceiling. Looking at areas like this in isolation the information can look distorted and unconvincing. Remember, perspective is only a strategy to be explored; an exciting overall pictorial space is more important than strict adherence to a technique.

▶ Instead of using one straight orthogonal to describe the side of the cable car station, I split the shape into different sections, each connected to a separate vanishing point along the horizon line. This produces a series of subtle arcs made from short straight lines connected together.

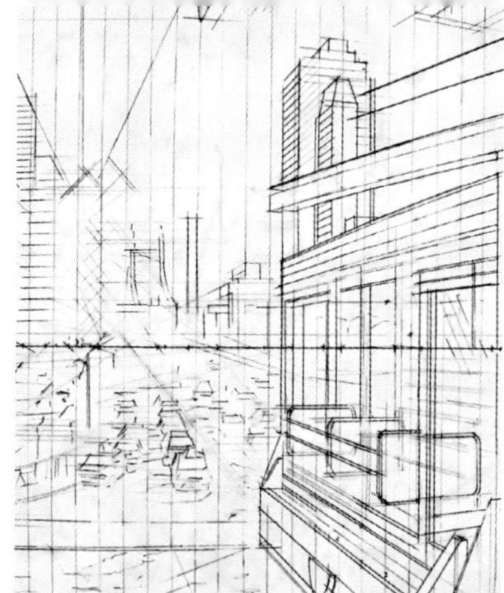

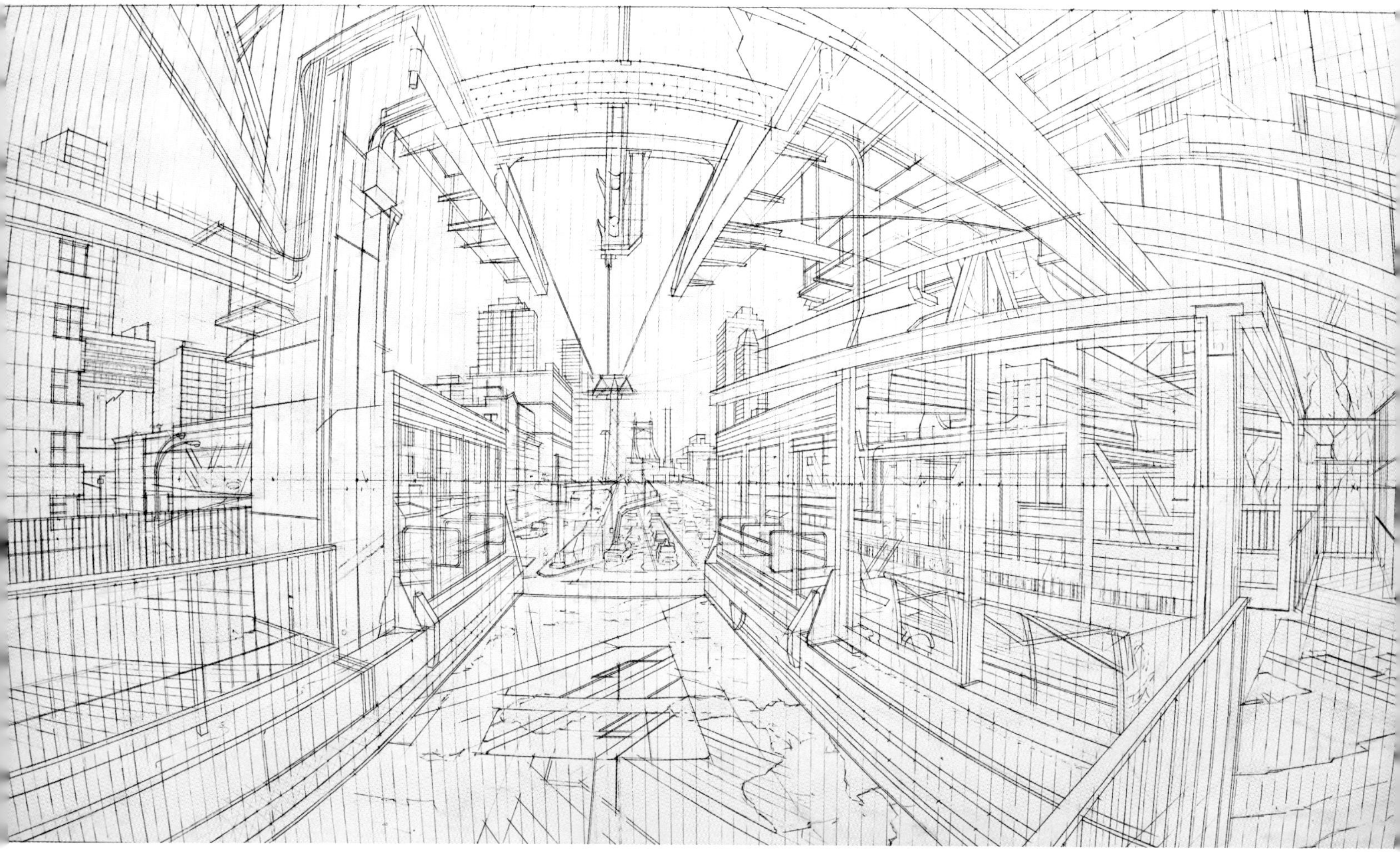

▲ COMPLETED DRAWING

At this point the drawing has been revised numerous times, as each visual element becomes more definite and fixed within the full composition. This leaves a history of markings, calculations and rubbings out, which, while of some interest to a viewer, can lead to some ambiguity of form. I therefore try not to overwork the drawing by adding extra bits of information or detail that are unlikely to add anything to the overall effect.

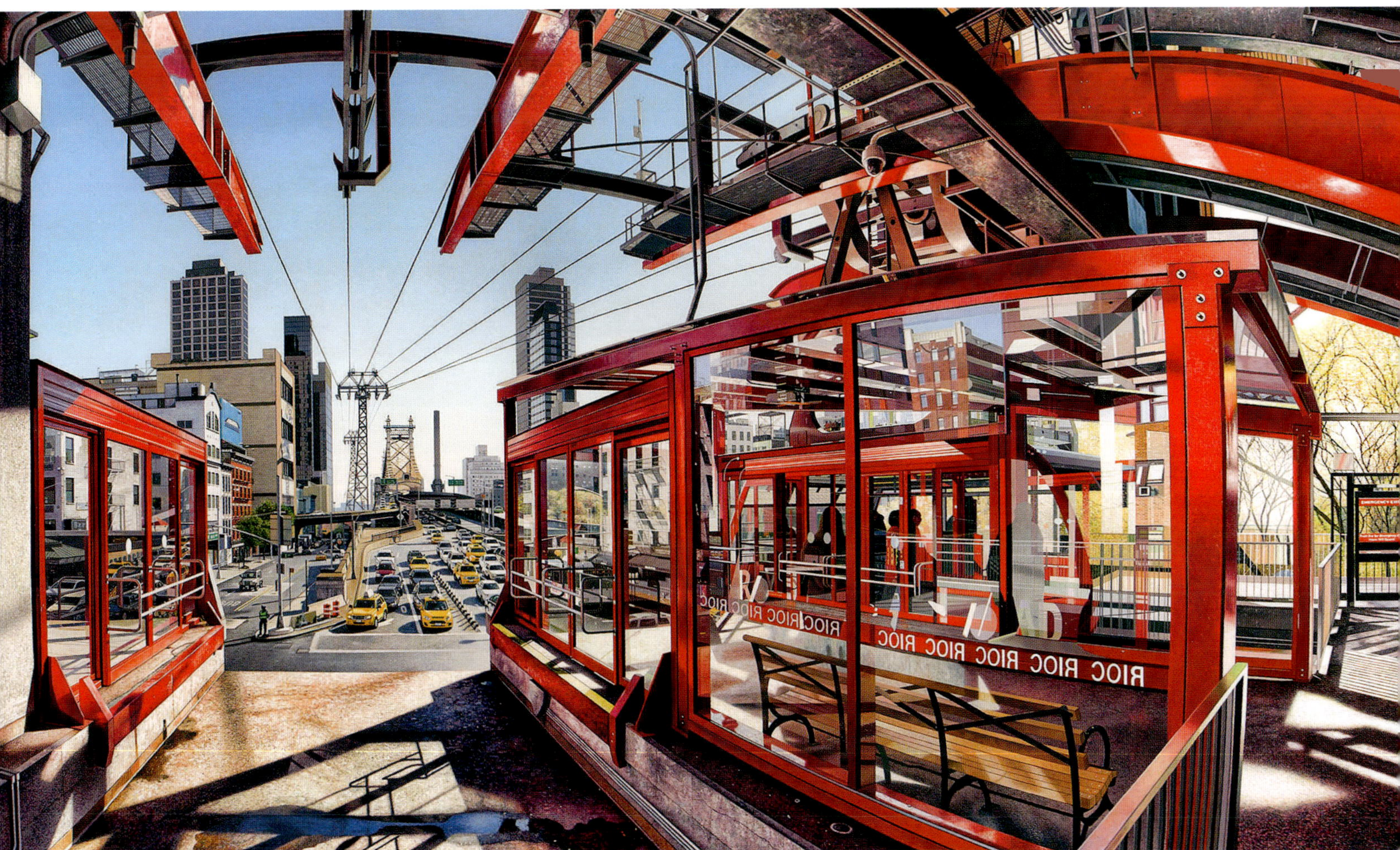

▲ FINISHED PAINTING

Layers of oil paint are built up over a number of months, thinly at first leading to more heavily textured and dense areas. Significant attention is paid to aerial perspective with colour, tone and edges being manipulated in order to create the illusion of depth. I will often mix small amounts of complementary colour into a colour mix to make it duller and push it back visually. Conversely I will also place small amounts of complementary colour against another colour to provide strong visual contrast. As the work progresses, I maintain a need to be flexible with the original structure. If the work suggests improvement through revision and change, then I remain open to the idea.

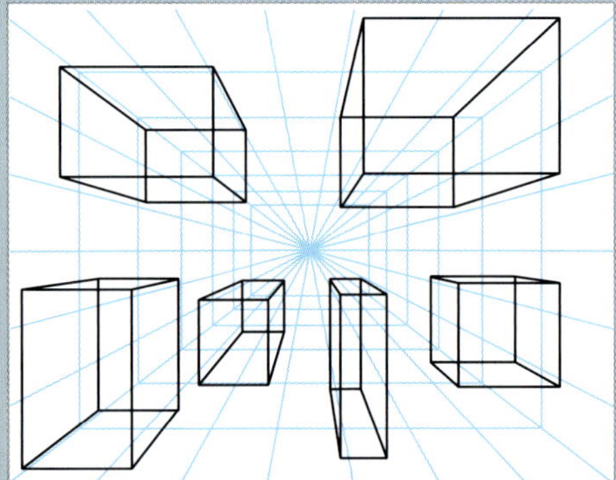

SIMPLE BOXES: demonstrate how shapes work in the space for each type of perspective.

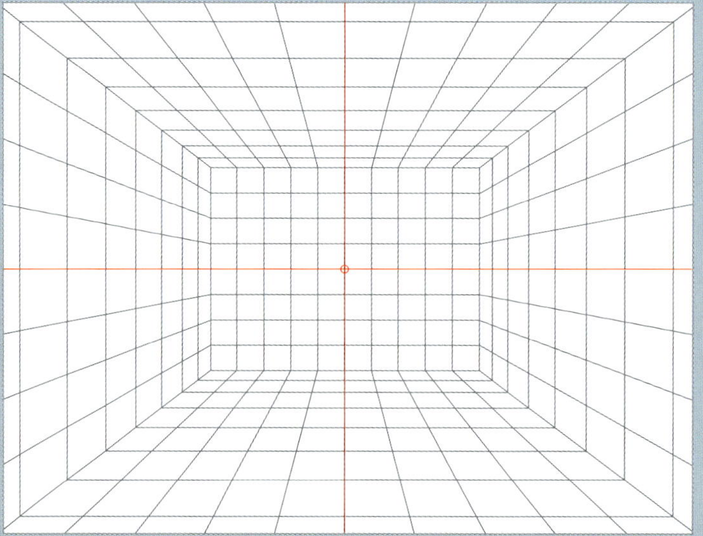

EXERCISE 1: These simple box shapes will give you an idea of how objects placed at different heights and distances from the vanishing points will appear. Using them as a guide, photocopy the blank grid and draw in your own scene.

WORKBOOK

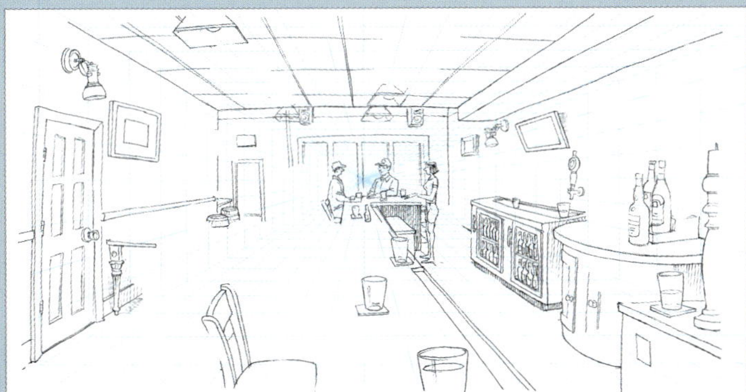

EXERCISE 2: Partial scenes are drawn inside the perspective grids and are designed for you to complete according to the list of missing objects. You can add the missing elements as you would imagine them to appear in the particular perspective type, but don't worry if they don't exactly match the completed scene. You can draw directly into the book, or photocopy the page and work on that instead.

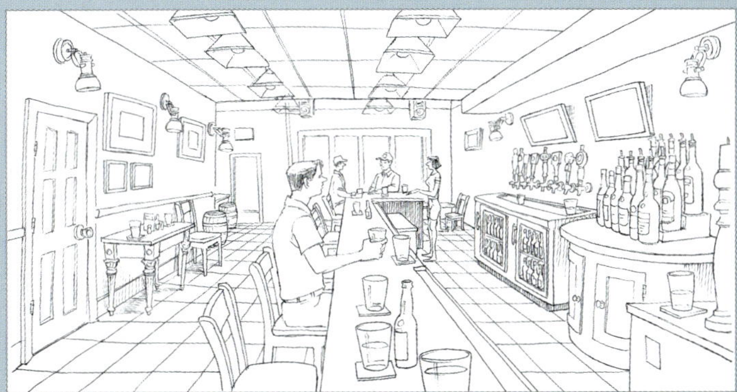

COMPLETED DRAWINGS: The finished scenes are in the back of the book (pages 138–140). However, try not to consult them until you finish each sketch, because your own interpretations are just as important as the 'right' answers.

This workbook section will help you to apply the principles of perspective using the exercises outlined above. These consist of established grids, simple box samples and partially finished drawings which apply the principles of all the types of perspective found in the book.

On pages 116, 119, 130 and 133 you'll find even bigger perspective chambers and grids that will allow you to plot really wide scenes.

Artwork Thomas Thorspecken
Grids John Woodcock

One-point perspective

Almost all sketches will include at least one vanishing point. Most of my sketches start by finding lines in the ceiling or floor that hint at the location of that vanishing point. If you are outside, that vanishing point might be on the horizon at the end of a road or rail tracks. If you are in a room, try and imagine that all the walls are mirrored. The vanishing point would be where you would see your own face in a reflection. Since few rooms have mirrored walls, guess how high your eyes are from the floor, and look straight ahead at a wall – that is where the vanishing point is.

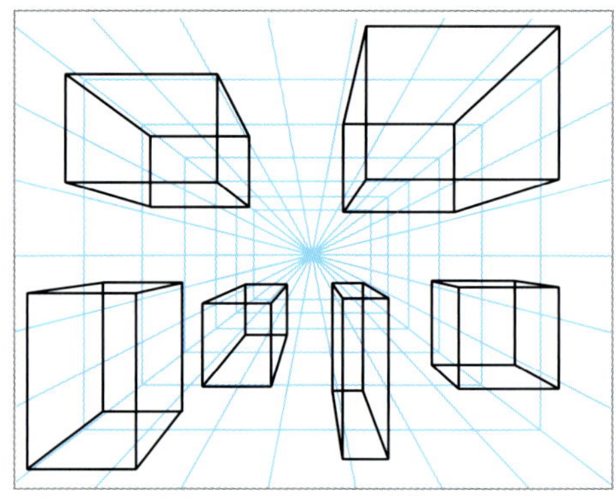

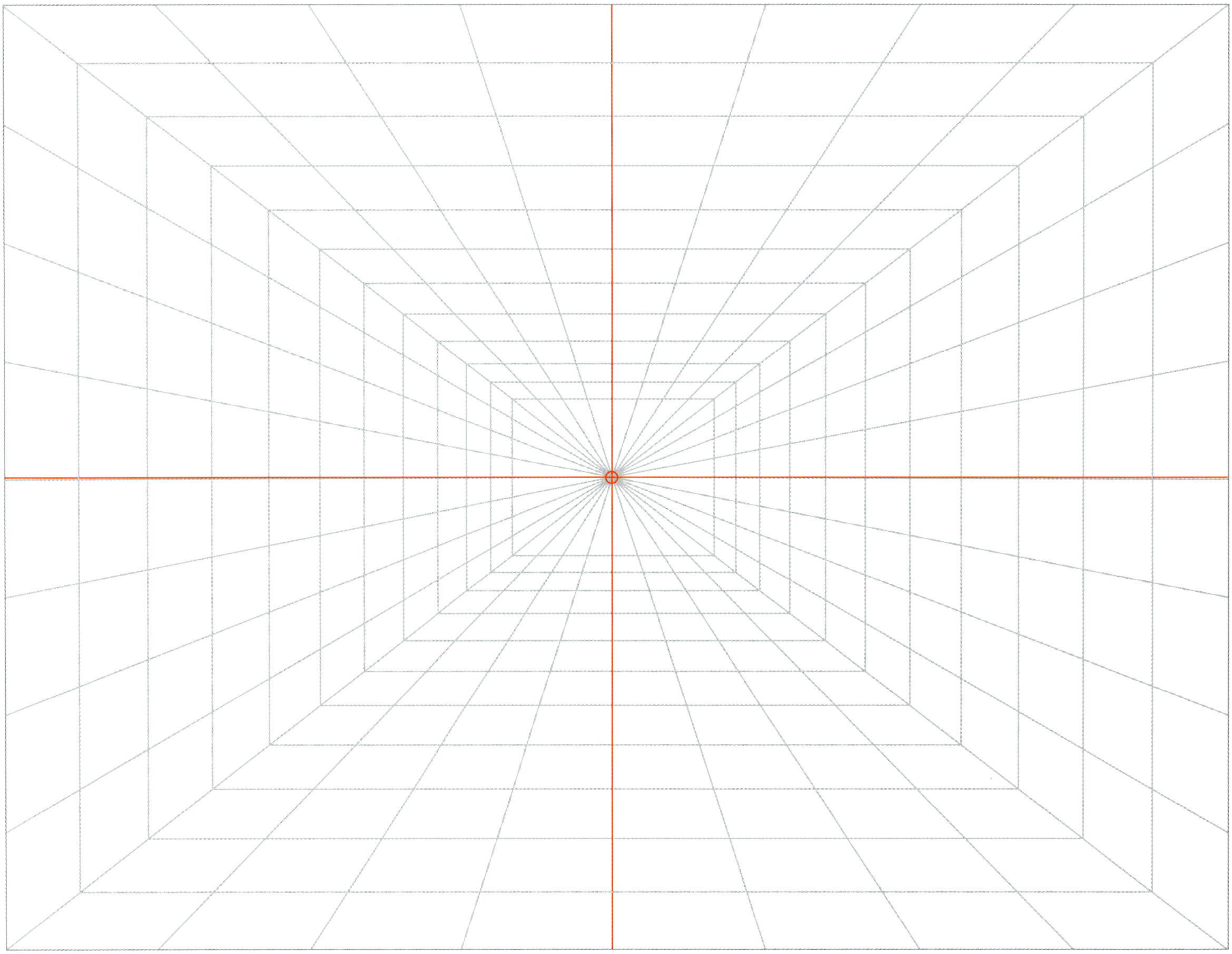

It is seldom a good idea to put the vanishing point directly in the centre of a composition. If you are seated it would be lower and if you are standing it would be higher. Using the box shapes as a guide, photocopy the grid below and draw in a scene; you could try an interior with furniture, windows and doors.

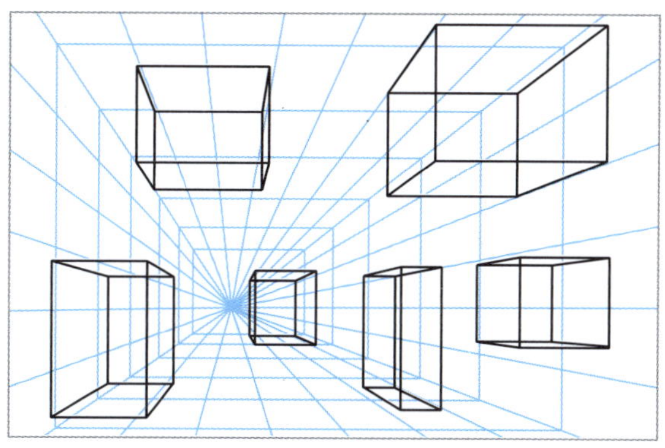

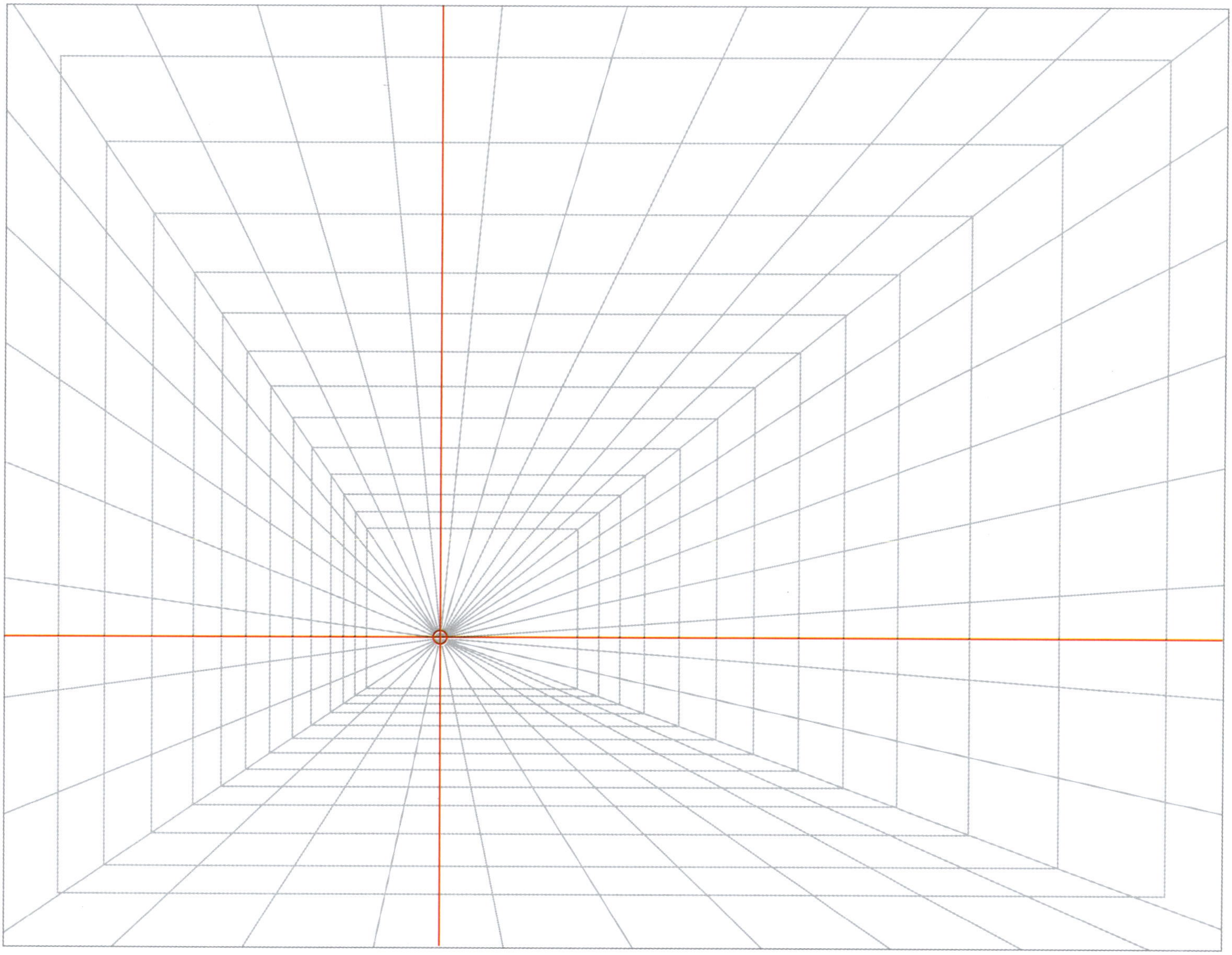

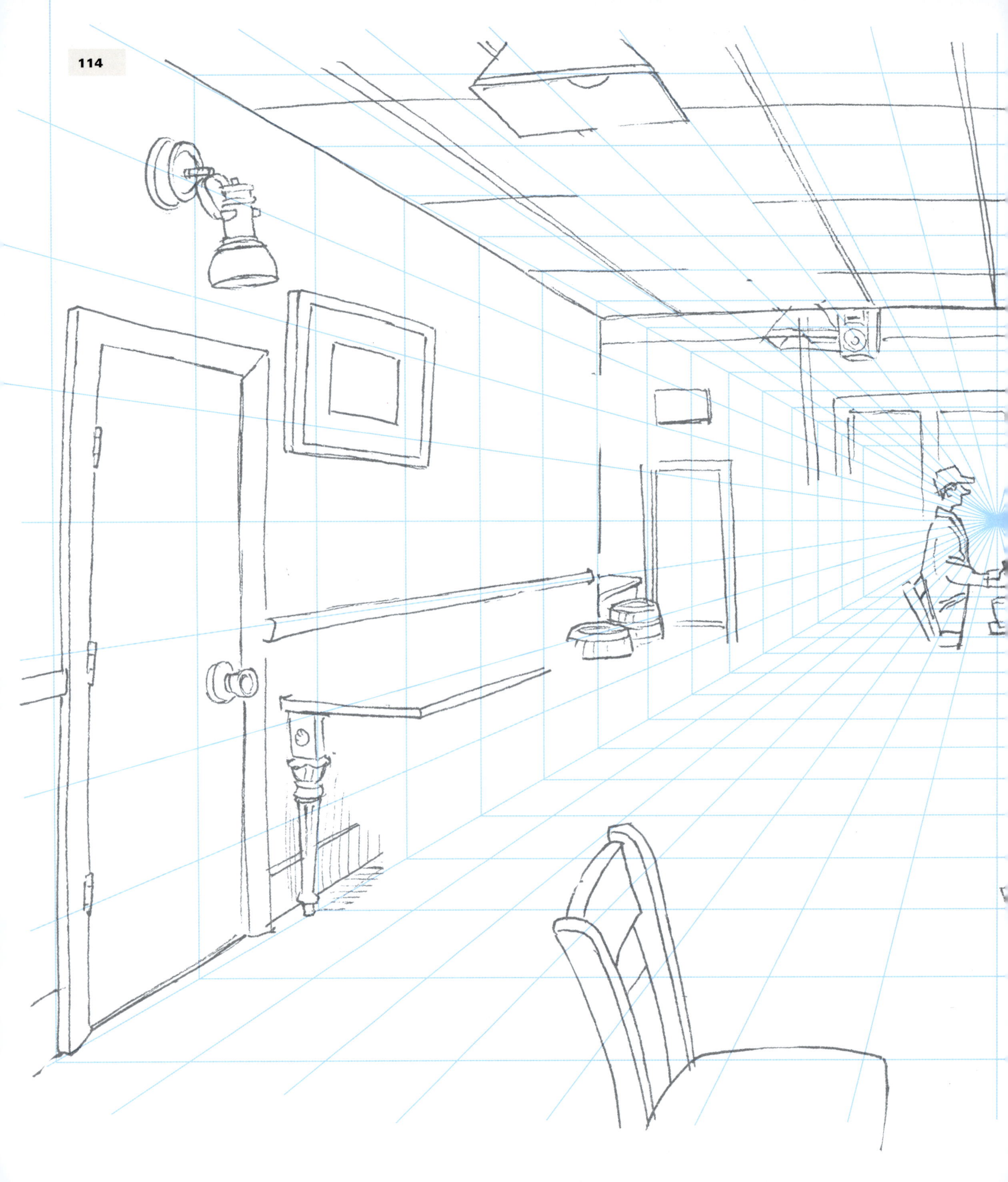

DRAW IN *(from left to right)*
• Four door panels
• Extra pictures and wall lights
• Finish the table against the wall and add some glasses and crockery
• Place a chair at the far end of the table; its back should be against the wall
• Finish drawing the two beer barrels
• Complete two rows of ceiling lights
• More bar chairs receding to the end of the bar and seat a figure on one of them
• Add glasses and bottles to the bar counter top
• On the right wall, add another TV and lights
• Add another door for the drinks cabinet and add bottles on top

(See page 138 for the completed drawing)

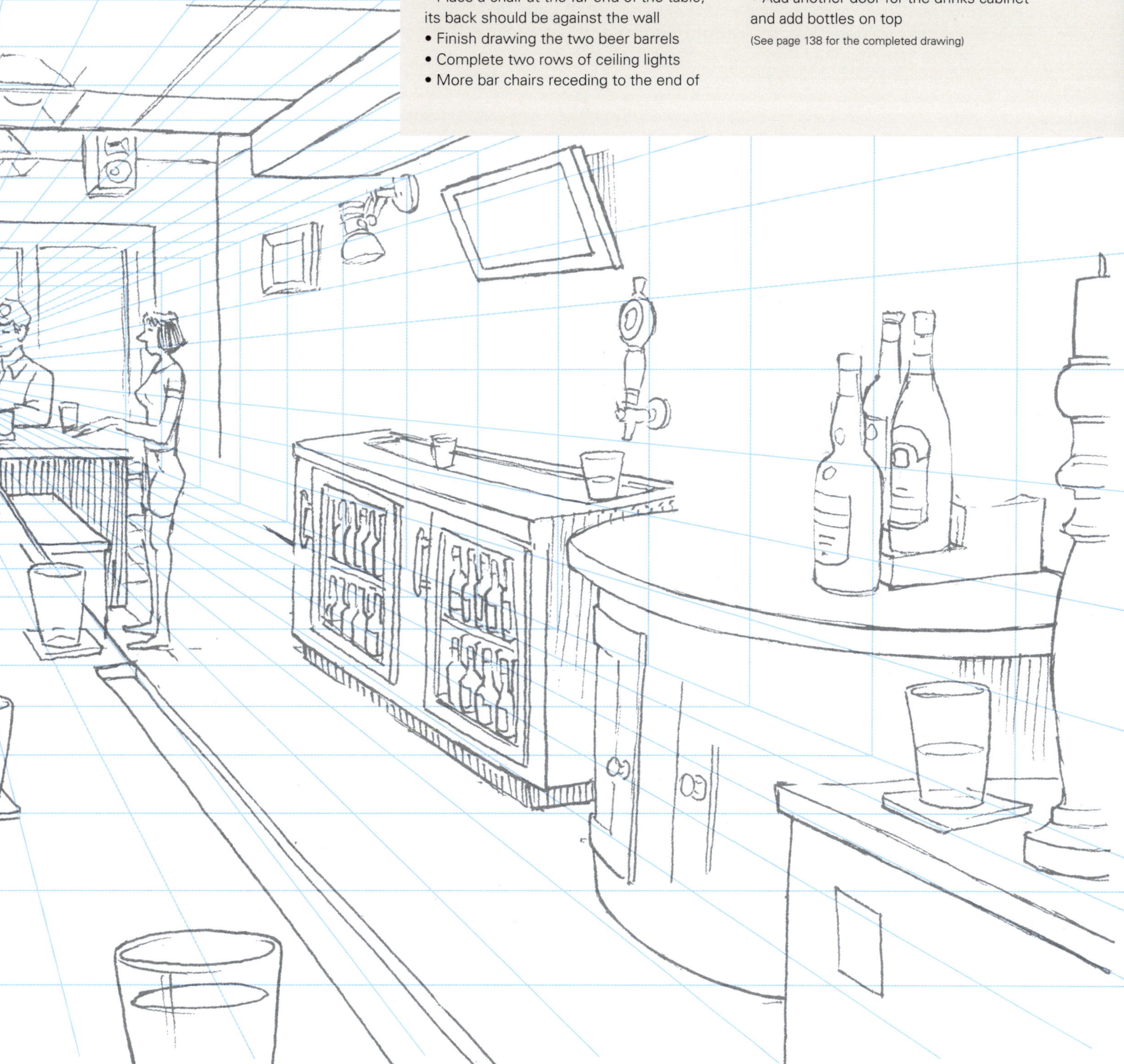

Two-point perspective

You can think of vanishing points much like the points on a compass. If you are at a crossroads looking north, then there will also be vanishing points due east and west. Our peripheral vision can usually see two vanishing points at a time. When you are inside, two vanishing points come into effect when you look at a corner of the room. Vanishing points relate perpendicularly to the walls of the room, assuming the walls are at 90-degree angles to each other.

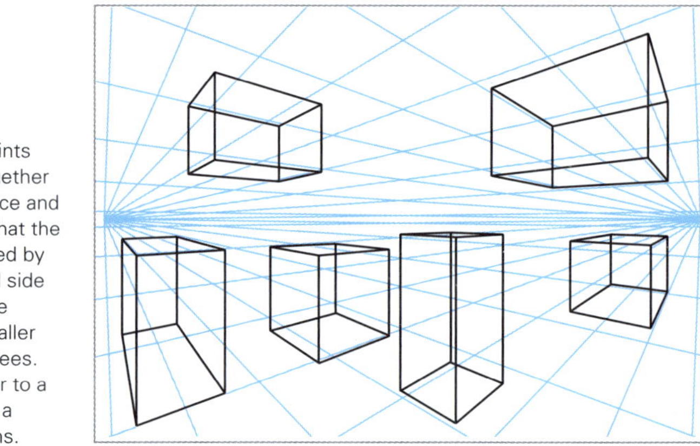

▶The two vanishing points are close together in this instance and this means that the angles created by the front and side planes will be acute, or smaller than 90 degrees. This is similar to a camera with a telephoto lens.

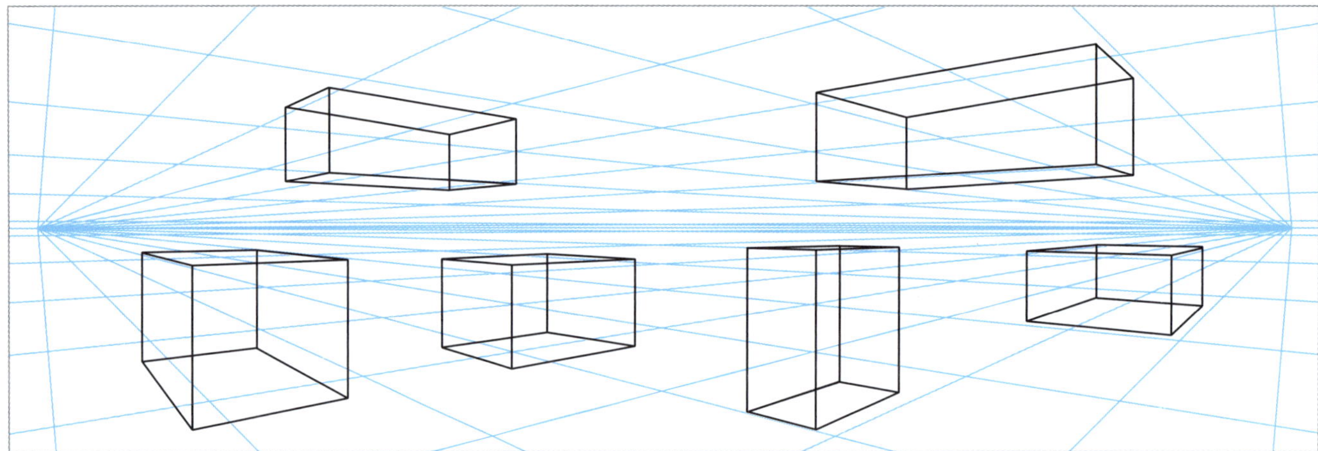

▲Here, the two vanishing points are at a greater distance from one another than in the first example. This means that the angles between the front and side planes are more oblique or wider than 90 degrees. This is similar to a camera with a wide-angle lens.

Exercise 3, pages 124–125: For this exercise you will need to draw in the missing elements given in the list, but this time there are specified co-ordinate points for you to follow. These points are where you should plot the missing item.

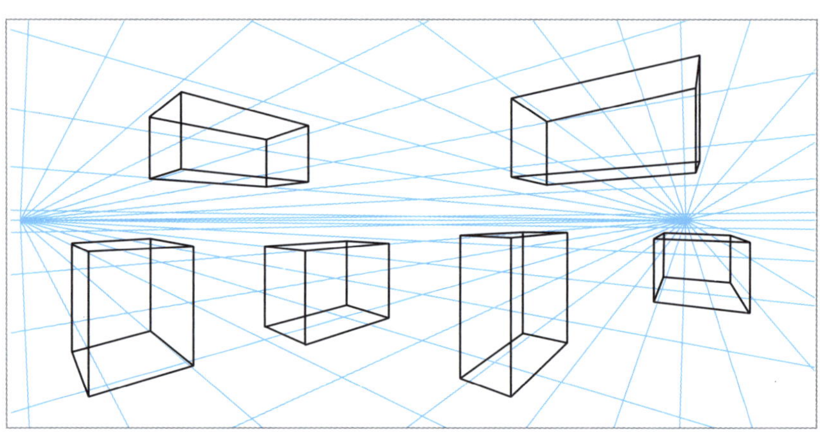

▲The vanishing points here lie at a distance between the two more extreme examples above. In addition, the vanishing points are not equidistant from the central axis, which provides a different pespectival view. All three solutions are plausible depending on the effect you wish to achieve.

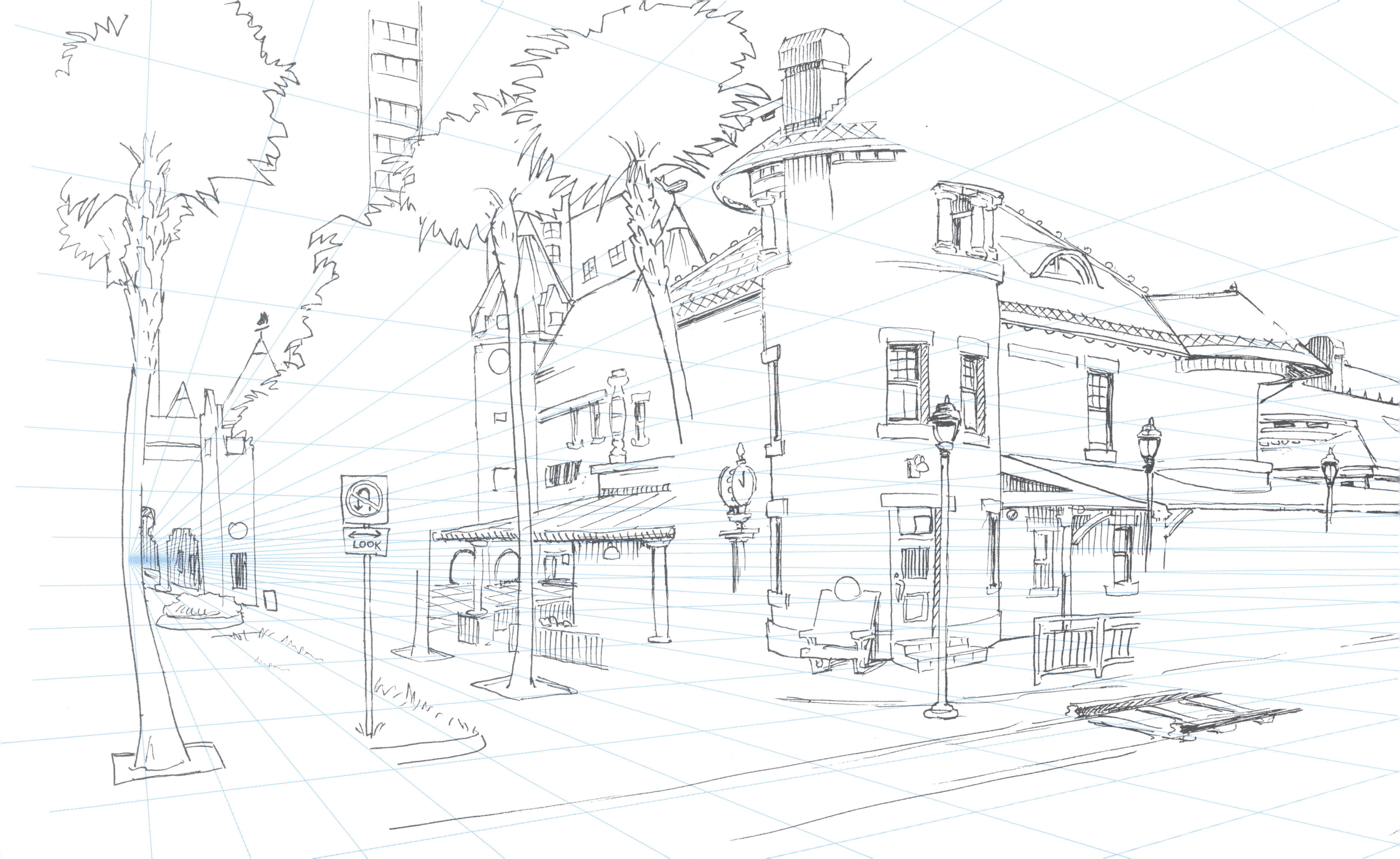

LOOK

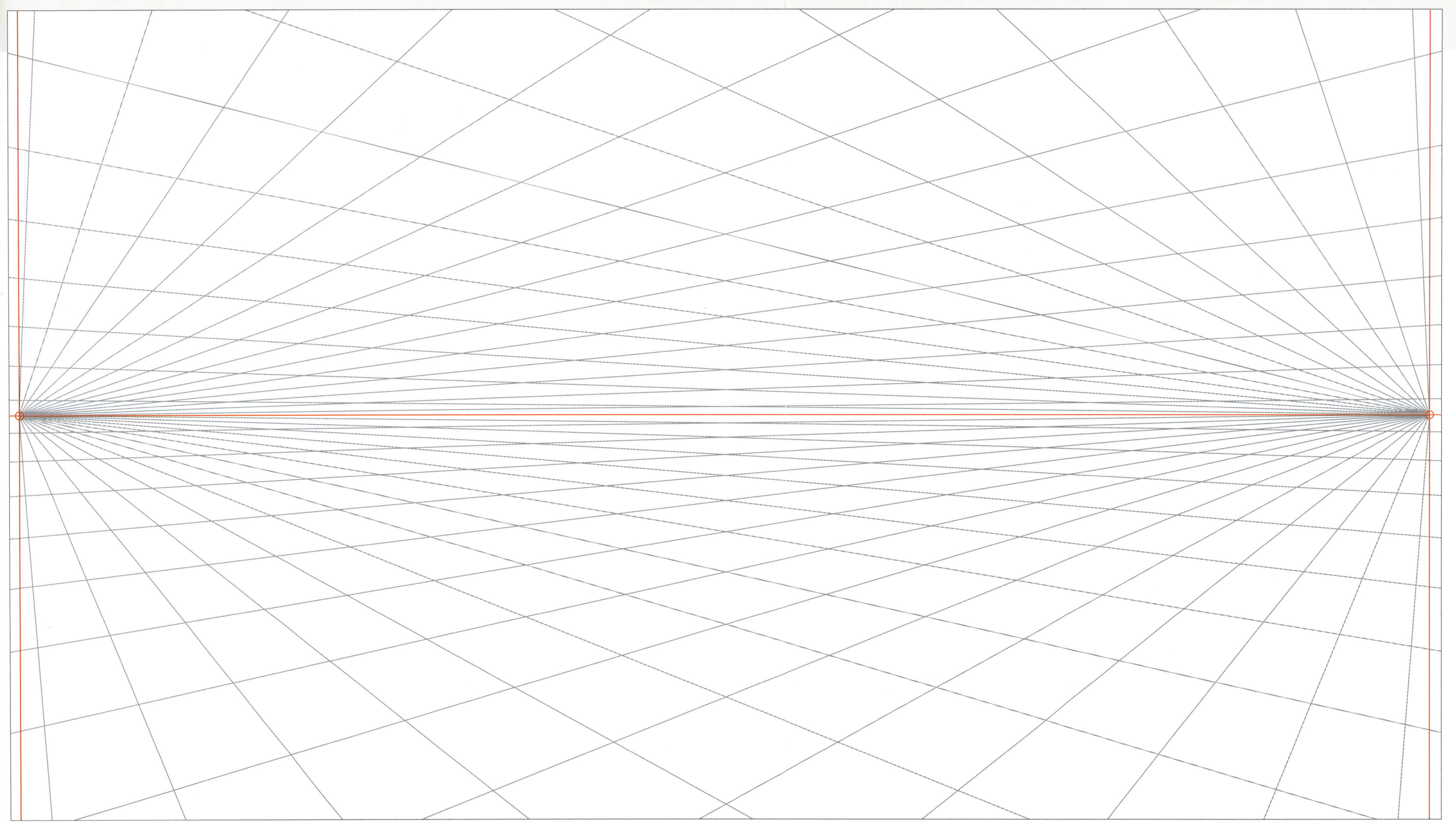

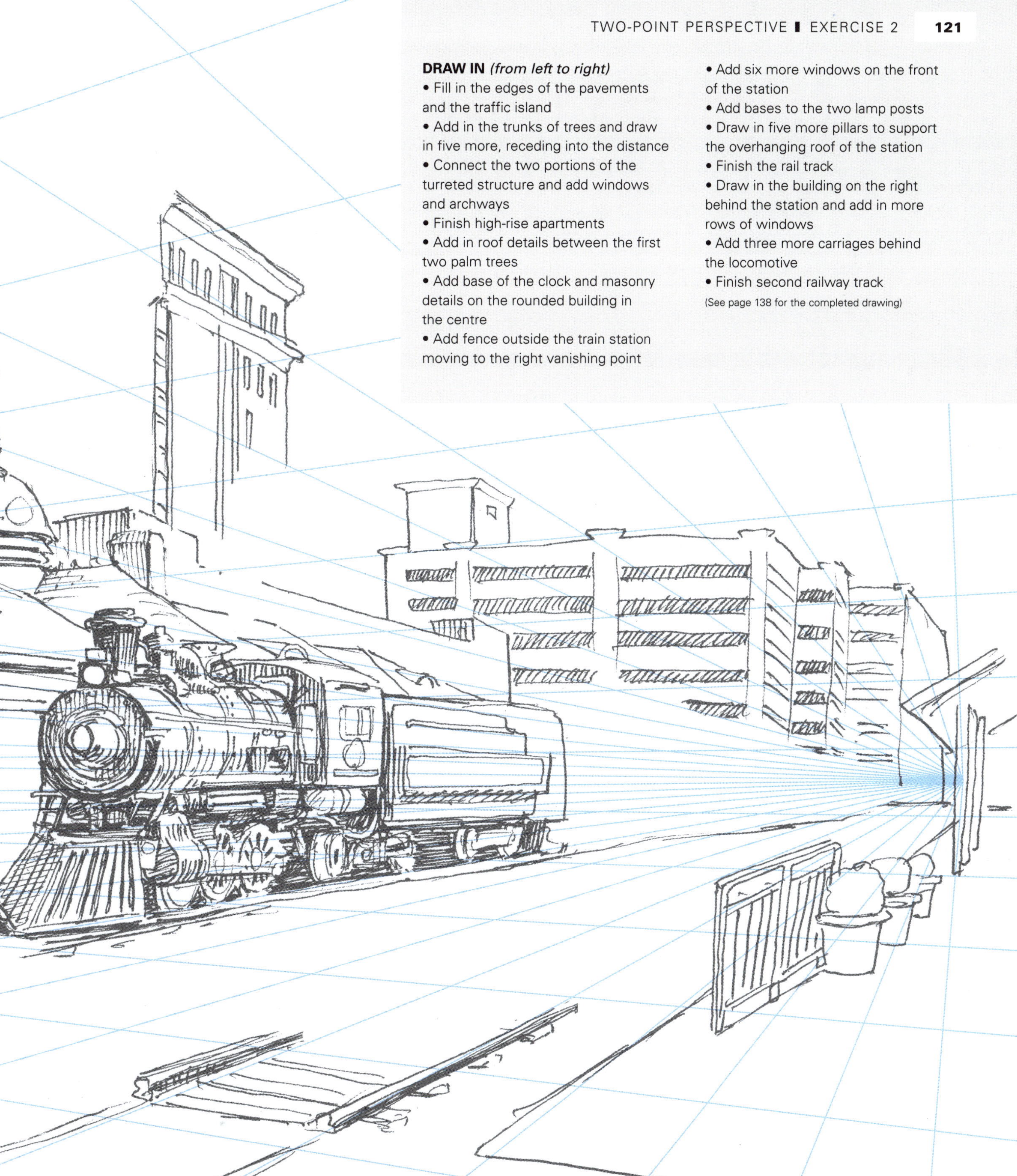

DRAW IN *(from left to right)*
• Fill in the edges of the pavements and the traffic island
• Add in the trunks of trees and draw in five more, receding into the distance
• Connect the two portions of the turreted structure and add windows and archways
• Finish high-rise apartments
• Add in roof details between the first two palm trees
• Add base of the clock and masonry details on the rounded building in the centre
• Add fence outside the train station moving to the right vanishing point

• Add six more windows on the front of the station
• Add bases to the two lamp posts
• Draw in five more pillars to support the overhanging roof of the station
• Finish the rail track
• Draw in the building on the right behind the station and add in more rows of windows
• Add three more carriages behind the locomotive
• Finish second railway track
(See page 138 for the completed drawing)

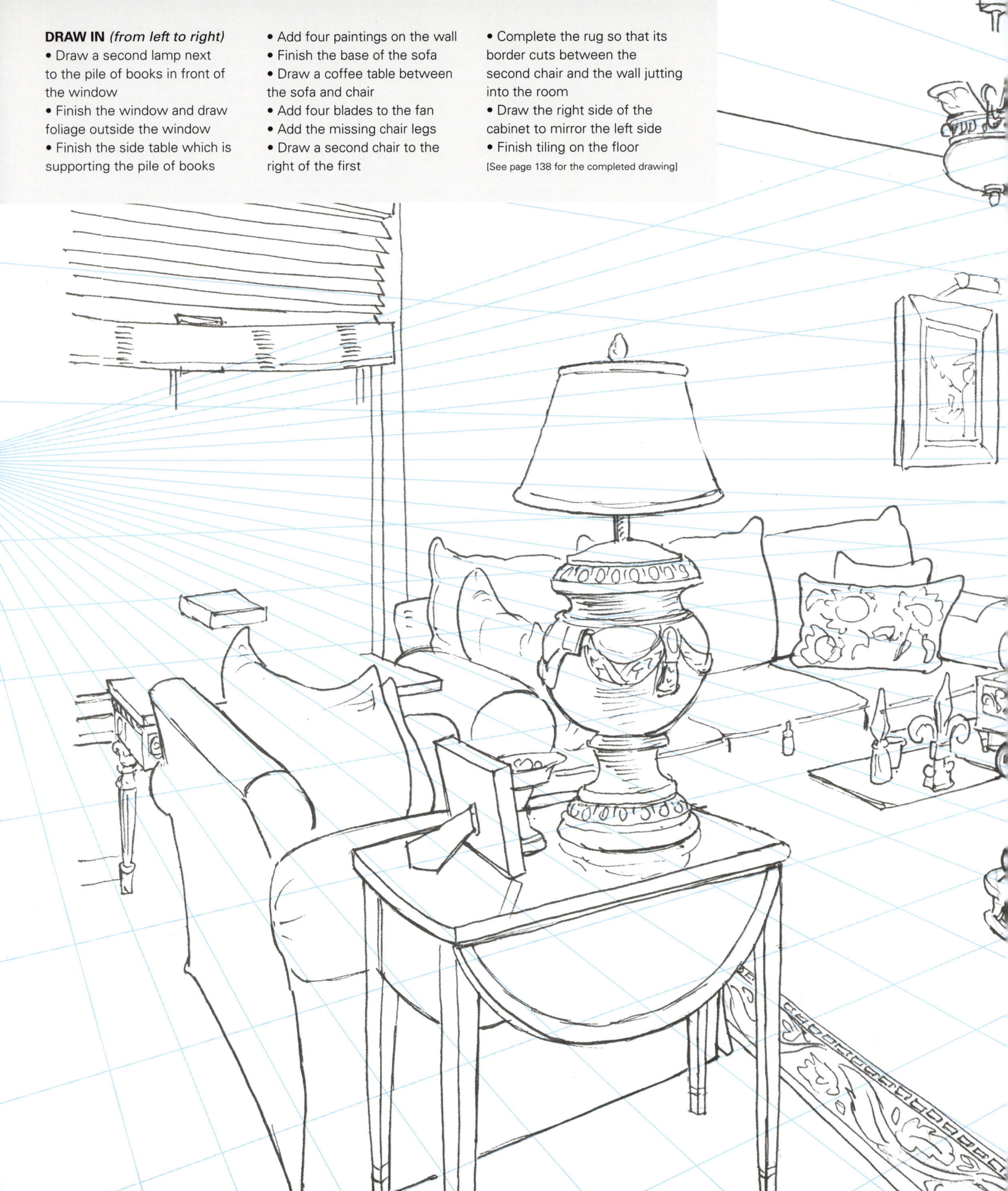

DRAW IN *(from left to right)*
- Draw a second lamp next to the pile of books in front of the window
- Finish the window and draw foliage outside the window
- Finish the side table which is supporting the pile of books
- Add four paintings on the wall
- Finish the base of the sofa
- Draw a coffee table between the sofa and chair
- Add four blades to the fan
- Add the missing chair legs
- Draw a second chair to the right of the first
- Complete the rug so that its border cuts between the second chair and the wall jutting into the room
- Draw the right side of the cabinet to mirror the left side
- Finish tiling on the floor

[See page 138 for the completed drawing]

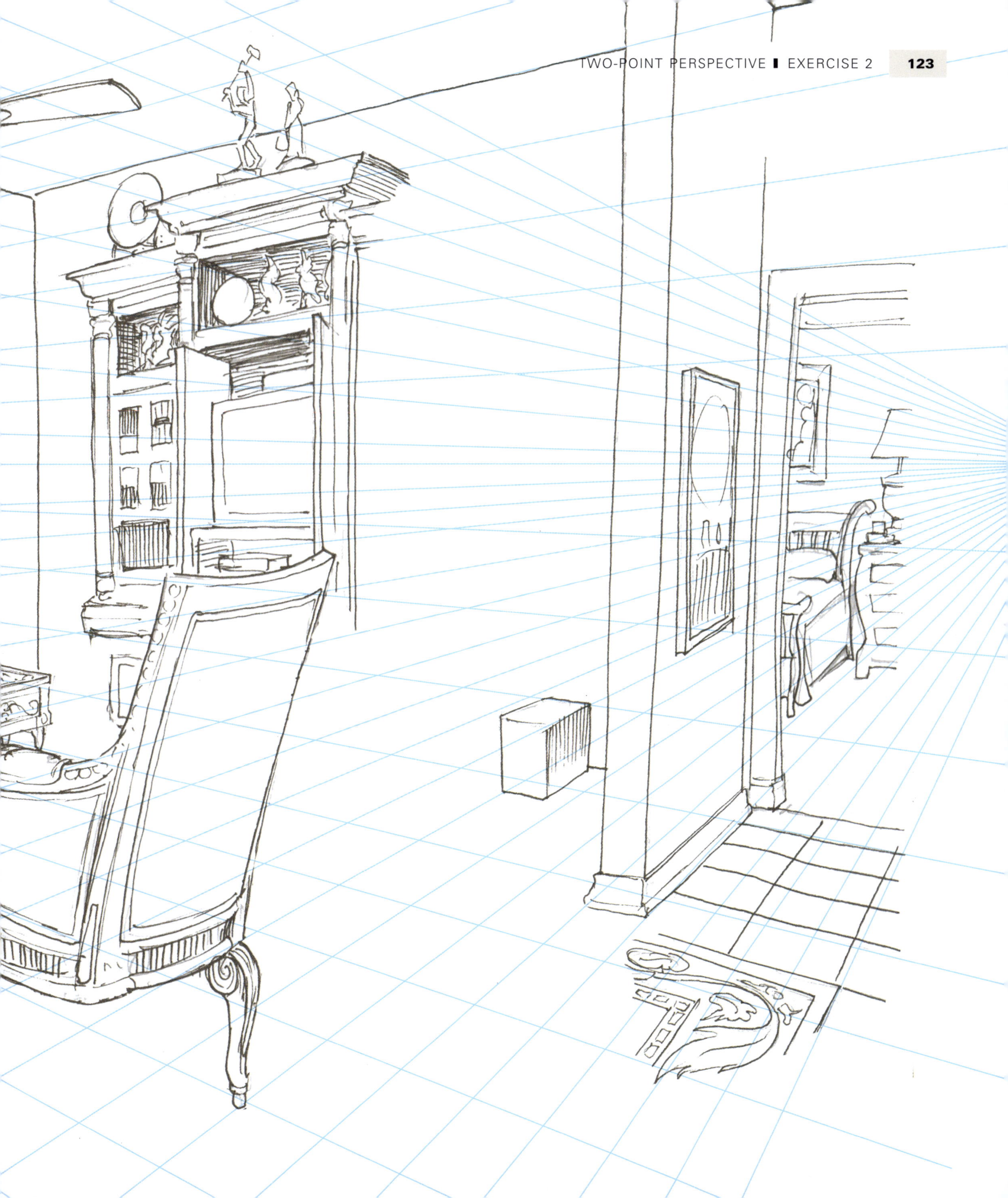

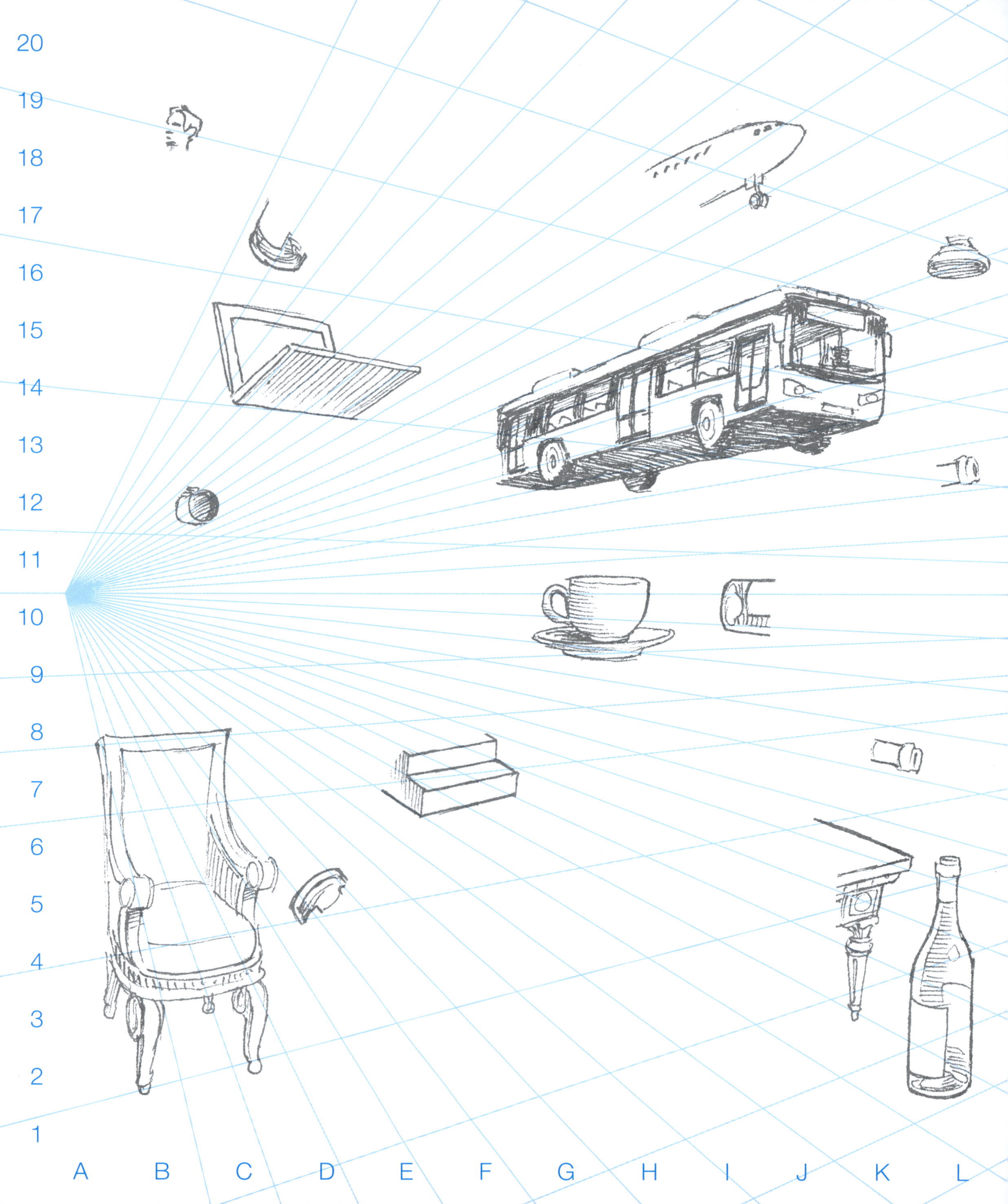

20
19
18
17
16
15
14
13
12
11
10
9
8
7
6
5
4
3
2
1
A B C D E F G H I J K L

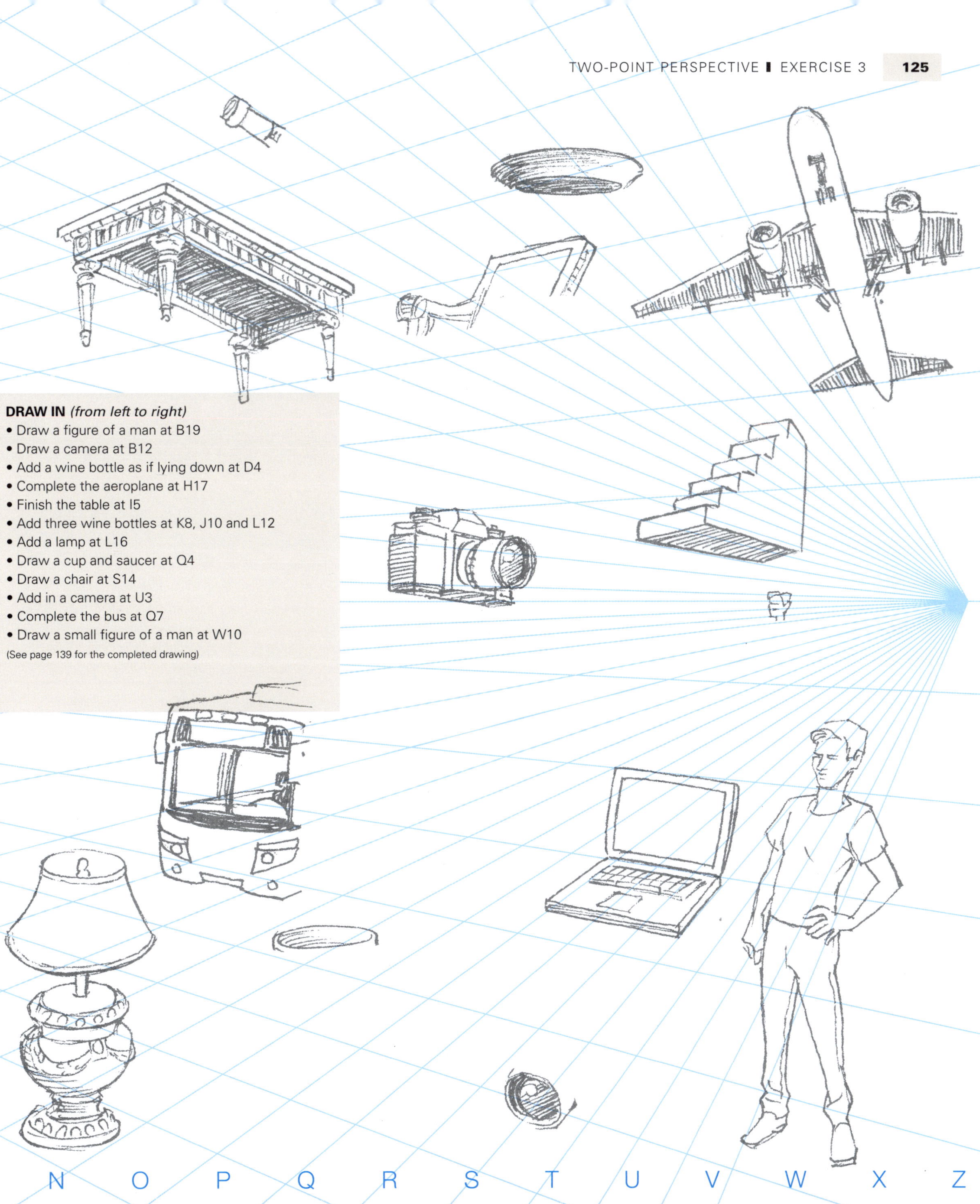

DRAW IN *(from left to right)*
- Draw a figure of a man at B19
- Draw a camera at B12
- Add a wine bottle as if lying down at D4
- Complete the aeroplane at H17
- Finish the table at I5
- Add three wine bottles at K8, J10 and L12
- Add a lamp at L16
- Draw a cup and saucer at Q4
- Draw a chair at S14
- Add in a camera at U3
- Complete the bus at Q7
- Draw a small figure of a man at W10

(See page 139 for the completed drawing)

Three-point perspective

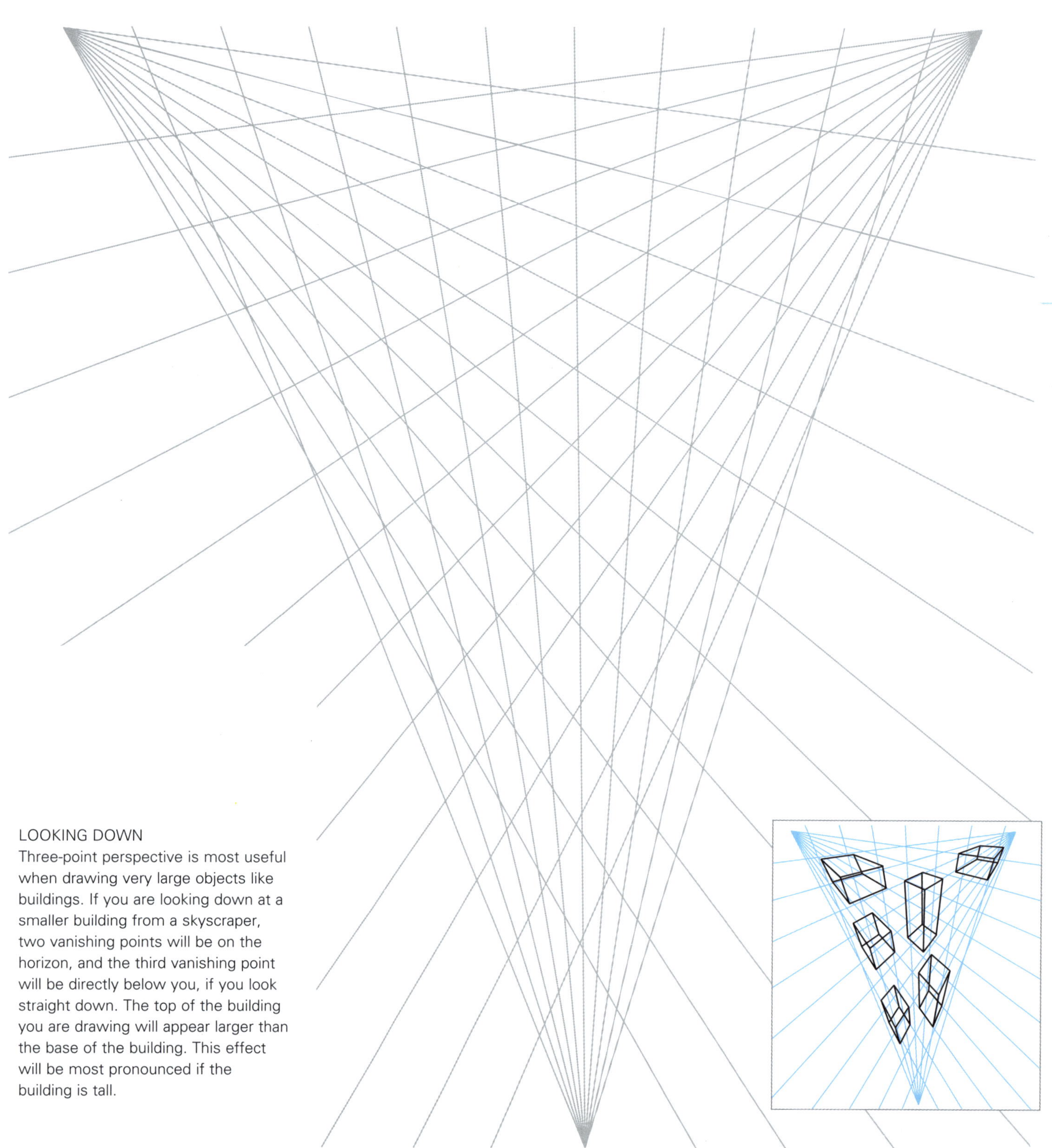

LOOKING DOWN
Three-point perspective is most useful when drawing very large objects like buildings. If you are looking down at a smaller building from a skyscraper, two vanishing points will be on the horizon, and the third vanishing point will be directly below you, if you look straight down. The top of the building you are drawing will appear larger than the base of the building. This effect will be most pronounced if the building is tall.

DRAW IN *(from left to right)*
• Extend the row of buildings in the background, adding rooftops and windows
• Draw an awning extending from the left side of the first building on the left
• Add a row of four windows to the same building, just below the roof
• Complete a row of four palm trees from the centre towards the right vanishing point
• Add a Coca-Cola ad on the front of the closest container
• Complete the lower roof on the building just behind the containers
and add windows as you did for the first building
• Draw two more containers
• Complete the roof on the third building

(See page 139 for the completed drawing)

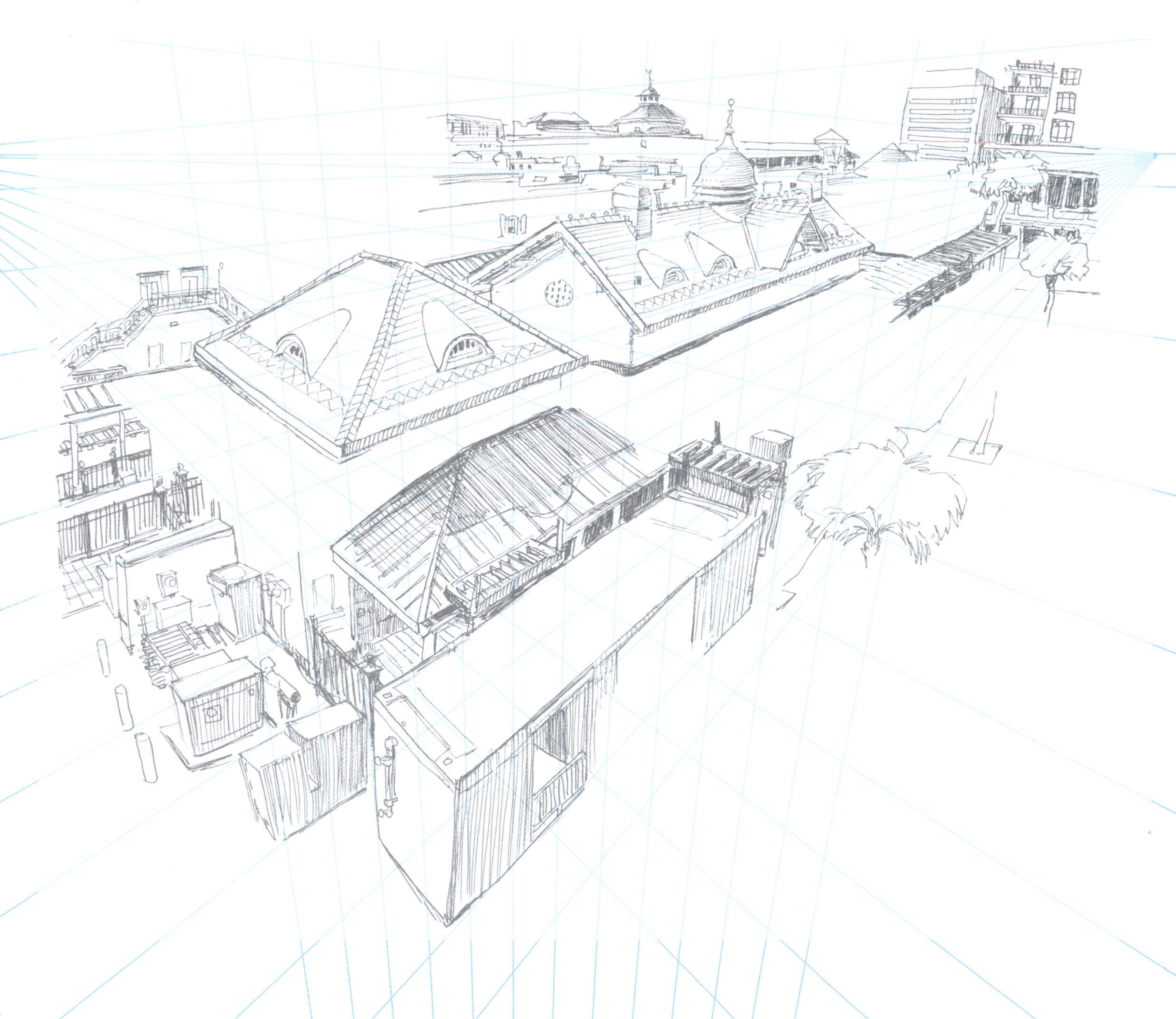

LOOKING UP

When looking up at a tall building, the top floor windows appear smaller than those on the ground floor. That is because the building is receding towards a third vanishing point high up in the sky. The two vanishing points on the horizon help to define where all the windows go, while the third vanishing point makes the building appear large and imposing.

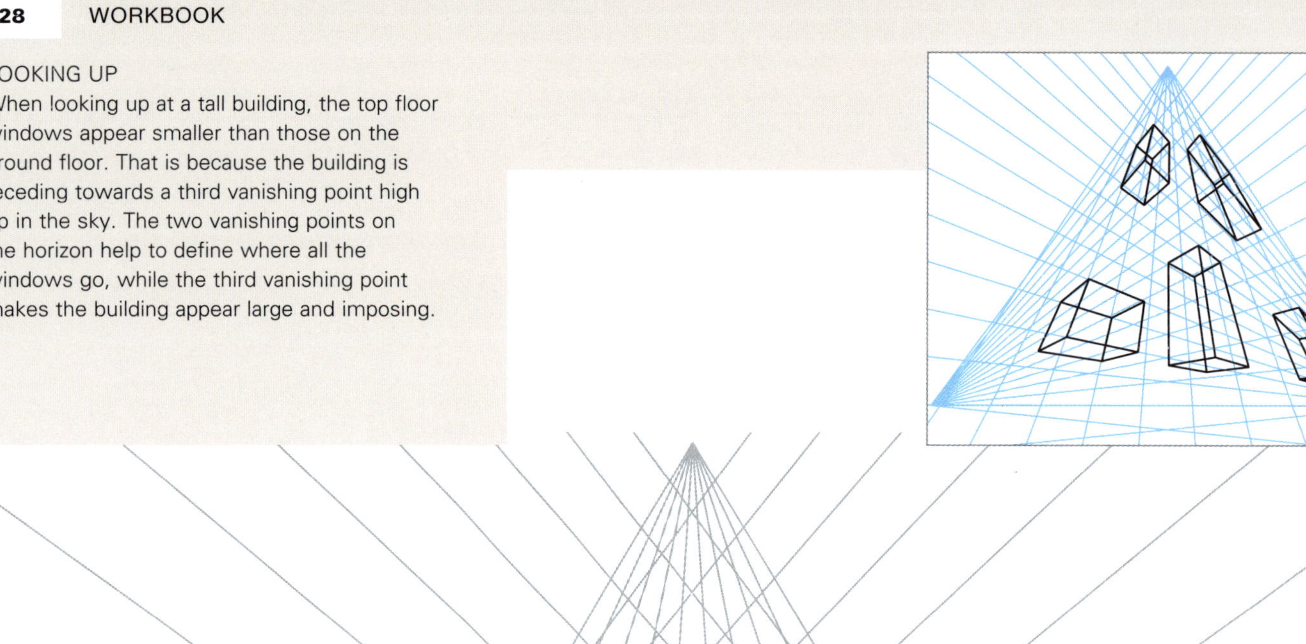

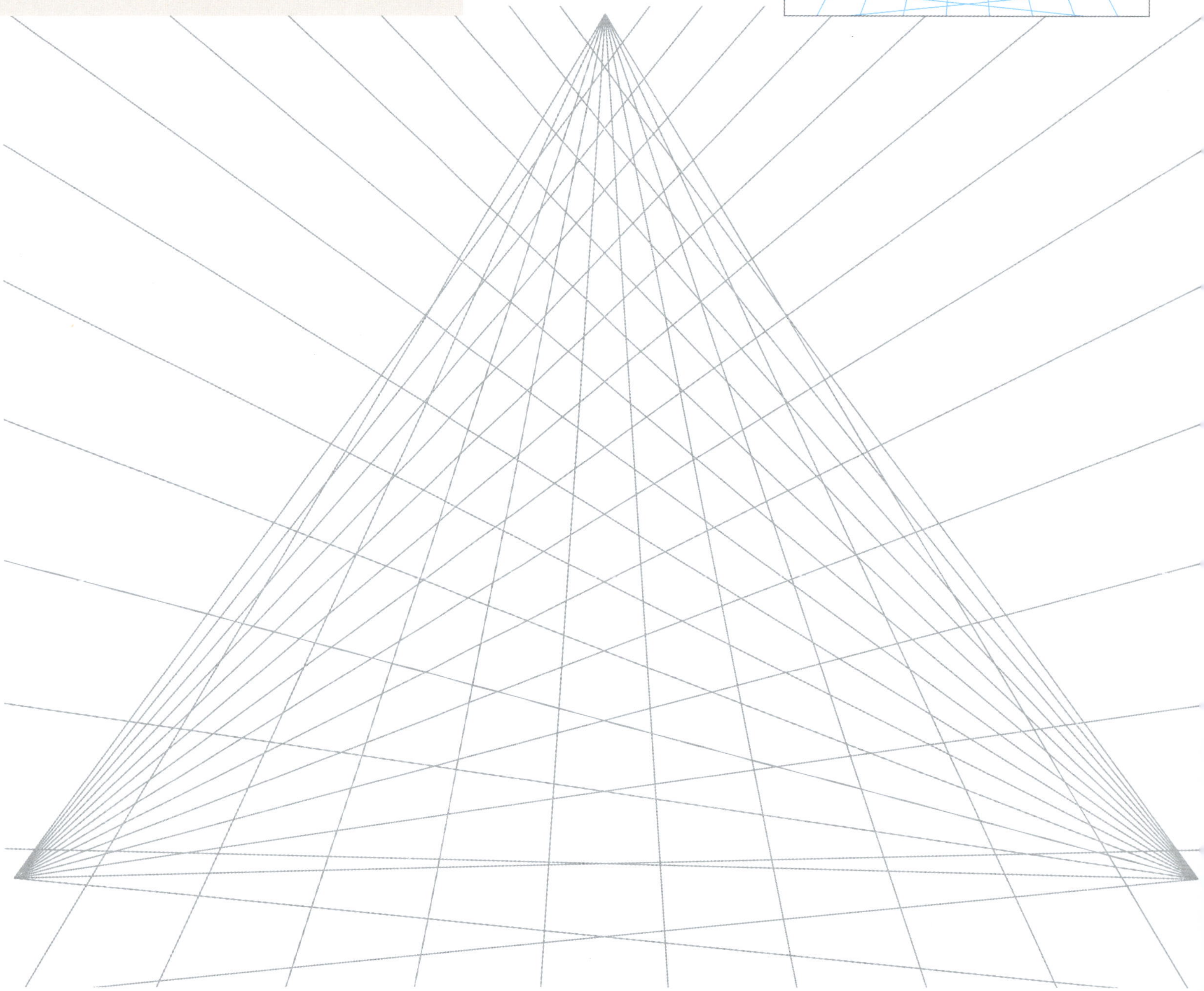

DRAW IN *(from left to right)*
- Add a car parked on the far side of the road
- Add two more trees on the far pavement
- Add a lamp post on the corner pavement
- Draw a man next to the lamp post and people walking on the pavement in the distance
- Complete the side of the building behind the trees and car
- Add eight more windows on the side of the main building
- Finish lettering on the building to read 'BOHEMIAN', going down
- Complete the right side of the building and the railing outside
- Finish the nine columns of windows on the right side

(See page 139 for the completed drawing)

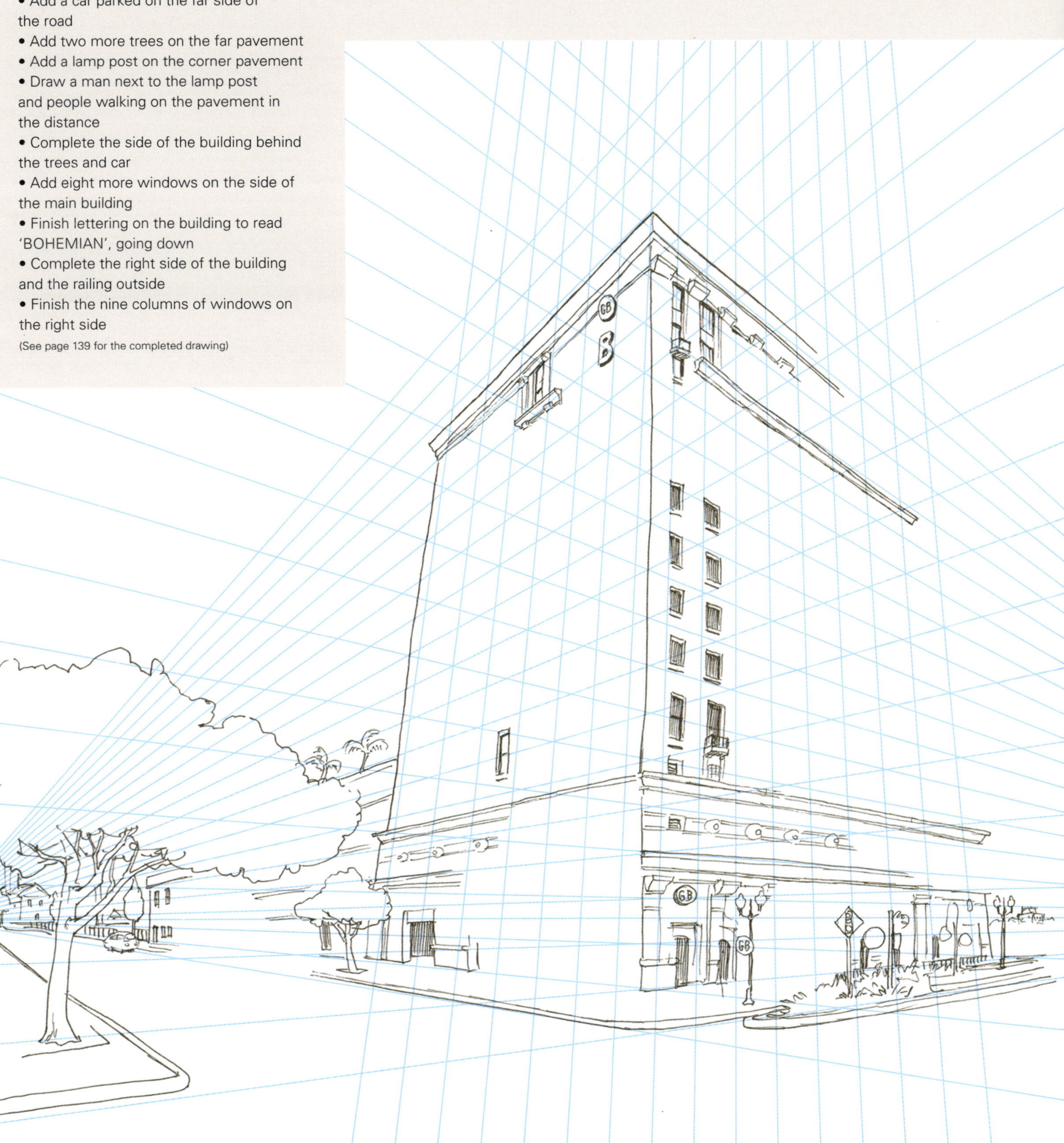

Curvilinear perspective

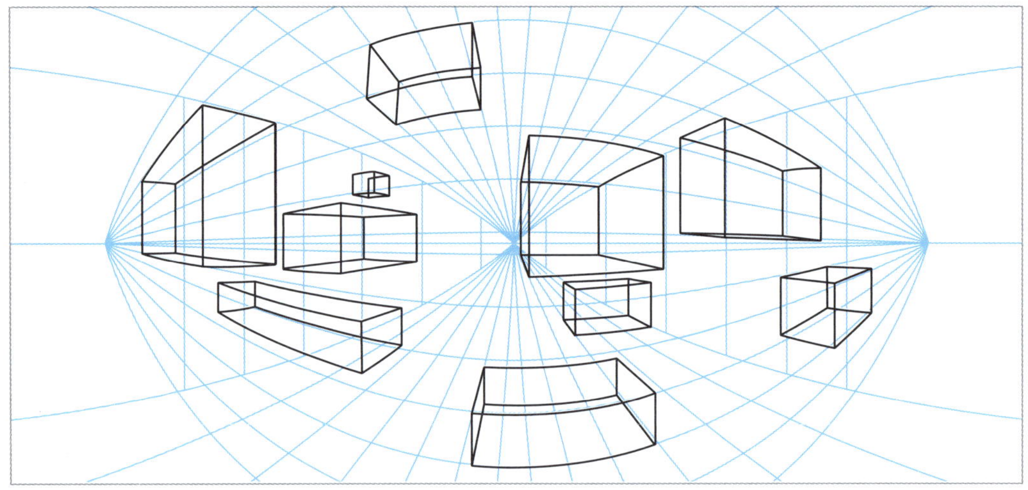

Curvilinear perspective is used when you want to try and fit a full 180-degree view into your sketch. It uses three vanishing points: one directly in front of you and then two at the far reaches of your peripheral vision. A fish-eye effect is achieved as you interpret the ground plane arching towards you.

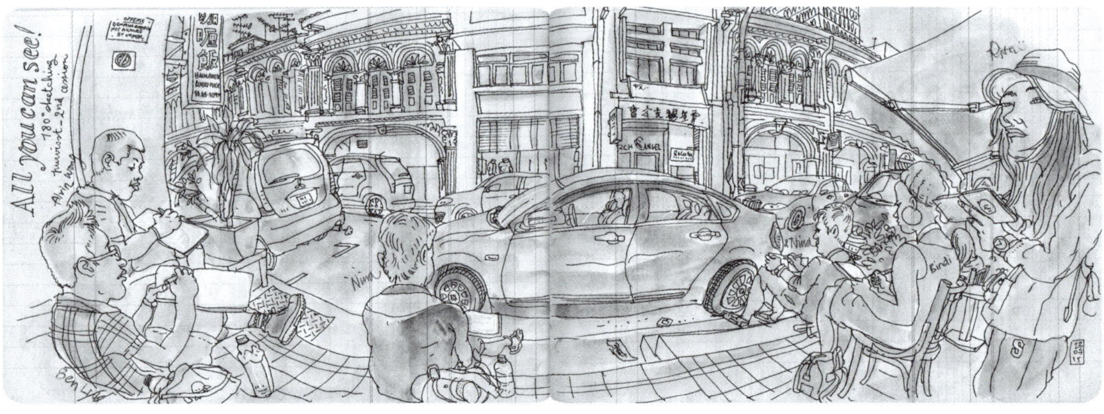

▲ In this street scene by Lapin, artists dominate the foreground while wonderfully ornate buildings arch towards the vanishing points to the right and left. By pushing the ground plane towards the viewer, he makes the far buildings seem closer.

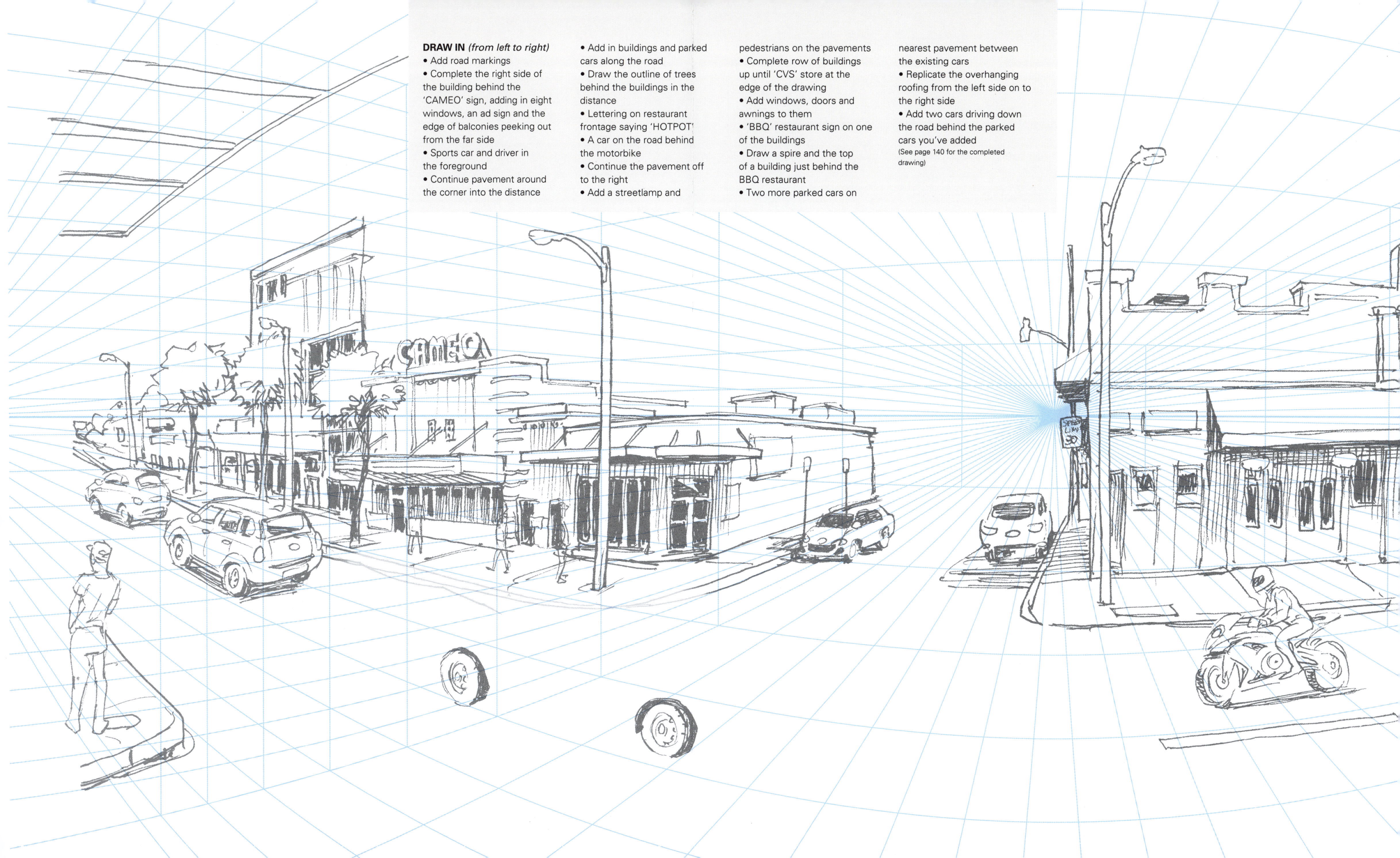

DRAW IN (from left to right)
• Add road markings
• Complete the right side of the building behind the 'CAMEO' sign, adding in eight windows, an ad sign and the edge of balconies peeking out from the far side
• Sports car and driver in the foreground
• Continue pavement around the corner into the distance
• Add in buildings and parked cars along the road
• Draw the outline of trees behind the buildings in the distance
• Lettering on restaurant frontage saying 'HOTPOT'
• A car on the road behind the motorbike
• Continue the pavement off to the right
• Add a streetlamp and pedestrians on the pavements
• Complete row of buildings up until 'CVS' store at the edge of the drawing
• Add windows, doors and awnings to them
• 'BBQ' restaurant sign on one of the buildings
• Draw a spire and the top of a building just behind the BBQ restaurant
• Two more parked cars on nearest pavement between the existing cars
• Replicate the overhanging roofing from the left side on to the right side
• Add two cars driving down the road behind the parked cars you've added
(See page 140 for the completed drawing)
CAMEO
BBQ
SPEED LIMIT 30

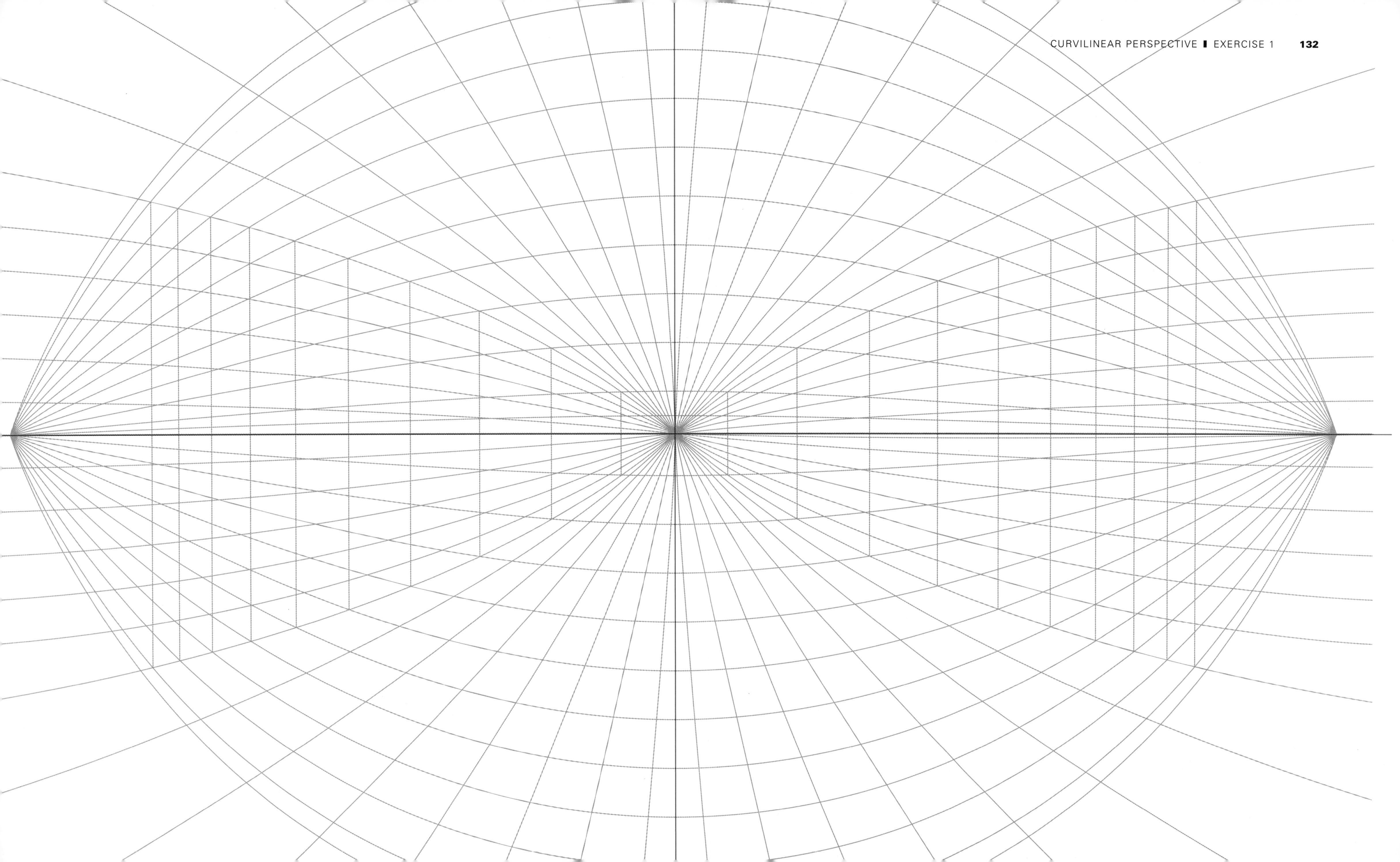

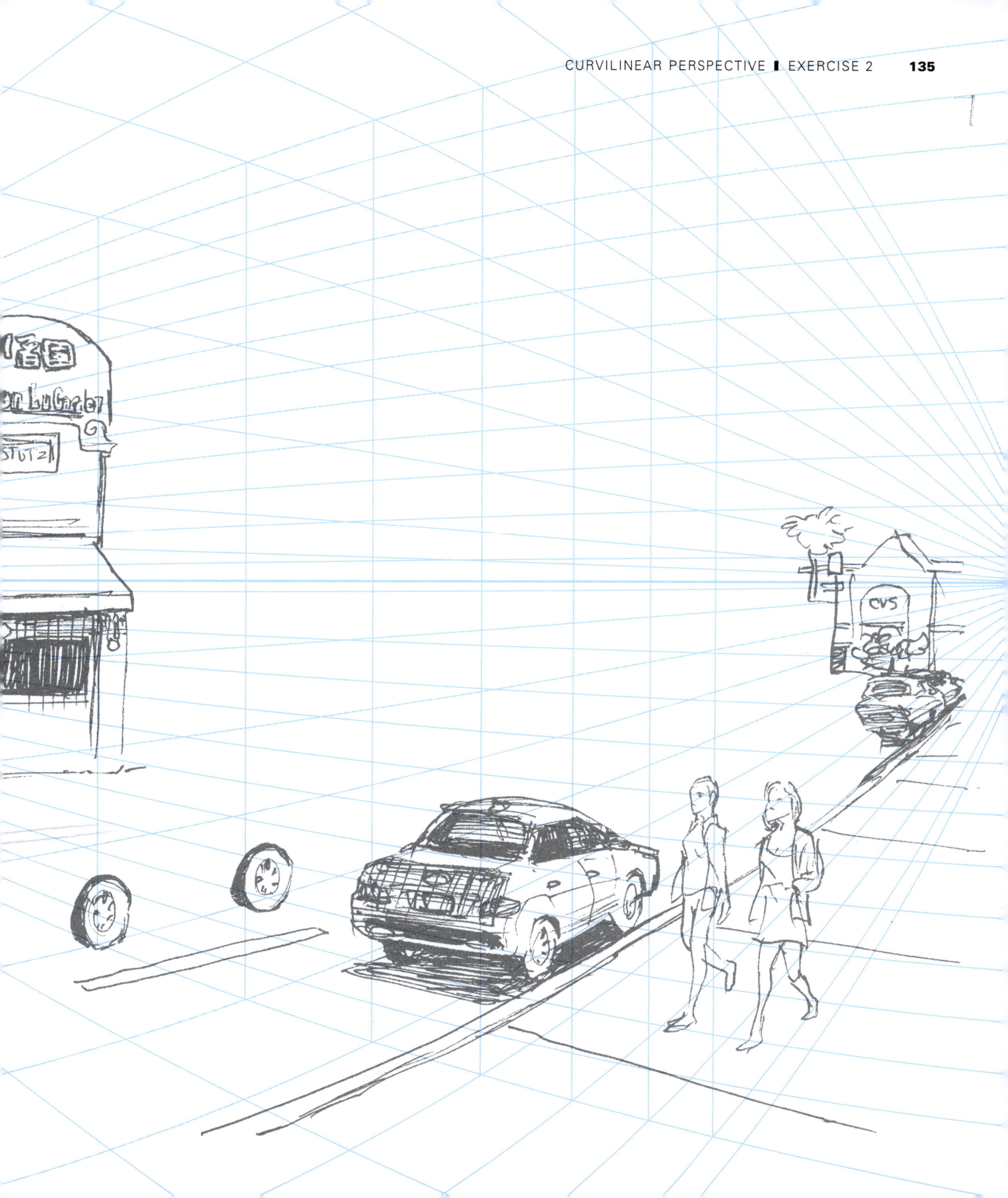
CVS

Extreme curvilinear

This view takes the curvilinear perspective and pushes it one step further. Besides the three vanishing points at the horizon, it adds a vanishing point above and below. The result is a sketch that looks like the world was seen in a mirrored ball.

DRAW IN *(from left to right, living room)*
- Add a sofa and a coffee table with ornaments
- Draw a two-doored cabinet on the back wall
- Side table with a lamp
- Add a picture on the wall above the cabinet

DRAW IN *(from left to right, kitchen)*
- Add a clock on left wall above cabinet
- Add plates and cups on the shelf
- Draw an assortment of objects on the table: wine glass, bowl and spoon, paper, envelopes, packets, pens

- Add two lights on ceiling
- Fill the store cupboard at the back with shelves and boxes
- Complete the doorway into the store cupboard
- Add a cupboard above the worktop on the right wall of the kitchen
- Draw four door panels

on the door to the right of the kitchen
- Complete the tiled flooring in the room on the right
(See page 140 for the completed drawing)

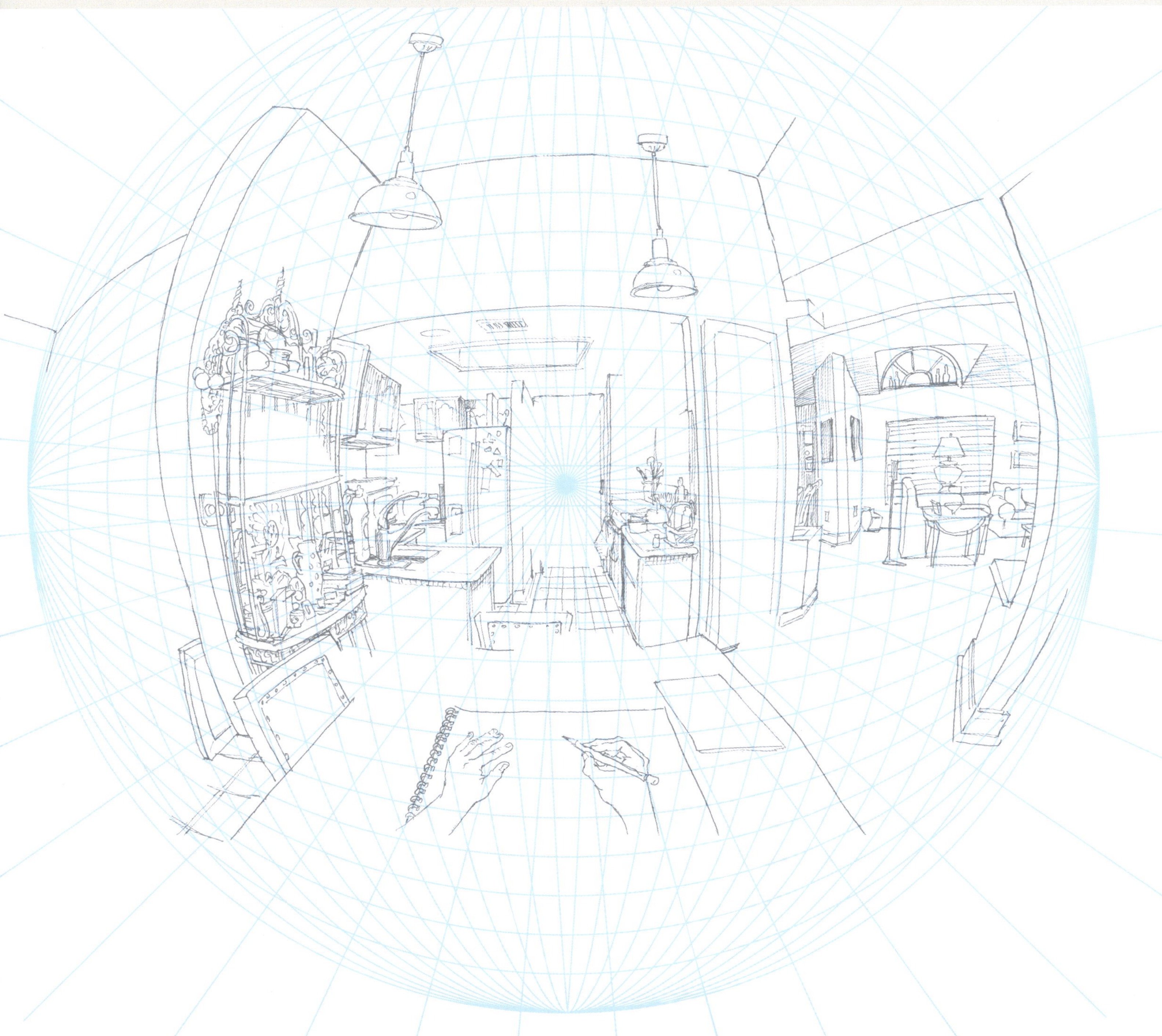

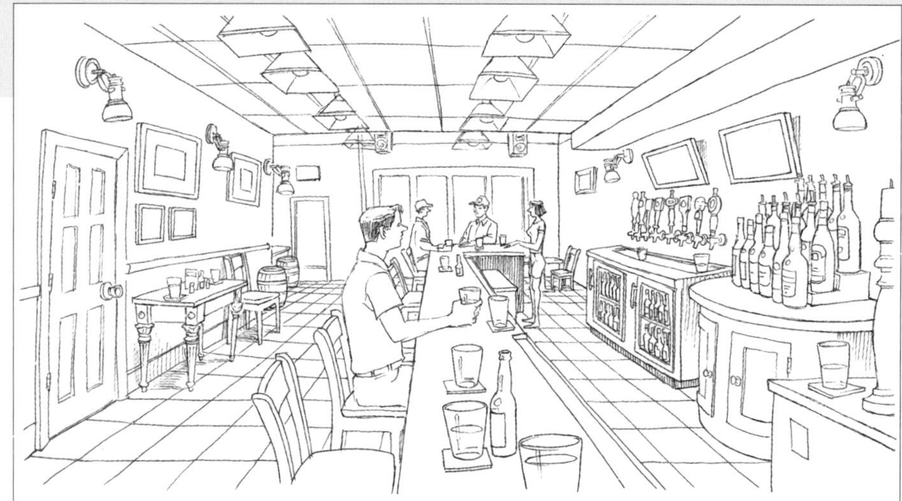

◀ One-point perspective.
Exercise is on pages 114–115

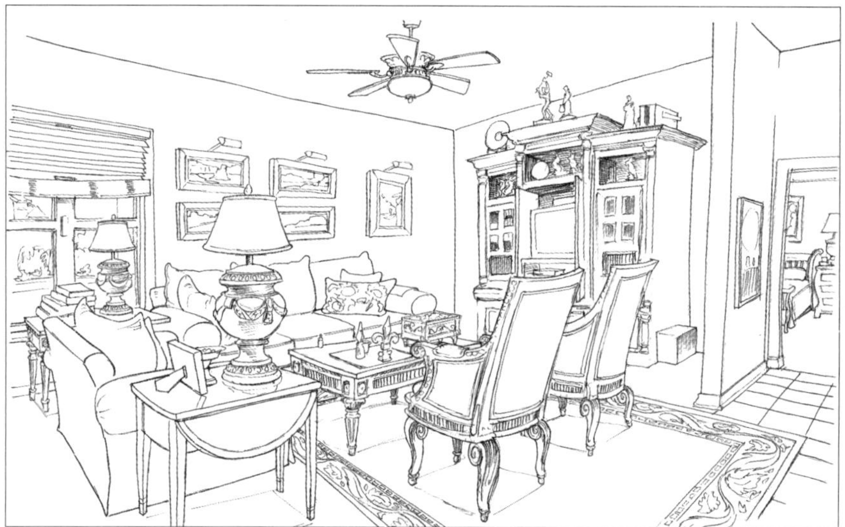

◀ Two-point perspective. Exercise
is on pages 122–123

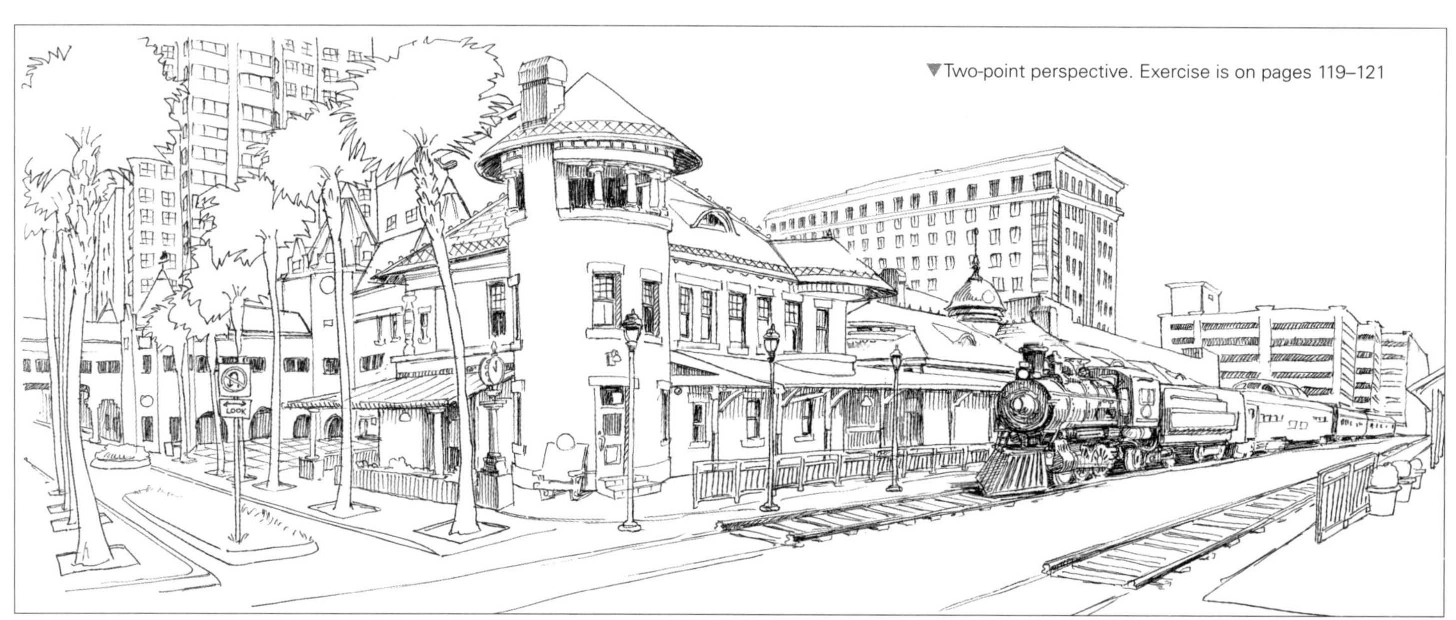

▼ Two-point perspective. Exercise is on pages 119–121

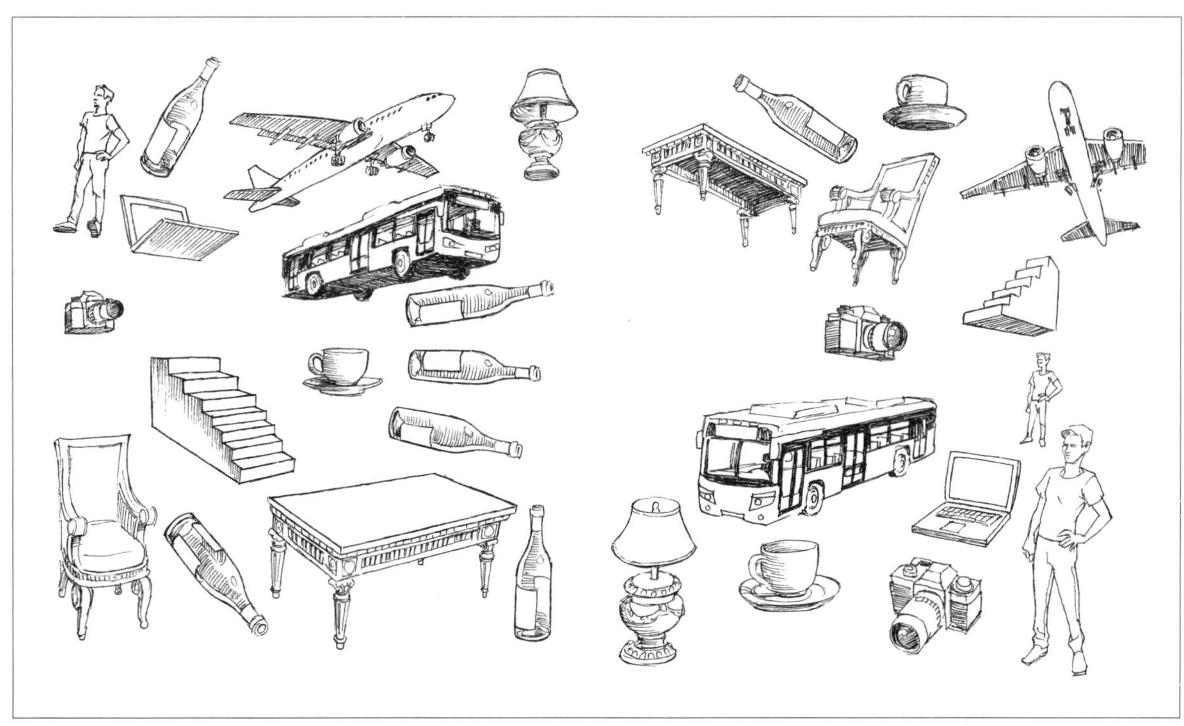

▲Two-point perspective. Exercise is on pages 124–125

▼Three-point perspective. Exercise is on page 127

▼Three-point perspective. Exercise is on page 129

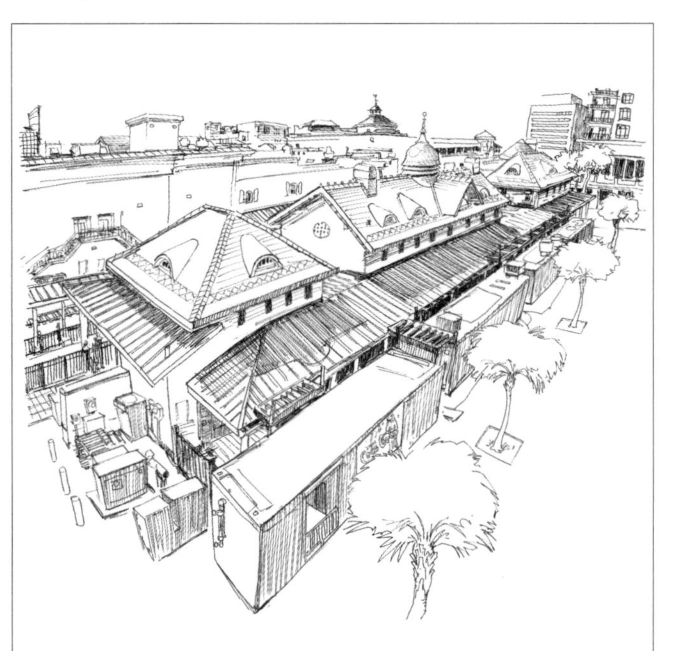

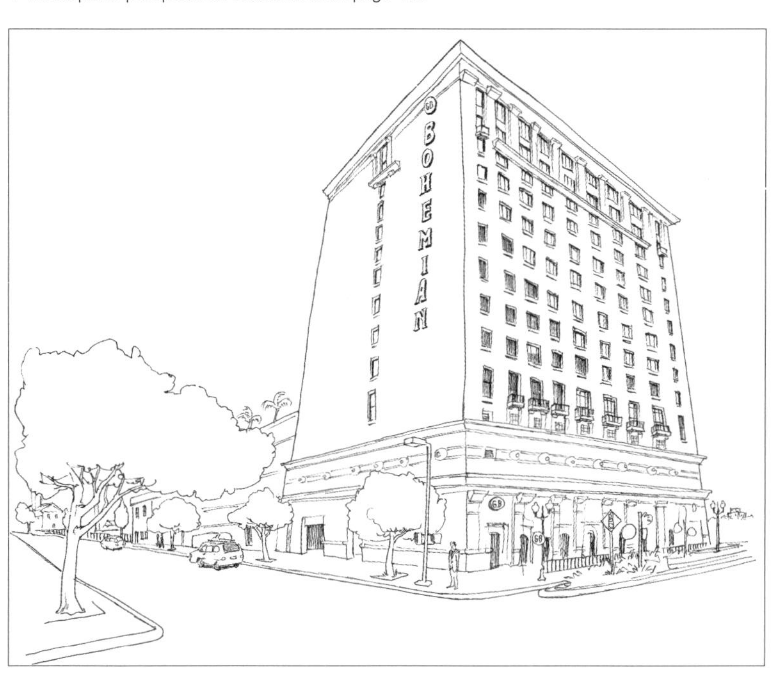

▼Curvilinear perspective. Exercises are on pages 133–135 and 137

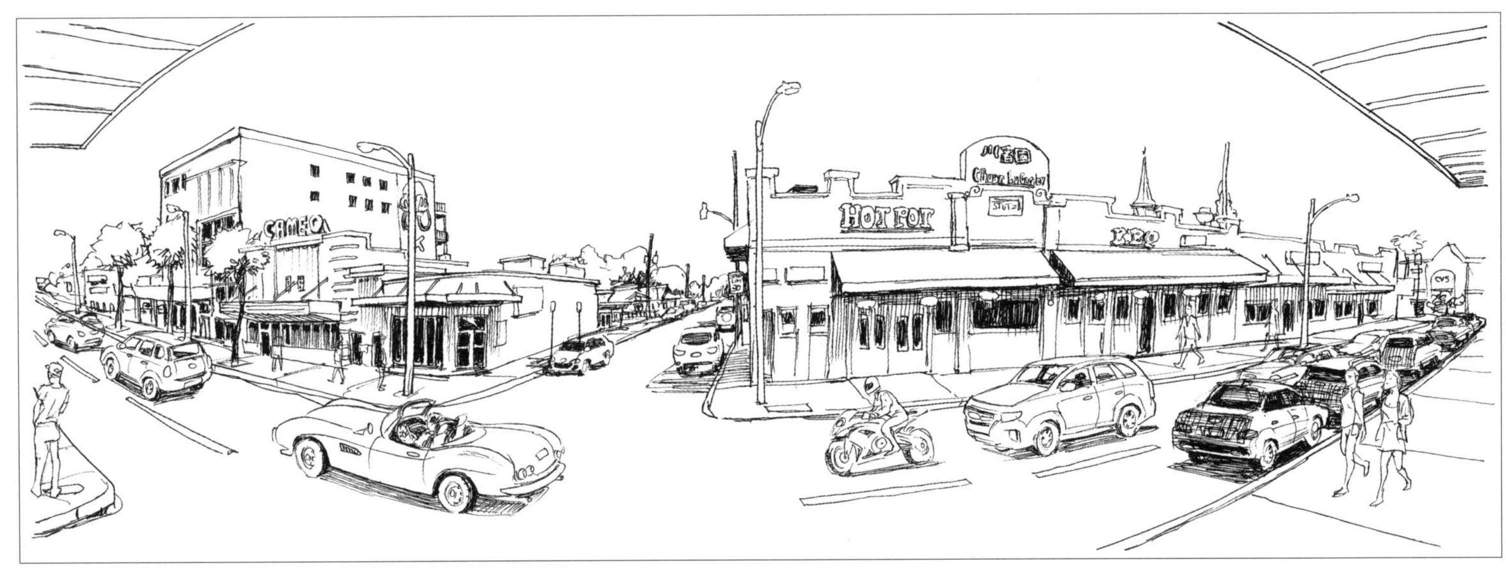

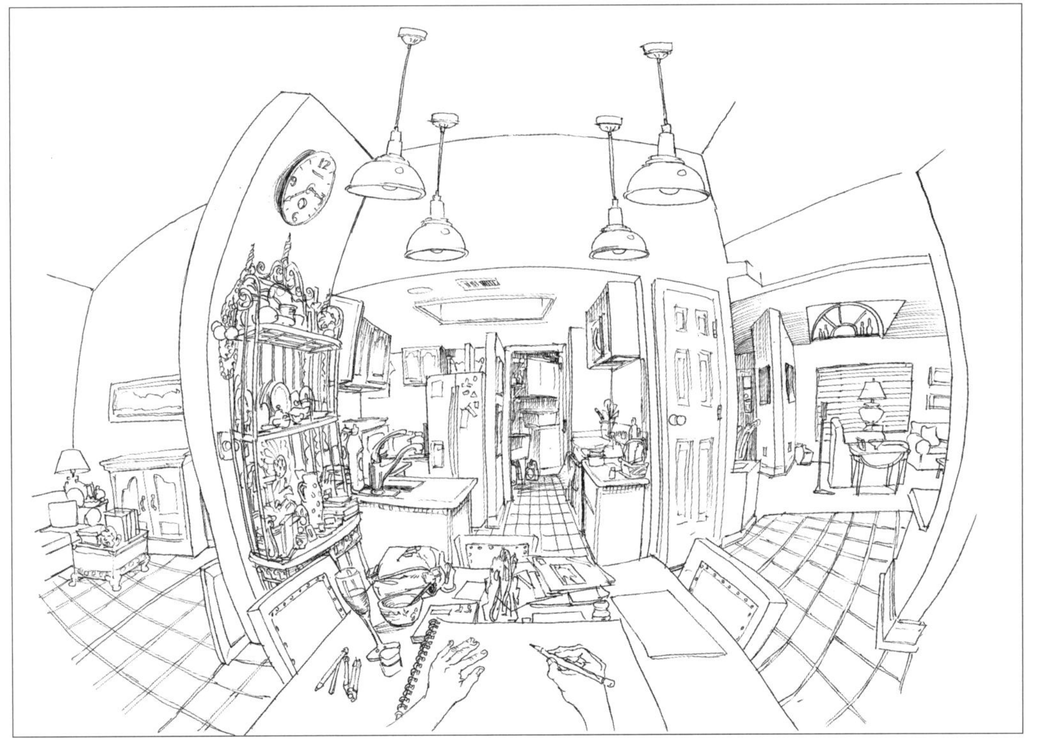

Glossary

Atmospheric perspective: 'Atmosphere' – dust particles and water vapour – affects how we see objects at a significant distance: the most distant objects appear to be fainter in value (less contrast between darks and lights), and sometimes cooler in colour (fewer warm tones). Conversely, objects at closer range appear to be sharper, showing more detail and value contrast, and exhibit a more complete range of warm colours.

Byzantine perspective: An approach to drawing that places the viewer between the subject and the vanishing point, so that objects appear to get larger rather than smaller as they recede into the distance. It is sometimes referred to as reverse perspective.

Cone of vision: The area of our vision with the greatest focus and least distortion. The cone is usually assumed to be about 60 degrees, but is somewhat variable as it relates to our peripheral vision, which is defined by a wider cone of approximately 140 degrees vertically and 180 degrees horizontally.

Curvilinear perspective: A way to represent what we can see in our peripheral vision. To make this type of drawing, we need to collapse a wide-angle view on to the page by distorting the ordinarily straight lines of other types of perspective.

Eye level: The height and orientation of our eyes at any given time and place.

Forced perspective: A grand scale optical illusion whereby the arrangement of spaces 'forces' our perception of spatial depth in one direction or the other.

Horizon line: A horizontal line where the earth and sky appear to meet in the extreme distance.

Line of sight: The specific direction in which we're looking at any given time. Think of it as a straight line emanating from a point right between your eyes and running outwards in the direction of view.

Linear perspective: When parallel lines that recede into the distance appear to get closer together or converge. It is also the type of perspective drawing in which lines that are straight in space are shown as straight in the drawing.

Lines of convergence: Two or more lines that are parallel to one another in space will appear to converge towards a common point as thier distance from the viewer increases.

Multi-point perspective: Takes into account objects and spaces that are not arranged solely on a two-dimensional grid. Many views include walls or other planes oriented at some other angle, requiring additional vanishing points to establish how they would appear to converge.

One-point perspective: When your line of sight is parallel to the horizontal set of lines that diminish to, or converge upon, a single point in the distance.

Overlap: When one object obscures another from view: if one object overlaps another, the object that is partially hidden will be understood to be further in the distance from the object that's obscuring our view.

Pencil sighting: The technique of using your pencil (or pen) as a rough measuring device. It's not necessary to hold your arm perfectly straight, as long as you keep the distance between the pencil and your eye consistent when making any set of measurements.

Perspective: A point of view, or the type of drawing that reproduces a particular point of view. Also the general term given for the science of how we understand and create these drawings.

Relative position: The unique position of a given object as something that helps us understand the distance between our viewpoint and our subject.

Relative size: Perhaps the most basic principle of visual depth, and the one that has the greatest affect on perspective drawing: objects appear to get smaller the further away they are from the viewer.

Reverse perspective: *See* 'Byzantine perspective'.

Sight sizing: The most effective way to check your progress as you're laying out the rough guidelines for any sketch: simply hold your sketch up, right next to the subject beyond, and move your book nearer to, or further from, your eyes until the sketch and the subject are about the same size. By directly comparing your view to your drawing, it's possible to identify inaccuracies and correct them before going any further.

Spatial depth: How near or far visible objects and spaces are from our position and point of view.

Three-point perspective: A linear perspective in which, in addition to the two typical vanishing points, we find a third – either directly overhead or directly below our vantage point.

Trompe l'œil: An optical illusion in art, especially as used to trick the eye into perceiving a painted or drawn two-dimensional surface as three-dimensional space.

Two-point perspective: A linear perspective in which there are two clearly identifiable vanishing points, with both most often occurring on the horizon line. Two-point perspective comes into play when your line of sight is at an angle to the horizontal sets of lines that converge upon, or 'vanish' towards, points in the distance.

Vanishing point: The precise spot at which a group of lines that are parallel in space will appear to converge.

Index

Credits

Quarto would like to thank and acknowledge the following artists for kindly supplying the illustrations and photographs reproduced in this book. All artists are credited in the caption to their work. Unless otherwise stated, all other artwork was produced by the author. While every effort has been made to credit contributors, Quarto would like to apologise should there have been any omissions or errors – and would be pleased to make the appropriate correction for future editions of the book.

A.Rmyth, www.flickr.com/photos/armyth, p.5c, 105t

Afflerbach, Florian, www.flaf.de, pp.26, 32–33, 34–35, 51b, 70–71, 72–73

Bajzek, Eduardo,www.ebbilustracoes.blogspot.com, photo by Alessandro Couto, www.alessandrocouto.com.br, pp.24, 46t/b, 85t, 86b

Blaukopf, Shari, www.shariblaukopf.com, p.29t

Campolongo, Marianne, Shutterstock.com, p.21tl

Castro Alonso, Daniel, www.flickr.com/photos/daniel-castro, pp.5, 49br, 63b, 66br, 67b, 84b, 89b, 101c

Curto, Cristina, www.cristinacurto.cat, p.30tl

Elisseeva, Elena, Shutterstock.com, p.40t

Getty Images, p.8t/b

Hartmann, Arno, www.arnohartmann.de, pp.29c, 45t, 50b

Herranz, Miguel, www.miguel-herranz.com, p.16

Jaramillo, Omar, www.omar-paint.blogspot.com, pp.29b, 66cl, 89tl/tr

Johnson, Richard, The Washington Post, www.washingtonpost.com/news/drawing-dc-together, pp.30br, 47t, 66t, 101t

Kerr, Stuart, www.flickr.com/photos/stu_kerr, p.31t, 82

Lapin, www.lesillustrationsdelapin.com, pp.30tr, 31b, 102t, 104t, 130b

Michel, Gérard, www.flickr.com/photos/gerard_michel, pp.11b, 25t, 49bl, 63t, 65t, 67t, 83b, 84t, 99b, 101b, 104c

Muerkens, Hans, www.flickr.com/photos/petervanayk/albums, p.36

Murray, Brenda, www.behance.net/brendamurray, p.69b

Nevans, Keith, www.flickr.com/photos/keithnevens, pp.3c, 48tr, 88l

Olgysha, Shutterstock.com, p.21b

Rojo, Ana, www.aidibus.blogspot.com.es, p.87l

Ruijters, Maarten, www.rtarchitekten.com, pp.68tl, 85b, 87b, 104b

Ruiz, Luis, www.luisrpadron.blogspot.com, pp.27b, 48b, 64t, 68b, 105b

Scully, Pete, www.petescully.com, pp.51t, 92–93, 98b

Smart, Sharon, www.shandysmart.com, pp.86t, 87t

Southern-Pearce, Pat, p.83t

Steel, Liz, www.lizsteel.com, pp.28b, 31c, 49t, 64b, 65b, 69t

Thorspecken, Thomas, www.analogartistdigitalworld.com, pp.5r, 90–91, 111, 114–115, 120–121, 122–123, 124–125, 127, 129, 134–135, 137, 138–139, 140

Tribastone, Christian, http://tribbie.blogspot.co.uk, pp.30bl, 50tl/r

Veron, Alexandre, http://alexandreveron.blogspot.co.uk, p.50cr

Walsh, Nathan, www.nathanwalsh.net, p.28t, 100

Watkins, Lis, http://lineandwash.blogspot.co.uk, p.47b

Wikipedia, p.9tl/tr/br, 10t/b, 11tl/tr

Woodcock, John, www.johnwoodcockillustration.co.uk, pp110–137 (Grids)

Author acknowledgments

I would like to give my most sincere thanks to the artists whose work appears throughout this book, and also to the many sketchers I've had the great fortune to know around the world. Your drawings and your generous friendship are a constant inspiration. Many thanks also to the folks at Quarto Publishing for their patience and enthusiasm throughout the development of this book. And of course deepest thanks to my family for their love, support, and humor.